Lauren Darcey
Shane Conder

D1402671

Sams **Teach Yourself**

Android™

Application Development

Second Edition

in **24 Hours**

SAMS 800 East 96th Street, Indianapolis, Indiana, 46240 USA

Sams Teach Yourself Android Application Development in 24 Hours, Second Edition

ISBN-13: 978-0-672-33569-3
ISBN-10: 0-672-33569-7

Library of Congress Cataloging-in-Publication Data
Darcey, Lauren, 1977-
  Sams teach yourself Android application development in 24 hours /
Lauren Darcey, Shane Conder. – 2nd ed.
     p. cm.
  ISBN 978-0-672-33569-3 (pbk. : alk. paper)
  1. Application software–Development. 2. Android (Electronic resource) 3. Mobile computing. I. Conder, Shane, 1975- II. Title. III. Title: Teach yourself Android application development in twenty-four hours.
  QA76.76.A65D26 2012
  004–dc23
                              2011025487

Printed in the United States of America

First Printing August 2011

Trademarks

Warning and Disclaimer

Bulk Sales

Sams Publishing offers excellent discounts on this book when ordered in quantity for bulk purchases or special sales. For more information, please contact

    U.S. Corporate and Government Sales

    1-800-382-3419

    corpsales@pearsontechgroup.com

For sales outside of the U.S., please contact

    International Sales

    international@pearson.com

Editor in Chief
Mark Taub

Acquisitions Editor
Trina MacDonald

Development Editor
Sheri Cain

Managing Editor
Sandra Schroeder

Project Editor
Mandie Frank

Copy Editor
Charlotte Kughen,
The Wordsmithery
LLC

Indexer
Larry Sweazy

Proofreader
Williams Woods
Publishing Services

Technical Editor
Jim Hathaway

Publishing Coordinator
Olivia Basegio

Designer
Gary Adair

Compositor
Bronkella Publishing

Contents at a Glance

Table of Contents

Sams Teach Yourself Android Application Development in 24 Hours, Second Edition

Sams Teach Yourself Android Application Development in 24 Hours, Second Edition

About the Authors

Lauren Darcey is responsible for the technical leadership and direction of a small software company specializing in mobile technologies, including Android, iPhone, BlackBerry, Palm Pre, BREW, and J2ME, and consulting services. With more than two decades of experience in professional software production, Lauren is a recognized authority in enterprise architecture and the development of commercial-grade mobile applications. Lauren received a B.S. in Computer Science from the University of California, Santa Cruz.

She spends her copious free time traveling the world with her geeky mobile-minded husband. She is an avid nature photographer, and her work has been published in books and newspapers around the world. In South Africa, she dove with 4-meter-long great white sharks and got stuck between a herd of rampaging hippopotami and an irritated bull elephant. She's been attacked by monkeys in Japan, gotten stuck in a ravine with two hungry lions in Kenya, gotten thirsty in Egypt, narrowly avoided a coup d'état in Thailand, geocached her way through the Swiss Alps, drank her way through the beer halls of Germany, slept in the crumbling castles of Europe, and gotten her tongue stuck to an iceberg in Iceland (while being watched by a herd of suspicious wild reindeer).

Shane Conder has extensive development experience and has focused his attention on mobile and embedded development for the past decade. He has designed and developed many commercial applications for Android, iPhone, BREW, BlackBerry, J2ME, Palm, and Windows Mobile—some of which have been installed on millions of phones worldwide. Shane has written extensively about the mobile industry and evaluated mobile development platforms on his tech blogs and is well known within the blogosphere. Shane received a B.S. in Computer Science from the University of California.

A self-admitted gadget freak, Shane always has the latest phone, laptop, or other mobile device. He can often be found fiddling with the latest technologies, such as cloud services and mobile platforms, and other exciting, state-of-the-art technologies that activate the creative part of his brain. He also enjoys traveling the world with his geeky wife, even if she did make him dive with 4-meter-long great white sharks and almost get eaten by a lion in Kenya. He admits that he has to take at least two phones and a tablet with him when backpacking, even though there is no coverage, that he snickered and whipped out his Android phone to take a picture when his wife got her tongue stuck to that iceberg in Iceland, and that he is catching on that he should be writing his own bio.

The authors have also published an intermediate/advanced book on Android development called *Android Wireless Application Development*, Second Edition, part of the Addison-Wesley Developer's Library series. Lauren and Shane have also published numerous articles on mobile software development for magazines, technical journals, and online publishers of educational content. You can find dozens of samples of their work in *Smart Developer* magazine (Linux New Media), Developer.com, *Network World*, Envato (MobileTuts+ and CodeCanyon), and InformIT, among others. They also publish articles of interest to their readers at their own Android website, http://androidbook.blogspot.com. You can find a full list of the authors' publications at http://goo.gl/f0Vlj.

Dedication

For Chickpea.

Acknowledgments

This book would never have been written without the guidance and encouragement we received from a number of very patient and supportive people, including our editorial team, co-workers, friends, and family.

Throughout this project, our editorial team at Pearson (Sams Publishing) has been top notch. Special thanks go to Trina MacDonald, Olivia Basegio, and Sheri Cain. Our technical reviewer, Jim Hathaway, helped us ensure that this book provides accurate information. With each edition, this book gets better. However, it wouldn't be here without the help of many folks on past editions. Thanks go out to past reviewers, technical editors, and readers for their valuable feedback. Finally, we'd like to thank our friends and family members who supported us when we needed to make our book deadlines.

We Want to Hear from You!

As the reader of this book, *you* are our most important critic and commentator. We value your opinion and want to know what we're doing right, what we could do better, what areas you'd like to see us publish in, and any other words of wisdom you're willing to pass our way.

You can email or write me directly to let me know what you did or didn't like about this book—as well as what we can do to make our books stronger.

Please note that I cannot help you with technical problems related to the topic of this book, and that due to the high volume of mail I receive, I might not be able to reply to every message.

When you write, please be sure to include this book's title and author as well as your name and phone or email address. I will carefully review your comments and share them with the author and editors who worked on the book.

Email: feedback@samspublishing.com

Mail: Mark Taub
            Editor in Chief
            Sams Publishing
            800 East 96th Street
            Indianapolis, IN 46240 USA

Reader Services

Visit our website and register this book at informit.com/register for convenient access to any updates, downloads, or errata that might be available for this book.

Introduction

The Android platform is packing some serious heat these days in the mobile marketplace and gaining traction worldwide. The platform has seen numerous advancements in terms of SDK functionality, handset availability, and feature set. A wide diversity of Android handsets and devices are now in consumers' hands—and we're not just talking about smartphones: The Android platform is used by tablets, netbooks, e-book readers (such as the Barnes & Noble nook), the much-hyped Google TV, digital photo frames, and a variety of other consumer electronics. Mobile operators and carriers are taking the platform seriously and spending big bucks on ad campaigns for Android devices.

In the past two years, the Android platform has transitioned from an early-adopter platform to providing some serious competition to more established platforms. (Yes, we're talking about platforms such as the iPhone and BlackBerry.) Not only is Android the number one global smartphone platform, having surpassed Symbian by the end of 2010 (http://goo.gl/EDrgz), but it's also gained standing among consumers as the most desired smartphone operating system in the U.S. (http://goo.gl/pVRgy)—a claim supported by 50% of all new smartphone sales (double the sales rate of second place iOS, with 25%) and 37% of all smartphones in the U.S. (second place is iOS, with 27%).

But let's not digress into an argument over which platform is better, okay? Because, honestly, you're wasting your time if you think there's one platform to rule them all. The reality is that people the world over use different phones, in different places, for different reasons—reasons such as price, availability, coverage quality, feature set, design, familiarity, compatibility. There is no one-size-fits-all answer to this debate.

Having developed for just about every major mobile platform out there, we are keenly aware of the benefits and drawbacks of each platform. We do not presume to claim that one platform is better than another in general; each platform has distinct advantages over the rest, and these advantages can be maximized. The trick is to know which platform to use for a given project. Sometimes, the answer is to use as many platforms as possible. Lately, we've been finding that the answer is the Android platform. It's inexpensive and easy to develop for; it's available to millions of potential users worldwide; and it has fewer limitations than other platforms.

Still, the Android platform is relatively young and has not yet reached its full-fledged potential. This means frequent SDK updates, an explosion of new devices on the market, and a nearly full-time job keeping track of everything going on in the Android world. In other words, it might be a bit of a bumpy ride, but there's still time to jump on this bandwagon, write some kick-butt applications, and make a name for yourself.

So let's get to it.

Who Should Read This Book?

There's no reason anyone with an Android device, a good idea for a mobile application, and some programming knowledge couldn't put this book to use for fun and
profit. Whether you're a programmer looking to break into mobile technology or an
entrepreneur with a cool app idea, this book can help you realize your goals of
making killer Android apps.

We make as few assumptions about you as a reader of this book as possible. No
wireless development experience is necessary. We do assume that you're somewhat
comfortable installing applications on a computer (for example, Eclipse, the Java
JDK, and the Android SDK) and tools and drivers (for USB access to a phone). We
also assume that you own at least one Android device and can navigate your way
around it, for testing purposes.

Android apps are written in Java. Therefore, we assume you have a reasonably solid
understanding of the Java programming language (classes, methods, scoping, OOP,
and so on), ideally using the Eclipse development environment. Familiarity with
common Java packages such as java.lang, java.net, and java.util will serve
you well.

Android can also be a fantastic platform for learning Java, provided you have some
background in object-oriented programming and adequate support, such as a pro-
fessor or some really good Java programming references. We have made every
attempt to avoid using any fancy or confusing Java in this book, but you will find
that with Android, certain syntactical Java wizardry not often covered in your typical beginner's Java book is used frequently: anonymous inner classes, method
chaining, templates, reflection, and so on. With patience, and some good Java references, even beginning Java developers should be able to make it through this book
alive; those with a solid understanding of Java should be able to take this book and
run with it without issue.

Finally, regardless of your specific skill set, we do expect you to use this book in conjunction with other supplementary resources, specifically the Android SDK reference
and the sample source code that accompanies each coding chapter. The Android
SDK reference provides exhaustive documentation about each package, class, and
method of the Android SDK. It's searchable online. If we were to duplicate this data
in book form, this book would weigh a ton, literally. Secondly, we provide complete,
functional code projects for each lesson in this book. If you're having trouble building the tutorial application as you go along, compare your work to the sample code
for that lesson. The sample code is not intended to be the "answers," but it is the
complete code listings that could not otherwise be reproduced in a book of this
length.

How This Book Is Structured

In 24 easy one-hour lessons, you design and develop a fully functional network-enabled Android application, complete with social features and LBS (location-based services) support. Each lesson builds on your knowledge of newly introduced Android concepts, and you iteratively improve your application from hour to hour.

This book is divided into six parts:

▶ **Part I, "Android Fundamentals"**—Here, you get an introduction to Android, become familiar with the Android SDK and tools, install the development tools, and write your first Android application. Part I also introduces the design principles necessary to write Android applications, including how Android applications are structured and configured, as well as how to incorporate application resources such as strings, graphics, and user interface components into your projects.

▶ **Part II, "Building an Application Framework"**—In this part, you begin developing an application framework that serves as the primary teaching-tool for the rest of the book. You start by developing an animated splash screen, followed by screens for the main menu, settings, help, and scores. You review basic user interface design principles, such as how to collect input from the user, and how to display dialogs to the user. Finally, you implement the core application logic of the game screen.

▶ **Part III, "Enhancing Your Application with Powerful Android Features"**—Here, you dive deeper into the Android SDK, adding more specialized features to the sample application. You learn how to work with graphics and the built-in camera, how to leverage LBS, how to network-enable your application, and how to enhance your application with social features.

▶ **Part IV, "Adding Polish to Your Android Application"**—In this part, you learn how to customize your application for different handsets, screen sizes, and foreign languages. You also review different ways to test your mobile applications.

▶ **Part V, "Publishing Your Application"**—Here, you find out what you need to do to prepare for and publish your Android applications to the Android Market.

▶ **Part VI, "Appendixes"**—In this part you can find several helpful references for setting up your Android development environment, using the Eclipse IDE, and accessing supplementary book materials, like the book website and downloadable source code.

What Is (and Isn't) in This Book

First and foremost, this book aims to provide a thorough introduction to the Android platform by providing a detailed walk-through of building a real application from start to finish. We begin with the fundamentals, try to cover the most important aspects of development, and provide information on where to go for more information. This is not an exhaustive reference on the Android SDK. We assume you are using this book as a companion to the Android SDK documentation, which is available for download as part of the SDK and online at http://developer.android.com.

We only have 24 "hours" to get you up to speed on the fundamentals of Android development, so forgive us if we stay strictly to the topic at hand. Therefore, we take the prerequisites listed earlier seriously. This book does not teach you how to program, does not explain Java syntax and programming techniques, and does not stray too far into the details of supporting technologies often used by mobile applications, such as algorithm design, network protocols, developing web servers, graphic design, database schema design, and other such peripheral topics; there are fantastic references available on each of these subjects.

The Android SDK and related tools are updated very frequently (every few months). This means that no matter how we try, some minor changes in step-by-step instructions may occur if you choose to use versions of the tools and SDK that do not exactly match those listed later in this introduction in the "What Development Environment Is Used?" section. When necessary, we point out areas where the Android SDK version affects the features and functionality available to the developer. Feel free to contact us if you have specific questions; we often post addendum information or tool change information on our book website, http://androidbook.blogspot.com.

Although we specifically targeted Android SDK Version 2.3.3 and 3.0 for the tutorial in this book, many of the examples were tested on handsets running a variety of Android SDK versions, as far back as Android 1.6. We have made every effort to make the content of this book compatible with all currently used versions of Android, as well as work smoothly regardless of what version of the Android SDK you want to target.

This book is written in a tutorial style. If you're looking for an exhaustive reference on Android development, with cookbook-style code examples and a more thorough examination of the many features of the Android platform, we recommend our more advanced Android book, *Android Wireless Application Development*, Second Edition, which is part of the Addison-Wesley Developer's Library series.

What Development Environment Is Used?

The code in this book was written using the following development environments:

▶ Windows 7 and Mac OS X 10.6.7.

▶ Eclipse Java IDE Version 3.6 (Helios).

▶ Android ADT Plugin for Eclipse, 10.0.1.

▶ Android SDK tools, Release 10.

▶ Sun Java SE Development Kit (JDK) 6 Update 21.

▶ Android SDK Version 2.3.3 and 3.0 (developed and tested on a variety of SDK versions).

▶ Various Android devices including smartphones and tablets (Android SDK 2.2, 2.3.3, 3.0). (Note: Tablet optimization is discussed in Hour 20.)

▶ The network portions of the sample application leverage Google App Engine, but you won't need these tools.

What Conventions Are Used in This Book?

This book presents several types of sidebars for special kinds of information:

▶ **Did You Know?** messages provide useful information or hints related to the current text.

▶ **By the Way** messages provide additional information that might be interesting or relevant.

▶ **Watch Out!** messages provide hints or tips about pitfalls that may be encountered and how to avoid them.

This book uses the following code-related conventions:

▶ Code and programming terms are set in a monospace font.

▶ ➥ is used to signify that the code that follows should appear on the same line as the preceding code.

▶ Exception handling and error checking are often removed from printed code samples for clarity and to keep the book a reasonable length.

This book uses the following conventions for step-by-step instructions and explanations:

▶ The core application developed in this book is developed iteratively. Generally, this means that the first time a new concept is explained, every item related to the new concept is discussed in detail. As we move on to more advanced topics in later lessons, we assume that you have mastered some of the more rudimentary aspects of Android development from previous hours, and we do not repeat ourselves much. In some cases, we instruct you to implement something in an early lesson and then help you improve it in a later hour.

▶ We assume that you'll read the hours of this book in order. As you progress through the book, note that we do not spell out each and every step that must be taken for each and every feature you implement to follow along in building the core application example. For example, if three buttons must be implemented on a screen, we walk you step-by-step through the implementation of the first button but leave the implementation of the other two buttons as an exercise for you. In a later hour on a different topic, we might simply ask you to implement some buttons on another screen.

▶ Where we tell you to navigate through menu options, we separate options using commas. For example, when we instruct you on how to open a new document, we might say "Select File, New Document."

An Overview of Changes in This Edition

When we first began writing the first edition of this book, there were few Android devices on the market. Today there are hundreds of devices shipping all over the world—smartphones, tablets, e-book readers, and specialty devices such as the Google TV. The Android platform has gone through extensive changes since the first edition of this book was published. The Android SDK has many new features and the development tools have received many much-needed upgrades. Android, as a technology, is now on solid footing within the mobile marketplace.

Within this new edition we took the opportunity to overhaul the content of this book based upon reader feedback—but don't worry, it's still the book readers loved the first time, just leaner, clearer, and more up-to-date. In addition to adding new content, we've retested and upgraded all existing content (text and sample code) for use with the newest Android SDKs, tools, and devices. Here are some of the highlights of the additions and enhancements we've made to this edition:

▶ Coverage of the latest and greatest Android tools and utilities

▶ Updates to all existing chapters, often with entirely new sections

▶ Improved all code listings, making them more complete and clear

▶ Ensured that each time a new class is discussed, its full package is specified for easy reference

▶ New, improved exercises based upon tremendously helpful reader feedback

▶ Completely overhauled sample code in a new companion CD

▶ Clarified several tricky areas where readers of the first edition struggled

▶ Coverage of hot topics such as tablet design, services, App Widgets, Android Market updates, and more

▶ Even more tips and tricks from the trenches to help you design, develop, and test applications for different device targets, including an all-new chapter on tackling compatibility issues

We didn't take this review lightly; we touched every chapter and appendix to make this book the most painless way possible to get started developing Android applications. Finally, we included many additions, clarifications, and, yes, even a few fixes based upon the feedback from our fantastic (and meticulous) readers. Thank you!

About the Short Links

We've chosen to make most links in the book short links. This benefits the readers of the print book by making typing links in far easier and far less prone to error. These links are all shortened with the goo.gl link shortener, a service provided by Google. If the target of the link goes away, neither the original link nor the shortened link will work. We're confident this is the easiest way for readers to effectively use the links we've provided. In addition, as authors, we get to see which links readers are actually using.

Sometimes link shorteners are used as a way to hide nefarious links. Please be assured that we have only included shortened links we believe to be good (and thoroughly tested). In addition, Google provides screening of the target URLs for malware, phishing, and spam sites. Should a target link change hands and become a bad link, using the shortened link provides you, the reader, with an extra layer of protection.

For more information on this subject, see http://www.google.com/support/web-search/bin/answer.py?answer=190768 (http://goo.gl/iv8c7).

Supplementary Tools Available

This book has an accompanying CD with all the sample source code for each lesson.

This source code is also available for download on the publisher website: http://www.informit.com/store/product.aspx?isbn=0672335697.

Shane Conder and Lauren Darcey also run a blog at http://androidbook.blogspot.com, where you can always download the latest source code for their books as well. This website also covers a variety of Android topics as well as reader discussions, questions, clarifications, the occasional exercise walk-through, and lots of other information about Android development. You can also find links to their various technical articles online and in print.

HOUR 1

Getting Started with Android

What You'll Learn in This Hour:

▶ A brief history of the Android platform
▶ Familiarizing yourself with Eclipse
▶ Creating Android projects
▶ Running and debugging applications

Android is the first *complete*, *open*, and *free* mobile platform. Developers enjoy a comprehensive software development kit, with ample tools for developing powerful, feature-rich applications. The platform is open source, relying on tried-and-true open standards developers will be familiar with. And best of all, there are no costly barriers to entry for developers: no required fees. (A modest fee is required to publish on third-party distribution mechanisms such as the Android Market.) Android developers have numerous options for distributing and commercializing their applications.

Introducing Android

To understand where Android fits in with other mobile technologies, let's take a minute to talk about how and why this platform came about.

Google and the Open Handset Alliance

In 2007, a group of handset manufacturers, wireless carriers, and software developers (notably, Google) formed the Open Handset Alliance, with the goal of developing the next generation of wireless platform. Unlike existing platforms, this new platform would be nonproprietary and based on open standards, which would lead to lower development costs and increased profits. Mobile software developers would also have unprecedented access to the handset features, allowing for greater innovation.

As proprietary platforms such as RIM BlackBerry and Apple iPhone gained traction, the mobile development community eagerly listened for news of this potential game-changing platform.

Android Makes Its Entrance

In 2007, the Open Handset Alliance announced the Android platform and launched a beta program for developers. Android went through the typical revisions of a new platform. Several prerelease revisions of the Android Software Development Kit (SDK) were released. The first Android handset (the T-Mobile G1) began shipping in late 2008. Throughout 2009 and 2010, new and exciting Android smartphones reached markets throughout the world and the platform proved itself to industry and consumers alike. Over the last three years, numerous revisions to the Android platform have been rolled out, each providing compelling features for developers to leverage and users to enjoy. Recently, mobile platforms have begun to consider devices above and beyond the traditional smartphone paradigm, to other devices like tablets, e-book readers, and set-top boxes like Google TV.

As of this writing, hundreds of varieties of Android devices are available to consumers around the world—from high-end smartphones to low-end "free with contract" handsets and everything in between. This figure does not include the numerous Android tablet and e-book readers also available, the dozens of upcoming devices already announced, or the consumer electronics running Android. (For a nice list of Android devices, check out this Wikipedia link: http://goo.gl/fU2X5.) There are more than 200,000 applications currently published on the Android Market. In the United States, all major carriers now carry Android phones prominently in their product lines, as do many in Asia, Europe, Central/South America, and beyond. The rate of new Android devices reaching the world markets has continued to increase.

Google has been a contributing member of the Open Handset Alliance from the beginning. The company hosts the Android open source project as well as the developer website at http://developer.android.com. This website is your go-to site for downloading the Android SDK, getting the latest platform documentation, and browsing the Android developer forums. Google also runs the most popular service for selling Android applications to end users: the Android Market. The Android mascot is the little green robot shown in Figure 1.1.

FIGURE 1.1
The Android
mascot.

By the Way

Although most Android applications are written in Java, developers do have other options for targeting apps for Android devices. Specifically, developers can design web applications for the Android platform using HTML5 and JavaScript and they can use the Android Native Development Kit (NDK) to include C/C++ code for porting and performance purposes.

Web developers can design web applications for the Android platform; these apps are run through the mobile browser instead of installed on the Android device. For more information about web applications for Android, see the Android developer website: http://goo.gl/ejCBB.

Developers seeking to port or leverage existing C/C++ applications or libraries might want to take a look at the Android NDK. This does not mean that if you know C/C++ and not Java, you should use the NDK. The NDK toolset enables developers to develop portions of their Android applications using C and C++ code; this technique has both benefits and drawbacks. To determine if your application is a good candidate for using the Android NDK, check out the Android developer website: http://goo.gl/UxTzH. Using the Android NDK is considered a fairly advanced topic suitable for those who already have mastered the basics of Android development.

Cheap and Easy Development

If there's one time when "cheap and easy" is a benefit, it's with mobile development. Wireless application development, with its ridiculously expensive compilers and preferential developer programs, has been notoriously expensive to break into compared to desktop development. Here, Android breaks the proprietary mold. Unlike with other mobile platforms, there are virtually no costs to developing Android applications.

The Android SDK and tools are freely available on the Android developer website, http://developer.android.com (http://goo.gl/K8GgD). The freely available Eclipse program has become the most popular integrated development environment (IDE) for Android application development; there is a powerful plug-in available on the Android developer site for facilitating Android development with Eclipse.

So we've covered cheap; now let's talk about why Android development is easy. Android applications are written in Java, one of the most popular development languages around. Java developers will be familiar with many of the packages provided as part of the Android SDK, such as java.net. Experienced Java developers will be pleased to find that the learning curve for Android is quite reasonable.

In this book, we focus on the most common, popular, and simple setup for developing Android applications:

▶ We use the most common and supported development language: Java. Although we do not teach you Java; we do try our best to keep the Java code in this book simple and straightforward so that beginners won't be wrestling with syntax. Even so, if you are very new to Java, we would recommend *Sam's Teach Yourself Java in 24 Hours* by Rogers Cadenhead and *Thinking in Java* by Bruce Eckel, 4th Edition in Print (3rd Edition free from http://goo.gl/tYoXd) books for reference.

▶ We use the most popular development environment: Eclipse. It's free, it's well supported by the Android team, and it's the only supported IDE that is compatible with the Android Development Tools plug-in. Did we mention it's free?

▶ We write instructions for the most common operating system used by developers: Windows. Users of Linux or Mac may need to translate some keyboard commands, paths, and installation procedures.

▶ We focus on the most recent Android platform versions available on devices throughout the world: Android 1.6 and beyond. Yes, numerous devices still run Android 1.6 and may never reach 2.0 and beyond, so we take a platform version neutral approach to Android development, enabling you to target the most, if not all, devices currently in existence, as well as those of the future.

If you haven't installed the development tools needed to develop Android applications or the Android SDK and tools yet then do so at this time.

By the Way

Installing the Android SDK and Tools

You can find all the details of how to install and configure your computer for Android application development in Appendix A, "Configuring Your Android Development Environment." You need to install and configure Java, Eclipse, the Android SDK, and the ADT plug-in for Eclipse. You might also need to install the USB drivers for any Android handsets you use for development.

Let's get started!

Familiarizing Yourself with Eclipse

Begin by writing a simple Android "Hello, World" application that displays a line of text to the user. As you do so, you will also take a tour through the Eclipse environment. Specifically, you will learn about some of the features offered by the Android Development Tools (ADT) plug-in for Eclipse. The ADT plug-in provides functionality for developing, compiling, packaging, and deploying Android applications. Specifically, the ADT plug-in provides the following features:

- ▶ The Android Project Wizard, which generates all the required project files

- ▶ Android-specific resource editors including a Graphical Layout editor for designing Android application user interfaces

- ▶ The Android SDK and AVD (Android Virtual Devices) Manager

- ▶ The Eclipse DDMS perspective for monitoring and debugging Android applications

- ▶ Integration with the Android LogCat logging utility

- ▶ Integration with the Android Hierarchy Viewer layout utility

- ▶ Automated builds and application deployment to Android emulators and handsets

- ▶ Application packaging and code-signing tools for release deployment, including ProGuard support for code optimization and obfuscation

Now let's take some of these features for a spin.

Creating Android Projects

The Android Project Wizard creates all the required files for an Android application. Open Eclipse and follow these steps to create a new project:

1. Choose File, New, Android Project or click the Android Project creator icon on the Eclipse toolbar.

> The first time you try to create an Android Project in Eclipse, you might need to choose File, New, Project... and then select the Android, Android Project. After you have done this once, it appears in the Eclipse project types and you can use the method described in Step 1.

2. Choose a project name. In this case, name the project Droid1.

3. Choose a location for the project source code. Because this is a new project, select the Create New Project in Workspace radio button.

> If you prefer to store your project files in a location other than the default, simply uncheck the Use Default Location check box and browse to the directory of your choice.

4. Select a build target for your application. For most applications, you want to select the version of Android most appropriate for the devices used by your target audience and the needs of your application. If you are planning to use the Google add-ons (for example, Google Maps), be sure to choose the Google APIs version for your target platform. For this example, the Android 2.3 (API level 9) build target is sufficient.

5. Specify an application name. This name is what users will see. In this case, call the application Droid #1.

6. Specify a package name, following standard package namespace conventions for Java. Because all code in this book falls under the com.androidbook.* namespace, use the package name com.androidbook.droid1.

7. Check the Create Activity check box, which instructs the wizard to create a default launch Activity class for the application. Call your activity DroidActivity. Your project settings should look much like Figure 1.2.

What Is an Activity?

An activity is a core component of the Android platform. Each activity represents a task the application can do, often tied to a corresponding screen in the application user interface.

The Droid #1 application has a single activity, called `DroidActivity`, which has a single responsibility: to display a `String` to the user. We talk more about activities in Hour 3, "Building Android Applications."

8. Confirm that the Min SDK Version field is correct. This field is set to the API level of the build target by default (for example, Android 2.3 is API level 9). If you want to support older versions of the Android SDK, you need to change this value. For example, to support devices with Android 1.6, set the Min SDK Version to API Level 4.

9. Click the Next button.

10. The Android project wizard enables you to create a test project in conjunction with your Android application. For this example, a test project is unnecessary. However, you can always add a test project later by clicking the Android Test Project creator icon, which is to the right of the Android Project Wizard icon (JU) on the Eclipse toolbar. Test projects are discussed in detail in Hour 22, "Testing Android Applications."

11. Click the Finish button.

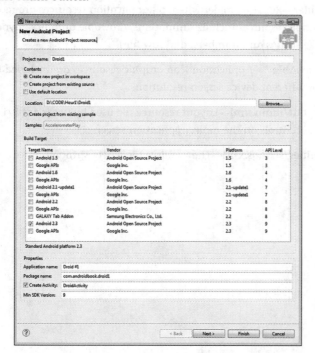

FIGURE 1.2
The Android Project Wizard in Eclipse.

Exploring the Android Project Files

You should now see a new Android project called Droid1 in the Eclipse File Explorer. In addition to linking the appropriate Android SDK jar file, the following core files and directories are created:

▶ **AndroidManifest.xml**—The central configuration file for the application.

▶ **default.properties**—A generated build file used by Eclipse and the Android ADT plug-in. Do not edit this file.

▶ **proguard.cfg**—A generated build file used by Eclipse, ProGuard, and the Android ADT plug-in. Edit this file to configure your code optimization and obfuscation settings for release builds.

▶ **/src folder**—Required folder for all source code.

▶ **/src/com.androidbook.droid1/DroidActivity.java**—Main entry point to this application, named `DroidActivity`. This activity has been defined as the default launch activity in the Android manifest file.

▶ **/gen/com.androidbook.droid1/R.java**—A generated resource management source file. Do not edit this file.

▶ **/assets folder**—Required folder where uncompiled file resources can be included in the project.

▶ **/res folder**—Required folder where all application resources are managed. Application resources include animations, drawable graphics, layout files, data-like strings and numbers, and raw files.

▶ **/res/drawable-***—Application icon graphic resources are included in several sizes for different device screen resolutions.

▶ **/res/layout/main.xml**—Layout resource file used by `DroidActivity` to organize controls on the main application screen.

▶ **/res/values/strings.xml**—The resource file where string resources are defined.

Editing Project Resources

The Android manifest file is the central configuration file for an Android application. Double-click the `AndroidManifest.xml` file within your new project to launch the Android manifest file editor (see Figure 1.3).

FIGURE 1.3
Editing an Android manifest file in Eclipse.

You can also add existing Android projects to Eclipse by using the Android Project Wizard. To do this, simply select Create Project from Existing Source instead of the default Create New Project in Workspace in the New Android Project dialog (refer to Figure 1.2). Several sample projects are provided in the `/samples` directory of the Android SDK, under the specific platform they support. For example, the Android SDK sample projects are found in the directory `/platforms/android-XXX/samples` (where *XXX* is the platform level number, such as "9").

You can also select a third option: Create Project from Existing Sample, which does what it says. However, make sure you choose the build target first option to get the list of sample projects you can create.

Because all Android resource files, including the Android manifest file, are simply XML files, you can always edit the XML instead of using the resource editors. You can create a new Android XML resource file by clicking the Android XML creator icon () on the Eclipse toolbar.

Editing the Android Manifest File

The Android manifest file editor organizes the manifest information into a number of tabs:

▶ **Manifest**—Use this tab, shown in Figure 1.3, for general application-wide settings such as the package name and application version information (used for installation and upgrade purposes).

▶ **Application**—Use this tab to define application details such as the name and icon the application displays, as well as the "guts" of the application, such as what activities can be run (including the default launch `DroidActivity`) and other functionality and services that the application provides.

▶ **Permissions**—Use this tab to define the application's permissions. For example, if the application requires the ability to read the contacts from the phone, then it must register a `Uses-Permission` tag within the manifest, with the name `android.permission.READ_CONTACTS`.

▶ **Instrumentation**—Use this tab for unit testing, using the various instrumentation classes available within the Android SDK.

▶ **AndroidManifest.xml**—Use this tab to access the XML editor to edit the manifest file manually.

If you switch to the AndroidManifest.xml tab, your manifest file should look something like this:

```xml
<?xml version="1.0" encoding="utf-8"?>
<manifest
    xmlns:android="http://schemas.android.com/apk/res/android"
    package="com.androidbook.droid1"
    android:versionCode="1"
    android:versionName="1.0">
    <application
        android:icon="@drawable/icon"
        android:label="@string/app_name">
        <activity
            android:name=".DroidActivity"
            android:label="@string/app_name">
            <intent-filter>
                <action
                    android:name="android.intent.action.MAIN" />
                <category
                    android:name="android.intent.category.LAUNCHER" />
            </intent-filter>
        </activity>
    </application>
    <uses-sdk
        android:minSdkVersion="9" />
</manifest>
```

Try It Yourself ▼

Edit the Android Manifest File

Now it's time to edit the Android manifest file. One setting you're going to want to know about is the `debuggable` attribute. You cannot debug your application until you set this value to true, so follow these steps:

1. Open the `AndroidManifest.xml` file in the Android manifest file editor.

2. Navigate to the Application tab.

3. Pull down the drop-down for the `debuggable` attribute and choose `true`.

4. Save the manifest file, either using Control+S or by pressing the Save icon (🖫) on the Eclipse toolbar.

If you switch to the AndroidManifest.xml tab and look through the XML, notice that the application tag now has the `debuggable` attribute:

```
android:debuggable="true"
```

▲

Editing Other Resource Files

Android applications are made up of functions (Java code, classes) and data (including resources such as graphics, strings, and so on). Most Android application resources are stored under the `/res` subdirectory of the project. The following subdirectories are also available by default in a new Android project:

▶ **/drawable-ldpi, /drawable-hdpi, /drawable-mdpi**—These subdirectories store graphics and drawable resource files for different screen densities and resolutions. If you browse through these directories using the Eclipse Project Explorer, you will find the `icon.png` graphics file in each one; this is your application's icon. You learn more about the difference between these directories in Hour 20, "Developing for Different Devices."

▶ **/layout**—This subdirectory stores user interface layout files. Within this subdirectory you will find the `main.xml` screen layout resource file that defines the user interface for the one activity in this simple application.

▶ **/values**—This subdirectory organizes the various types of resources, such as text strings, color values, and other primitive types. Here you find the `strings.xml` resource file, which contains all the string resources used by the application.

If you double-click any of resource files, the resource editor launches. Remember, you can always edit the XML directly.

▼   **Try It Yourself**

Edit a String Resource

If you inspect the `main.xml` layout file of the project, you will notice that it displays a simple layout with a single `TextView` control. This user interface control simply displays a string. In this case, the string displayed is defined in the string resource called `@string/hello`.

To edit the string resource called `@string/hello`, using the string resource editor, follow these steps:

1. Open the `strings.xml` file in the resource editor by double-clicking it in the Package Explorer of Eclipse.

2. Select the `String` called `hello` and note the name (`hello`) and value (`Hello World, DroidActivity!`) shown in the resource editor.

3. Within the Value field, change the text to `Hello, Dave`.

4. Save the file.

If you switch to the strings.xml tab and look through the raw XML, you will notice that two string elements are defined within a `<resources>` block:

```
<?xml version="1.0" encoding="utf-8"?>
<resources>
    <string name="hello">Hello, Dave</string>
    <string name="app_name">Droid #1</string>
</resources>
```

The first resource is the string called `@string/hello`. The second resource is the string called `@string/app_name`, which contains the name label for the application. If you look at the Android manifest file again, you should see `@string/app_name` used in the application configuration.

▲

We talk much more about project resources in Hour 4, "Managing Application Resources." For now, let's move on to compiling and running the application.

Running and Debugging Applications

To build and debug an Android application, you must first configure your project for debugging. The ADT plug-in enables you to do this entirely within the Eclipse development environment. Specifically, you need to do the following:

▶ Create and configure an Android Virtual Device (AVD)

▶ Create an Eclipse debug configuration for your project

▶ Build the Android project and launch the Emulator with the AVD

When you have completed each of these tasks, Eclipse attaches its debugger to the Android emulator (or Android device connected via USB), and you are free to run and debug the application as desired.

Managing Android Virtual Devices

To run an application in the Android emulator, you must configure an Android Virtual Device (AVD). The AVD profile describes the type of device you want the emulator to simulate, including which Android platform to support. You can specify different screen sizes and resolutions, and you can specify whether the emulator has an SD card and, if so, its capacity. In this case, an AVD for the default installation of Android 2.3 suffices. Here are the steps for creating a basic AVD:

1. Launch the Android SDK and AVD Manager from within Eclipse by clicking the little green Android icon with the arrow (🔳) on the toolbar. You can also launch the manager by selecting Window, Android SDK and AVD Manager in Eclipse.

2. Click the Virtual Devices menu item on the left menu. The configured AVDs will be displayed as a list. There are no default AVDs.

3. Click the New button to create a new AVD.

4. Choose a name for the AVD. Because you are going to take all the defaults, name this AVD VanillaAVD.

5. Choose a build target. For example, to support Android 2.3, choose the item build target called Android 2.3 – API Level 9 from the drop-down.

6. Choose an SD card capacity, in either kibibytes or mibibytes. (Not familiar with kibibytes? See this Wikipedia entry: http://goo.gl/N3Rdd.) Each SD card image takes up space on your hard drive, so choose a reasonable size, such as

a 1024MiB. (The minimum is 9MiB, but keep in mind that the full size of the
SD card is stored on your machine.)

7. Choose a skin. This option controls the different visual looks of the emulator.
   In this case, go with the default screen skin, which displays in portrait mode.

   Your project settings should look as shown in Figure 1.4.

8. Click the Create AVD button and wait for the operation to complete. This
   might take a few seconds if your SD card capacity is large, as the memory
   allocated for the SD card emulation is formatted as part of the AVD creation
   process.

9. Check the Snapshot checkbox to enable much faster emulator restart times at
   the expense of some storage space.

10. Click Finish. You should now see your newly created AVD in the list.

FIGURE 1.4
Creating a new
AVD in Eclipse.

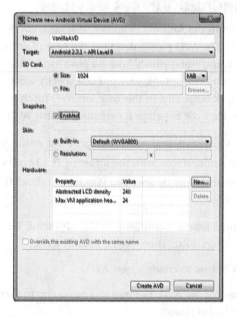

Creating Debug and Run Configurations in Eclipse

You are almost ready to launch your application. You have one last task remaining:
You need to create a Debug configuration (or a Run configuration) for your project
in Eclipse. To do this, take the following steps:

1. In Eclipse, choose Run, Debug Configurations from the menu, or, alternatively, click the drop-down menu next to the Debug icon (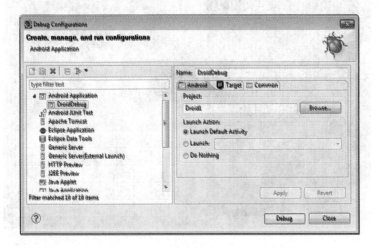) on the Eclipse toolbar and choose the Debug Configurations option.

2. Double-click the Android Application item to create a new entry.

3. Edit that new entry, currently called New_configuration.

4. Change the name of the configuration to DroidDebug.

5. Set the project by clicking the Browse button and choosing the Droid1 project.

6. On the Target tab, check the box next to the AVD you created.

> If you choose Manual on the Target tab, instead of choosing Automatic and selecting an AVD, you will be prompted to choose a target each time you launch this configuration. This is useful when you're testing on a variety of devices and emulator configurations. See "Launching Android Applications on a Device," later in this hour, for more information.

7. Apply your changes by clicking the Apply button. Your Debug Configurations dialog should look as shown in Figure 1.5.

FIGURE 1.5
The DroidDebug debug configuration in Eclipse.

Launching Android Applications Using the Emulator

It's launch time, and your application is ready to go! To launch the application, you can simply click the Debug button from within the Launch Configuration screen, or you can do it from the project by clicking the little green bug icon (🐞) on the Eclipse toolbar. Then select DroidDebug debug configuration from the list.

By the Way

> On some older emulators, you might need to click the Menu button on the emulator or drag the lock slider to the right when you come to the Screen Locked view.
>
> The first time you try to select DroidDebug debug configuration from the little green bug drop-down, you have to navigate through the debug configuration manager. Future attempts show the DroidDebug configuration for convenient access.

After you click the Debug button, the emulator launches, as shown in Figure 1.6. This can take some time, so be patient.

FIGURE 1.6
An Android emulator launching (Startup view).

Now the Eclipse debugger is attached, and your application runs, as shown in Figure 1.7.

As you can see, the application is very simple. It displays a single TextView control, with a line of text. The application does nothing else.

FIGURE 1.7
The Droid #1
Android applica-
tion running in
the emulator.

Debugging Android Applications Using DDMS

In addition to the normal Debug perspective built into Eclipse for stepping through
code and debugging, the ADT plug-in adds the DDMS perspective. While you have
the application running, take a quick look at this perspective in Eclipse. You can get
to the DDMS perspective (see Figure 1.8) by clicking the Android DDMS icon
(**DDMS**) in the top-right corner of Eclipse. To switch back to the Eclipse Project
Explorer, simply choose the Java perspective from the top-right corner of Eclipse.

FIGURE 1.8
The DDMS per-
spective in
Eclipse with
both an emula-
tor (running
Android 2.3)
and a physical
device (running
Android 2.3.1).

If the DDMS perspective is not visible in Eclipse, you can add it to your workspace by clicking the Open Perspective button in the top right-hand corner next to the available perspectives (or, alternatively, choose Window, Open Perspective). To see a complete list of available perspectives, select the Other option from the Open Perspective drop-down menu. Select the DDMS perspective and press OK.

You can use the DDMS perspective to monitor application processes, as well as interact with the emulator. You can simulate voice calls and send SMS messages to the emulator. You can send a mock location fix to the emulator to mimic location-based services. You learn more about DDMS (Dalvik Debug Monitor Service) and the other tools available to Android developers in Hour 2, "Mastering the Android Development Tools."

The LogCat logging tool is displayed on both the DDMS perspective and the Debug Perspective. This tool displays logging information from the emulator or the device, if a device is plugged in via USB.

Launching Android Applications on a Device

It's time to load your application onto a real handset. To do this, you need to plug an Android device into your computer using the USB data cable. Make sure you have configured this device for debugging purposes, as discussed in Appendix A.

To ensure that you debug using the correct settings, follow these steps:

1. In Eclipse, from the Java perspective (as opposed to the DDMS perspective), choose Run, Debug Configurations.

2. Double-click DroidDebug Debug Configuration.

3. On the Target tab, change Deployment Target Selection Mode to Manual. You can always change it back to Automatic later, but choosing Manual mode forces you to choose whether to debug within the emulator (with a specific AVD) or a device, if one is plugged in via USB, whenever you choose to deploy and debug your application from Eclipse.

4. Apply your changes by clicking the Apply button.

5. Plug an Android device into your development computer, using a USB cable.

6. Click the Debug button within Eclipse. A dialog (Figure 1.9) appears, showing all available configurations for running and debugging your application. All physical devices are listed, as are existing emulators that are running. You can also launch new emulator instances by using other AVDs you have created.

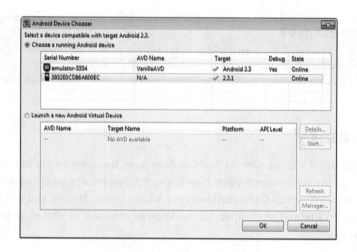

FIGURE 1.9
The Eclipse dialog for choosing an application deployment target, including a running emulator instance r
unning the VanillaAVD configuration and a physical device running Android 2.3.1.

7. Choose the running Android device instance. There should be one listed for each handset plugged into the machine via USB. If you do not see the handset listed, check your cables and make sure you installed the appropriate drivers, as explained in Appendix A.

Eclipse will now install the Android application on the device, attach the debugger, and run your application. Your device should show a screen very similar to the one you saw in the emulator, as shown in Figure 1.10. If you look at the DDMS perspective in Eclipse, you see that logging information is available, and many features of the DDMS perspective work with real handsets as well as the emulator.

FIGURE 1.10
The Droid #1 application running on the Nexus S, an Android device.

New to Eclipse?

If you're still learning the ropes of the Eclipse development environment, now is a great time to check out Appendix B, "Eclipse IDE Tips and Tricks."

Summary

Congratulations! You are now an Android developer. You have begun to learn your way around the Eclipse development environment. You created your first Android project. You reviewed and compiled working Android code. Finally, you ran your newly created Android application on the Android emulator as well as on a real Android device.

Q&A

Q. *What programming languages are supported for Android development?*

A. Right now, Java is the only programming language fully supported for Android development. Other languages, such as C++, may be added in the future. Although applications must be Java, C and C++ can be used for certain routines that need higher performance by using the Android NDK. Web developers can also write web applications that run in the Android web browser instead of being installed on the device.

Q. *I want to develop with the latest and greatest version of the Android platform. Why would I want to create AVDs for older target platforms such as Android 1.6 when newer versions of the Android SDK are available?*

A. Although handset firmware may be updated over-the-air, not every Android device will support every future firmware version. Verify the firmware version available on each of your target devices carefully before choosing which Android SDK version(s) your application will support and be tested on. You learn more about targeting different platform versions in Hour 20.

Q. *The Android resource editors can be cumbersome for entering large amounts of data, such as many string resources. Is there any way around this?*

A. Android project files, such as the Android manifest, layout files, and resource values (for example, /res/values/strings.xml), are stored in specially formatted XML files. You can edit these files manually by clicking on the XML tab of the resource editor. We talk more about the XML formats in Hour 4.

Workshop

Quiz

1. Who are the members of the Open Handset Alliance?

   A. Handset manufacturers

   B. Wireless operators and carriers

   C. Mobile software developers

   D. All of the above

2. What is the most popular IDE for Android development?

   A. Eclipse

   B. IntelliJ

   C. Emacs

3. True or False: You can simply launch the Android emulator to use default settings right after the SDK is installed.

4. True or False: You can use Eclipse for debugging when your application is running on an Android device.

Answers

1. D. The Open Handset Alliance is a business alliance that represents all levels of the handset supply chain.

2. A. Eclipse is the most popular IDE for Android development. You can use other IDEs, but they do not enable you to use the specially-designed Android ADT plug-in that is integrated with Eclipse.

3. False. You must first create an Android Virtual Device configuration, or AVD, to specify the device characteristics that the emulator should emulate.

4. True. Eclipse supports debugging within the emulator and on the device, provided that device is configured properly and connected to your development machine via a USB connection.

Exercises

1. Visit the Android website at http://developer.android.com and look around. Check out the online Developer's Guide and reference materials. Check out the Community tab and seriously consider signing up for the Android Beginners and Android Developers Google Groups.

2. Visit the Eclipse website and take a look around. Check out the online documentation at http://www.eclipse.org/documentation/ (http://goo.gl/fc406). Eclipse is an open-source project, made freely available. Check out the Contribute link (http://www.eclipse.org/contribute/) and consider how you might give back to this great project in some way, either by reporting bugs, or one of the many other options provided.

3. Within Eclipse, create a second AVD for a different platform version, or a different screen size/resolution. Try launching the Droid #1 application using your new AVD and see what happens.

4. If you downloaded the Android sample projects using the Android SDK and AVD Manager, try adding one of the Android sample projects to your Eclipse workspace. To do this within Eclipse, follow the steps to create a new Android project, except choose Create Project from Existing Source and set the project location to the specific Android sample project you want to load. Sample projects are located in the /samples subdirectory wherever you installed the Android SDK. For example, try sample projects such as LunarLander or APIDemos. Browse through the project files and then create a debug configuration and then compile and launch the sample application in the emulator as you did your own applications.

HOUR 2

Mastering the Android Development Tools

What You'll Learn in This Hour:

▶ Using the Android documentation
▶ Debugging applications with DDMS
▶ Working with the Android Emulator
▶ Using the Android Debug Bridge (ADB)
▶ Working with Android virtual devices

Android developers are fortunate to have more than a dozen development tools at their disposal to help facilitate the design of quality applications. Understanding what tools are available and what they can be used for is a task best done early in the Android learning process, so that when you are faced with a problem, you have some clue as to which utility might be able to help you find a solution. Most of the Android development tools are integrated into Eclipse using the ADT plug-in, but you can also launch them independently—you can find the executables in the /tools subdirectory of the Android SDK installation. During this hour, we walk through a number of the most important tools available for use with Android. This information will help you develop Android applications faster and with fewer roadblocks.

Using the Android Documentation

Although it is not a tool, per se, the Android documentation is a key resource for Android developers. An HTML version of the Android documentation is provided in the /docs subfolder of the Android SDK documentation, and this should always be your first stop when you encounter a problem. You can also access the latest help documentation online at the

Android Developer website, http://developer.android.com (http://goo.gl/K8GgD, see Figure 2.1 for a screenshot of the Dev Guide tab of this website).

FIGURE 2.1
Android developer documentation (online version).

The Android documentation is divided into seven sections:

▶ **Home**—This tab provides some high-level news items for Android developers, including announcements of new platform versions. You can also find quick links for downloading the latest Android SDK, publishing your applications on the Android Market, and other helpful information.

▶ **SDK**—This tab provides important information about the SDK version installed on your machine. One of the most important features of this tab is the release notes, which describe any known issues for the specific installation. This information is also useful if the online help has been upgraded but you want to develop to an older version of the SDK.

▶ **Dev Guide**—This tab links to the Android Developer's Guide, which includes a number of FAQs for developers, best practice guides and a useful glossary of Android terminology for those new to the platform. The appendix section also lists all Android platform versions (API Levels), supported media formats, and lists of intents.

▶ **Reference**—This tab includes, in a Javadoc-style format, a searchable package and class index of all Android APIs provided as part of the Android SDK.

▶ **Resources**—This tab includes links to articles, tutorials, and sample code. It also acts as a gateway to the Android developer forums. There are a number of Google groups you can join, depending on your interests.

▶ **Videos**—This tab, which is available online only, is your resource for Android training videos. Here, you can find videos about the Android platform, developer tips, and the Google I/O conference sessions.

▶ **Blog**—This tab links to the official Android developer blog. Check here for the latest news and announcements about the Android platform. This is a great place to find how-to examples, learn how to optimize Android applications, and hear about new SDK releases and Android Developer Challenges.

Now is a good time to get to know your way around the Android SDK documentation. First, check out the online documentation and then try the local documentation (available in the /docs subdirectory of your Android SDK installation).

Debugging Applications with DDMS

The Dalvik Debug Monitor Service (DDMS) is a debugging utility that is integrated into Eclipse through a special Eclipse perspective. The DDMS perspective provides a number of useful features for interacting with emulators and handsets and debugging applications (Figure 2.2).

The features of DDMS are roughly divided into five functional areas:

▶ Task management

▶ File management

▶ Emulator interaction

▶ Logging

▶ Screen captures

FIGURE 2.2
The DDMS perspective, with one emulator and two Android devices connected (the Nexus S running 2.3.1 and the Samsung Galaxy Tablet running 2.2).

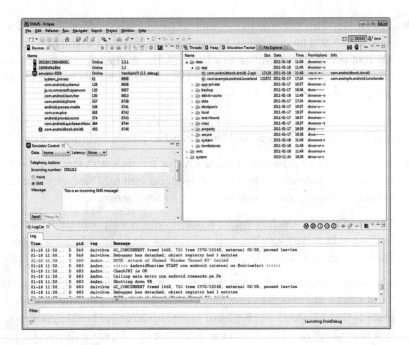

DDMS and the DDMS perspective are essential debugging tools. Now let's take a look at how to use these features in a bit more detail.

> The DDMS tool can be launched separately from Eclipse. You can find it in the Android SDK /tools directory.

Managing Tasks

The top-left corner of the DDMS perspective lists the emulators and handsets currently connected. You can select individual instances and view its processes and threads. You can inspect threads by clicking on the device process you are interested in—for example, com.androidbook.droid1—and clicking the Update Threads button ( ), as shown in Figure 2.3. You can also prompt garbage collection on a process and then view the heap updates by clicking the Update Heap button ( ). Finally, you can stop a process by clicking the Stop Process button ( ).

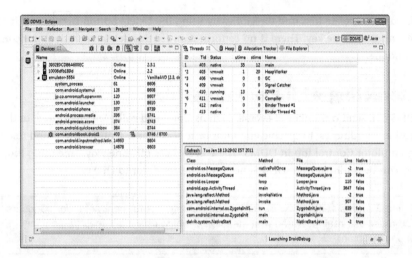

FIGURE 2.3
Using DDMS to examine thread activity for the Droid1 application.

Debugging from the DDMS Perspective

Within the DDMS perspective, you can choose a specific process on an emulator or a handset and then click the Debug button (🐞) to attach a debugger to that process. You need to have the source code in your Eclipse workspace for this to work properly. This works only in Eclipse, not in the standalone version of DDMS.

Browsing the Android File System

You can use the DDMS File Explorer to browse files and directories on the emulator or a device (Figure 2.4). You can copy files between the Android file system and your development machine by using the Push (📱) and Pull (📲) buttons available in the top right-hand corner of the File Explorer tab.

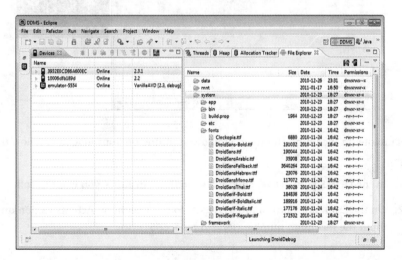

FIGURE 2.4
Using the DDMS File Explorer to browse system fonts on the handset.

You can also delete files and directories by using the Delete button ( ) or just pressing the Delete key. There is no confirmation for this delete operation, nor can it be undone.

Interacting with Emulators

DDMS can send a number of events, such as simulated calls, SMS messages, and location coordinates, to specific emulator instances. These features are found under the Emulator Control tab in DDMS. These events are all "one way," meaning that they can be initiated from DDMS, not from the emulator to DDMS.

By the Way

> These features generally work for emulators only, not for handsets. For handsets, you must use real calls and real messages, which may incur fees (depending upon your plan).

Simulating Incoming Calls to the Emulator

You can simulate incoming voice calls by using the DDMS Emulator Control tab (see Figure 2.5). This is not a real call; no data (voice or otherwise) is transmitted between the caller and the receiver.

FIGURE 2.5
Using the DDMS Emulator Control tab (left) to place a call to the emulator (right).

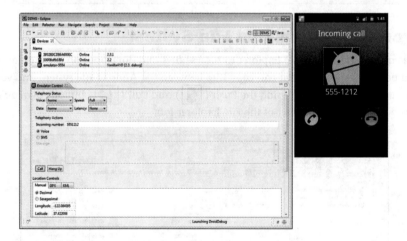

To simulate an incoming call to an emulator running on your machine, follow these steps:

1. In the DDMS perspective, choose the emulator instance you want to call.

2. On the Emulator Control tab, navigate to the Telephony Actions section and input the incoming number (for example, 5551212).

3. Select the Voice radio button.

4. Click the Call button.

5. In the emulator, you should see an incoming call. Answer the call by clicking the Send button in the emulator or sliding the slider to the right.

6. End the call at any time by clicking the End button in the emulator or by clicking the Hang Up button in the DDMS perspective.

Simulating Incoming SMS Messages to the Emulator

You can simulate incoming SMS messages by using the Emulator DDMS Emulator Control tab (see Figure 2.6). You send an SMS much as you initiate a voice call.

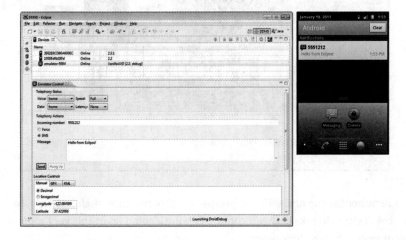

FIGURE 2.6
Using the DDMS Emulator Control tab (left) to send an SMS message to the emulator (right).

To send an SMS message to an emulator running on your machine, follow these steps:

1. In the DDMS perspective, choose the emulator instance you want a send an SMS message to.

2. On the Emulator Control tab, navigate to the Telephony Actions section and input the Incoming number (for example, 5551212).

3. Select the SMS radio button.

4. Type an SMS message in the Message textbox.

5. Click the Send button. In the emulator, you should see an incoming SMS notification on the notification bar. Pull down the bar to view the SMS message details.

Taking Screenshots of the Emulator or Handset

One feature that can be particularly useful for debugging both handsets and emulators is the ability to take screenshots of the current screen (see Figure 2.7).

FIGURE 2.7
Using the DDMS Screen Capture button to take a screenshot of the Nexus S handset, which happens to be displaying some old photo albums in the Gallery.

The screenshot feature of the DDMS perspective is particularly useful when used with real devices. To take a screen capture of what's going on at this very moment on your device, follow these steps:

1. In the DDMS perspective, choose the device (or emulator) you want a screenshot of. The device must be connected via USB.

2. On that device or emulator, make sure you have the screen you want. Navigate to it, if necessary.

3. Press the Screen Capture button ( ) to take a screen capture. This launches a capture screen dialog.

4. Within the capture screen, click the Save button to save the screenshot to your local hard drive. The Rotate button rotates the Device Screen Capture tool to display in landscape mode. This tool does not show a live view, just a snapshot; click the Refresh button to update the capture view if you make changes on the device. The Copy button places the image on your system's clipboard

for pasting into another application, such as an image editor. Click the Done button to exit the tool and return to the DDMS perspective.

Viewing Log Information

The LogCat logging utility that is integrated into the DDMS perspective enables you to view the Android logging console. You might have noted the LogCat logging tab, with its diagnostic output, in Figure 2.2 earlier in this chapter. We talk more about how to implement your own custom application logging in Hour 3, "Building Android Applications."

Filtering Log Information

Eclipse has the ability to filter logs by log severity. You can also create custom log filters by using tags. For more information on how to do this, see Appendix B, "Eclipse IDE Tips and Tricks."

Working with the Android Emulator

The Android emulator is probably the most powerful tool at a developer's disposal. It is important for developers to learn to use the emulator and understand its limitations. The Android emulator is integrated with Eclipse, using the ADT plug-in for the Eclipse IDE.

Emulator Limitations

The Android emulator is a convenient tool, but it has a number of limitations:

- ▶ The emulator is not a device. It simulates general handset behavior, not specific hardware implementations or limitations.
- ▶ Sensor data, such as satellite location information, battery and power settings, and network connectivity, are all simulated using your computer.
- ▶ Peripherals such as camera hardware are not fully functional.
- ▶ Phone calls cannot be placed or received but are simulated. SMS messages are also simulated and do not use a real network.
- ▶ No USB or Bluetooth support is available.
- ▶ Using the Android emulator is not a substitute for testing on a true Android device.

Providing Input to the Emulator

As a developer, you can provide input to the emulator in a number of ways:

▶ Use your computer mouse to click, scroll, and drag items (for example, sliding volume controls) onscreen as well as on the emulator skin.

▶ Use your computer keyboard to input text into controls.

▶ Use your mouse to simulate individual finger presses on the soft keyboard or physical emulator keyboard.

▶ Use a number of emulator keyboard commands to control specific emulator states.

▼ **Try It Yourself**

Try out some of the methods of interacting with the emulator:

1. In Eclipse, launch the Droid1 application you created in Hour 1, "Getting Started with Android."

2. While your application is running, press Ctrl+F11 and Ctrl+F12 to toggle the emulator between portrait and landscape modes. Note how your application redraws the simple application screen to accommodate different screen orientations.

3. Press Alt+Enter to enter full screen mode with the emulator. Then press Alt+Enter again to return to exit full screen mode.

Many useful commands are available for the emulator. For an exhaustive list, see the official emulator documentation that was installed with the Android SDK documentation or online at http://goo.gl/aDnxD.

▲

Exploring the Android System

If you're not already familiar with how Android devices work, now is a good time to learn your way around Android devices as users see them. Keep in mind that we're focusing on the "Google experience" or the "Google Android" user interface here, as opposed to the specific user interface changes and additions made by some device manufacturers and carriers.

Table 2.1 lists some important features of Android devices. The features described in this table apply to the traditional smartphone UI most users are familiar. The Android 3.0/3.1 release (which was tablet-centric) introduced a new holographic UI design, which has similar features.

TABLE 2.1 Android System Screens and Features

Feature	Description	Appearance
Home screen	Default screen. This is a common location for app widgets and live folders. You will also find a quick launch bar for the Dialer ( ) and Browser ( ) applications as well as the Application menu.	
Dialer application	Built-in application for making and receiving phone calls. Note: The emulator has limited phone features.	
Messaging application	Built-in application for sending and receiving SMS messages. Note: The emulator has limited messaging features.	
Browser application	Built-in web browser. Note that the emulator has an Internet connection, provided that your machine has one.	
Contacts application	Database of contact information. Leveraged by many applications on the platform for sharing purposes. Consider adding some "test contacts" to your favorite emulator AVD instance for easy development and testing.	

TABLE 2.1   Continued

Feature	Description	Appearance
Application menu	Shows all installed applications. From the Home screen, click the Application menu button (▦) to see all installed applications.	
Settings application	Built-in application to configure a wide variety of "phone" settings for the emulator, such as application management, sound and display settings, and localization.	
Dev Tools application	Built-in application to configure development tool settings.	

Using SD Card Images with the Emulator

If you want to transfer files to your emulator instance (running a specific AVD) then you likely want to use the SD card image associated with that AVD to store those files. The same holds true for downloading content such as images using the Browser application.

To copy file data to a specific instance of the emulator, use the File Explorer tab of the DDMS perspective to push or pull files. For developers, most file transfers occur either between the /mnt/sdcard directories, or to and from specific application's directory (for example, /data/data/com.androidbook.droid1).

> If you've added media files (for example, images, audio, and so on) to the device, you might need to force the Android operating system to rescan for new media. The most convenient way to do this is by using the Dev Tools application to run the Media Scanner. After you force a scan, you should see any new images you copied to the `/mnt/sdcard/download` directory, for example, show up in the Gallery application.

Using Other Android Tools

Although we've already covered the most important tools, a number of other special-purpose utilities are included with the Android SDK. A list of the tools that come as part of the Android SDK is available on the Android developer website at http://goo.gl/yzFHz. Here you can find a description of each tool as well as a link to its official documentation.

Summary

The Android SDK ships with a number of powerful tools to help with common Android development tasks. The Android documentation is an essential reference for developers. The DDMS debugging tool, which is integrated into the Eclipse development environment as a perspective, is useful for monitoring emulators and devices. The Android emulator can be used for running and debugging Android applications virtually, without the need for an actual device. There are also a number of other tools for interacting with handsets and emulators in a variety of situations.

Q&A

Q. *Is the Android documentation installed with the Android SDK the same as the documentation found at http://developer.android.com (http://goo.gl/K8GgD)?*

A. No. The documentation installed with the SDK was "frozen" at the time the SDK was released, which means it is specific to the version of the Android SDK you installed. The online documentation is always the latest version of the Android SDK. We recommend using the online documentation, unless you are working offline or have a slow Internet connection, in which case the local SDK documentation should suffice.

Q. *Do you have to develop Android applications with Eclipse?*

A. No. Eclipse is the preferred development environment for Android (and the IDE used by this book), but it is not required for Android development. The ADT plug-in for Eclipse provides a convenient entry point for many of the underlying development tools for creating, debugging, packaging, and signing Android applications. Developers who do not use Eclipse (or simply want access to these tools outside of the IDE) can run the underlying tools directly from the command line. For more information about developing using other IDEs, see the Android developer website at http://goo.gl/KXcZj.

Q. *Is testing your application on the emulator alone sufficient?*

A. No. The Android emulator simulates the functionality of a real device and can be a big time- and cost-saving tool for Android projects. It is a convenient tool for testing, but it can only pretend at real device behavior. The emulator cannot actually determine your real location or make a phone call. Also, the emulator is a generic device simulation and does not attempt to emulate any quirky details of a specific device or user experience. Just because your application runs fine on the emulator does not guarantee that it will work on the device.

Workshop

Quiz

1. Which features are available in the DDMS perspective?

    A. Taking screenshots of emulator and handset screens

    B. Browsing the file system of the emulator or handset

    C. Monitoring thread and heap information on the Android system

    D. Stopping processes

    E. Simulating incoming phone calls and SMS messages to emulators

    F. All of the above

2. True or False: You must use the Android emulator for debugging.

3. Which target platforms can Android applications be written for?

4. True or False: The Android emulator is a generic device that supports only one screen configuration.

Answers

1. F. All of the above. The DDMS perspective can be used to monitor, browse, and interact with emulators and handsets in a variety of ways.

2. False. The Android emulator is useful for debugging, but you can also connect the debugger to an actual device and directly debug applications running on real hardware.

3. There are a number of target platforms available and more are added with each new SDK release. Some important platform targets include Android 1.6, Android 2.1, Android 2.2, Android 2.3, and Android 3.0. Targets can include the Google APIs, if desired. These targets map to the AVD profiles you must create in order to use the Android emulator.

4. False. The Android emulator is a generic device, but it can support several different skins. For a complete list of skins supported, see the Android SDK and AVD Manager.

Exercises

1. Launch the Android emulator and customize your home screen. Change the wallpaper. Install an AppWidget. Get familiar with how the emulator tries to mimic a real handset. Note the limitations, such as how the dialer works.

2. Launch the Android emulator and browse the Settings application. Try changing a setting and see what happens. Uninstall an application (Settings, Applications, Manage Applications, click on an application and press the UnInstall button, then confirm with the OK button to uninstall an application). Under the About phone submenu, check the Android version.

3. Launch the Android emulator and browse the Dev Tools application. Review the settings available, especially those within the Development Settings submenu. Check out the documentation for this tool on the Android Developer website at http://goo.gl/QcScV.

4. Launch the Android emulator and add a few test contacts to your Contacts database for this AVD. If you give a contact the phone number you like to use for incoming calls from the DDMS perspective, the contact's name and picture display whenever that phone number is used for testing purposes.

5. Add a new image file to your emulator instance. Find a JPG graphic file, such as a photo, and use the DDMS perspective's File Explorer to push the file to the `/mnt/sdcard/download` directory of the emulator. Launch the Gallery application and if the image does not immediately appear, then use the Dev Tools application to perform a media scan and re-launch the Gallery application. After the graphic is visible in the Gallery, go create a contact and set the contact's photo to that photo.

HOUR 3

Building Android Applications

What You'll Learn in This Hour:

▶ Designing a typical Android application
▶ Using the application context
▶ Working with activities, intents, and dialogs
▶ Logging application information

Every platform technology uses different terminology to describe its application components. The three most important classes on the Android platform are `Context`, `Activity`, and `Intent`. Although there are other, more advanced, components developers can implement, these three components form the building blocks for each and every Android application. This hour focuses on understanding how Android applications are put together and gives you a look at some handy utility classes that can help developers debug applications.

Designing a Typical Android Application

An Android application is a collection of tasks, each of which is called an activity. Each activity within an application has a unique purpose and user interface. To understand this more fully, imagine a theoretical game application called Chippy's Revenge.

Some past readers have assumed that they were to perform all the tasks discussed in this chapter on their own and build an app in one hour without any help whatsoever. Not so! This chapter is meant to give you the 10,000 foot view of Android application development so that you have a good idea of what to expect when you'll begin implementing an application from the ground up a few chapters from now. The application provided in this hour is simply a sample, not the full-fledged application we build throughout later chapters. We do this so you get an idea of how another application might be built, too.

So get yourself a cup of coffee, tea, or your "brain fuel" of choice, sit back, relax, and let's discuss the building blocks of Android apps!

Designing Application Features

The design of the Chippy's Revenge game is simple. It has five screens:

> ▶ **Splash**—This screen acts as a startup screen, with the game logo and version. It might also play some music.

> ▶ **Menu**—On this screen, a user can choose from among several options, including playing the game, viewing the scores, and reading the help text.

> ▶ **Play**—This screen is where game play actually takes place.

> ▶ **Scores**—This screen displays the highest scores for the game (including high scores from other players), providing players with a challenge to do better.

> ▶ **Help**—This screen displays instructions for how to play the game, including controls, goals, scoring methods, tips, and tricks.

Starting to sound familiar? This is a generic design you might recognize from many a mobile application, game or otherwise, on any platform.

By the Way

You can find some helpful user interface guidelines stated on the Android developer website at http://goo.gl/a6MFa. Certainly, you are free to implement any kind of user interface you desire, provided that the application is stable, responsive, and plays nice with the rest of the Android system.

The best and most popular applications leverage the users' existing experience with user interfaces. It's best to improve upon those features, when necessary, rather than reinvent them, so you don't force the user to exert time and effort to learn your application in order to use it properly.

Determining Application Activity Requirements

You need to implement five activity classes, one for each feature of the game:

▶ SplashActivity—This activity serves as the default activity to launch. It simply displays a layout (maybe just a big graphic), plays music for several seconds, and then launches MenuActivity.

▶ MenuActivity—This activity is pretty straightforward. Its layout has several buttons, each corresponding to a feature of the application. The onClick() handlers for each button trigger cause the associated activity to launch.

▶ PlayActivity—The real application guts are implemented here. This activity needs to draw stuff onscreen, handle various types of user input, keep score, and generally follow whatever game dynamics the developer wants to support.

▶ ScoresActivity—This activity is about as simple as SplashActivity. It does little more than load a bunch of scoring information into a TextView control within its layout.

▶ HelpActivity—This activity is almost identical to ScoresActivity, except that instead of displaying scores, it displays help text. Its TextView control might possibly scroll.

Each activity class should have its own corresponding layout file stored in the application resources. You could use a single layout file for ScoresActivity and HelpActivity, but it's not necessary. If you did, though, you would simply create a single layout for both and set the image in the background and the text in the TextView control at runtime, instead of within the layout file.

Figure 3.1 shows the resulting design for your game, Chippy's Revenge Version 0.0.1 for Android.

FIGURE 3.1
Application
design of a sim-
ple Android
application
(Chippy's
Revenge).

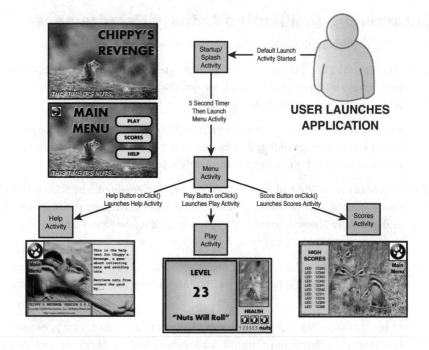

Implementing Application Functionality

Now that you understand how a typical Android application might be designed,
you're probably wondering how to go about implementing that design.

We've talked about how each activity has its own user interface, defined within a
separate layout resource file. You might be wondering about implementation hurdles such as the following:

▶ How do I control application state?

▶ How do I save settings?

▶ How do I launch a specific activity?

With our theoretical game application in mind, it is time to dive into the implementation details of developing an Android application. A good place to start is the
application context.

Using the Application Context

The application context is the central location for all top-level application functionality. You use the application context to access settings and resources shared across multiple activity instances.

You can retrieve the application context for the current process by using the getApplicationContext() method, like this:

```
Context context = getApplicationContext();
```

Because the Activity class is derived from the Context class, you can use the this object instead of retrieving the application context explicitly when you're writing code inside your Activity class.

> You might be tempted to just use your Activity context in all cases. Doing so can lead to memory leaks, though. The subtleties of why this happens are beyond the scope of this book, but there is a great official Android blog post on this topic at http://goo.gl/JI3Jj.

After you have retrieved a valid application context, you can use it to access application-wide features and services.

Retrieving Application Resources

You can retrieve application resources by using the getResources() method of the application context. The most straightforward way to retrieve a resource is by using its unique resource identifier, as defined in the automatically generated R.java class. The following example retrieves a String instance from the application resources by its resource ID:

```
String greeting = getResources().getString(R.string.hello);
```

Accessing Application Preferences

You can retrieve shared application preferences by using the getSharedPreferences() method of the application context. You can use the SharedPreferences class to save simple application data, such as configuration settings. You can give each SharedPreferences object a unique name, enabling you to organize preference values into categories, or store preferences together in one large, unnamed set.

For example, you might want to keep track of each user's name and some simple game state information, such as whether the user has credits left to play. The following code creates a set of shared preferences called `GamePrefs` and saves a few such preferences:

```
SharedPreferences settings = getSharedPreferences("GamePrefs", MODE_PRIVATE);
SharedPreferences.Editor prefEditor = settings.edit();
prefEditor.putString("UserName", "Spunky");
prefEditor.putBoolean("HasCredits", true);
prefEditor.commit();
```

To retrieve preference settings, you simply retrieve `SharedPreferences` and read the values back out:

```
SharedPreferences settings = getSharedPreferences("GamePrefs", MODE_PRIVATE);
String userName = settings.getString("UserName", "Chippy Jr. (Default)");
```

Accessing Other Application Functionality Using Contexts

The application context provides access to a number of top-level application features. Here are a few more things you can do with the application context:

▶ Launch `Activity` instances

▶ Retrieve assets packaged with the application

▶ Request a system-level service provider (for example, location service)

▶ Manage private application files, directories, and databases

▶ Inspect and enforce application permissions

The first item on this list—launching `Activity` instances—is perhaps the most common reason you will use the application context.

Working with Activities

The `Activity` class is central to every Android application. Much of the time, you'll define and implement an activity for each screen in your application.

In the Chippy's Revenge game application, you have to implement five different `Activity` classes. In the course of playing the game, the user transitions from one activity to the next, interacting with the layout controls of each activity.

Launching Activities

There are a number of ways to launch an activity, including the following:

- ▶ Designating a launch activity in the manifest file
- ▶ Launching an activity using the application context
- ▶ Launching a child activity from a parent activity for a result

Designating a Launch Activity in the Manifest File

Each Android application must designate a default activity within the Android manifest file. If you inspect the manifest file of the Droid1 project, you will notice that DroidActivity is designated as the default activity.

> Other Activity classes might be designated to launch under specific circumstances. You manage these secondary entry points by configuring the Android manifest file with custom filters.

Did you Know?

In Chippy's Revenge, SplashActivity is the most logical activity to launch by default.

Launching Activities Using the Application Context

The most common way to launch an activity is to use the startActivity() method of the application context. This method takes one parameter, called an Intent. We talk more about the Intent class in a moment, but for now, let's look at a simple startActivity() call.

The following code calls the startActivity() method with an explicit intent:

```
startActivity(new Intent(getApplicationContext(), MenuActivity.class));
```

This intent requests the launch of the target activity, named MenuActivity, by its class. This class must be implemented elsewhere within the package.

Because the MenuActivity class is defined within this application's package, it must be registered as an activity within the Android manifest file. In fact, you could use this method to launch every activity in your theoretical game application; however, this is just one way to launch an activity.

Launching an Activity for a Result

Sometimes you want to launch an activity, have it determine something such as a user's choice, and then return that information to the calling activity. When an

activity needs a result , it can be launched using the
`Activity.startActivityForResult()` method. The result is returned in the `Intent`
parameter of the calling activity's `onActivityResult()` method. We talk more
about how to pass data using an `Intent` parameter in a moment.

Managing Activity State

Applications can be interrupted when various higher-priority events, such as phone
calls, take precedence. There can be only one active application at a time; specifically, a single application activity can be in the foreground at any given time.

Android applications are responsible for managing their state, as well as their memory, resources, and data. The Android operating system may terminate an activity
that has been paused, stopped, or destroyed when memory is low. This means that
any activity that is not in the foreground is subject to shutdown. In other words, an
Android application must keep state and be ready to be interrupted and even shutdown at any time.

Using Activity Callbacks

The `Activity` class has a number of callbacks that provide an opportunity for an
activity to respond to events such as suspending and resuming. Table 3.1 lists the
most important callback methods.

TABLE 3.1   Key Callback Methods of Android Activities

Callback Method	Description	Recommendations
`onCreate()`	Called when an activity starts or restarts.	Initializes static activity data. Binds to data or resources required. Sets layout with `setContentView()`.
`onResume()`	Called when an activity becomes the foreground activity.	Acquires exclusive resources. Starts any audio, video, or animations.
`onPause()`	Called when an activity leaves the foreground.	Saves uncommitted data. Deactivates or releases exclusive resources. Stops any audio, video, or animations.
`onDestroy()`	Called when an application is shutting down.	Cleans up any static activity data. Releases any resources acquired.

The main thread is often called the UI thread, because this is where the processing
for drawing the UI takes place internally. An activity must perform any processing

that takes place during a callback reasonably quickly, so that the main thread is not blocked. If the main UI thread is blocked for too long, the Android system may decide toshut down the activity due to a lack of response. This is especially important to respond quickly during the onPause() callback, when a higher-priority task (for example, an incoming phone call) is entering the foreground.

Figure 3.2 shows the order in which activity callbacks are called.

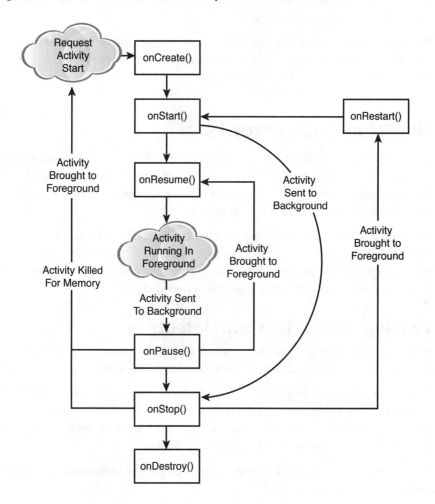

FIGURE 3.2
Important call-back methods of the activity life cycle.

Saving Activity State

An activity can have private preferences—much like shared application preferences. You can access these preferences by using the getPreferences() method of the activity. This mechanism is useful for saving state information. For example,

`PlayActivity` for your game might use these preferences to keep track of the current level and score, player health statistics, and game state.

Shutting Down Activities

To shut down an activity, you make a call to the `finish()` method. There are several different versions of this method to use, depending whether the activity is shutting itself down or shutting down another activity.

Within your game application, you might return from the Scores, Play, and Help screens to the Menu screen by finishing `ScoresActivity`, `PlayActivity`, or `HelpActivity`.

Working with Intents

An `Intent` object encapsulates a task request used by the Android operating system. When the `startActivity()` method is called with the `Intent` parameter, the Android system matches the `Intent` action with the appropriate activity on the Android system. That activity is then launched.

The Android system handles all intent resolution. An intent can be very specific, including a request for a specific activity to be launched, or somewhat vague, requesting that any activity matching certain criteria be launched. For the finer details on intent resolution, see the Android documentation.

Passing Information with Intents

Intents can be used to pass data between activities. You can use an intent in this way by including additional data, called extras, within the intent.

To package extra pieces of data along with an intent, you use the `putExtra()` method with the appropriate type of object you want to include. The Android programming convention for intent extras is to name each one with the package prefix (for example, `com.androidbook.chippy.NameOfExtra`).

For example, the following intent includes an extra piece of information, the current game level, which is an integer:

```
Intent intent = new Intent(getApplicationContext(), HelpActivity.class);
intent.putExtra("com.androidbook.chippy.LEVEL", 23);
startActivity(intent);
```

When the `HelpActivity` class launches, the `getIntent()` method can be used to retrieve the intent. Then the extra information can be extracted using the appropriate methods. Here's an example. This little piece of information could be used to give special Help hints, based on the level.

```
Intent callingIntent = getIntent();
int helpLevel = callingIntent.getIntExtra("com.androidbook.chippy.LEVEL", 1);
```

For the parent activity that launched a subactivity using the `startActivityForResult()` method, the result is passed in as a parameter to the `onActivityResult()` method with an `Intent` parameter. The intent data can then be extracted and used by the parent activity.

Using Intents to Launch Other Applications

Initially, an application may only be launching activity classes defined within its own package. However, with the appropriate permissions, applications may also launch external activity classes in other applications.

There are well-defined intent actions for many common user tasks. For example, you can create intent actions to initiate applications such as the following:

▶ Launching the built-in web browser and supplying a URL address

▶ Launching the web browser and supplying a search string

▶ Launching the built-in Dialer application and supplying a phone number

▶ Launching the built-in Maps application and supplying a location

▶ Launching Google Street View and supplying a location

▶ Launching the built-in Camera application in still or video mode

▶ Launching a ringtone picker

▶ Recording a sound

Here is an example of how to create a simple intent with a predefined action (ACTION_VIEW) to launch the web browser with a specific URL:

```
Uri address = Uri.parse("http://www.perlgurl.org");
Intent surf = new Intent(Intent.ACTION_VIEW, address);
startActivity(surf);
```

This example shows an intent that has been created with an action and some data. The action, in this case, is to view something. The data is a uniform resource identifier (URI), which identifies the location of the resource to view.

For this example, the browser's activity then starts and comes into foreground, causing the original calling activity to pause in the background. When the user finishes with the browser and clicks the Back button, the original activity resumes.

Applications may also create their own intent types and allow other applications to call them, which makes it possible to develop tightly integrated application suites.

Working with Dialogs

Handset screens are small, and user interface real estate is valuable. Sometimes you want to handle a small amount of user interaction without creating an entirely new activity. In such instances, creating an activity dialog can be very handy. Dialogs can be helpful for creating very simple user interfaces that do not necessitate an entirely new screen or activity to function. Instead, the calling activity dispatches a dialog, which can have its own layout and user interface, with buttons and input controls.

Table 3.2 lists the important methods for creating and managing activity dialog windows.

TABLE 3.2   Important Dialog Methods of the Activity Class

Method	Purpose
`Activity.showDialog()`	Shows a dialog, creating it if necessary.
`Activity.onCreateDialog()`	Is a callback when a dialog is being created for the first time and added to the activity dialog pool.
`Activity.onPrepareDialog()`	Is a callback for updating a dialog on-the-fly. Dialogs are created once and can be used many times by an activity. This callback enables the dialog to be updated just before it is shown for each `showDialog()` call.
`Activity.dismissDialog()`	Dismisses a dialog and returns to the activity. The dialog is still available to be used again by calling `showDialog()` again.
`Activity.removeDialog()`	Removes the dialog completely from the activity dialog pool.

Activity classes can include more than one dialog, and each dialog can be created and then used multiple times.

There are quite a few types of ready-made dialog types available for use in addition to the basic dialog. These are `AlertDialog`, `CharacterPickerDialog`, `DatePickerDialog`, `ProgressDialog`, and `TimePickerDialog`.

You can also create an entirely custom dialog by designing an XML layout file and using the `Dialog.setContentView()` method. To retrieve controls from the dialog layout, you simply use the `Dialog.findViewById()` method.

Working with Fragments

The concept of fragments is relatively new to Android. A fragment is simply a block of UI, with its own life cycle, that can be reused within different activities. Fragments allow developers to create highly modular user interface components that can change dramatically based on screen sizes, orientation, and other aspects of the display that might be relevant to the design.

Table 3.3 shows some important lifecycle calls that are sent to the Fragment class.

TABLE 3.3   Key Fragment Lifecycle Callbacks

Method	Purpose
onCreateView()	Called when the fragment needs to create its view
onStart()	Called when the fragment is made visible to the user
onPause()	Similar to `Activity.onPause()`
onStop()	Called when the fragment is no longer visible
onDestroy()	Final fragment cleanup

Although the lifecycle of a fragment is similar to that of an activity, a fragment only exists within an activity. A common example of fragment usage is to change the UI flow between portrait and landscape modes. If an interface has a list of items and a details view, the list and the details could both be fragments. In portrait orientation, the screen would show the list view followed by the details view, both full screen. But in landscape mode, the view could show the list and details side-by-side.

The modular nature of fragments makes them a very powerful user interface building block. The Fragment API is also available as a static compatibility library for use with older versions of Android as far back as Android 1.6, thus Fragment features can be leveraged by most Android applications.

Logging Application Information

Android provides a useful logging utility class called android.util.Log. Logging messages are categorized by severity (and verbosity), with errors being the most severe. Table 3.4 lists some commonly used logging methods of the Log class.

TABLE 3.4   Commonly Used Log Methods

Method	Purpose
Log.e()	Logs errors
Log.w()	Logs warnings
Log.i()	Logs informational messages
Log.d()	Logs debug messages
Log.v()	Logs verbose messages
Log.wtf()	Logs messages for events that should not happen (like during a failed assert)

Excessive use of the Log utility can result in decreased application performance. Debug and verbose logging should be used only for development purposes and removed before application publication.

The first parameter of each Log method is a string called a tag. One common Android programming practice is to define a global static string to represent the overall application or the specific activity within the application such that log filters can be created to limit the log output to specific data.

For example, you could define a string called TAG, as follows:

```
private static final String TAG = "MyApp";
```

Now anytime you use a Log method, you supply this tag. An informational logging message might look like this:

```
Log.i(TAG, "In onCreate() callback method");
```

You can use the LogCat utility from within Eclipse to filter your log messages to the tag string. See Appendix B, "Eclipse IDE Tips and Tricks," for details.

Summary

In this hour, you've seen how different Android applications can be designed using three application components: Context, Activity, and Intent. Each Android application comprises one or more activities. Top-level application functionality is accessible through the application context. Each activity has a special function and (usually) its own layout, or user interface. An activity is launched when the Android system matches an intent object with the most appropriate application activity, based on the action and data information set in the intent. Intents can also be used to pass data from one activity to another.

In addition to learning the basics of how Android applications are put together, you've also learned how to take advantage of useful Android utility classes, such as application logging, which can help streamline Android application development and debugging.

Q&A

Q. *Do I need to have an Activity class for each screen in my application?*

A. It's common practice to organize screens by Activity, but not a requirement. For example, you might use the same Activity class to handle similar tasks, adjusting the screen layout as needed.

Q. *How do I design a responsive application that will not be shut down during low-memory conditions?*

A. Applications can limit (but never completely eradicate) the risk of being shut down during low-memory situations by prudently managing activity state. This means using the appropriate activity callbacks and following the recommendations. Most importantly, applications should acquire resources only when necessary and release those resources as soon as possible.

Q. *How should I design an input form for an Android application?*

A. Mobile applications need to be ready to pause and resume at any time. Typical web form style—with various fields and Submit, Clear, and Cancel buttons—isn't very well suited to mobile development. Instead, consider committing data as it is entered. This will keep data housekeeping to a minimum as activity state changes, without frustrating users.

Q. *Where can I find a list of intents exposed by other applications?*

A. The OpenIntents.org website keeps a list of intent actions at www.openintents.org/en/intentstable. This list includes those built into Android as well as those available from third-party applications.

Workshop

Quiz

1. Which of these screens does it make the most sense to show to a user first?

   A. Menu screen

   B. Splash screen

   C. Play screen

2. True or False: Android provides a simple method for storing application settings.

3. What is the recommended way to get a context instance, required by many Android calls?

   A. `Context context = (Context) this;`

   B. `Context context = getAndroidObject(CONTEXT);`

   C. `Context context = getApplicationContext();`

4. True or False: The `android.util.Log` class supports five types of logging messages.

Answers

1. B. The splash screen shows the game logo before the user starts to play.

2. True. Simply use the `SharedPreferences` class to store simple settings.

3. C. This retrieves the context tied to your application. Using the activity context, as shown in A, works but is not recommended.

4. False. The `Log` class supports six log message types: error, warning, informational, debug, verbose and wtf (what a terrible failure).

Exercises

1. Add a logging tag to the `DroidActivity` class you created in the Droid1 project in Hour 1. Within the `onCreate()` callback method, add an informational logging message, using the `Log.i()` method. Run the application and view the log output in the Eclipse DDMS or Debug perspectives within the LogCat tab.

2. Within the DroidActivity class you created in the Droid1 project in Hour 1, add method stubs for the Activity callback methods in addition to onCreate(), such as onStart(), onRestart(), onResume(), onPause(), onStop(), and onDestroy(). To do this easily from within Eclipse, right-click the DroidActivity.java class and choose Source, Override/Implement methods. Under the Activity class methods, select the suggested methods (such as onStart() and so on) and hit the OK button. You should see appropriate method stubs added for each of the methods you selected.

3. Add a log message to each Activity class callback method you created in Exercise 2. For example, add an informational log message such as "In method onCreate()" to the onCreate() method. Run the application normally and view the log output to trace the application life cycle. Next, try some other scenarios, such as pausing or suspending the application and then resuming. Simulate an incoming call using the Eclipse DDMS perspective while running your application and see what happens.

HOUR 4

Managing Application Resources

What You'll Learn in This Hour:

▶ Using application and system resources
▶ Working with simple resource values
▶ Working with drawable resources
▶ Working with layouts
▶ Working with files
▶ Working with other types of resources

Android applications rely upon strings, graphics, and other types of resources to generate robust user interfaces. Android projects can include these resources, using a well-defined project resource hierarchy. In this hour, you review the most common types of resources used by Android applications, how they are stored, and how they can be accessed programmatically. This hour prepares you for working with resources in future chapters, but you are not directly asked to write code or create resources.

Using Application and System Resources

Resources are broken down into two types: application resources and system resources. Application resources are defined by the developer within the Android project files and are specific to the application. System resources are common resources defined by the Android platform and accessible to all applications through the Android SDK. You can access both types of resources at runtime.

You can load resources in your Java code, usually from within an activity. You can also reference resources from within other resources; for example, you might reference numerous string, dimension, and color resources from inside an XML layout resource, to define the properties and attributes of specific controls like background colors and text to display.

Working with Application Resources

Application resources are created and stored within the Android project files under the /res directory. Using a well-defined but flexible directory structure, resources are organized, defined, and compiled with the application package. Application resources are not shared with the rest of the Android system.

Storing Application Resources

Defining application data as resources (as opposed to at runtime in code) is good programming practice. Grouping application resources together and compiling them into the application package has the following benefits:

- ▶ Code is cleaner and easier to read, leading to fewer bugs.

- ▶ Resources are organized by type and guaranteed to be unique.

- ▶ Resources are conveniently located for handset customization.

- ▶ Localization and internationalization are straightforward.

The Android platform supports a variety of resource types (see Figure 4.1), which can be combined to form different types of applications.

Android applications can include many different kinds of resources. The following are some of the most common resource types:

- ▶ Strings, colors, and dimensions

- ▶ Drawable graphics files

- ▶ Layout files

- ▶ Raw files of all types

Resource types are defined with special XML tags and organized into specially named project directories. Some /res subdirectories, such as the /drawable, /layout, and /values directories, are created by default when a new Android project is created, but others must be added by the developer when required.

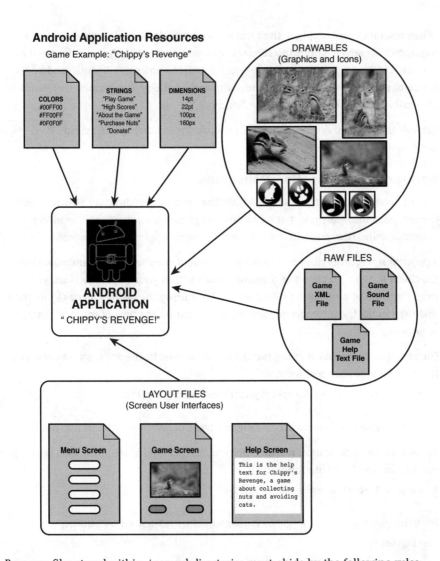

FIGURE 4.1
Android applications can use a variety of resources.

Resource files stored within /res subdirectories must abide by the following rules:

▶ Resource filenames must be lowercase.

▶ Resource filenames may contain letters, numbers, underscores, and periods only.

▶ Resource filenames (and XML name attributes) must be unique.

When resources are compiled, their name dictates their variable name. For example, a graphics file saved within the /drawable directory as mypic.jpg is referenced as @drawable/mypic. It is important to name resource names intelligently and be aware of character limitations that are stricter than file system names. (For example, dashes cannot be used in image filenames.)

Consult the Android documentation for specific project directory naming conventions.

Referencing Application Resources

All application resources are stored within the /res project directory structure and are compiled into the project at build time. Application resources can be used programmatically. They can also be referenced in other application resources.

Application resources can be accessed programmatically using the generated class file called R.java. To reference a resource from within your Activity class, you must retrieve the application's Resources object using the getResources() method and then make the appropriate method call, based on the type of resource you want to retrieve.

For example, to retrieve a string named hello defined in the strings.xml resource file, use the following method call:

```
String greeting = getResources().getString(R.string.hello);
```

We talk more about how to access different types of resources later in this hour.

To reference an application resource from another compiled resource, such as a layout file, use the following format:

```
@[resource type]/[resource name]
```

For example, the same string used earlier would be referenced as follows:

```
@string/hello
```

We talk more about referencing resources later in the hour, when we talk about layout files.

Working with System Resources

Applications can access the Android system resources in addition to their private resources. This "standardized" set of resources is shared across all applications, providing users with common styles, and other useful templates as well as commonly used strings and colors.

System resources are stored within the `android.R` package. There are classes for each of the major resource types. For example, the `android.R.string` class contains the system string resources. For example, to retrieve a system resource string called ok from within an `Activity` class, you first need to use the static method of the `Resources` class called `getSystem()` to retrieve the global system `Resource` object. Then you call the `getString()` method with the appropriate string resource name, like this:

```
String confirm = Resources.getSystem().getString(android.R.string.ok);
```

To reference a system resource from another compiled resource, such as a layout resource file, use the following format:

```
@android:[resource type]/[resource name]
```

For example, you could use the system string for ok by setting the appropriate string attribute as follows:

```
@android:string/ok
```

Working with Simple Resource Values

Simple resources such as string, color, and dimension values should be defined in XML files under the `/res/values` project directory in XML files. These resource files use special XML tags that represent name/value pairs. These types of resources are compiled into the application package at build time. You can manage string, color, and dimension resources by using the Eclipse Resource editor, or you can edit the XML resource files directly.

Working with Strings

You can use string resources anywhere your application needs to display text. You define string resources with the `<string>` tag, identify them with the name property, and store them in the resource file `/res/values/strings.xml`.

Here is an example of a string resource file:

```
<?xml version="1.0" encoding="utf-8"?>
<resources>
    <string name="app_name">Name this App</string>
    <string name="hello">Hello</string>
</resources>
```

String resources have a number of formatting options. Strings that contain apostrophes or single straight quotes must be escaped or wrapped within double straight quotes. Table 4.1 shows some simple examples of well-formatted string values.

TABLE 4.1   String Resource Formatting Examples

String Resource Value	Will Be Displayed As
Hello, World	Hello, World
"Hello, World"	Hello, World
Mother\'s Maiden Name:	Mother's Maiden Name:
He said, \"No.\"	He said, "No."

There are several ways to access a string resource programmatically. The simplest way is to use the getString() method within your Activity class:

```
String greeting = getResources().getString(R.string.hello);
```

Working with Colors

You can apply color resources to screen controls. You define color resources with the <color> tag, identify them with the name attribute, and store them in the file /res/values/colors.xml. This XML resource file is not created by default and must be created manually.

You can add a new XML file, such as this one, by choosing File, New, Android XML File and then fill out the resulting dialog with the type of file (such as values). This automatically sets the expected folder and type of file for the Android project.

Here is an example of a color resource file:

```
<?xml version="1.0" encoding="utf-8"?>
<resources>
    <color name="background_color">#006400</color>
    <color name="app_text_color">#FFE4C4</color>
</resources>
```

The Android system supports 12-bit and 24-bit colors in RGB format. Table 4.2 lists the color formats that the Android platform supports.

TABLE 4.2   Color Formats Supported in Android

Format	Description	Example
#RGB	12-bit color	#00F (blue)
#ARGB	12-bit color with alpha	#800F (blue, alpha 50%)
#RRGGBB	24-bit color	#FF00FF (magenta)
#AARRGGBB	24-bit color with alpha	#80FF00FF (magenta, alpha 50%)

The following Activity class code snippet retrieves a color resource named app_text_color using the getColor() method:

```
int textColor = getResources().getColor(R.color.app_text_color);
```

> Don't know your hex color values? No problem! There are lots of color pickers on the web. For example, http://goo.gl/uP5QP provides a simple color chart and a clickable color picker.

By the Way

Working with Dimensions

To specify the size of a user interface control such as a Button or TextView control, you need to specify different kinds of dimensions. Dimension resources are helpful for font sizes, image sizes and other physical or pixel-relative measurements. You define dimension resources with the <dimen> tag, identify them with the name property, and store them in the resource file /res/values/dimens.xml. This XML resource file is not created by default and must be created manually.

Here is an example of a dimension resource file:

```
<?xml version="1.0" encoding="utf-8"?>
<resources>
    <dimen name="thumbDim">100px</dimen>
</resources>
```

Each dimension resource value must end with a unit of measurement. Table 4.3 lists the dimension units that Android supports.

TABLE 4.3   Dimension Unit Measurements Supported in Android

Type of Measurement	Description	Unit String
Pixels	Actual screen pixels	px
Inches	Physical measurement	in
Millimeters	Physical measurement	mm
Points	Common font measurement	pt

TABLE 4.3   Continued

Type of Measurement	Description	Unit String
Density-independent pixels	Pixels relative to 160dpi	dp
Scale-independent pixels	Best for scalable font display	sp

The following `Activity` class code snippet retrieves a dimension resource called `thumbDim` using the `getDimension()` method:

```
float thumbnailDim = getResources().getDimension(R.dimen.thumbDim);
```

Working with Drawable Resources

Drawable resources, such as image files, must be saved under the `/res/drawable` project directory hierarchy. Typically, applications provide multiple versions of the same graphics for different pixel density screens. A default Android project contains three drawable directories: drawable-ldpi (low density), drawable-mdpi (medium density), and drawable-hdpi (high density). The system picks the correct version of the resource based on the device the application is running on. All versions of a specific resource must have the same name in each of the drawable directories. You learn more about these directories in Hour 20, "Developing for Different Devices." These types of resources are then compiled into the application package at build time and are available to the application.

You can drag and drop image files into the `/res/drawable` directory by using the Eclipse Project Explorer. Again, remember that filenames must be unique within a particular drawable directory, lowercase and contain only letters, numbers, and underscores.

Working with Images

The most common drawable resources used in applications are bitmap-style image files, such as PNG and JPG files. These files are often used as application icons and button graphics but may be used for a number of user interface components.

As shown in Table 4.4, Android supports many common image formats.

TABLE 4.4   Image Formats Supported in Android

Supported Image Format	Description	Required Extension
Portable Network Graphics	Preferred format (lossless)	`.png` (PNG)
Nine-Patch Stretchable Images	Preferred format (lossless)	`.9.png` (PNG)
Joint Photographic Experts Group	Acceptable format (lossy)	`.jpg` (JPEG/JPG)
Graphics Interchange Format	Discouraged but supported (lossless)	`.gif` (GIF)

Using Image Resources Programmatically

Image resources are encapsulated in the class `BitmapDrawable`. To access a graphic resource file called `/res/drawable/logo.png` within an `Activity` class, use the `getDrawable()` method, as follows:

```
BitmapDrawable logoBitmap =
    (BitmapDrawable)getResources().getDrawable(R.drawable.logo);
```

Most of the time, however, you don't need to load a graphic directly. Instead, you can use the resource identifier as the source attribute on a control such as an `ImageView` control within a compiled layout resource and it will be displayed on the screen. However, there are times when you might want to programmatically load, process, and set the drawable for a given ImageView control at runtime. The following `Activity` class code sets and loads the `logo.png` drawable resource into an `ImageView` control named `LogoImageView`, which must be defined in advance:

```
ImageView logoView = (ImageView)findViewById(R.id.LogoImageView);

logoView.setImageResource(R.drawable.logo);
```

Working with Other Types of Drawables

In addition to graphics files, you can also create specially formatted XML files to describe other `Drawable` subclasses, such as `ShapeDrawable`. You can use the `ShapeDrawable` class to define different shapes, such as rectangles and ovals. See the Android documentation for the `android.graphics.drawable` package for further information.

Working with Layouts

Most Android application user interface screens are defined using specially format-ted XML files called layouts. Layout XML files can be considered a special type of resource; they are generally used to define what a portion of, or all of, the screen will look like. It can be helpful to think of a layout resource as a template; you fill a layout resource with different types of view controls, which may reference other resources, such as strings, colors, dimensions, and drawables.

In truth, layouts can be compiled into the application package as XML resources or be created at runtime in Java from within your `Activity` class using the appropri-ate layout classes within the Android SDK. However, in most cases, using the XML layout resource files greatly improves the clarity, readability, and reusability of code and flexibility of your application.

Layout resource files are stored in the `/res/layout` directory hierarchy. You compile layout resources into your application as you would any other resources.

Here is an example of a layout resource file:

```
<?xml version="1.0" encoding="utf-8"?>
<LinearLayout
    xmlns:android="http://schemas.android.com/apk/res/android"
    android:orientation="vertical"
    android:layout_width="fill_parent"
    android:layout_height="fill_parent">
    <TextView
        android:layout_width="fill_parent"
        android:layout_height="wrap_content"
        android:text="@string/hello" />
</LinearLayout>
```

You might recognize this layout: It is the default layout, called `main.xml`, created with any new Android application. This layout file describes the user interface of the only activity within the application. It contains a `LinearLayout` control that is used as a container for all other user interface controls—in this case, a single `TextView` control. The `main.xml` layout file also references another resource: the string resource called `@string/hello`, which is defined in the `strings.xml` resource file.

Designing Layouts Using the Layout Resource Editor

You can design and preview compiled layout resources in Eclipse by using the layout resource editor (see Figure 4.2). Double-click the project file `/res/layout/main.xml`, within Eclipse to launch the layout resource editor. The layout resource editor has two tabs: Graphical Layout and main.xml. The Graphical Layout tab provides drag-

and-drop visual design and the ability to preview the layout in various device configurations. The main.xml tab enables you to edit the layout XML directly.

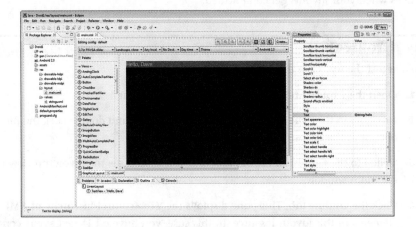

FIGURE 4.2
The layout resource editor in Eclipse.

Chances are, you'll switch back and forth between the graphical and XML modes frequently. There are also several other Eclipse panes that are helpful for using with the layout resource editor: the Outline pane and the Properties pane. You can add and remove controls to the specific layout using the Outline pane (Figure 4.2, bottom). You can set individual properties and attributes of a specific control by using the Properties pane (Figure 4.2, right). Note that Eclipse panes are not fixed—drag them around and configure them in a way that works for you. Eclipse actually calls these panes "views" (confusing for Android folks). You can also add different types of view "panes" from the Windows menu of Eclipse.

Like most other user interface designers, the layout resource editor works well for basic layout design but it has some limitations. For some of the more complex user interface controls, you might be forced to edit the XML by hand. You might also lose the ability to preview your layout if you add a control to your layout that is not supported by the Graphical Layout tool. In such a case, you can still view your layout by running your application in the emulator or on a handset. Displaying an application correctly on a handset, rather than the Eclipse layout editor, should always be a developer's primary objective.

Designing Layouts Using XML

You can edit the raw XML of a layout file. As you gain experience developing layouts, you should familiarize yourself with the XML layout file format. Switch to the XML view frequently and accustom yourself to the XML generated by each type of control. Do not rely on the Graphical Layout editor alone—that would be equivalent to a web designer who knows how to use a web design tool but doesn't know HTML. The Graphical Layout editor is still relatively new and not always the most reliable of tools when your layouts get complicated.

▼　**Try It Yourself**

Tired of just theory? Give the Eclipse Layout editor a spin:

1. Open the Droid1 Android project you created in Hour 1.

2. Navigate to the /res/layout/main.xml layout file and double-click the file to open it in the Eclipse layout resource editor.

3. Switch to the Graphical Layout tab, and you should see the layout preview in the main window.

4. Click the Outline tab. This pane displays the View control hierarchy of XML elements in this layout resource. In this case, you have a LinearLayout control. If you expand it, you see that it contains a TextView control.

5. Select the TextView control on the Outline tab. You see a colored box highlight the TextView control in the layout preview.

6. Click the Properties tab. This tab displays all the properties and attributes that can be configured for the TextView control you just selected. Scroll down to the property called Text and note that it has been set to a string resource called @string/hello.

7. Click the Text property called @string/hello on Properties tab. You can now modify the field. You can type in a string directly, manually enter a different string resource (@string/app_name, for example), or click the little button with the three dots and choose an appropriate resource from the list of string resources available to your application. Each time you change this field, note how the Graphical Layout preview updates automatically.

8. Switch to the main.xml tab and note how the XML is structured. Changes you make in the XML tab are immediately reflected in the Graphical Layout tab. If you save and run your project in the emulator, you should see results similar to those displayed in the preview.

Feel free to continue to explore the layout resource editor. You might want to try adding additional view controls, such as an ImageView control or another TextView control, to your layout. We cover designing layouts in much more detail later in this book.

▲

Using Layout Resources Programmatically

Layout controls, whether `Button`, `ImageView`, `TextView` controls, or `LinearLayout` controls are derived from the `View` class. In most instances, you do not need to load and access a whole layout resource programmatically. Instead, you simply want to modify specific `View` controls within it. For example, you might want to change the text being displayed by the `TextView` control in the `main.xml` layout resource.

The default layout file created with the Droid1 project contains one `TextView` control. However, this `TextView` control does not have a default name attribute. The easiest way to access the correct `View` control is by its unique name, so take a moment and set the `id` attribute of the `TextView` control using the layout resource editor. Call it `@+id/TextView01`.

Now that your `TextView` control has a unique identifier, you can find it from within your `Activity` class using the `findViewById()` method. After you have found the `TextView` you were looking for, you are free to call its methods, such as the `TextView` class's `setText()` method. Here's how you would retrieve a `TextView` object named `TextView01` that has been defined in the layout resource file:

```
TextView txt = (TextView)findViewById(R.id.TextView01);
```

Note that the `findViewById()` method takes a resource identifier—the same one you just configured in your layout resource file. Here's what's happening behind the scenes: When you save the layout resource file as XML, Eclipse automatically recompiles the generated `R.java` file associated with your project, making the identifier available for use within your Java classes. (If you don't have the Build Automatically setting in the Project menu turned on, you have to do build the project manually.)

Working with Files

In addition to string, graphic, and layout resources, Android projects can contain files as resources. These files may be in any format. However, some formats are more convenient than others.

Working with XML Files

As you might expect, the XML file format is well supported on the Android platform. Arbitrary XML files can be included as resources. These XML files are stored in the `/res/xml` resource directory. XML file resources are the preferred format for any structured data your application requires.

How you format your XML resource files is up to you. A variety of XML utilities are available as part of the Android platform, as shown in Table 4.5.

TABLE 4.5   XML Utility Packages

Package	Description
android.sax.*	Framework to write standard SAX handlers
android.util.Xml.*	XML utilities, including the XMLPullParser
org.xml.sax.*	Core SAX functionality (see www.saxproject.org)
javax.xml.*	SAX and limited DOM, Level 2 core support
org.w3c.dom	Interfaces for DOM, Level 2 core
org.xmlpull.*	XmlPullParser and XMLSerializer interfaces (see www.xmlpull.org)

To access an XML resource file called /res/xml/default_values.xml programmatically from within your Activity class, you can use the getXml() method of the Resources class, like this:

```
XmlResourceParser defaultDataConfig =

    getResources().getXml(R.xml.default_values);
```

After you have accessed the XML parser object, you can parse your XML, extract the appropriate data elements, and do with it whatever you wish.

Working with Raw Files

An application can include raw files as resources. Raw files your application might use include audio files, video files, and any other file formats you might need. All raw resource files should be included in the /res/raw resource directory. All raw file resources must have unique names, excluding the file suffix (meaning that file1.txt and file1.dat would conflict).

If you plan to include media file resources, you should consult the Android platform documentation to determine what media formats and encodings are supported on your application's target handsets. A general list of supported formats for Android devices is available at http://goo.gl/wMNS9.

The same goes for any other file format you want to include as an application resource. If the file format you plan on using is not supported by the native Android system, your application must do all file processing itself.

To access a raw file resource programmatically from within your `Activity` class, simply use the `openRawResource()` method of the `Resources` class. For example, the following code creates an `InputStream` object to access to the resource file `/res/raw/file1.txt`:

```
InputStream iFile = getResources().openRawResource(R.raw.file1);
```

> There are times when you might want to include files within your application but not have them compiled into application resources. Android provides a special project directory called `/assets` for this purpose. This project directory resides at the same level as the `/res` directory. Any files included in this directory are included as binary resources, along with the application installation package, and are not compiled into the application.
>
> Uncompiled files, called *application assets*, are not accessible through the `getResources()` method. Instead, you must use `AssetManager` to access files included in the `/assets` directory.

Did you know?

Working with Other Types of Resources

We have covered the most common types of resources you might need in an application. There are numerous other types of resources available as well. These resource types may be used less often and may be more complex. However, they allow for very powerful applications. Some of the other types of resources you can take advantage of include the following:

- ▶ Primitives (boolean values, integers)
- ▶ Arrays (string arrays, integer arrays, typed arrays)
- ▶ Menus
- ▶ Animation sequences
- ▶ Shape drawables
- ▶ Styles and themes
- ▶ Custom layout controls

When you are ready to use these other resource types, consult the Android documentation for further details. A good place to start is http://goo.gl/X9XZj.

Summary

Android applications can use many different types of resources, including application-specific resources and system-wide resources. The Eclipse resource editors facilitate resource management, but XML resource files can also be edited manually. Once defined, resources can be accessed programmatically as well as referenced, by name, by other resources. String, color, and dimension values are stored in specially formatted XML files, and graphic images are stored as individual files. Application user interfaces are defined using XML layout files. Raw files, which can include custom data formats, may also be included as resources for use by the application. Finally, applications may include numerous other types of resources as part of their packages.

Q&A

Q. *Can I tell what all the system resources are, just by their names?*

A. Sometimes you can't. The official documentation for the Android system resources does not describe each resource. If you are confused about what a specific system resource is or how it works, you can either experiment with it or examine its resource definition in the Android SDK directory hierarchy. Where it's located exactly depends on your Android SDK and tool versions, so your best bet is to find a uniquely named resource and do a File Search.

Q. *Must string, color, and dimension resources be stored in separate XML files?*

A. Technically, no. However, we do recommend this practice. For example, string internationalization might require you to create alternative resource files, but the colors or dimensions might remain the same across all languages. Keeping the resource types separate keeps them organized.

Q. *Which XML parser should I use?*

A. The Android SDK is updated and improved frequently. Our tests have shown that the SAX parser is the most efficient XML parser (closely followed by XMLPullParser), and we recommend this parser for most purposes. However, the choice is yours, and you should test your specific XML implementation to determine the appropriate parser for your application's needs.

Workshop

Quiz

1. What color formats are supported for color resources?

   A. 12-bit color

   B. 24-bit color

   C. 64-bit color

2. True or False: You can include files of any format as a resource.

3. Which graphics formats are supported and encouraged on Android?

   A. Joint Photographic Experts Group (JPG)

   B. Portable Network Graphics (PNG)

   C. Graphics Interchange Format (GIF)

   D. Nine-Patch Stretchable Images (.9.PNG)

4. True or False: Resource filenames can be uppercase.

5. True or False: Naming resources is arbitrary.

Answers

1. A and B. Both 12-bit and 24-bit color are supported.

2. True. Simply include a file as a raw resource.

3. B and D. Although all four formats are supported, they are not all encouraged. PNG graphics, including Nine-Patch Stretchable graphics, are highly encouraged for Android development because they are lossless and efficient. JPG files are acceptable but lossy, and GIF file use is outright discouraged.

4. False. Resource filenames may contain letters, numbers, and underscores and must be lowercase.

5. False. The resource names dictate the variable names used to reference the resources programmatically.

Exercises

1. Add a new color resource with a value of #00ff00 to your Droid1 project. Within the main.xml layout file, use the Properties pane to change the textColor attribute of the TextView control to the color resource you just created. View the layout in the Eclipse Layout Resource Editor and then rerun the application and view the result on an emulator or device—in all three cases, you should see green text.

2. Add a new dimension resource with a value of 22pt to your Droid1 project. Within the main.xml layout file, use the Properties pane to change the textSize attribute of the TextView control to the dimension resource you just created. View the layout in the Eclipse Layout Resource Editor and then rerun the application and view the result on an emulator or device—in all three cases, you should see larger font text (22pt). What happens if you try it with different screen density settings in the emulator? What about use of px, dp, or sp as the unit type?

3. Add a new drawable graphics file resource to your Droid1 project (for example, a small PNG or JPG file). Within the main.xml layout resource file, use the Outline pane to add an ImageView control to the layout. Then use the Properties pane to set the ImageView control's src attribute to the drawable resource you just created. View the layout in the Eclipse Layout Resource Editor and then rerun the application and view the result on an emulator or device—in all three cases, you should see an image below the text on the screen.

HOUR 5

Configuring the Android Manifest File

What You'll Learn in This Hour:

▶ Exploring the Android manifest file

▶ Configuring basic application settings

▶ Defining activities

▶ Managing application permissions

▶ Managing other application settings

Every Android project includes a special file called the Android manifest file. The Android system uses this file to determine application configuration settings, including the application's identity as well as what permissions the application requires to run. In this hour, we examine the Android manifest file in detail and look at how different applications use its features.

Exploring the Android Manifest File

The Android manifest file, named `AndroidManifest.xml`, is an XML file that must be included at the top level of any Android project. The Android system uses the information in this file to do the following:

▶ Install and upgrade the application package

▶ Display application details to users

▶ Launch application activities

▶ Manage application permissions

▶ Handle a number of other advanced application configurations, including acting as a service provider or content provider

If you use Eclipse with the ADT plug-in for Eclipse, the Android Project Wizard creates the initial `AndroidManifest.xml` file with default values for the most important configuration settings.

You can edit the Android manifest file by using the Eclipse manifest file resource editor or by manually editing the XML.

The Eclipse manifest file resource editor organizes the manifest information into categories presented on five tabs:

▶ Manifest

▶ Application

▶ Permissions

▶ Instrumentation

▶ AndroidManifest.xml

Using the Manifest Tab

The Manifest tab (see Figure 5.1) contains package-wide settings, including the package name, version information, and minimum Android SDK version information. You can also set any hardware configuration requirements here.

Using the Application Tab

The Application tab (see Figure 5.2) contains application-wide settings, including the application label and icon, as well as information about application components such as activities, intent filters, and other application functionality, including configuration for service and content provider implementations.

FIGURE 5.1
The Manifest
tab of the
Eclipse
manifest file
resource editor.

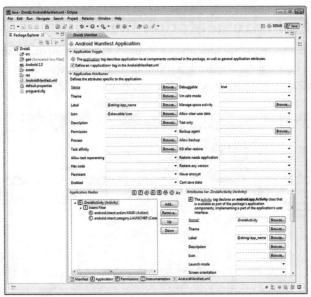

FIGURE 5.2
The Application
tab of the
Eclipse
manifest file
resource editor.

Using the Permissions Tab

The Permissions tab (see Figure 5.3) contains any permission rules required by the application. This tab can also be used to enforce custom permissions created for the application.

FIGURE 5.3
The Permissions
tab of the
Eclipse manifest
file resource
editor.

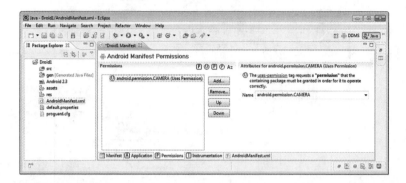

Do not confuse the application Permission field (a drop-down list on the Application tab) with the Permissions tab features. Use the Permissions tab to define the permissions required for the application to access the resources or APIs it needs. The application Permission field is used to define permissions required by other applications to access exposed resources and APIs in your application.

Using the Instrumentation Tab

You can use the Instrumentation tab (see Figure 5.4) to declare any instrumentation classes for monitoring the application. We talk more about testing and instrumentation in Hour 22, "Testing Android Applications."

FIGURE 5.4
The instrumen-
tation tab of the
Eclipse
manifest file
resource editor.

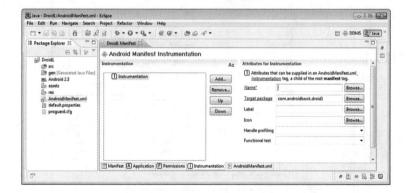

Using the AndroidManifest.xml Tab

The Android manifest file is a specially formatted XML file. You can edit the XML manually in the AndroidManifest.xml tab of the manifest file resource editor (see Figure 5.5).

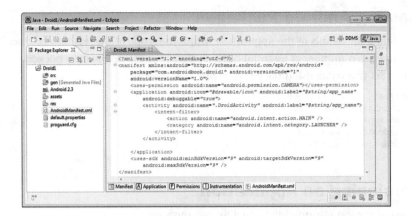

FIGURE 5.5
The AndroidManifest .xml tab of the Eclipse manifest file resource editor.

Figure 5.5 shows the Android manifest file for the Droid1 project you created in the first hour, which has fairly simple XML.

Note that the file has a single `<manifest>` tag, within which all the package-wide settings appear. Within this tag is one `<application>` tag, which defines the specific application, with its single activity, called `.DroidActivity`, with an `Intent` filter. In addition, the `<uses-sdk>` tag is set to target only API Level 9 (Android 2.3), for this example.

Now let's talk about each of these settings in a bit more detail.

Configuring Basic Application Settings

If you use the Android Project Wizard in Eclipse to create a project, then an Android manifest file is created for you by default. However, this is just a starting point. It is important to become familiar with how the Android Manifest file works; if your application's manifest file is configured incorrectly then your application will not run properly.

In terms of the XML definition for the Android manifest file, it always starts with an XML header like this one:

```
<?xml version="1.0" encoding="utf-8"?>
```

Many of the important settings your application requires are set using attributes and child tags of the `<manifest>` and `<application>` blocks. Now let's look at a few of the most common manifest file configurations.

Naming Android Packages

You define the details of the application within the scope of the <manifest> tag. This tag has a number of essential attributes, such as the application package name. Set this value using the package attribute, as follows:

```
<manifest
    xmlns:android="http://schemas.android.com/apk/res/android"
    package="com.androidbook.droid1"
    android:versionCode="1"
    android:versionName="1.0">
```

Versioning an Application

Manifest version information is used for two purposes:

▶ To organize and keep track of application features

▶ To manage application upgrades

For this reason, the <manifest> tag has two separate version attributes: a version name and a version code.

Setting the Version Name

The version name is the traditional versioning information, used to keep track of application builds. Smart versioning is essential when publishing and supporting applications. The <manifest> tag android:versionName attribute is a string value provided to keep track of the application build number. For example, the Droid1 project has the version name 1.0. The format of the version name field is up to the developer. However, note that this field is visible to the user.

Setting the Version Code

The version code enables the Android platform to programmatically upgrade and downgrade an application. The <manifest> tag android:versionCode attribute is a whole number integer value that the Android platform and Android marketplaces use to manage application upgrades and downgrades. android:versionCode generally starts at a value of 1. This value must be incremented with each new version of the application deployed to users. The version code field is not visible to the user and need not stay in sync with the version name. For example, an update might have a version name of 1.0.1 but the version code would be incremented to 2.

The version code needs to be incremented for published applications or testing purposes only, not each time you deploy an application onto a device for debugging.

Setting the Minimum Android SDK Version

Android applications can be compiled for compatibility with several different SDK versions. You use the <uses-sdk> tag to specify the minimum SDK required on the handset in order for the application to build and run properly. The android:minSdkVersion attribute of this tag is an integer representing the minimum Android SDK version required. Table 5.1 shows the Android SDK versions available for shipping applications.

TABLE 5.1 Android SDK Versions

Android SDK Version	Value
Android 1.0 SDK	1
Android 1.1 SDK	2
Android 1.5 SDK	3
Android 1.6 SDK	4
Android 2.0 SDK	5
Android 2.0.1 SDK	6
Android 2.1 SDK	7
Android 2.2 SDK	8
Android 2.3 SDK	9
Android 2.3.3/2.3.4 SDK	10
Android 3.0 SDK	11
Android 3.1 SDK	12

For example, in the Droid1 project, you specified the minimum SDK as Android 2.3 SDK:

```
<uses-sdk android:minSdkVersion="9" />
```

Did you know?

Each time a new Android SDK is released, you can find the SDK version number in the SDK release notes. This is often referred to as the API Level within the tools, especially the Android SDK and AVD Manager. For an up-to-date list of the available API Levels, see http://goo.gl/n0fUZ. The value need not be a number, as witnessed by the Honeycomb Preview SDK with an API Level of Honeycomb.

Naming an Application

The <application> tag android:label attribute is a string representing the application name. You can set this name to a fixed string, as in the following example:

```
<application android:label="My application name">
```

You can also set the android:label attribute to a string resource. In the Droid1 project, you set the application name to the string resource as follows:

```
<application android:label="@string/app_name">
```

In this case, the resource string called app_name in the strings.xml file supplies the application name.

Providing an Icon for an Application

The <application> tag attribute called android:icon is a Drawable resource representing the application. In the Droid1 project, you set the application icon to the Drawable resource as follows:

```
<application android:icon="@drawable/icon">
```

Providing an Application Description

The <application> tag android:description attribute is a string representing a short description of the application. You can set this name to a string resource:

```
<application
    android:label="My application name"
    android:description="@string/app_desc">
```

The Android system and application marketplaces use the application description to display information about the application to the user.

Setting Debug Information for an Application

The <application> tag android:debuggable attribute is a Boolean value that indicates whether the application can be debugged using a debugger such as Eclipse. You cannot debug your application until you set this value. You will also need to reset this value to false before you publish your application. If you forget, the publishing tools warn you to adjust this setting.

Setting Other Application Attributes

Numerous other settings appear on the Application tab, but they generally apply only in very specific cases, such as when you want to link secondary libraries or apply a theme other than the default to your application. There are also settings for handling how the application interacts with the Android operating system. For most applications, the default settings are acceptable.

You will spend a lot of time on the Application tab in the Application Nodes box, where you can register application components—most commonly, each time you register a new activity.

Defining Activities

Recall that Android applications comprise a number of different activities. Every activity must be registered within the Android manifest file by its class name before it can be run on the device. You therefore need to update the manifest file each time you add a new activity class to an application.

Each activity represents a specific task to be completed, often with its own screen. Activities are launched in different ways, using the Intent mechanism. Each activity can have its own label (name) and icon but uses the application's generic label and icon by default.

Registering Activities

You must register each activity in the Application Nodes section of the Application tab. Each activity has its own `<activity>` tag in the resulting XML. For example, the following XML excerpt defines an activity class called `DroidActivity`:

```
<activity
    android:name=".DroidActivity" />
```

This activity must be defined as a class within the application package. If needed, you may specific the entire name, including package, with the activity class name.

Try It Yourself ▼

To register a new activity in the Droid1 project, follow these steps:

1. Open the Droid1 project in Eclipse.

2. Right-click `/src/com.androidbook.droid1` and choose New, Class. The New Java Class window opens.

3. Name your new class `DroidActivity2`.

▼

▼

4. Click the Browse button next to the Superclass field and set the superclass to `android.app.Activity`. You might need to type several letters of the class/package name before it resolves and you can choose it from the list.

5. Click the Finish button. You see the new class in your project.

6. Make a copy of the `main.xml` layout file in the `/res/layout` resource directory for your new activity and name it `second.xml`. Modify the layout so that you know it's for the second activity. For example, you could change the text string shown. Save the new layout file.

7. Open the `DroidActivity2` class. Right-click within the class and choose Source, Override/Implement Methods.

8. Check the box next to the `onCreate(Bundle)` method. This method is added to your class.

9. Within the `onCreate()` method, set the layout to load for the new activity by adding and calling the `setContentView(R.layout.second)` method. Save the class file.

10. Open the Android manifest file and click the Application tab of the resource editor.

11. In the Application Nodes section of the Application tab, click the Add button and choose the Activity element. Make sure you are adding a top-level activity. The attributes for the activity are shown in the right side of the screen.

12. Click the Browse button next to the activity Name field. Choose the new activity you created, `DroidActivity2`.

13. Save the manifest file. Switch to the AndroidManifest.xml tab to see what the new XML looks like.

You now have a new, fully registered `DroidActivity2` activity that you can use in your application.

▲

Designating the Launch Activity

You can use an `Intent` filter to designate an activity as the primary entry point of the application. The `Intent` filter for launching an activity by default must be configured using an `<intent-filter>` tag with the MAIN action type and the LAUNCHER category. In the Droid1 project, the Android project wizard set `DroidActivity` as the primary launching point of the application:

```
<activity
    android:name=".DroidActivity"
    android:label="@string/app_name">
    <intent-filter>
        <action
            android:name="android.intent.action.MAIN" />
        <category
            android:name="android.intent.category.LAUNCHER" />
    </intent-filter>
</activity>
```

This <intent-filter> tag instructs the Android system to direct all application launch requests to the DroidActivity activity.

Managing Application Permissions

The Android platform is built on a Linux kernel and leverages its built-in system security as part of the Android security model. Each Android application exists in its own virtual machine and operates within its own Linux user account (see Figure 5.6).

Applications that want access to shared or privileged resources on the handset must declare those specific permissions in the Android manifest file. This security mechanism ensures that no application can change its behavior on-the-fly or perform any operations without the user's permission.

> Because each application runs under a different user account, each application has its own private files and directories, just as a Linux user would.

Did you Know?

Android applications can access their own private files and databases without any special permissions. However, if an application needs to access shared or sensitive resources, it must declare those permissions using the <uses-permission> tag within the Android manifest file. These permissions are managed on the Permissions tab of the Android manifest file resource editor.

FIGURE 5.6
Simplified
Android platform
architecture
from a security
perspective.

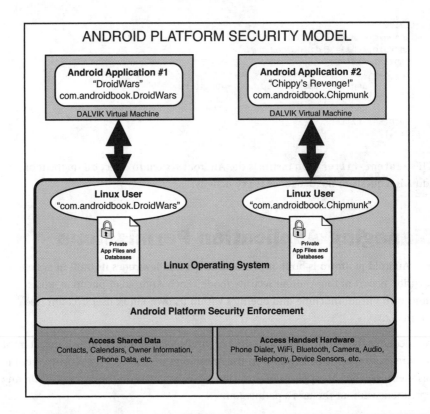

Try It Yourself

To give your application permission to access the built-in camera, use the following
steps:

1. Open the Droid1 project in Eclipse.

2. Open the Android manifest file and click the Permissions tab of the resource
   editor.

3. Click the Add button and choose Uses Permission. The Name attribute for the
   permission is shown in the right side of the screen as a drop-down list.

4. Choose android.permission.CAMERA from the drop-down list.

5. Save the manifest file. Switch to the AndroidManifest.xml tab to see what the
   new XML looks like.

Now that you have registered the camera permission, your application can access
the camera APIs within the Android SDK without causing security exceptions to be
thrown.

Table 5.2 lists some of the most common permissions used by Android applications.

TABLE 5.2   Common Permissions Used by Android Applications

Permission Category	Useful Permissions
Location-based services	android.permission.ACCESS_COARSE_LOCATION
	android.permission.ACCESS_FINE_LOCATION
Accessing contact database	android.permission.READ_CONTACTS
	android.permission.WRITE_CONTACTS
Making calls	android.permission.CALL_PHONE
	android.permission.CALL_PRIVILEGED
Sending and receiving	android.permission.READ_SMS
messages	android.permission.RECEIVE_MMS
	android.permission.RECEIVE_SMS
	android.permission.RECEIVE_WAP_PUSH
	android.permission.SEND_SMS
	android.permission.WRITE_SMS
Using network sockets	android.permission.INTERNET
Accessing audio settings	android.permission.RECORD_AUDIO
	android.permission.MODIFY_AUDIO_SETTINGS
Accessing network settings	android.permission.ACCESS_NETWORK_STATE
	android.permission.CHANGE_NETWORK_STATE
Accessing Wi-Fi settings	android.permission.ACCESS_WIFI_STATE
	android.permission.CHANGE_WIFI_STATE
Accessing device hardware	android.permission.BLUETOOTH
	android.permission.CAMERA
	android.permission.FLASHLIGHT
	android.permission.VIBRATE
	android.permission.BATTERY_STATS

During the application installation process, the user is shown exactly what permissions the application uses. The user must agree to install the application after reviewing these permissions. For a complete list of the permissions used by Android applications, see the android.Manifest.permission class documentation.

> Applications can define and enforce their own permissions. This can be critically important for certain types of applications, such as banking and commerce applications.

By the Way

Managing Other Application Settings

In addition to the features already discussed in this hour, a number of other specialized features can be configured in the Android manifest file. For example, if your application requires a hardware keyboard or a touch screen, you can specify these hardware configuration requirements in the Android manifest file.

You must also declare any other application components—such as whether your application acts as a service provider, content provider, or broadcast receiver—in the Android manifest file.

Summary

The Android manifest file (`AndroidManifest.xml`) exists at the root of every Android project. It is a required component of any application. The Android manifest file can be configured using the manifest file editor built into Eclipse by the ADT plug-in, or you can edit the manifest file XML directly. The file uses a simple XML schema to describe what the application is, what its components are, and what permissions it has. The Android platform uses this information to manage the application and grant its activities certain permissions on the Android operating system.

Q&A

Q. *Can application names be internationalized?*

A. Yes. You simply define the `android:label` attribute as a string resource and create resource files for each locale you want to support. We talk more about localizing resources in Hour 19, "Internationalizing Your Application."

Q. *I added a new* `Activity` *class to my project, and my application keeps crashing. What did I do wrong?*

A. Chances are, you forgot to register the activity in the Android manifest file. If you don't register the activity by using an `<activity>` tag, your application will likely crash upon launch. You will not necessarily see an error message that specifically says "You forgot to register this Activity in your manifest file!," so always check first before suspecting any other problems.

Q. *If I can use the Eclipse resource editor to edit the Android manifest file, why do I need to know about the raw XML?*

A. When making straightforward configuration changes to the manifest file, using the resource editor is the most straightforward method. However, when bulk changes must be made, editing the XML directly can be much faster.

Q. *Do I need specific permissions to forward requests to other applications (for example, implementing a "Share" feature)?*

A. You only need permissions for tasks your application code performs, not those that you "outsource" to other applications. Therefore, you do not usually need permissions to forward requests to other applications via documented exposed intents. The "Share" feature many Android users are familiar with is achieved by dispatching requests to other apps. Those apps would need the appropriate permissions to perform the specific job.

Workshop

Quiz

1. True or False: Every Android application needs an Android manifest file.

2. True or False: The android:versionCode numbers must correspond with the application android:versionName.

3. What is the permission for using the camera?

   A. android.permission.USE_CAMERA

   B. android.permission.CAMERA

   C. android.permission.hardware.CAMERA

4. True or False: When installing an application, the user is shown the permissions requested in the Android manifest file.

Answers

1. True. The Android manifest file is an essential part of every Android project. This file defines the application's identity, settings, and permissions.

2. False. The android:versionCode attribute must be incremented each time the application is deployed, and it can be upgraded. This number need not match the android:versionName setting.

3. B. You use the android.permission.CAMERA permission to access the camera.

4. True. This way, the user knows what the application might attempt to do, such as take a picture or access the user's contacts.

Exercises

1. Review the complete list of available permissions for Android applications in the Android SDK documentation. You can do this with your local copy of the documentation, or online at the Android Developer website http://goo.gl/II3Uv.

2. Edit the Android manifest file for the Droid1 application again. Add a second permission (any will do, this is just for practice) to the application. Look up what that permission is used for in the documentation, as discussed in the previous exercise.

3. Begin with the Try It Yourself exercise earlier in this chapter. Add another Activity class to the Droid1 application and register this new `Activity` within the Android manifest file. Take this exercise a step further and make this new Activity your application's default launch activity with the proper intent filter. (More than one activity can be a launcher activity. Each one with the launcher category appears in the application list with an icon. This is not typical, so you might want to move the intent filter rather than copy it.) Save your changes and run your application.

HOUR 6

Designing an Application Framework

What You'll Learn in This Hour:

▶ Designing an Android trivia game
▶ Implementing an application prototype
▶ Running the game prototype

It's time to put the skills you have learned so far to use and write some code. In this hour, you design an Android application prototype—the basic framework upon which you build a full application. Taking an iterative approach, you add many exciting features to this application over the course of this book. So let's begin.

Designing an Android Trivia Game

Social trivia-style games are always popular. They are also an application category where you can, from a development perspective, explore many different features of the Android SDK. So let's implement a fairly simple trivia game, and by doing so, learn all about designing an application user interface, working with text and graphics, and, eventually, connecting with other users.

We need a theme for our game. How about travel? In our soon-to-be-viral game, the user is asked questions about travel and related experiences, such as:

▶ Have you ever visited the pyramids in Egypt?
▶ Have you ever milked a cow?
▶ Have you ever gone diving with great white sharks?
▶ Have you climbed a mountain?

The user with the highest score is the most well traveled and well seasoned. Let's call the game *Been There, Done That!*.

Determining High-Level Game Features

First, you need to roughly sketch out what you want this application to do. Imagine what features a good application should have and what features a trivia application needs. In addition to the game question screen, the application likely needs the following:

▶ A splash sequence that displays the application name, version, and developer

▶ A way to view scores

▶ An explanation of the game rules

▶ A way to store game settings

You also need a way to transition between these different features. One way to do this is to create a traditional main menu screen that the user can use to navigate throughout the application.

Reviewing these requirements, you need six primary screens within the Been There, Done That! application:

▶ A startup screen

▶ A main menu screen

▶ A game play screen

▶ A settings screen

▶ A scores screen

▶ A help screen

These six screens make up the core user interface for the Been There, Done That! application.

Determining Activity Requirements

Each screen of the Been There, Done That! application has its own `Activity` class. Figure 6.1 shows the six activities required, one for each screen.

A good design practice is to implement a base `Activity` class with shared components, which you can simply call `QuizActivity`. Consider employing this practice as you define the activities needed by the Been There, Done That! game, like this:

▶ `QuizActivity`—Derived from `android.app.Activity`, this is the base class. Here, define application preferences and other application-wide settings and features.

▶ `QuizSplashActivity`—Derived from `QuizActivity`, this class represents the splash screen.

▶ `QuizMenuActivity`—Derived from `QuizActivity`, this class represents the main menu screen.

▶ `QuizHelpActivity`—Derived from `QuizActivity`, this class represents the help screen.

▶ `QuizScoresActivity`—Derived from `QuizActivity`, this class represents the scores screen.

▶ `QuizSettingsActivity`—Derived from `QuizActivity`, this class represents the settings screen.

▶ `QuizGameActivity`—Derived from `QuizActivity`, this class represents the game screen.

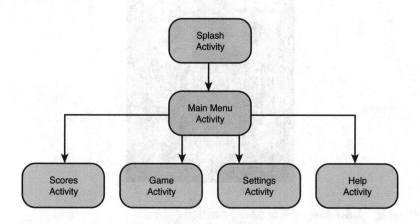

FIGURE 6.1
A rough design of the activity workflow in the Been There, Done That! application.

Determining Screen-Specific Game Features

Now it's time to define the basic features of each activity in the Been There, Done That! application.

Defining Splash Screen Features

The splash screen serves as the initial entry point for the Been There, Done That! game. Its functionality should be encapsulated within the `QuizSplashActivity` class. This screen should do the following:

▶ Display the name and version of the application

▶ Display an interesting graphic or logo for the game

▶ Transition automatically to the main menu screen after a period of time

Figure 6.2 shows a mockup of the splash screen.

FIGURE 6.2
The Been There, Done That! splash screen.

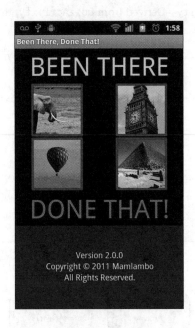

Defining Main Menu Screen Features

The main menu screen serves as the main navigational screen in the game. This screen displays after the splash screen and requires the user to choose where to go next. Its functionality should be encapsulated within the `QuizMenuActivity` class. This screen should do the following:

▶ Automatically display after the splash screen

▶ Allow the user to choose Play Game, Settings, Scores, or Help

Figure 6.3 shows a mockup of the main menu screen.

FIGURE 6.3
The Been There,
Done That!
main menu
screen.

Defining Help Screen Features

The help screen tells the user how to play the game. Its functionality should be encapsulated within the QuizHelpActivity class. This screen should do the following:

▶ Display help text to the user and enable the user to scroll through text

▶ Provide a method for the user to suggest new questions

Figure 6.4 shows a mockup of the help screen.

Defining Scores Screen Features

The scores screen enables the user to view game scores. Its functionality should be encapsulated within the QuizScoresActivity class. This screen should do the following:

▶ Display top score statistics

▶ Show the latest score if the user is coming from the game screen

Figure 6.5 shows a mockup of the scores screen.

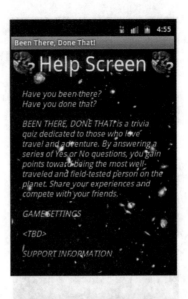

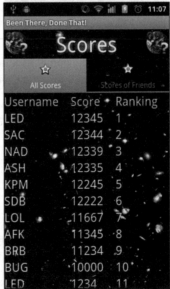

Defining Settings Screen Features

The settings screen allows users to edit and save game settings, including username
and other important features. Its functionality should be encapsulated within the
QuizSettingsActivity class. This screen should do the following:

▶ Allow the user to input game settings

▶ Allow the user to invite friends to play

Figure 6.6 shows a mockup of the basic settings screen.

FIGURE 6.6
The Been There,
Done That! set-
tings screen.

Defining Game Screen Features

The game screen displays the trivia quiz. Its functionality should be encapsulated within the QuizGameActivity class. This screen should do the following:

▶ Display a series of yes/no questions

▶ Handle input and keep score and state of the quiz

▶ Transition to the scores screen when the user is finished playing

Figure 6.7 shows a mockup of the game screen.

FIGURE 6.7
The Been There,
Done That!
game screen.

Implementing an Application Prototype

Now that you have a rough idea what the Been There, Done That! application will do and how it will look, it's time to start coding. This involves the following steps:

1. Creating a new Android project in Eclipse

2. Adding some application resources, including strings and graphics

3. Creating a layout resource for each screen

4. Implementing a Java class (derived from the `Activity` class) for each screen

5. Creating a set of application-wide preferences for use in all activities

Reviewing the Accompanying Source Code

Because of length limitations and other practical reasons, we cannot provide full code listings in every hour of this book—they would take more than an hour to review and be incredibly repetitive. Instead, we provide inline code excerpts based upon the Android topic at hand and provide the complete Java source code project for each hour (the hour is denoted by the project name, package name, and application icon) on the accompanying book CD as well as online at the publisher's website, http://goo.gl/G43H7 and the authors' website, http://goo.gl/fYC7v.

These source files are not meant to be the "answers" to quizzes or questions. The full source code is vital for providing context and complete implementations of the topics discussed in each hour of this book. We expect you will follow along with the source code for a given hour and, if you feel inclined, you can build your own incarnation of the Been There, Done That! application in parallel. The full source code helps give context to developers less familiar with Java, Eclipse or mobile development topics. Also, there may be times when the source code does not exactly match the code provided in the book—this is normally because we strip comments, error checking, and exception handling from book code, again for readability and length.

The application package names also vary by chapter. For example, for Hour 6 code, the source code Eclipse project name is BTDT_Hour6, with a package name of `com.androidbook.btdt.hour6` and an icon that clearly indicates the hour number (6). This enables you to keep multiple projects in Eclipse and install multiple applications on a single device without conflicts or naming clashes. However, if you are building your own version in parallel, you may only have one version—one Eclipse project, one application you revise and improve in each hour, using the downloaded project for reference.

Creating a New Android Project

You can begin creating a new Android project for your application by using the Eclipse Android Project Wizard.

The project has the following settings:

- ▶ Project name: BTDT (Note: For this hour's source code, this hour's project is named BTDT_Hour6.)

- ▶ Build target: Android 2.3.3 + Google APIs (API Level 10)

- ▶ Application name: Been There, Done That!

- ▶ Package name: `com.androidbook.btdt` (Note: For this hour's source code, the package is actually named `com.androidbook.btdt.hour6.`)

- ▶ Create activity: `QuizSplashActivity`

Using these settings, you can create the basic Android project. However, you need to make a few adjustments.

Adding Project Resources

The Been There, Done That! project requires some additional resources. Specifically, you need to add a Layout file for each activity and a text string for each activity name, and you need to change the application icon to something more appropriate.

Adding String Resources

Begin by modifying the `strings.xml` resource file. Delete the `hello` string and create six new string resources—one for each screen. For example, create a string called `help` with a value of `"Help Screen"`. When you are done, the `strings.xml` file should look like this:

```
<?xml version="1.0" encoding="utf-8"?>
<resources>
    <string
        name="app_name">Been There, Done That!</string>
    <string
        name="help">Help Screen</string>
    <string
        name="menu">Main Menu Screen</string>
    <string
        name="splash">Splash Screen</string>
    <string
        name="settings">Settings Screen</string>
    <string
        name="game">Game Screen</string>
    <string
        name="scores">Scores Screen</string>
</resources>
```

Adding Layout Resources

Next, you need layout resource files for each activity. Begin by renaming the `main.xml` layout to `splash.xml`. Then copy the `splash.xml` file five more times, resulting in one layout for each activity: `game.xml`, `help.xml`, `menu.xml`, `scores.xml`, and `settings.xml`.

You might notice that there is an error in each Layout file. This is because the `TextView` control in the layout refers to the `@string/hello` string, which no longer exists. For each layout file, you need to use the Eclipse layout editor to change the String resource loaded by the `TextView` control. For example, `game.xml` needs to replace the reference to `@string/hello` with the new string you created called `@string/game`. Now when each layout loads, it displays the screen it is supposed to represent.

Adding Drawable Resources

While you are adding resources, you should change the icon for your application to something more appropriate. To do this, create a 48×48 pixel PNG file called `quiz-icon.png` and add this resource file to the `/drawable` resource directory. Then you can delete the `icon.png` files used by default.

For the book source code, we've only created a single application icon in the `/drawable` directory. However, even if you've created three differently sized icons and placed them in the three default directories (/drawable-ldpi, /drawable-mdpi, and /drawable-hdpi), only a single reference to the icon is required. Just make sure all of the icons are named identically. This enables the Android operating system to choose the most appropriate icon version for the device.

Implementing Application Activities

To implement a base `Activity` class, simply copy the source file called `QuizSplashActivity.java`. Name this new class file `QuizActivity` and save the file. This class should look very simple for now:

```
package com.androidbook.btdt;
import android.app.Activity;
public class QuizActivity extends Activity {
    public static final String GAME_PREFERENCES = "GamePrefs";
}
```

You will add to this class later. Next, update the `QuizSplashActivity` class to extend from the `QuizActivity` class instead of directly from the `Activity` class.

Creating the Rest of the Application Activities

Now perform the same steps five more times, once for each new activity: `QuizMenuActivity`, `QuizHelpActivity`, `QuizScoresActivity`, `QuizSettingsActivity`, and `QuizGameActivity`. Note the handy way that Eclipse updates the class name when you copy a class file. You can also create class files by right-clicking the package name `com.androidbook.btdt` and choosing New Class. Eclipse presents a dialog where you can fill in class file settings.

> For more tips on working with Eclipse, check out Appendix B, "Eclipse IDE Tips and Tricks."

By the Way

Note that there is an error in each Java file. This is because each activity is trying to load the `main.xml` layout file—a resource that no longer exists. You need to modify each class to load the specific layout associated with that activity. For example, in the `QuizHelpActivity` class, modify the `setContentView()` method to load the layout file you created for the help screen as follows:

```
setContentView(R.layout.help);
```

You need to make similar changes to the other activity files, such that each call to `setContentView()` loads the corresponding layout file.

Updating the Android Manifest File

You now need to make some changes to the Android manifest file. First, modify the application icon resource to point at the @drawable/quizicon icon you created. Second, you need to register all your new activities in the manifest file so they run properly. Finally, set the Debuggable application attribute to true and verify that you have QuizSplashActivity set as the default activity to launch.

Creating Application Preferences

The Been There, Done That! application needs a simple way to store some basic state information and user data. You can use Android's shared preferences (android.content.SharedPreferences) to add this functionality.

You can access shared preferences, by name, from any activity within the application. Therefore, declare the name of your set of preferences in the base class QuizActivity so that they are easily accessible to all subclasses:

```
public static final String GAME_PREFERENCES = "GamePrefs";
```

There is no practical limit to the number of sets of shared preferences you can create. You can use the preference name string to divide preferences into categories, such as game preferences and user preferences. How you organize shared preferences is up to you.

To add shared preferences to the application, follow these steps:

1. Use the getSharedPreferences() method to retrieve an instance of a SharedPreferences object within your Activity class.

2. Create a SharedPreferences.Editor object to modify preferences.

3. Make changes to the preferences by using the editor.

4. Commit the changes by using the commit() method in the editor.

Saving Specific Shared Preferences

Each preference is stored as a key/value pair. Preference values can be the following types:

▶ Boolean

▶ Float

▶ Integer

▶ Long

▶ String

After you decide what preferences you want to save, you need to get an instance of the `SharedPreferences` object and use the `Editor` object to make the changes and commit them. In the following sample code, when placed within your `Activity` class, illustrates how to save two preferences—the user's name and age:

```
SharedPreferences settings =
    getSharedPreferences(GAME_PREFERENCES, MODE_PRIVATE);
SharedPreferences.Editor prefEditor = settings.edit();
prefEditor.putString("UserName", "JaneDoe");
prefEditor.putInt("UserAge", 22);
prefEditor.commit();
```

You can also use the shared preferences editor to clear all preferences, using the `clear()` method, and to remove specific preferences by name, using the `remove()` method.

Retrieving Shared Preferences

Retrieving shared preference values is even simpler than creating them because you don't need an editor. The following example shows how to retrieve shared preference values within your `Activity` class:

```
SharedPreferences settings =
    getSharedPreferences(GAME_PREFERENCES, MODE_PRIVATE);
if (settings.contains("UserName") == true) {
    // We have a user name
    String user = Settings.getString("UserName", "Default");
}
```

You can use the `SharedPreferences` object to check for a preference by name, retrieve strongly typed preferences, or retrieve all the preferences and store them in a map.

Although you have no immediate needs for shared preferences yet in Been There, Done That!, you now have the infrastructure set up to use them as needed within any of the activities within your application. This will be important later when you implement each activity in full in subsequent hours.

Running the Game Prototype

You are almost ready to run and test your application. But first, you need to create a debug configuration for your new project within Eclipse.

Creating a Debug Configuration

Each new Eclipse project requires a debug configuration. Be sure to set the preferred AVD for the project to one that is compatible with the Google APIs and within the API Level target range you set in your application (check the Manifest file if you are unsure). If you do not have one configured appropriately, simply click the Android SDK and AVD Manager button in Eclipse. From here, determine which AVDs are appropriate for the application and create new ones, as necessary.

Launching the Prototype in the Emulator

It's time to launch the Been There, Done That! application in the Android emulator. You can do this by using the little bug icon in Eclipse or by clicking the Run button on the debug configuration you just created.

As you can see in Figure 6.8, the application does very little so far. It has a pretty icon, which a user can click to launch the default activity, `QuizSplashActivity`. This activity displays its `TextView` control, informing you that you have reached the splash screen. There is no real user interface to speak of yet for the application, and you still need to wire up the transitions between the different activities. However, you now have a solid framework to build on. In the next few hours, you will flesh out the different screens and begin to implement game functionality.

FIGURE 6.8
The prototype for Been There, Done That! in the application listing.

Exploring the Prototype Installation

The Been There, Done That! application does very little so far, but you can use helpful applications that run on the Android emulator to peek at all you've done up to this point:

▶ **Application Manager**—This application is helpful for determining interesting information about Android applications running on the system. In the emulator, navigate to the home screen, click the Menu button and choose Settings, Applications, Manage applications and then choose the Been There, Done That! application from the list of applications. Here you can see some basic information about the application, including storage and permissions used, as well as information about the cache and so on. You can also kill the app or uninstall it.

▶ **Dev Tools**—This application helps you inspect other Android applications in more detail. In the emulator, pull up the application drawer, launch the Dev Tools application, and choose Package Browser. Navigate to the package name `com.androidbook.btdt`. This tool reads information out of the manifest and enables you to inspect the settings of each activity registered, among other features.

Of course, you can also begin to investigate the application by using the DDMS perspective of Eclipse. For example, you could check out the application directory for the `com.androidbook.btdt` package on the Android file system. You could also step through the code of `QuizSplashActivity`.

Summary

In this hour, you built a basic prototype on which you can build in subsequent hours. You designed a prototype and defined its requirements in some detail. Then you created a new Android project, configured it, and created an activity for each screen. You also added custom layouts and implemented shared preferences for the application.

Q&A

Q. *What class might you inherit from to provide an application activity with consistent shared components?*

A. By creating your own shared `Activity` base class, you can implement behavior that will exist within each screen of your application. You can also use common Activity subclasses for specific types of functionality that users are familiar with, such as lists and tab sets.

Q. *Can an activity have its own preferences?*

A. Yes, preferences can be shared among activities, and an activity can have its own preferences. To access shared preferences, use the `getSharedPreferences()` method. To access activity-level preferences, use the `getPreferences()` method.

Q. *What two things need to be configured before you can run and debug an Android application in Eclipse?*

A. You need to have configured both an AVD and the debug configuration. Then you can easily launch your application straight from Eclipse for debugging and testing.

Workshop

Quiz

1. True or False: The Been There, Done That! application has three activities.

2. What data types are supported within application shared preferences?

A. Boolean, Float, Integer, Long, and String

B. Boolean, Integer, and String

C. All types that are available in Java

3. True or False: You only need to put your base activity class (for example, `QuizActivity`) in the Android manifest file.

Answers

1. False. The Been There, Done That! application has an activity for each screen. It also has a base class activity, from which all other activities are derived. The design has seven total activity classes.

2. A. Boolean, Float, Integer, Long, and String preferences are possible.

3. False. Each activity needs its own entry in the Android manifest file.

Exercises

1. Add a log message to the onCreate() method of each Activity class in your Been There, Done That! application prototype. For example, add an informational log message such as "In Activity QuizSplashActivity" to the QuizSplashActivity class.

2. Add an additional application preference string to the application prototype: lastLaunch. In the onCreate() method of QuizSplashActivity class, make the following changes. Whenever this method runs, read the old value the lastLaunch preference and print its value to the log output. Then update the preference with the current date and time.

HINTS: The default Date class (java.util.Date) constructor can be used to get the current date and time, and the SimpleDateFormat class (java.text.SimpleDateFormat) can be used to format date and time information in various string formats. See the Android SDK for complete details on these classes.

3. Sketch out an alternate design for the Been There, Done That! application. Consider options such as not including a Main Menu Screen. Look over similar applications in the Android Market for inspiration. You can post links to alternative designs for the application on our book website at http://goo.gl/dyyus or email them directly to us at androidwirelessdev+btdt@gmail.com.

HOUR 7

Implementing an Animated Splash Screen

What You'll Learn in This Hour:

▶ Designing a splash screen
▶ Updating the splash screen layout
▶ Working with animation

This hour focuses on implementing the splash screen of the Been There, Done That! application. After roughly sketching out the screen design, you determine exactly which Android View controls you need to implement the splash.xml layout file. When you are satisfied with the screen layout, you add some tweened animations to give the splash screen some pizzazz. Finally, after your animations have completed, you must implement a smooth transition from the splash screen to the main menu screen.

Designing the Splash Screen

You implement the Been There, Done That! application from the ground up, beginning with the screen users see first: the splash screen. Recall from Hour 6, "Designing an Application Framework," that you had several requirements for this screen. Specifically, the screen should display some information about the application (title and version information) in a visually-appealing way and then, after some short period of time, automatically transition to the main menu screen. Figure 7.1 provides a rough design for the splash screen.

FIGURE 7.1
Rough design
for the Been
There, Done
That! splash
screen.

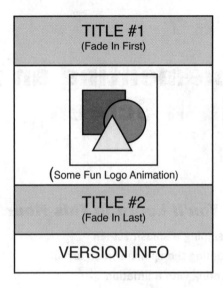

For the time being, focus on designing the splash screen in portrait mode, but try to avoid making the porting effort difficult for landscape orientations. For now, a simple layout design should suffice. Different devices will display this layout in different ways. We discuss porting issues and how to support different devices later in this book.

Recall as well that the full source code associated with this hour is available on the CD that accompanies this book; you can also download the latest code from the book websites.

Implementing the Splash Screen Layout

Now that you know how your splash screen should look, you need to translate the rough design into the appropriate layout design. Recall that the /res/layout/splash.xml layout file is used by QuizSplashActivity. You need to update the default layout, which simply displays a single TextView control (informing us it is the splash screen) to contain controls for each of the elements in the rough design.

Screen layout controls come in many forms. Each control is a rectangle that can control a specific part of the screen. You are using two common screen controls on your splash screen:

▶ A TextView control displays a text string.

▶ An ImageView control displays a graphic.

You also need some way to organize various View controls on the screen in an orderly fashion. For this, you use Layout controls. For example, LinearLayout enables placement of child views in a vertical or horizontal stack.

In addition to LinearLayout, there are a number of other Layout controls. Layouts may be nested and control only part of the screen, or they may control the entire screen. It is quite common for a screen to be encapsulated in one large parent layout—often a LinearLayout control. Table 7.1 lists the available Layout controls.

TABLE 7.1 Common Layout Controls

Layout Control Name	Description	Key Attributes/Elements
LinearLayout	Each child view is placed after the previous one, in a single row or column.	Orientation (vertical or horizontal).
RelativeLayout	Each child view is placed in relation to the other views in the layout, or relative to the edges of the parent layout.	Many alignment attributes to control where a child view is positioned relative to other child View controls.
FrameLayout	Each child view is stacked within the frame, relative to the top-left corner. View controls may overlap.	The order of placement of child View controls is important, when used with appropriate gravity settings.
TableLayout	Each child view is a cell in a grid of rows and columns.	Each row requires a TableRow element.

Layouts and their child View controls have certain attributes that help control their behavior. For example, all layouts share the attributes android:layout_width and android:layout_height, which control how wide and high an item is. These attribute values can be dimensions, such as a number of pixels, or use a more flexible approach: fill_parent or wrap_content. Using fill_parent instructs a layout to scale to the size of the parent layout, and using wrap_content "shrink wraps" the child View control within the parent, giving it only the space of the child View control's dimensions. You can use a number of other interesting properties to control specific layout behavior, including margin settings and type-specific layout attributes.

Let's use a TableLayout control to display some ImageView controls as part of the splash screen.

In the splash screen design, you can use a vertical `LinearLayout` control to organize the screen elements, which are, in order, a `TextView` control, a `TableLayout` control with some `TableRow` control elements of `ImageView` controls, and then two more `TextView` controls. Figure 7.2 shows the layout design of the splash screen.

FIGURE 7.2
Layout design for the Been There, Done That! splash screen.

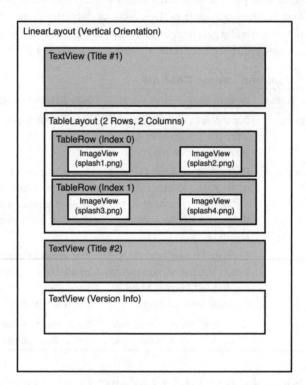

Adding New Project Resources

Now that you have your layout design for the splash screen, you need to create the string, color, and dimension resources to use within the layout.

Begin by adding four new graphic resources (in three resolutions) to the /res/draw-able directory hierarchy. Specifically, you must add the following files: splash1.png, splash2.png, splash3.png, and splash4.png to each of the draw-able directories: lpdi, mdpi, and hdpi. Figure 7.3 shows what the directory structure now looks like within the Eclipse project. These graphics will be displayed in the `TableLayout` control in the center of the splash screen.

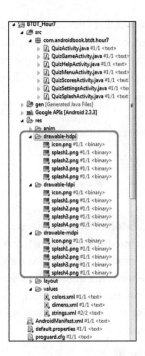

FIGURE 7.3
The resource
directory hierar-
chy of the
Been There,
Done That!
application.

Then add three new strings to the `/res/values/strings.xml` resource file: one for
the top title (Been There), one for the bottom title (Done That!), and one for some
version information (multiple lines). Remove the `splash` string because you are no
longer using it. Your string resource file should now look like the following:

```xml
<?xml version="1.0" encoding="utf-8"?>
<resources>
    <string
        name="app_name">Been There, Done That!</string>
    <string
        name="help">Help Screen</string>
    <string
        name="menu">Main Menu Screen</string>
    <string
        name="settings">Settings Screen</string>
    <string
        name="game">Game Screen</string>
    <string
        name="scores">Scores Screen</string>
    <string
        name="app_logo_top">BEEN THERE</string>
    <string
        name="app_logo_bottom">DONE THAT!</string>
    <string
        name="app_version_info">Version 2.0.0\nCopyright © 2011 Mamlambo\nAll
Rights Reserved.</string>
</resources>
```

Next, create a new resource file called `/res/values/colors.xml` to contain the three color resources you need: one for the title text color (a golden yellow), one for the version text color (grayish white), and one for the version text background color (deep blue). Your color resource file should now look like the following:

```xml
<?xml version="1.0" encoding="utf-8"?>
<resources>
    <color
        name="logo_color">#FFFF0F</color>
    <color
        name="version_color">#f0f0f0</color>
    <color
        name="version_bkgrd">#1a1a48</color>
</resources>
```

Finally, you need to create some dimension resources in a new resource file called `/res/values/dimens.xml`. Create three new dimension values: one to control the title font size (48dp), one to control the version text font size (15dp), and one to allow for nice line spacing between the lines of the version text (3dp). We use the dp units so that the dimensions are flexible, device-independent values and therefore appropriate for many different resolution devices. Your dimension resource file should now look like the following:

```xml
<?xml version="1.0" encoding="utf-8"?>
<resources>
    <dimen
        name="logo_size">48dp</dimen>
    <dimen
        name="version_size">15dp</dimen>
    <dimen
        name="version_spacing">3dp</dimen>
</resources>
```

Save the resource files now. After you've saved them, you can begin to use your new resources in the `splash.xml` layout resource file.

Updating the Splash Screen Layout

Before taking the following steps, first use the editor to remove all existing controls from the `splash.xml` layout. The file should be empty except for the XML header. You can delete unwanted controls in the Graphical Layout view by right-clicking them and choosing Delete from either the visual view or the Outline view. However, we find that the simplest way is to delete the controls from the XML mode. After you've removed any unnecessary controls, take the following steps to generate the desired layout, based on your intended design (these steps may seem overwhelming at first, but important for seeing how to build up a layout; the resulting XML is shown after the steps):

1. Begin by adding a LinearLayout control and setting its background attribute to @android:color/black (a built-in color resource) and its orientation to vertical. Add all subsequent controls as child views inside this control.

2. Add a TextView control called TextViewTopTitle. Set layout_width to match_parent and layout_height to wrap_content. Set the control's text attribute to the appropriate string resource, its textColor attribute to the appropriate color resource, and its textSize to the dimension resource you created for that purpose.

3. Add a TableLayout control called TableLayout01. Set its layout_width attribute to match_parent and its layout_height attribute to wrap_content. Also, set the stretchColumns attribute to * to stretch any column, as necessary, to fit the screen.

4. Within the TableLayout control add a child TableRow control. Within this TableRow control, add two ImageView controls. For the first ImageView control, set the src attribute to the splash1.png drawable resource called @drawable/splash1. Add a second ImageView control and set its src attribute to the @drawable/splash1 drawable resource.

5. Repeat step 4, creating a second TableRow. Again, add ImageView controls for splash3.png and splash4.png.

6. Add another TextView control called TextViewBottomTitle within the parent LinearLayout. Set its layout_width attribute to match_parent and layout_height to wrap_content. Set its text attribute to the appropriate string, its textColor attribute to the appropriate color resource, and its textSize attribute to the dimension you created for that purpose.

7. For the version information, create one last TextView control, called TextViewBottomVersion. Set its layout_width attribute to match_parent and layout_height to match_parent. Set its text attribute to the appropriate string, its textColor attribute to the grayish color, and its textSize attribute to the dimension resource you created. Also, set its background attribute to the color resource (dark blue) and lineSpacingExtra to the spacing dimension resource value you created for that purpose.

8. Finally, tweak the layout_gravity and gravity settings on the various controls until you think the layout looks reasonable in the Eclipse resource editor preview.

The resulting splash.xml layout resource should now look like this:

```xml
<?xml version="1.0" encoding="utf-8"?>
<LinearLayout

    xmlns:android="http://schemas.android.com/apk/res/android"
    android:orientation="vertical"
    android:layout_width="match_parent"
    android:layout_height="match_parent"
    android:background="@android:color/black">
    <TextView
        android:layout_width="match_parent"
        android:layout_height="wrap_content"
        android:id="@+id/TextViewTopTitle"
        android:text="@string/app_logo_top"
        android:textColor="@color/logo_color"
        android:layout_gravity="center_vertical|center_horizontal"
        android:gravity="top|center"
        android:textSize="@dimen/logo_size"></TextView>
    <TableLayout
        android:id="@+id/TableLayout01"
        android:stretchColumns="*"
        android:layout_height="wrap_content"
        android:layout_width="match_parent">
        <TableRow
            android:id="@+id/TableRow01"
            android:layout_height="wrap_content"
            android:layout_width="wrap_content"
            android:layout_gravity="center_vertical|center_horizontal">
            <ImageView
                android:id="@+id/ImageView2_Left"
                android:layout_width="wrap_content"
                android:layout_height="wrap_content"
                android:layout_gravity="center_vertical|center_horizontal"
                android:src="@drawable/splash1"></ImageView>
            <ImageView
                android:id="@+id/ImageView2_Right"
                android:layout_width="wrap_content"
                android:layout_height="wrap_content"
                android:layout_gravity="center_vertical|center_horizontal"
                android:src="@drawable/splash2"></ImageView>
        </TableRow>
        <TableRow
            android:id="@+id/TableRow02"
            android:layout_height="wrap_content"
            android:layout_width="wrap_content"
            android:layout_gravity="center_vertical|center_horizontal">
            <ImageView
                android:id="@+id/ImageView3_Left"
                android:layout_width="wrap_content"
                android:layout_height="wrap_content"
                android:layout_gravity="center_vertical|center_horizontal"
                android:src="@drawable/splash3"></ImageView>
            <ImageView
                android:id="@+id/ImageView3_Right"
                android:layout_width="wrap_content"
                android:layout_height="wrap_content"
                android:layout_gravity="center_vertical|center_horizontal"
```

```
            android:src="@drawable/splash4"></ImageView>
        </TableRow>
    </TableLayout>
    <TextView
        android:layout_width="match_parent"
        android:layout_height="wrap_content"
        android:id="@+id/TextViewBottomTitle"
        android:text="@string/app_logo_bottom"
        android:textColor="@color/logo_color"
        android:gravity="center"
        android:textSize="@dimen/logo_size"></TextView>
    <TextView
        android:id="@+id/TextViewBottomVersion"
        android:text="@string/app_version_info"
        android:textSize="@dimen/version_size"
        android:textColor="@color/version_color"
        android:background="@color/version_bkgrd"
        android:layout_height="match_parent"
        android:lineSpacingExtra="@dimen/version_spacing"
        android:layout_width="match_parent"
        android:layout_gravity="center_vertical|center_horizontal"
        android:gravity="center"></TextView>
</LinearLayout>
```

At this point, save the `splash.xml` layout file and run the Been There, Done That! application in the Android emulator. The Splash screen should look as shown in Figure 7.4.

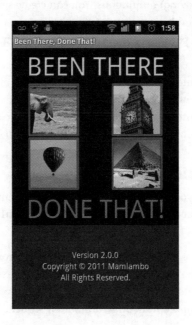

FIGURE 7.4
The Been There,
Done That!
splash screen.

Working with Animation

One great way to add zing to your splash screen is to add some animation. The Android platform supports four types of graphics animation:

▶ **Animated GIF images**—Animated GIFs are self-contained graphics files with multiple frames.

▶ **Frame-by-frame animation**—The Android SDK provides a similar mechanism for frame-by-frame animation in which the developer supplies the individual graphic frames and transitions between them (see the `AnimationDrawable` class).

▶ **Tweened animation**—Tweened animation is a simple and flexible method of defining specific animation operations that can then be applied to any view or layout.

▶ **OpenGL ES**—Android's OpenGL ES API provides advanced three-dimensional drawing, animation, lighting, and texturing capabilities.

For the Been There, Done That! application, tweened animation makes the most sense. Android provides tweening support for alpha (transparency), rotation, scaling, and translating (moving) animations. You can create sets of animation operations to be performed simultaneously, in a timed sequence, and after a delay. Thus, tweened animation is a perfect choice for your splash screen.

With tweened animation, you create an animation sequence, either programmatically or by creating animation resources in the /res/anim directory. Each animation sequence needs its own XML file, but the same animation may be applied to any number of View controls within your application. You can also take advantage of built-in animation resources as well, provided in the android.R.anim class.

Adding Animation Resources

For your splash screen, you need to create three custom animations in XML and save them to the /res/anim resource directory: fade_in.xml, fade_in2.xml, and custom_anim.xml.

The first animation, fade_in.xml, simply fades its target from an alpha value of 0 (transparent) to an alpha value of 1 (opaque) over the course of 2500 milliseconds, or 2.5 seconds. There is no built-in animation editor in Eclipse. Instead, it's up to the developer to create the appropriate XML animation sequence.

An animation resource looks much like the other types of resources available. The fade_in.xml resource file simply has a single animation applied using the <alpha>

tag. For complete details on the tags and attributes available for animation resources, revisit Hour 4, "Managing Application Resources," or see the Android Developer online reference on the topic at http://goo.gl/K3aZ7.

The XML for the `fade_in.xml` animation should look something like this:

```
<?xml version="1.0" encoding="utf-8" ?>
<set
    xmlns:android="http://schemas.android.com/apk/res/android"
    android:shareInterpolator="false">
    <alpha
        android:fromAlpha="0.0"
        android:toAlpha="1.0"
        android:duration="2500">
    </alpha>
</set>
```

You can apply this animation to the top `TextView` control with your title text.

Next, you create the `fade_in2.xml` animation. This animation does exactly the same thing as the `fade_in` animation, except that the `startOffset` attribute should be set to `2500` milliseconds. This means that this animation actually takes 5 seconds total: It waits for 2.5 seconds and then fades in for 2.5 seconds. Because 5 seconds is long enough to display the entire splash screen, you should plan to listen for `fade_in2` to complete and then react by transitioning to the main menu screen (more on this in a few moments).

Finally, you need to create a fun animation sequence for the `TableLayout` graphics. In this case, the animation set should contain multiple, simultaneous operations: a rotation, some scaling, and an alpha transition. As a result, the target `View` spins into existence. The `custom_anim.xml` file looks like this:

```
<?xml version="1.0" encoding="utf-8" ?>
<set
    xmlns:android="http://schemas.android.com/apk/res/android"
    android:shareInterpolator="false">
    <rotate
        android:fromDegrees="0"
        android:toDegrees="360"
        android:pivotX="50%"
        android:pivotY="50%"
        android:duration="2000" />
    <alpha
        android:fromAlpha="0.0"
        android:toAlpha="1.0"
        android:duration="2000">
    </alpha>
    <scale
        android:pivotX="50%"
        android:pivotY="50%"
        android:fromXScale=".1"
        android:fromYScale=".1"
```

```
        android:toXScale="1.0"
        android:toYScale="1.0"
        android:duration="2000" />
</set>
```

As you can see, the rotation operation takes 2 seconds to rotate from 0 to 360 degrees, pivoting around the center of the view. The alpha operation should look familiar; it simply fades in over the same 2-second period. Finally, the scale operation scales from 10% to 100% over the same 2-second period. This entire animation takes 2 seconds to complete.

After you have saved all three of your animation files, you can begin to apply the animations to specific views.

Animating Specific Views

Animation sequences must be applied and managed programmatically within your Activity class—in this case, the QuizSplashActivity class. Remember, costly operations, such as animations, should be stopped if the application is paused. The animation can resume when the application comes back into the foreground.

Let's start with a simplest case: applying the fade_in animation to your title TextView control, called TextViewTopTitle. All you need to do is retrieve an instance of your TextView control in the onCreate() method of the QuizSplashActivity class, load the animation resource into an Animation object, and call the startAnimation() method of the TextView control:

```
TextView logo1 = (TextView) findViewById(R.id.TextViewTopTitle);
Animation fade1 = AnimationUtils.loadAnimation(this, R.anim.fade_in);
logo1.startAnimation(fade1);
```

When an animation must be stopped—for instance, in the onPause() callback method of the activity—you can simply call the clearAnimation() method. For instance, the following onPause() method implementation demonstrates this for the corner logos:

```
@Override
protected void onPause() {
    super.onPause();
    // Stop the animation
    TextView logo1 = (TextView) findViewById(R.id.TextViewTopTitle);
    logo1.clearAnimation();

    TextView logo2 = (TextView) findViewById(R.id.TextViewBottomTitle);
    logo2.clearAnimation();

    // ... stop other animations
}
```

Animating All Views in a Layout

In addition to applying animations to individual View controls, you can also apply them to all child View controls within a parent control (usually a layout such as TableLayout), using a LayoutAnimationController object.

To animate View controls in this fashion, you must load the animation, create an instance of a LayoutAnimationController, configure it, and then pass it to the layout's setLayoutAnimation() method. For example, the following code loads the custom_anim animation, creates a LayoutAnimationController, and then applies it to each TableRow in the TableLayout control:

```
Animation spinin = AnimationUtils.loadAnimation(this, R.anim.custom_anim);
LayoutAnimationController controller =
    new LayoutAnimationController(spinin);
TableLayout table = (TableLayout) findViewById(R.id.TableLayout01);
for (int i = 0; i < table.getChildCount(); i++) {
    TableRow row = (TableRow) table.getChildAt(i);
    row.setLayoutAnimation(controller);
}
```

There is no need to call any startAnimation() method in this case because LayoutAnimationController handles it for you. Using this method, the animation is applied to each child view, but each starts at a different time. (The default is 50% of the duration of the animation—which, in this case, would be 1 second.) This gives you the nice effect of each ImageView spinning into existence in a cascading fashion.

Stopping LayoutAnimationController animations is no different from stopping individual animations; simply use the clearAnimation() method as discussed for each TableRow. The additional lines to do this in the existing onPause() method are shown here:

```
TableLayout table = (TableLayout) findViewById(R.id.TableLayout01);
for (int i = 0; i < table.getChildCount(); i++) {
    TableRow row = (TableRow) table.getChildAt(i);
    row.clearAnimation();
}
```

Handling Animation Life Cycle Events

Now that your splash screen has some nice animations, all that's left is to handle the activity transition between QuizSplashActivity and QuizMenuActivity when the animations are complete. To do this, create a new Intent control to launch the QuizMenuActivity class and pass it into the startActivity() method. Then call the finish() method of QuizSplashActivity, as you do not want to keep the QuizSplashActivity on the activity stack (that is, you do not want the Back button to return to the splash screen).

Of your animations, the `fade_in2` animation takes the longest, at 5 seconds total. This animation is therefore the one you want to trigger your transition upon. You do so by creating an `AnimationListener` object, which has callbacks for the animation life cycle events such as start, end, and repeat. In this case, only the `onAnimationEnd()` method needs to be implemented; simply drop the code for starting the new Activity here. The following code listing shows how to create the `AnimationListener` and implement the `onAnimationEnd()` callback:

```
Animation fade2 = AnimationUtils.loadAnimation(this, R.anim.fade_in2);
fade2.setAnimationListener(new AnimationListener() {
    public void onAnimationEnd(Animation animation) {
        startActivity(new Intent(QuizSplashActivity.this,
            QuizMenuActivity.class));
        QuizSplashActivity.this.finish();
    }
});
```

Now you run the Been There, Done That! application again, either on the emulator or on the handset. You now see some nice animation on the splash screen. The screen then transitions smoothly to the main menu, which is the next screen on your to-do list.

Summary

Congratulations! You've implemented the first screen of the Been There, Done That! application. In this hour, you designed a screen and then identified the appropriate layout and view components needed to implement your design. After you created the appropriate resources, you were able to configure the `splash.xml` layout file with various `View` controls like `TextView` and `ImageView`. Finally, you added some tweened animations to the screen and then handled the transition between `QuizSplashActivity` and `QuizMenuActivity`.

Q&A

Q. *How well does the Android platform perform with regard to animation?*

A. The Android platform has reasonable performance with animations and the newest SDKs and hardware available allow for such things to be accelerated through hardware. However, it is very easy to overload a screen with animations and `View` controls. For example, if you were to place a `VideoView` control in the middle of the screen with all the animations, you would likely notice distinct performance degradation. Always test operations, such as animations, on a handset to be sure your implementation is feasible.

Q. *Why did you iterate through each child view of the* `TableLayout` *control instead of accessing each* `TableRow` *control (*`R.id.TableRow01` *and* `R.id.TableRow02`*) by name?*

A. It would be perfectly acceptable to access each `TableRow` element by name if each one is guaranteed to exist in all cases. You will be able to take advantage of this iterative approach later when you port your project to different screen orientations. For now, the Splash screen draws reasonably well only in portrait mode. We discuss how to tweak your application to display on different devices and screen orientations in Hour 20, "Developing for Different Devices." If you are having trouble getting the application to display reasonably on a device you own, feel free to adjust the dimension resource values, or skip ahead to Hour 20 for more tips and tricks.

Q. *What would happen if you applied* `LayoutAnimationController` *to* `TableLayout` *instead of each* `TableRow`*?*

A. If you applied `LayoutAnimationController` to `TableLayout`, each `TableRow` control—instead of each `ImageView` control—would spin into existence. It would be a different, less visually appealing, effect.

Workshop

Quiz

1. True or False: There is no way to stop an animation once it has started.

2. What types of operations are supported with tweened animation?

   A. Transparency, motion, and 3D rotation

   B. Alpha, scale, rotate, and translate

   C. Dance, sing, and be merry

3. True or False: `LinearLayout` can be used to draw `View` controls in a single row or column.

4. Which of these classes is not a built-in layout in the Android SDK?

   A. `FrameLayout`

   B. `CircleLayout`

   C. `HorizontalLayout`

   D. `RelativeLayout`

Answers

1. False. Use the `clearAnimation()` method to clear all pending and executing animations on a given view.

2. B. Tweened animation can include any combination of alpha transitions (transparency), scaling (growth or shrinking), two-dimensional rotation, and translation (moving) from one point to another.

3. True. `LinearLayout` can be used to display child `View` objects in a horizontal or vertical orientation.

4. B and C. `FrameLayout` and `RelativeLayout` are both included in the Android SDK.

Exercises

1. Modify the `LayoutAnimationController` in the `QuizSplashActivity` class to apply animations of each child view within a `TableRow` control in random order by using the `setOrder()` method with a value of `LayoutAnimationController.ORDER_RANDOM`. View the resulting animation.

2. Create a new animation resource. Modify the `LayoutAnimationController` in the `QuizSplashActivity` class to apply your new animation instead of the one designed in this lesson. View the resulting animation.

3. **[Challenging!]** Design an alternative splash screen layout, perhaps using a `RelativeLayout` instead of a `TableLayout` and `LinearLayout` combination. Consider modifying the animation sequences to suit your alternative layout.

HOUR 8

Implementing the Main Menu Screen

What You'll Learn in This Hour:

▶ Designing the main menu screen
▶ Implementing the main menu screen layout
▶ Working with `ListView` controls
▶ Working with other menu types

In this hour, you learn about some of the different menu mechanisms available in Android. You begin by implementing the main menu screen of the Been There, Done That! application, using new layout controls, such as `RelativeLayout`. You also learn about a powerful control called a `ListView`, which is used to provide variable length scrolling list of items with individual click actions. Finally, you learn about other special types of menus available for use in your applications, such as the options menu.

Designing the Main Menu Screen

To design the main menu screen, begin by reviewing what its functions are and then roughly sketch what you want it to look like. If you review the screen requirements discussed in Hour 6, "Designing an Application Framework," you see that this screen provides essential navigation to the features of the rest of the application. Users can choose from four different options: play the game, review the help, configure the settings, or view the high scores. Figure 8.1 shows a rough design of the main menu screen.

FIGURE 8.1
Rough design
for the Been
There, Done
That! main
menu screen.

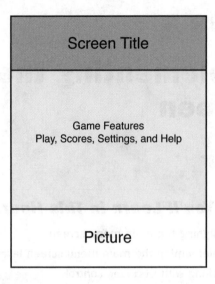

There are a number of different ways you could implement the main menu screen. For example, you could create a button for each option, listen for clicks, and funnel the user to the appropriate screen. However, if the number of options grows, this method does not scale well. Therefore, a list of the options, in the form of a ListView control, is more appropriate. This way, if the list becomes longer than the screen, you have built-in scrolling capability.

In addition to the screen layout, you want the main menu screen to have some bells and whistles. Therefore, begin with the default behavior of each layout control and then add some custom flair to those controls using optional attributes. For example, you could add a nice background image behind the menu and add a custom selection graphic to the ListView control.

Finally, you wire up the ListView control to ensure that when a user clicks on a specific list option, he or she is taken to the appropriate activity within the application. This enables users to access the rest of the screens you need to implement within the Been There, Done That! application.

Recall as well that the full source code associated with this hour is available on the CD that accompanies this book; the latest code can also be downloaded from the book websites.

Determining Main Menu Screen Layout Requirements

Now that you know how you want your main menu screen to look, you need to translate your rough design into the appropriate layout design. In this case, you need to update the `/res/layout/menu.xml` layout file that is used by `QuizMenuActivity`. In the case of the main menu layout, you want some sort of header, followed by a `ListView` control and then an `ImageView` control.

Designing the Screen Header with `RelativeLayout`

You know you want to display a `TextView` control for the screen title in the header. Wouldn't it be nice if you also included graphics on each side of the `TextView` control? This is a perfect time to try out `RelativeLayout`, which allows each child view to be placed in relation to the parent layout or other child view controls. Therefore, you can easily describe the header as a `RelativeLayout` control with three child layouts:

- ▶ An `ImageView` control aligned to the top left of the parent control
- ▶ A `TextView` control aligned to the top center of the parent control
- ▶ An `ImageView` control aligned to the top right of the parent control

Designing the `ListView` Control

Next in your layout includes the `ListView` control. A `ListView` control is simply a container that holds a list of `View` objects. The default is for a `ListView` control to contain `TextView` controls, but `ListView` controls may contain many different `View` controls.

A `ListView` control of `TextView` controls works fine for this example. To override the default behavior of each child `TextView`, you need to make a layout resource to act as the template for each `TextView` control in the `ListView` control. Also, you can make the menu more interesting by adding a custom divider and selector to the `ListView` control.

Finishing Touches for the Main Menu Layout Design

You finish off the layout by adding the `ImageView` control after the `ListView` control. As before, you need to wrap your screen in a parent layout—in this case, a `RelativeLayout`, within which you place the `RelativeLayout` with the header content, then the `ListView`, and finally the bottom `ImageView` control. Figure 8.2 shows the layout design of the main menu screen.

FIGURE 8.2
Layout design
for the Been
There, Done
That! main
menu screen.

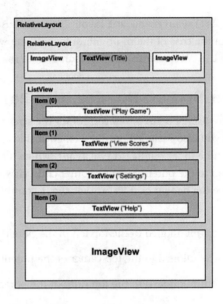

Implementing the Main Menu Screen Layout

To implement the main menu screen, you begin by adding new resources to the project. Then, you must update the menu.xml layout resource to reflect the main menu screen design.

Watch Out!

> The Eclipse layout resource editor does not always display complex controls, or dynamic controls such as ListView controls, properly in design mode. Use XML mode for these cases. You must view a ListView control by using the Android emulator or a device. In this case, the layout designer does not reflect actual application look and feel.

Adding New Project Resources

Now that you have your layout designed, you need to create the drawable, string, color, and dimension resources you use in the layouts used by the main menu screen. For specific resource configurations, you can use the values provided in the book source code as a guide, or configure your own custom values.

Begin by adding four new graphic resources (in various resolutions) to the /res/drawable directory hierarchy: bkgrnd.png, divider.png, half.png, and selector.png. The RelativeLayout uses the bkgrnd.png graphic file as the background image. The ListView control uses the divider.png and selector.png graphics for the custom divider and selector, respectively. The ImageView control uses the half.png graphic of the Earth at the bottom of the screen.

Continue by adding and modifying several new strings in the /res/values/strings.xml resource file so that you have a string for each menu option, as well as one for the title TextView control. For example, the following string resources suffice:

```
<string
    name="menu">MAIN MENU</string>
<string
    name="menu_item_settings">Settings</string>
<string
    name="menu_item_play">Play Game</string>
<string
    name="menu_item_scores">View Scores</string>
<string
    name="menu_item_help">Help</string>
```

Finally, update the color resources in /res/menu/colors.xml to include colors for the screen title TextView attributes as well as the TextView items displayed within the ListView. For example, we used the following color resources:

```
<color
    name="title_color">#f0f0f0</color>
<color
    name="title_glow">#F00</color>
<color
    name="menu_color">#FFFF0F</color>
<color
    name="menu_glow">#F00</color>
```

Update the resources in /res/values/dimens.xml to include dimensions for the title text and the ListView item text. For example, the following dimension resources work well:

```
<dimen
    name="screen_title_size">40dp</dimen>
<dimen
    name="menu_item_size">34dp</dimen>
```

Save the resource files. After you've saved the files, you can begin to use them in the layout resource files used by the main menu screen.

Updating the Main Menu Screen Layout Files

Perhaps you have noticed by now that the main menu screen relies on layout resource files—plural. The master layout file, `menu.xml`, defines the layout of the overall screen. You must separately create a new layout file used by the `ListView` control as a template for each item.

Updating the Master Layout

Again, open the Eclipse layout resource editor and remove all existing controls from the `menu.xml` layout file. Then follow these steps to generate the layout you want, based on your intended layout design:

1. Add a new `RelativeLayout` control and set its background attribute to `@drawable/bkgrnd`. All subsequent controls should be added inside this control.

2. Add a second `RelativeLayout` control to contain the screen header information. Set its `layout_width` attribute to `wrap_content` and its `layout_height` attribute to `wrap_content`. Also, set its `layout_alignParentTop` attribute to `true` so that the header sticks to the top of the parent `RelativeLayout`.

3. Within the `RelativeLayout` control, add an `ImageView` control. Set the `ImageView` control's `layout_alignParentLeft` and `layout_alignParentTop` attributes to `true`. Set the image's `src` attribute to the `@drawable/icon` graphic.

4. Still within the `RelativeLayout` control, add a `TextView` control for the title text. Set the `TextView` control's `text`, `textSize`, and `textColor` attributes to the resources you just created. Then set the `layout_centerHorizontal` and `layout_alignParentTop` attributes to `true`.

Did you Know?

> You can make `TextView` text "glow" by setting the shadow attributes, including `shadowColor`, `shadowDx`, `shadowDy`, and `shadowRadius`. See the menu layout resource in the sample source code for an example.

5. Finish the `RelativeLayout` control by adding one more `ImageView` control. Set the control's `layout_alignParentRight` and `layout_alignParentTop` attributes to `true`. Set the image's `src` attribute to the `@drawable/icon` graphic.

6. Outside the header `RelativeLayout`, but still within the parent `RelativeLayout`, add the `ListView` and `ImageView` controls. Begin by adding a `ListView` control called `ListView_Menu`. Set its `layout_width` attribute to

match_parent and layout_height attribute to wrap_content. Additionally, set its layout_centerHorizontal attribute to true. Finally, set its layout_below attribute to @+id/RelativeLayout01 (the header RelativeLayout control id).

7. Finally, add the last ImageView control. Set its src attribute to the @drawable/half graphic, its layout_width attribute to match_parent, and its layout_height attribute to wrap_content to ensure that the control fills the bottom of the screen. Additionally, set its layout_alignParentBottom attribute to true, its scaleType attribute to centerInside, and its adjustViewBounds attribute to true so that the graphic scales and draws nicely.

At this point, save the menu.xml layout file. You can find a full XML listing for this layout in the sample code for Hour 8, available on the accompanying CD as well as downloadable from the book websites.

Adding the ListView **Template Layout**

A ListView control has a variable number of items, where each item is displayed using a simple layout template. You now need to create this new layout resource for your project. For example, the /res/layout/menu_item.xml layout resource file can serve as a template for your ListView in the menu.xml layout resource. In this case, the menu_item.xml layout file contains a TextView control to display the menu item name (scores, help, and so on).

The TextView control has all the typical attributes assigned except for one: the text itself. The text attribute is supplied by the ListView control. At this point, you can tweak the TextView attributes for textColor and textSize, which you created as color and dimension resources earlier.

The menu_item.xml file looks like this:

```
<TextView
    xmlns:android="http://schemas.android.com/apk/res/android"
    android:layout_width="match_parent"
    android:textSize="@dimen/menu_item_size"
    android:layout_gravity="center_horizontal"
    android:layout_height="wrap_content"
    android:shadowRadius="5"
    android:gravity="center"
    android:textColor="@color/menu_color"
    android:shadowColor="@color/menu_glow"
    android:shadowDy="3"
    android:shadowDx="3" />
```

At this point, save the menu_item.xml layout file.

Working with the `ListView` Control

Now it's time to switch your focus to the `QuizMenuActivity.java` file. Here you need to wire up the `ListView` control. First, you need to fill the `ListView` control with content, and then you need to listen for user clicks on specific items in the `ListView` control and send the user to the appropriate activity (and screen) in the application.

Filling a `ListView` Control

Your `ListView` control needs content. `ListView` controls can be populated from a variety of data sources, including arrays and databases, using data adapters. In this case, you have a fixed list of four items, so a simple `String` array is a reasonable choice for your `ListView` data.

All `ListView` setup occurs in the `onCreate()` method of the `QuizMenuActivity` class, just after the `setContentView()` method call. To populate your `ListView` control, you must first retrieve it by its unique identifier by using the `findViewById()` method, as follows:

```
ListView menuList = (ListView) findViewById(R.id.ListView_Menu);
```

Next, define the `String` values you will use to populate the individual `TextView` items within the `ListView` control. In this case, load the four resource strings representing the choices:

```
String[] items = { getResources().getString(R.string.menu_item_play),
    getResources().getString(R.string.menu_item_scores),
    getResources().getString(R.string.menu_item_settings),
    getResources().getString(R.string.menu_item_help) };
```

Alternatively, you could create a string array resource and load it instead. For more information on string array resources, see Hour 4, "Managing Application Resources," or the Android SDK reference at http://goo.gl/fbiYQ.

Now that you have retrieved the `ListView` control and have the data you want to stuff into it, use a data adapter to map the data to the layout template you created (menu_item.xml). The choice of adapter depends on the type of data being used. In this case, use an `ArrayAdapter`:

```
ArrayAdapter<String> adapt = new ArrayAdapter<String>(this,
    R.layout.menu_item, items);
```

Next, tell the `ListView` control to use this data adapter using the `setAdapter()` method:

```
menuList.setAdapter(adapt);
```

At this point, save the `QuizMenuActivity.java` file and run the Been There, Done That! application in the Android emulator. After the splash screen finishes, the main menu screen should look similar to the screen shown in Figure 8.3.

FIGURE 8.3
The Been There, Done That! splash screen.

As you see, the main menu screen is beginning to take shape. However, clicking the menu items doesn't yet have the desired response. Nothing happens!

If you get tired of watching the splash screen appear when you launch the application, simply modify the `AndroidManifest.xml` file to launch `QuizMenuActivity` by default until you are done testing.

By the Way

Listening for `ListView` Events

You need to listen for and respond to specific events within the `ListView` control. Although there are a number of events to choose from, you are most interested in the event that occurs when a user clicks a specific menu item in the `ListView` control.

To listen for item clicks, use the `setOnItemClickListener()` method of the `ListView`. Specifically, implement the `onItemClick()` method of the `AdapterView.OnItemClickListener` class. Here is a sample implementation of the `onItemClick()` method, which simply checks which item was clicked and launches the appropriate application activity in response:

```
menuList.setOnItemClickListener(new AdapterView.OnItemClickListener() {
    public void onItemClick(AdapterView<?> parent, View itemClicked,
        int position, long id) {
        TextView textView = (TextView) itemClicked;
        String strText = textView.getText().toString();
        if (strText.equalsIgnoreCase(getResources().getString(
            R.string.menu_item_play))) {
            // Launch the Game Activity
            startActivity(new Intent(QuizMenuActivity.this,
                QuizGameActivity.class));
        } else if (strText.equalsIgnoreCase(getResources().getString(
            R.string.menu_item_help))) {
            // Launch the Help Activity
            startActivity(new Intent(QuizMenuActivity.this,
                QuizHelpActivity.class));
        } else if (strText.equalsIgnoreCase(getResources().getString(
            R.string.menu_item_settings))) {
            // Launch the Settings Activity
            startActivity(new Intent(QuizMenuActivity.this,
                QuizSettingsActivity.class));
        } else if (strText.equalsIgnoreCase(getResources().getString(
            R.string.menu_item_scores))) {
            // Launch the Scores Activity
            startActivity(new Intent(QuizMenuActivity.this,
                QuizScoresActivity.class));
        }
    }
});
```

The `onItemClick()` method passes in all the information needed to determine which item was clicked. In this case, one of the simplest ways is to cast the `View` clicked (the incoming parameter named `itemClicked`) to a `TextView` control (because you know all items are `TextView` controls, although you might want to verify this by using `instanceof`) and just extract the specific `TextView` control's text attribute contents and map it to the appropriate screen. Another way to determine which item was clicked is to check the `View` control's id attribute.

Now implement the `OnItemClickListener()` method and rerun the application in the emulator. You can now use the main menu to transition between the screens in the Been There, Done That! application.

Customizing `ListView` **Control Characteristics**

Now you're ready to customize the rather boring default `ListView` control with a custom divider and selection graphics. A `ListView` control has several parts—a header, the list of items, and a footer. By default, the `ListView` control displays no header or footer.

Adding a Custom Divider

A `ListView` divider is displayed between each `ListView` item. The `divider` attribute can be either a color or a drawable graphic resource. If a color is specified, then a horizontal line (the thickness is configurable) is displayed between items in the list. If a drawable graphic resource is used, the graphic appears between items. By default, no divider is displayed above the first list item or below the last.

To add a divider to the `ListView` control, simply open the `menu.xml` layout file and change the `ListView` control's `divider` attribute to the `@drawable/divider` graphic resource (two comets streaking away from each other) you added earlier.

Adding a Custom Selector

A `ListView` selector indicates which list item is currently selected within the list. The `ListView` selector is controlled by the `listSelector` attribute. The default selector of a `ListView` control is a bright orange band.

To add a custom selector to the `ListView` control, open the `menu.xml` layout file and change the `ListView` control's `listSelector` attribute to the `@drawable/selector` graphic resource (a textured orange halo) you added earlier.

Save these changes to the `ListView` divider and selector and re-launch the Been There, Done That! application in the emulator. The main menu screen now looks similar to Figure 8.4. (You might have to click the down-arrow or tap an item to see the selector.)

FIGURE 8.4
The Been There,
Done That!
main menu
screen with a
customized
`ListView`
control.

Working with Other Menu Types

The Android platform has several other types of useful menu mechanisms, including the following:

- ▶ **Context menus**—A context menu pops up when a user performs a long-click
  on any `View` object. This type of menu is often used in conjunction with
  `ListView` controls filled with similar items, such as songs in a playlist. The
  user can then long-click on a specific song to access a context menu with
  options such as Play, Delete, and Add to Playlist for that specific song.

- ▶ **Options menus**—An options menu pops up whenever a user clicks the Menu
  button on the handset. This type of menu is often used to help the user handle
  application settings and such.

By the Way

Still confused about the difference between context and options menus? Check
out the nice write-up on the Android Developer website: http://goo.gl/OrfZP.

Because we've been focusing on application screen navigation in this hour, let's consider where these different menus are appropriate in the Been There, Done That!
application. This application design lends itself well to an options menu for the
game screen, which would enable the user to pause while answering trivia questions
to access the settings and help screens easily and then return to the game screen.

Adding an Options Menu to the Game Screen

To add an options menu to the game screen, you need to add a special type of resource called a menu resource. You can then update the QuizGameActivity class (which currently does nothing more than display a string of text saying it's the Game screen) to enable an options menu and handle menu selections.

Adding Menu Resources

For your options menu, create a menu definition resource in XML and save it to the /res/menu resource directory as gameoptions.xml.

A menu resource is a special type of resource that contains a <menu> tag followed by a number of <item> child elements. Each <item> element represents a menu option and has a number of attributes. The following are some commonly used attributes:

- ► id—This attribute enables you to easily identify the specific menu item.

- ► title—This attribute is the string shown for the options menu item.

- ► icon—This is a drawable resource representing the icon for the menu item.

Your options menu will contain only two options: Settings and Help. Therefore, your gameoptions.xml menu resource is fairly straightforward:

```
<menu
    xmlns:android="http://schemas.android.com/apk/res/android">
    <item
        android:id="@+id/settings_menu_item"
        android:title="@string/menu_item_settings"
        android:icon="@android:drawable/ic_menu_preferences"></item>
    <item
        android:id="@+id/help_menu_item"
        android:title="@string/menu_item_help"
        android:icon="@android:drawable/ic_menu_help"></item>
</menu>
```

Set the title attribute of each menu option by using the same String resources you used on the main menu screen. Note that instead of adding new drawable resources for the options menu icons, you use built-in drawable resources from the Android SDK to have a common look and feel across applications.

> You can use the built-in drawable resources provided in the android.R.drawable class just as you would use resources you include in your application package. If you want to see what each of these shared resources looks like, check the Android SDK directory installed on your machine. There is a /res/drawable directory containing the layout resource files that define the available resources; the specific directory path varies depending on the version of the tools and SDK you have installed, so a file search is most efficient.

Did you Know?

Adding an Options Menu to an Activity

For an options menu to show when the user presses the Menu button on the game screen, you must provide an implementation of the onCreateOptionsMenu() method in the QuizGameActivity class. Specifically, you need to inflate (load) the menu layout resource into the options menu and set the appropriate Intent information for each menu item. Here is a sample implementation of the onCreateOptionsMenu() method for you to add to QuizGameActivity:

```
@Override
public boolean onCreateOptionsMenu(Menu menu) {
    super.onCreateOptionsMenu(menu);
    getMenuInflater().inflate(R.menu.gameoptions, menu);
    menu.findItem(R.id.help_menu_item).setIntent(
        new Intent(this, QuizHelpActivity.class));
    menu.findItem(R.id.settings_menu_item).setIntent(
        new Intent(this, QuizSettingsActivity.class));
    return true;
}
```

Handling Options Menu Selections

To listen for when the user launches the options menu and selects a menu option, implement the onOptionsItemSelected() method of the activity. For example, start the appropriate activity by extracting the intent from the menu item selected as follows:

```
@Override
public boolean onOptionsItemSelected(MenuItem item) {
    super.onOptionsItemSelected(item);
    startActivity(item.getIntent());
    return true;
}
```

> The method given here for handling onOptionsItemSelected() works as designed. It's not technically required if the only thing your menu does is launch the Intent set via the setIntent() method. However, to add any other functionality to each MenuItem requires the implementation of this method.

There you have it: You have created an options menu on the game screen. Save your changes and run the application once more. Navigate to the game screen, press the Menu button, and see that you can now use a fully functional options menu (see Figure 8.5).

FIGURE 8.5
The Been There,
Done That!
game screen
with an options
menu.

Summary

You've made excellent progress. The main menu screen of the Been There, Done That! application is now fully functional. You've learned important skills for developing Android applications, including how to use layouts such as RelativeLayout, as well as how to use the powerful ListView control. You've also learned about the other types of navigation mechanisms available in Android and implemented an options menu on the game screen.

Q&A

Q. *What is the difference between a* ListView *control's* setOnClickListener() *method and the* setOnItemClickListener() *method?*

A. The setOnClickListener() method listens for a click anywhere in the entire ListView control. The setOnItemClickListener() method listens for a click in a specific View item within the ListView control.

Q. *There is no default item selected in the* ListView *control I created. How can I have it default to a specific item?*

A. To have a ListView control highlight a specific list item by default, use the setSelection() method.

Q. *What is the* `ListActivity` *class for?*

A. If you have a screen with only a `ListView` control, consider using the `ListActivity` class, which simplifies `ListView` management. However, if your layout has more than just a `ListView` control, your best bet is to incorporate the `ListView` control into a layout file as we did in this hour.

Workshop

Quiz

1. True or False: Context menus are launched using the Menu button.

2. What mechanism acts as the "glue" between a data source and a `ListView` control?

   A. A database

   B. An interpolator

   C. A data adapter

3. What type of layout is most appropriate for aligning child `View` controls in relation to the parent control?

   A. `RelativeLayout`

   B. `AbsoluteLayout`

   C. `LinearLayout`

4. True or False: Using `ListActivity` is a convenient way to build screens that are just `ListView` objects.

Answers

1. False. Options menus are launched using the Menu button. Context menus are launched using a long-click on a `View` control.

2. C. A data adapter, such as `ArrayAdapter`, is used to match a data source to the layout template used by a `ListView` control to display each list item.

3. A. RelativeLayout is especially handy when its child View controls need to be aligned to the top, bottom, left, right, and center of the parent layout. RelativeLayout can also be used to position child View controls relative to one another inside the parent layout.

4. True. ListActivity simplifies the handling of ListView controls.

Exercises

1. Create a string array resource made up of the individual string resources for the menu and load it using the getStringArray() method of the Resources class. Hint: Load a string array resource by identifier using R.array.name_of_string_array.

2. Add a third option to the game screen's options menu to allow the user to access the scores screen.

3. Modify the outer RelativeLayout control of menu.xml to include an animation that fades in so that the entire main menu screen fades in.

HOUR 9

Developing the Help and Scores Screens

What You'll Learn in This Hour:

▶ Designing and implementing the help screen
▶ Working with files
▶ Designing and implementing the scores screen
▶ Designing screens with tabs
▶ Working with XML

In this hour, you implement two more screens of the Been There, Done That! application: the help and scores screens. You begin by implementing the help screen using a TextView control with text supplied from a text file, which enables you to explore some of the file support classes of the Android SDK. Next, you design and implement the scores screen. With its more complicated requirements, the scores screen is ideal for trying out the tab set control called TabHost. Finally, you test the scores screen by parsing XML score data.

Designing the Help Screen

The help screen requirements are straightforward: This screen must display a large quantity of text and should have scrolling capabilities. Figure 9.1 shows a rough design of the help screen.

FIGURE 9.1
Rough design
for the Been
There, Done
That! help
screen

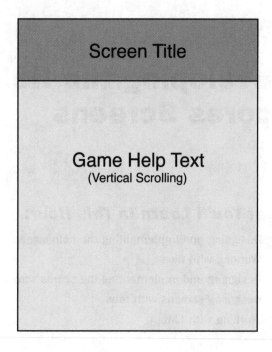

For consistency and familiarity, application screens share some common features. Therefore, the help screen mimics some of the menu screen features such as a header. To translate your rough design into the appropriate layout design, update the /res/layout/help.xml layout file and the QuizHelpActivity class.

Use the same title header you used in the menu screen (using a RelativeLayout), followed by a TextView control with scrolling capability. Figure 9.2 shows the layout design for the help screen.

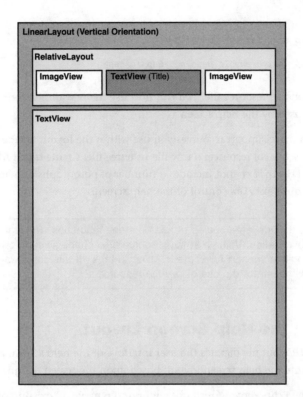

FIGURE 9.2
Layout design
for the Been
There, Done
That! help
screen.

Implementing the Help Screen Layout

To implement the help screen, begin by adding new resources to the project. Then update the help.xml layout resource to reflect the help screen design.

Adding New Project Resources

As with the other screens in the Been There, Done That! application, you need to add numerous string, color, and dimension resources to your project to support the help screen. Specifically for this implementation, you want to add four dimension resources in /res/values/dimens.xml for the help text sizes and padding attributes:

```
<dimen
    name="help_text_padding">20dp</dimen>
<dimen
    name="help_text_size">7pt</dimen>
```

```
<dimen
    name="help_text_fading">25dp</dimen>
<dimen
    name="help_text_drawable_padding">5dp</dimen>
```

Save the dimension resource file. You can now use the new dimensions in the layout resource files used by the help screen.

In addition to these support resources you use within the layout for the help screen, also add a new type of resource: a raw file resource file. Create a text file called /res/raw/quizhelp.txt that includes a number of paragraphs of help text to display in the main TextView control of the help screen.

You can also include large bodies of text as string resources. This can be helpful for internationalization. Using a string resource also enables you to take advantage of the built-in support for some HTML-style tags. In this case, we've used a text file to demonstrate the use of raw file resources.

Updating the Help Screen Layout

The help.xml layout file dictates the user interface of the help screen. Follow these steps to generate the help screen layout, based upon the screen design:

1. Open the Eclipse layout resource editor and remove all existing controls from the layout resource file.

2. Add a LinearLayout control and set its background attribute to @drawable/bkgrnd and its orientation attribute to vertical. Set its layout_width and layout_height attributes both to match_parent to fill the screen. Add all subsequent controls inside the LinearLayout control.

3. Add the same header you created in the menu.xml layout. It contains a RelativeLayout control with two ImageView controls and a TextView control. Set the TextView control's text attribute to the string resource called @string/help to reflect the appropriate screen title.

4. Outside the RelativeLayout control but still within the LinearLayout control, add a TextView control called TextView_HelpText. This control contains the help text. Set its layout_width attribute to match_parent and its layout_height attribute to match _parent. Set any text colors and optional attributes, as desired.

> You can make text in a `TextView` control bold or italic by using the `textStyle` attribute. In the source code example provided, we make the help text italic using this handy attribute.
>
> You can also automatically link phone numbers, web addresses, email addresses, and postal addresses that show in the `TextView` control to the Android Phone Dialer, Web Browser, Email, and Map applications by setting the `linksClickable` attribute to `true` and the `autoLink` attribute to `all` for the `TextView` control.

5. Enable simple scrolling abilities within the `TextView` control you just created and configure how the scrollbar looks and behaves by setting the following attributes: set the `isScrollContainer` attribute to `true`, set the `scrollbars` attribute to `vertical`, set the `fadingEdgeLength` attribute to a reasonable dimension (see the dimension resource created for this purpose), and set the `scrollbarStyle` to `outsideOverlay`. Other attribute settings are certainly acceptable, but these are the settings used in the application provided.

At this point, save the `help.xml` layout file. You can find the Android SDK documentation for the XML attributes for `TextView` controls at http://goo.gl/a1N2T. You might also have to look at the attributes for View controls for some of the inherited attributes, such as the scrollbar attributes.

Working with Files

Now that the `help.xml` layout file is complete, the `QuizHelpActivity` class must be updated to read the `quizhelp.txt` file and place the resulting text into the `TextView` control called `TextView_HelpText`.

Each Android application has its own private directory on the Android file system for storing application files. In addition to all the familiar `File` and `Stream` classes available, you can access private application files and directories by using the following Context class methods: `fileList()`, `getFilesDir()`, `getDir()`, `openFileInput()`, `openFileOutput()`, `deleteFile()`, and `getFileStreamPath()`. These features can be very helpful if your application needs to generate files or download them from the Internet.

Adding Raw Resource Files

Raw resource files, such as the `quizhelp.txt` text file, are added to a project by simply including them in the `/raw` resources project directory. This can be done by either creating them as a new file, dragging them in from a file management tool, or any other way you're accustomed to adding files to Android projects in Eclipse.

For the purposes of this exercise, we created a text file that contained some basic help text, as well as a website, street address, and phone number. This way, when we enable the `linksClickable` attribute within the `TextView` control that contains the help text, these pieces of information are "clickable" and launch the appropriate application, such as Maps, the Phone Dialer, and so on. This text file is included in the source code for this hour for you to use.

Accessing Raw File Resources

The Android platform includes many of the typical Java file I/O classes, including stream operations. To read string data from a file, use the `openRawResource()` method of the `Resources` class from within your activity, as in the following example:

```
InputStream iFile = getResources().openRawResource(R.raw.quizhelp);
```

Now that you have an `InputStream` object, you can read the file, line-by-line or byte-by-byte, and create a string. There are a number of ways to do this in Java. Here's a simple Java method that reads an `InputStream` and returns a `String` with its contents:

```
public String inputStreamToString(InputStream is) throws IOException {
    StringBuffer sBuffer = new StringBuffer();
    DataInputStream dataIO = new DataInputStream(is);
    String strLine = null;
    while ((strLine = dataIO.readLine()) != null) {
        sBuffer.append(strLine + "\n");
    }

    dataIO.close();
    is.close();

    return sBuffer.toString();
}
```

This helper method should be used within a try/catch block. See this hour's sample code if you require further explanation. Use the `inputStreamToString()` method with the `InputStream` of the help file to retrieve the help text. Then retrieve the `TextView` control using the `findViewById()` method and set the help text to it using the `TextView` control's `setText()` method, as follows:

```
TextView helpText = (TextView) findViewById(R.id.TextView_HelpText);
String strFile = inputStreamToString(iFile);
helpText.setText(strFile);
```

At this point, save the `QuizHelpActivity.java` file and run the Been There, Done That! application in the Android emulator. After the splash screen finishes, choose the help screen option from the main menu. The help screen should now look like Figure 9.3.

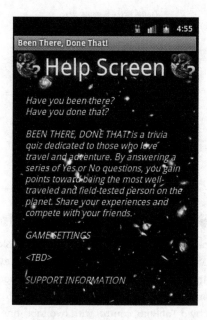

FIGURE 9.3
The Been There, Done That! help screen.

Designing the Scores Screen

Now that you've created the help screen, it's time to turn your attention to another screen: the scores screen. The requirements for this screen include showing several different scores to the user. There are two types of scores: the all-time-high scores and the user's friends' scores. The same screen handles both categories of scores. For each user shown, the data includes the name, score, and overall ranking.

There are a number of ways you could implement the scores screen. For example, you could use string formatting with a `TextView` control or `ListView` control to display the score information. However, you are working with a small screen, and you don't want to overwhelm the user with too much information. Because you have two different sets of data to display, two tabs are ideal for this screen. Figure 9.4 shows a rough design of the scores screen.

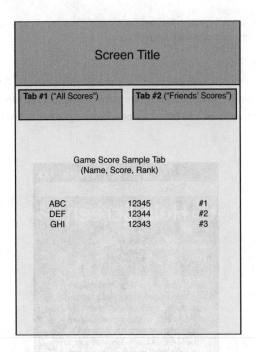

Determining Scores Screen Layout Requirements

Now that you have the rough design of the scores screen, translate the design to use the appropriate layout controls. To do this, update the /res/layout/scores.xml layout file that is used by the QuizScoresActivity class. Once again, take advantage of the RelativeLayout control to add a familiar title bar to the top of the scores screen. This header is followed by a TabHost control with two tabs: one tab for all user scores and one for friends' scores. Each tab contains a TableLayout control to display scores in neat rows and columns. Although you could use a ListView, this is as good a place as any to teach you about the TableLayout control—you already learned about the ListView control in Hour 8, "Implementing the Main Menu Screen."

Adding the TabHost Control

To add tabbing support to the scores screen, you must include a TabHost control, which is a container view with child tabs, each of which may contain layout content. The TabHost control is a somewhat complex object and you might want to review the Android SDK documentation regarding this class if you run into problems or require clarification about how to configure it properly, above and beyond the steps discussed here. In order to configure tab controls within an XML layout resource file, you need to follow these guidelines:

▶ Include a `TabHost` control

▶ Ensure that there is a `LinearLayout` within the `TabHost` control

▶ Ensure that there is a specially named `TabWidget` control and `FrameLayout` control within the `LinearLayout` control

▶ Define the contents of each tab in a `FrameLayout` control

Figure 9.5 shows the layout design for the scores screen.

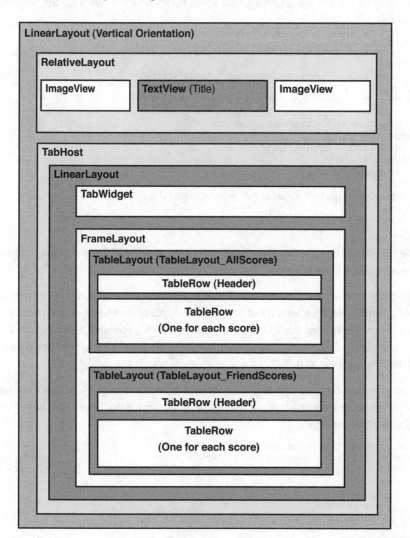

FIGURE 9.5
Layout design for the Been There, Done That! scores screen.

Implementing the Scores Screen Layout

To implement the scores screen, begin by adding new resources to the project. Then update the `scores.xml` layout resource to reflect the scores screen design. Let's walk through how to do each of these tasks now.

Adding New Project Resources

As with the other screens in the Been There, Done That! application, you need to add several new string, color, and dimension resources to your project to support the scores screen. Start by adding string resources to `/res/values/strings.xml` for the score column names, status string, and when no scores exist. We used the following strings:

```xml
<string
    name="all_scores">"All Scores"</string>
<string
    name="friends_scores">"Scores of Friends"</string>
<string
    name="no_scores">"No scores to show."</string>
<string
    name="username">"Username"</string>
<string
    name="rank">"Ranking"</string>
<string
    name="score">"Score"</string>
<string
    name="wait_msg">"Retrieving Scores..."</string>
<string
    name="wait_title">"Loading..."</string>
```

Save the string resource file. Now these strings are available for use in the scores screen layout resource file.

The scores for the Been There, Done That! application will eventually be retrieved from a remote network server, but for now the application will use some mock score data. Android supports the XML resource file type. XML resource files can contain this mock score data, so you can mimic the structure that the real network scores will be available in: XML.

To achieve this, add two files to the `/res/xml/` resource directory—`allscores.xml` and `friendscores.xml`—that represent the mock score data. These files have the following XML structure:

```xml
<?xml version="1.0" encoding="utf-8"?>
    <!-- This is a mock score XML chunk -->
<scores>
    <score
        username="LED"
        score="12345"
```

```
        rank="1" />
   <score
       username="SAC"
       score="12344"
       rank="2" />
   <score
       username="NAD"
       score="12339"
       rank="3" />
</scores>
```

The score data uses a very simple schema. A single <scores> element has a number of child <score> elements. Each <score> element has three attributes: username, score, and rank. For this example, assume that the score data is sorted and limited to the top 20 or so scores. A server will enforce these restrictions in the future.

Updating the Scores Screen Layout

The scores screen user interface is defined in the scores.xml layout file. To update this layout to your intended layout design, follow these steps:

> The Eclipse layout resource editor does not display TabHost controls properly in design mode—it throws a NullPointerException. To design this kind of layout, you should stick to the XML layout mode. You must use the Android emulator or an Android device to view the tabs.

1. Remove all the old controls and start fresh.

2. Add a new LinearLayout control, setting its android:background attribute to @drawable/bkgrnd. Set its orientation attribute to vertical and its layout_width and layout_height attributes to match_parent to fill the screen. All subsequent controls are added inside this LinearLayout control.

3. Add the same header you created in other layouts. Recall that it contains a RelativeLayout control with two ImageView controls and a TextView control. Set the TextView control's text attribute to the string resource @string/scores to reflect the appropriate screen title.

4. Outside the RelativeLayout control but still within the LinearLayout, add a TabHost control with an id attribute of @+id/TabHost1. Set its layout_width and layout_height attributes to match_parent.

5. Inside the TabHost control, add another LinearLayout control, with its orientation attribute set to vertical. Set its layout_width and layout_height attributes to match_parent.

6. Inside the inner `LinearLayout` control, add a `TabWidget` control. Set the control's id attribute to `@android:id/tabs`, its `layout_width` to `match_parent`, and its `layout_height` to `wrap_content`.

7. Within the inner `LinearLayout` control at the same level as the `TabWidget` control, add a `FrameLayout` control. Set the `FrameLayout` control's id attribute to `@android:id/tabcontent` and its `layout_width` and `layout_height` attributes to `match_parent`.

By the Way

When creating a tabbed view in this way, you must name the `FrameLayout` control as listed: `@android:id/tabcontent`; otherwise, exceptions are thrown at runtime. This identifier is expected by the `TabHost` control and references a special Android package resource. It is not the same as using `@+id/tabcontent`. That would create a new identifier for a layout object in your own application package.

8. Define the content of your tabs. Within the `FrameLayout` control, add two `TableLayout` controls, one for each tab. The scores are displayed in neat rows and columns using these `TableLayout` controls. Name the first `TableLayout` control `TableLayout_AllScores` and the second `TableLayout_FriendScores`. Set each `TableLayout` control's `layout_width` and `layout_height` attributes to `match_parent`. Set the `stretchColumns` attribute to * to allow columns to resize based on the content.

9. **The list of scores may grow longer than the available vertical space on the screen.** The `ScrollView` controls solves this problem by allowing its children to grow virtually beyond its own bounds by providing a scrollable area and a scrollbar to indicate the scrolling. Give a `TableLayout` control a vertical scrollbar, wrap it in a `ScrollView` control (inside the `FrameLayout`, encompassing a single `TableLayout`) and set the `scrollbars` attribute to `vertical`. You also need to set its `layout_width` and `layout_height` attributes.

The `TabHost` section of the scores screen layout file (with optional scrolling `TableLayout` tabs) should now look something like this:

```
<TabHost
    android:id="@+id/TabHost1"
    android:layout_width="match_parent"
    android:layout_height="match_parent">
    <LinearLayout
        android:orientation="vertical"
        android:layout_width= match_parent"
        android:layout_height="match_parent">
        <TabWidget
            android:id="@android:id/tabs"
            android:layout_width="match_parent"
            android:layout_height="wrap_content" />
```

```
    <FrameLayout
        android:id="@android:id/tabcontent"
        android:layout_width="match_parent"
        android:layout_height="match_parent">
        <ScrollView
            android:id="@+id/ScrollViewAllScores"
            android:layout_width="match_parent"
            android:layout_height="match_parent"
            android:scrollbars="vertical">
            <TableLayout
                android:id="@+id/TableLayout_AllScores"
                android:layout_width="match_parent"
                android:layout_height="match_parent"
                android:stretchColumns="*">
            </TableLayout>
        </ScrollView>
        <ScrollView
            android:id="@+id/ScrollViewFriendScores"
            android:layout_width="match_parent"
            android:layout_height="match_parent"
            android:scrollbars="vertical">
            <TableLayout
                android:id="@+id/TableLayout_FriendScores"
                android:layout_width="match_parent"
                android:layout_height="match_parent"
                android:stretchColumns="*"></TableLayout>
        </ScrollView>
    </FrameLayout>
    </LinearLayout>
</TabHost>
```

Save the `scores.xml` layout file.

Building a Screen with Tabs

It's time to switch your focus to the `QuizScoresActivity.java` file and wire up the
controls needed by the `TabHost` control. First, initialize the `TabHost` control and
then add the two tabs, making the default tab the All Scores tab. Finally, parse the
mock XML score data and populate the `TableLayout` control for each tab. Let's now
discuss how to do these tasks.

Configuring the `TabHost` Control

The `TabHost` control must be initialized before it will function properly. Therefore,
start by retrieving the control by using the `findViewById()` method. Next, call the

TabHost control's `setup()` method to initialize the TabHost and "glue" the specially named `TabWidget` and `FrameLayout` controls together to form a tab set, as follows:

```
TabHost host = (TabHost) findViewById(R.id.TabHost1);
host.setup();
```

Adding Tabs to the `TabHost` Control

Now that the `TabHost` control is initialized, configure each tab and add the configured tabs to the `TabHost` using the `addTab()` method. The `addTab()` method takes a `TabSpec` parameter to describe the tab contents. To create the All Scores tab, add the following code right after the `setup()` method call:

```
TabSpec allScoresTab = host.newTabSpec("allTab");
allScoresTab.setIndicator(getResources().getString(R.string.all_scores),
    getResources().getDrawable(android.R.drawable.star_on));
allScoresTab.setContent(R.id.ScrollViewAllScores);
host.addTab(allScoresTab);
```

The `TabSpec` control called `allScoresTab` has the tag spec reference of `"allTab"`. The actual tab label contains both a `TextView` control label and a drawable icon (in this case, a star from the built-in Android resources). Finally, the contents of the tab are set to `ScrollViewAllScores` using a call to the `setContent()` method, which contains the `TableLayout` control called `TableLayout_AllScores`, defined in the `scores.xml` layout resource.

Implement the tab for friends' scores using this same mechanism. The sample code for this chapter uses `friendsTab` as the `TabSpec` name. Change the content around to use the appropriate label for the tab indicator and the appropriate content with the `setContent()` method.

Setting the Default Tab

At this point, you need to identify which tab to show by default. To do this, call the `setCurrentTabByTag()` method and pass in the tag name of the tab you want to display by default. For example, to display the all scores tab first, use the following method call, placed after the code for adding the tabs to the `TabHost`:

```
host.setCurrentTabByTag("allTab");
```

Save the `QuizScoresActivity.java` file and try to run the application in the Android emulator. Navigate to the scores screen. You should see the two tabs, and blank space beneath. Let's now fill that in with the scores.

Working with XML

The Android platform has a number of mechanisms for working with XML data, including support for the following:

- ▶ SAX (Simple API for XML)
- ▶ XML Pull Parser
- ▶ Limited DOM Level 2 core support

The XML technology you use depends on your specific project. For this example, you simply want to read through a simple XML file and extract the mock score data.

Retrieving XML Resources

First, write code to access the mock XML data you saved in the project resources. The Android SDK includes an easy method to retrieve XML resources into an object time that is used to parse the XML files: the XMLResourceParser object. Initialize two instances of this object, one for each score file, using the following code

```
XmlResourceParser mockAllScores =
    getResources().getXml(R.xml.allscores);
XmlResourceParser mockFriendScores =
    getResources().getXml(R.xml.friendscores);
```

Now you've got an XMLResourceParser object that is used to parse the XML.

Parsing XML Files with XmlResourceParser

The mock score files have a very simple schema with only two tags: <scores> and <score>. To parse the file, you want to find each <score> tag and extract its user-name, rank, and score attributes. Because you can assume a small amount of data (we guarantee it here), implement your parsing routine by using a simple while() loop to iterate through the events by using the next() method, as follows:

```
int eventType = -1;
boolean bFoundScores = false;
// Find Score records from XML
while (eventType != XmlResourceParser.END_DOCUMENT) {
    if (eventType == XmlResourceParser.START_TAG) {
        // Get the name of the tag (eg scores or score)
        String strName = scores.getName();
        if (strName.equals("score")) {
            bFoundScores = true;
            String scoreValue = scores.getAttributeValue(null, "score");
            String scoreRank = scores.getAttributeValue(null, "rank");
            String scoreUserName =
                scores.getAttributeValue(null, "username");
```

```
        insertScoreRow(scoreTable, scoreValue, scoreRank,
            scoreUserName);
    }
  }
  eventType = scores.next();
}
```

Within the loop, watch for the START_TAG event. When the tag name matches the
<score> tag, a piece of score data is ready. Extract the score data by using the
getAttributeValue() method. For each score, add a new TableRow control to the
appropriate TableLayout control (in the appropriate tab); in this case, we implemented a helper function called insertScoreRow(). This method simply creates a
new TableRow control with three new TextView controls (username, score, ranking)
and adds the row to the TableLayout using the addView() method. For the complete implementation of this helper method, see the source code that accompanies
this hour.

Now we said that this method would work for small amounts of data, and it does.
But when you have time-intensive processing, always perform the hard work asynchronously to the main thread. We discuss methods of doing this later in the book,
but it's worth noting now that parsing is just such an operation. For this hour, we
keep it simple.

Applying Finishing Touches to the Scores Screen

After you have written the code to parse the two mock XML files and populate the
two TableLayout controls in the TabHost control, you need only make a few minor
additions to QuizScoresActivity. Add a header TableRow to each TableLayout
control, with nicely styled column headers using the string resources you created
earlier in this hour. Then implement special handling for the case where no score
data is available. These tasks are a little different from populating the rows with
scores; you're simply getting the text data from a different source.

When you're done applying these finishing touches, save the class and run the
application in the emulator or on the device. Navigate to the scores screen. Both
tabs are now populated with data and look similar to Figure 9.6.

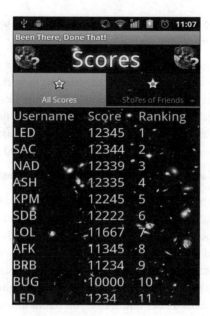

FIGURE 9.6
The Been There,
Done That!
scores screen.

Summary

You've made excellent progress on building the Been There, Done That! application in this hour, including the implementation of two new screens. As you implemented the help screen, you learned how to display large amounts of data by using a scrolling `TextView` control. You learned how to enable links to websites, street addresses, and phones numbers within `TextView` controls, as well as how to access a file resource and change layout characteristics programmatically. By implementing the scores screen, you learned about the `TabHost` control, the `TableLayout` control, and even how to parse XML to display some mock score data to the screen.

Q&A

Q. *What is the* `TabActivity` *class for?*

A. If you have a screen with only a `TabHost` control, consider using the `TabActivity` class, which simplifies `TabHost` management. However, if your layout has more than just a `TabHost` control (for example, a header), your best bet is to incorporate the `TabHost` control into a layout file as we did in this Hour.

Q. *Why do I need to name certain controls within the* `TabHost` *control with specific Android* `id` *attributes?*

A. Occasionally, you will find situations in which you need to name layout controls with specific names in order for the controls to work properly with the Android SDK. The more complex a control, the more likely it requires a bit of "glue" (or "magic") for the Android system to load the right templates and resources to display the control in a familiar way. Almost always, these kinds of naming requirements are documented in the Android SDK.

Q. *There is a bit of a delay when loading the scores screen. Why?*

A. There are a number of reasons this screen may be less responsive than other screens. First, you are parsing XML, which can be a costly operation. Second, you create a large number of `View` controls to display the score data. You must always be careful to offload intense processing from the main UI thread to make the application more responsive and avoid unnecessary shutdown by the Android system. You could easily add a worker thread to handle the XML (in fact, we do this in a later hour), and you might also consider other, more efficient, controls for displaying the score data. Finally, with Eclipse, when the debugger is attached, performance of an application greatly degrades.

Workshop

Quiz

1. True or False: A `TextView` control can display a large amount of text.

2. What class can you use to simplify tab screens?

   A. `Tabify`

   B. `TabActivity`

   C. `TabController`

3. True or False: XML files are handled by the XML Resource Manager, so no parsing is necessary.

4. What type of control can you use to enable scrolling?

   A. `ScrollLayout`

   B. `Scroller`

   C. `ScrollView`

Answers

1. True. The `TextView` control can display large quantities of text, with optional horizontal and vertical scrollbars.

2. B. A screen that requires only a tab set can use the `TabActivity` class to handle tabbing setup and tasks efficiently.

3. False. XML files can be included but still need to be parsed. Three parsers are available, with the default resource parser being XML Pull Parser.

4. C. The `ScrollView` control can be used to wrap child `View` controls within a scrolling area.

Exercises

1. Launch the application and click each of the links in the help screen text. Note how easy it can be to integrate with other applications such as web browsers, the phone dialer, and the Maps application.

2. Change the indicator icon used by the All Scores tab to another drawable resource, either another built-in resource (for example, `star_big_on`) or a drawable resource you supply to the project.

3. Experiment with the scrollbars implemented on both the help and scores screens. The scrolling functionality of the help screen is derived from the built-in scroll abilities every `View` control inherits; the scrolling ability on the score tabs is achieved using the `ScrollView` control. There are numerous scrollbar-related attributes that you can configure in different ways, colors and styles. Try some of them out within your application. Which scrollbar style do you prefer?

HOUR 10

Building Forms to Collect User Input

What You'll Learn in This Hour:

▶ Designing and implementing the settings screen
▶ Working with `EditText` controls
▶ Working with `Button` controls
▶ Working with `Spinner` controls
▶ Saving form data with `SharedPreferences`

In this hour, you begin implementation of the settings screen of the Been There, Done That! application. The settings screen displays a form for entering application configuration information, including the user's login and profile settings. Different settings necessitate the use of different input controls, including `EditText`, `Spinner`, and `Button` controls, among others. Finally, you need to ensure that each setting is saved and stored in a persistent manner as part of the application's preferences.

Designing the Settings Screen

The settings screen must allow the user to configure any number of game settings. Game settings may be text input fields, drop-down lists, or other, more complex, controls. You will eventually need to handle the social gaming settings as well, but we deal with this requirement in a later hour. For now, begin by implementing a simple settings screen with five basic game settings:

▶ `Nickname`—The name to be displayed on score listings. This text field should be no more than 20 characters long—an arbitrary but reasonable length for the purposes of this application.

▶ Email—The unique identifier for each user. This is a text field.

▶ Password—A mechanism to handle user verification. This is a password text field. When setting the password, the user should input the password twice for verification. The password text may be stored as plaintext.

▶ Date of Birth—To verify minimum age, when necessary. This is a date field but often displayed in a friendly way users understand and can easily configure.

▶ Gender—A piece of demographic information, which could be used for special score listings or to target ads to the user. This can be set to three different settings: Male (1), Female (2), or Prefer Not to Say (0).

Figure 10.1 shows a rough design for the settings screen.

FIGURE 10.1
Rough design for the Been There, Done That! settings screen.

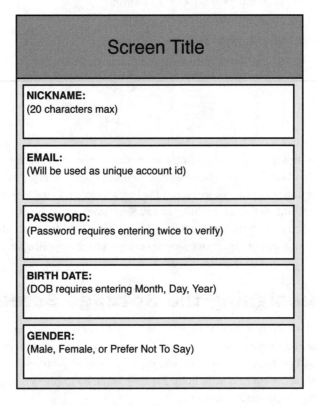

The application settings screen contains quite a few different controls, so you need to be especially careful with screen real estate. Begin with the customary header bar that contains the title of the screen.

Below the title, add a `ScrollView` control to contain all of the settings. This way, when the settings controls no longer fit on a single screen, the user can easily scroll up and down to find the setting they require. A `ScrollView` control can have only a single child control, so place a vertical `LinearLayout` control within it to align the settings within.

Each setting requires two "rows" in the `LinearLayout` control: a `TextView` row that displays the setting name label and a row for the input control to capture its value. For example, the Nickname setting requires a row with a `TextView` control to display the label string ("Nickname:") and a second row for an `EditText` control to enable the user to input a string of text.

Now determine which input control is most appropriate for each setting:

▶ The Nickname and Email fields are simply different types of single-line text input, so they can be `EditText` controls.

▶ The Password setting requires two `EditText` controls to request the password and confirm it. Use a `Dialog` for these two input controls. This way, the entries aren't shown on the settings screen nor do they take up extra room on the screen. The main settings screen can just display whether or not the password has been set in a simple `TextView` control and a `Button` control to launch the password dialog.

▶ The Date of Birth setting requires a `DatePicker` input control. Because the `DatePicker` control is actually three separate controls—a month picker, a day picker, and a year picker—it takes up a lot of space on the screen. Therefore, instead of including it directly on the settings screen, you can add a `Button` control to launch a `DatePickerDialog` control in a `Dialog`. The user then selects the appropriate date from the picker and closes the dialog. The resulting date is then displayed (but not editable) on the settings screen using a simple `TextView` control.

▶ The Gender setting is simply a choice between three values, so a `Spinner` (drop-down) control is most appropriate.

Figure 10.2 shows the layout design of the basic settings screen.

FIGURE 10.2
Layout design for the Been There Done That! settings screen.

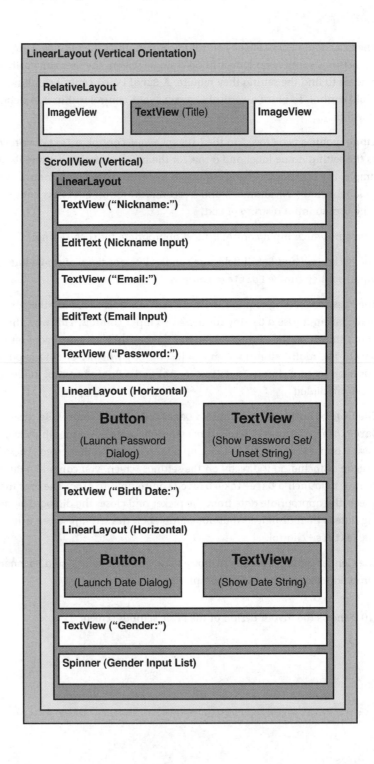

Implementing the Settings Screen Layout

To implement the settings screen, begin by adding new resources to the project. Then update the `settings.xml` layout resource to reflect the settings screen design. In this hour, you focus on the controls specific to the settings screen, but you won't implement the Dialog controls for the password and date picker until the next hour.

Adding New Project Resources

Screens with form fields seem to rely on more resources than most other screen types. You need to add a number of new resources to support the settings screen. In addition to the string and color resources, you also need to add a new type of resource: a string array.

Adding New Color Resources

The settings screen relies on one new color resource to display error text. This text color would be used when the two passwords do not match. Therefore, add the following color resource to the `colors.xml` resource file:

```
<color
    name="error_color">#F00</color>
```

Now save the `colors.xml` resource file.

Adding New String Resources

The settings screen relies on numerous new string resources. Add the following text resources to the `strings.xml` resource file:

- ▶ Text label for each setting's `TextView` control (for example, `"Nickname:"`)
- ▶ Text label for each `Button` control (for example, "Set Password")
- ▶ Text to display in a `TextView` control when the password is set or not set
- ▶ Text to display in a `TextView` control when the Date of Birth field is not set
- ▶ Text to display in a `TextView` control when the two Password fields match or don't match
- ▶ Text for each Gender option in the `Spinner` control (for example, `"Male"`)

Save the `strings.xml` resource file. For a complete list of the new strings required for the settings screen, see the sample source code provided on the CD that accompanies this book, or download the source code from the book website.

Adding New String Array Resources

Spinner controls can use data adapters as the source for the information they display. They can also directly use arrays for static sets of information. Android resources can be grouped together as arrays. This is a convenient way to prepare simple data for use with Spinner controls.

To group the gender string resources ("Male", "Female", "Prefer Not To Say") together into an array, create a new resource type called a string array.

To create a string array resource, add a new resource file called /res/values/arrays.xml. Within this file, create a new <string-array> element called genders. Within this <string-array> element, add three <item> elements, one for each string resource.

For example, let's assume that you created the following string resources in the strings.xml resource file:

```
<string
    name="gender_male">Male</string>
<string
    name="gender_female">Female</string>
<string
    name="gender_neutral">Prefer Not To Say</string>
```

Within the arrays.xml resource file, add each string resource as an item in the genders string array. For example, the first item in the array (with an index of 0) would have the value @string/gender_neutral. The resulting arrays.xml resource file would then look like this:

```
<?xml version="1.0" encoding="utf-8"?>
<resources>
    <string-array
        name="genders">
        <item>@string/gender_neutral</item>
        <item>@string/gender_male</item>
        <item>@string/gender_female</item>
    </string-array>
</resources>
```

Save the arrays.xml resource file. To load the genders string array resource, access it programmatically by using the R.array.genders resource identifier as the identifier parameter to the createFromResource() method of the ArrayAdapter class.

Updating the Settings Screen Layout

The settings.xml layout file dictates the user interface of the settings screen. Follow these steps to generate the settings screen layout desired, based on your earlier design:

1. Open the settings.xml layout resource in the Eclipse resource designer and remove all existing controls.

2. Add the customary LinearLayout control, with its background attribute set to @drawable/bkgrnd. Set its orientation attribute to vertical and its layout_width and layout_height attributes to match_parent, so that the control fills the screen. All subsequent controls should be added inside this control.

3. Add the same header you've added to other screens, using the RelativeLayout with the ImageView control, TextView control, and second ImageView control.

4. Below the title bar, add a ScrollView control to encapsulate your settings. Set its isScrollContainer attribute to true and its scrollbars attribute to vertical. Try setting its scrollbarAlwaysDrawVerticalTrack attribute to true as well. Set its layout_width and layout_height attributes to match_parent.

5. Within the ScrollView control, add a LinearLayout control to encapsulate your settings. Set its orientation attribute to vertical. Set its layout_width and layout_height attributes to match_parent. All subsequent settings controls should be added within this LinearLayout control.

6. Now within the LinearLayout control, begin adding the settings sections themselves. Start by adding a TextView control to display the Nickname label text. Below the TextView control, add an EditText input control. Set its id attribute to EditText_Nickname, its maxLength attribute to 20, its maxLines attribute to 1, and its inputType attribute to textPersonName.

7. Add a TextView control to display the Email label text and then another EditText control below it, setting its id attribute to EditText_Email, its maxLines attribute to 1, and its inputType attribute to textEmailAddress.

8. Now add the Password settings region of the form by adding another TextView control to display the Password label text. Below it, add a horizontal LinearLayout control (whose layout_height should be wrap_content, layout_width should be match_parent) with two child controls: a Button control and a TextView control. Configure the Button control with the id attribute Button_Password and the text attribute set to the Password button text string resource; its layout_width and layout_height attributes should be set to wrap_content. Configure the TextView control to display the Password setting state string ("Password not set", for now, until we wire up the dialog).

9. At the same level as the Password setting region, add a region for the Date of Birth setting. Start by adding another `TextView` control to display the Date of Birth label text. Next, add another horizontal `LinearLayout` control with two controls: a `Button` control and a `TextView` control. Configure the `Button` control with the `id` attribute `Button_DOB` and the `text` attribute set to the Date of Birth button text string resource. Configure the `TextView` control to display the Date of Birth setting state string (`"Date not set"`, for now, until we wire up the dialog).

10. Add one last settings region for the Gender drop-down by adding a `TextView` control to display the Gender label text. Then add a `Spinner` control and set its `id` attribute to `Spinner_Gender`.

11. Before saving, adjust any text sizes, styles, colors, and dimension atrributes until the screen draws as desired.

At this point, save the `settings.xml` layout file.

Using Common Form Controls

Now that the `settings.xml` layout file is complete, you need to update the `QuizSettingsActivity` class to wire up the controls and allow editing and saving of form data. Different controls are handled in different ways. Begin with `EditText` control, and then work through `Button` and `Spinner` controls.

Working with `EditText` Controls

The `EditText` control, which is derived from the `TextView` control, is used to collect textual input from the user. Figure 10.3 shows a simple `EditText` control.

FIGURE 10.3
An `EditText`
control for text
input.

This is an input field..|

Configuring `EditText` Controls

All the typical attributes of a `TextView` control (for example, `textColor`, `textSize`) are available to `EditText` controls. The following are some `EditText` attributes that are commonly used for the settings screen:

▶ `inputType`—This attribute instructs the Android system about how to help the user fill in the text. Set the `inputType` attribute of the `EditText` control for the Email field to `textEmailAddress`, which instructs the Android system to use the email-oriented soft keyboard (with the @ sign). The inputType value called textPassword automatically masks the user's password as it is typed. You see this in action when you create the password dialog in the next hour.

▶ minLines and maxLines—These attributes restrict the number of lines of text allowed in the control.

▶ maxLength—This attribute restricts the number of characters of text allowed in the control. For example, you can limit the number of characters allowed in the Nickname setting by setting the maxLength attribute of the Nickname setting's EditText control to 20.

Handling Text Input

As with a TextView control, you can access the text stored in an EditText control by using the getText() and setText() methods. For example, to extract the string typed into the EditText control called EditText_Nickname, you use the getText() method as follows:

```
EditText nicknameText = (EditText) findViewById(R.id.EditText_Nickname);
String strNicknameToSave = nicknameText.getText().toString();
```

The getText() method returns an Editable object, but because you simply want its String value equivalent, use the toString() method to get the String representation of the inputted text.

Working with Button Controls

The Android platform actually supports two kinds of button controls: the basic Button control and the ImageButton control. An ImageButton control behaves much like a regular Button control, only instead of displaying a text label, it displays a drawable graphic. The Button control on the Android platform is relatively straightforward, as form controls go. Generally speaking, a Button control is simply a clickable area of the screen, generally with a text label. Figure 10.4 shows a Button control.

FIGURE 10.4
A Button control.

Configuring Button Controls

Many of the typical attributes of TextView controls, such as textColor and textSize, are available for the Button text label. You need two simple Button controls for the settings screen: one for launching the Password dialog and one for launching the date picker dialog. Configure these Button controls by giving each a unique identifier and setting each control's text attribute label. Also set each Button control's layout_width and layout_height attributes to wrap_content so that each control scales appropriately, based on the text label.

By default, a Button control looks like a silver rectangle with slightly rounded corners. You can use various attributes to modify the look of a Button control. For example, you can change the shape of the button by setting the background, drawableTop, drawableBottom, drawableLeft, and drawableRight attributes of the Button control to drawable resources.

▼   Try It Yourself

Try changing the look of the Button control called Button_DOB by taking the following steps in the settings.xml layout file:

1. Change the background property of the Button control to the Drawable graphic resource called @drawable/selector.

2. Change the drawableTop property of the Button control to the Drawable graphic resource called @drawable/divider.

3. Change the drawableBottom property of the Button control to the Drawable graphic resource called @drawable/divider. Note that the Button control is now an ugly orange menace on the screen. You've created a monster.

4. Change the Button control back to the default Button control look and feel by removing the background, drawableTop, and drawableBottom properties from Button_DOB.

▲

Handling Button Clicks

Handling button clicks is easy with Eclipse. First, add a method to your activity class that takes a single View parameter, does not return any values (void), and performs the desired action when the user presses the button. Then, modify the layout file with the Button control and place a reference to this method as the control's onClick attribute.

Let's make these changes for both the Pick Date button and the Set Password button. First, add two methods to the QuizSettingsActivity class. Name one onPickDateButtonClick() and name the other onSetPasswordButtonClick(). Both take a single parameter of type View and don't return any values.

You are not yet ready to implement the dialogs that will ultimately be launched when the buttons are clicked. For the moment, it makes sense to display a debug message using a Toast. A Toast is a view that pops up in the foreground to display a message for a few seconds and then disappears. The two new methods should now look like this:

```java
public void onSetPasswordButtonClick(View view) {
    Toast.makeText(QuizSettingsActivity.this,
        "TODO: Launch Password Dialog", Toast.LENGTH_LONG).show();
}
// ...
public void onPickDateButtonClick(View view) {
    Toast.makeText(QuizSettingsActivity.this,
        "TODO: Launch DatePickerDialog", Toast.LENGTH_LONG).show();
}
```

Save the Java file now and then switch over to the settings.xml layout resource file. Modify both the Set Password button and the Pick Date button controls by adding a value for the android:onClick property. For the button with the id of Button_Password, set this value to the string onSetPasswordButtonClick and for the button with the id of Button_DOB, set this value to the string onPickDateButtonClick. Make this change using either the Graphic Layout view and the properties panel in Eclipse or by directly editing the XML file. Either way, when the change is done, the two button entries look like this:

```xml
<Button
    android:id="@+id/Button_Password"
    android:layout_width="wrap_content"
    android:layout_height="wrap_content"
    android:text="@string/settings_button_pwd"></Button>
<... >
<Button
    android:id="@+id/Button_DOB"
    android:layout_width="wrap_content"
    android:layout_height="wrap_content"
    android:text="@string/settings_button_dob"
    android:onClick="onPickDateButtonClick"></Button>
```

Save the layout file and run the application. When you click one of the buttons, you see the toast message like the one shown in Figure 10.5.

FIGURE 10.5
A Toast mes-
sage triggered
by a button
click.

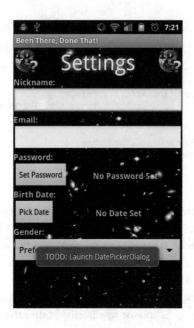

Working with Spinner Controls

The Spinner control is basically the Android platform's version of a drop-down list.
The Spinner control looks much like a drop-down when closed (see Figure 10.6,
left), but when the control is activated, it displays a chooser window (see Figure 10.6,
right) instead of drawing the drop-down on the main screen.

FIGURE 10.6
A Spinner
control closed
(left) and open
(right).

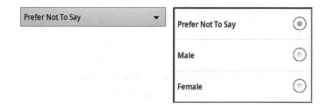

Configuring Spinner Controls

Earlier in this hour, you created a string array resource of genders for the specific
purpose of using it with the Spinner control. It is now time to use it.

Open up the settings.xml layout resource file and located the Spinner control
with the id of Spinner_Gender. Change its entries attribute to @array/genders.
If you made this change in the Graphical Layout, you immediately see the first
option, Prefer Not To Say, displayed on the preview. The XML for the Spinner control now looks like this:

```
<Spinner
    android:id="@+id/Spinner_Gender"
    android:layout_height="wrap_content"
    android:layout_width="match_parent"
    android:entries="@array/genders"></Spinner>
```

Save the layout file. If you run the application now, you see the Spinner behave much like Figure 10.6.

Handling Spinner Selections

After the Spinner control has been filled with data, you can control which item is selected using the setSelection() method. For example, you know that the option for female gender is stored in the string array at index 2 because you use a 0-based string array. Because you mapped the indexes directly to the gender values, you can set the Spinner control to the Female option by using the setSelection() method, as follows:

```
spinner.setSelection(2);
```

The Spinner class also includes a number of methods for retrieving the current item selected.

Listening for Spinner Selection Events

You need to save the Spinner control selection to the application preferences. To do this, use the setOnItemSelectedListener() method of the Spinner control to register the appropriate listener for selection events. Specifically, implement the onItemSelected() callback method of AdapterView.OnItemSelectedListener, like this:

```
spinner.setOnItemSelectedListener(
    new AdapterView.OnItemSelectedListener() {
        public void onItemSelected(AdapterView<?> parent, View itemSelected,
            int selectedItemPosition, long selectedId) {
            // TODO: Save item index (selectedItemPosition) as Gender setting
        }

        // … Other required overrides
    });
```

Depending on the version of the Android SDK you are developing for, you may also need to provide stub implementations of the other methods provided for the listener. At this point, save the QuizSettingsActivity.java file and run the Been There, Done That! application in the Android emulator. You're almost done; now you need to commit the form data to the application shared preferences.

Saving Form Data with SharedPreferences

You can use the persistent storage mechanism called SharedPreferences to store the application game settings. Using these preferences, you can save all the form values on the settings screen.

Defining SharedPreferences Entries

Earlier, you added a string to the QuizActivity base class for your game preferences:

```
public static final String GAME_PREFERENCES = "GamePrefs";
```

Now add a String variable for each of the settings to store to the QuizActivity class preferences:

```
public static final String GAME_PREFERENCES_NICKNAME = "Nickname"; // String
public static final String GAME_PREFERENCES_EMAIL = "Email"; // String
public static final String GAME_PREFERENCES_PASSWORD = "Password"; // String
public static final String GAME_PREFERENCES_DOB = "DOB"; // Long
public static final String GAME_PREFERENCES_GENDER = "Gender"; // Int
```

Saving Settings to SharedPreferences

Now that you have defined the preference settings, it's time to save the form fields to the game preferences. Within the QuizSettingsActivity class, begin by defining a SharedPreferences member variable:

```
SharedPreferences mGameSettings;
```

Within the onCreate() method of the activity, initialize this member variable as follows:

```
mGameSettings =
    getSharedPreferences(GAME_PREFERENCES, Context.MODE_PRIVATE);
```

Pass in the name of your SharedPreferences (the String called GAME_PREFERENCES found in the QuizActivity class). The mode called MODE_PRIVATE is the default permission used for private application files.

Now any time you need to save a preference within your application, simply open a SharedPreferences.Editor, assign a specific preference setting, and commit the change. For example, to save the Nickname EditText information, retrieve the text by using the EditText control's getText() method:

```
final EditText nicknameText =
    (EditText) findViewById(R.id.EditText_Nickname);
String strNickname = nicknameText.getText().toString();
```

After you have extracted the String value from the EditText input field, save it to SharedPreferences.Editor, using the putString() method:

```
Editor editor = mGameSettings.edit();
editor.putString(GAME_PREFERENCES_NICKNAME, strNickname);
editor.commit();
```

The Nickname, Email, and Password settings are saved as string values, but the Date of Birth and Gender settings are of long and integer types, respectively. To save these settings, extract the value from the appropriate control, convert it if necessary, and save it using the SharedPreferences.Editor methods putLong() and putInt().

For now, commit the input from the Nickname, Email, and Gender fields. Add the Nickname and Email commit code to the onPause() method of the QuizSettingsActivity class (you may need to create the method stub first, if you haven't already). The Gender setting can be saved within the Spinner listener you implemented earlier.

Further work needs to be done with the Date of Birth and Password fields before you can collect the user's input and save it to the settings. You revisit this in the next hour when you implement the Pick Date and Set Password dialogs.

Reading Settings from SharedPreferences

When you begin saving settings in a persistent fashion, you need to be able to read them back out and load them into the form for editing. To do this, access the game preferences and check whether specific settings exist. Do this for the Nickname setting by using the contains() and getString() methods of SharedPreferences as follows:

```
final EditText nicknameText =
    (EditText) findViewById(R.id.EditText_Nickname);
if (mGameSettings.contains(GAME_PREFERENCES_NICKNAME)) {
    nicknameText.setText(mGameSettings.getString(
        GAME_PREFERENCES_NICKNAME, ""));
}
```

This code first checks for the existence of a specific setting name defined as GAME_PREFERENCES_NICKNAME in the shared preferences by using the contains() method. If the contains() method returns true, extract the value of that setting (a String setting) from shared preferences by using the getString() method.

The Nickname, Email, and Password settings are strings and can be extracted using the getString() method. However, the Date of Birth setting must be extracted using the getLong() method, and the Gender setting requires the getInt() method.

Finally, for testing purposes, consider overriding the `onDestroy()` method of QuizSettingsActivity to log all current settings whenever the settings screen is destroyed:

```
@Override
protected void onDestroy() {
    Log.d(DEBUG_TAG, "SHARED PREFERENCES");
    Log.d(DEBUG_TAG, "Nickname is: "
        + mGameSettings.getString(GAME_PREFERENCES_NICKNAME, "Not set"));
    Log.d(DEBUG_TAG, "Email is: "
        + mGameSettings.getString(GAME_PREFERENCES_EMAIL, "Not set"));
    Log.d(DEBUG_TAG, "Gender (M=1, F=2, U=0) is: "
        + mGameSettings.getInt(GAME_PREFERENCES_GENDER, 0));
    // We are not saving the password yet
    Log.d(DEBUG_TAG, "Password is: "
        + mGameSettings.getString(GAME_PREFERENCES_PASSWORD, "Not set"));
    // We are not saving the date of birth yet
    Log.d(DEBUG_TAG, "DOB is: "
        + DateFormat.format("MMMM dd, yyyy", mGameSettings.getLong(
            GAME_PREFERENCES_DOB, 0)));
    super.onDestroy();
}
```

Now whenever QuizSettingsActivity is destroyed (for example, when a user presses the Back button), the preferences that have been committed are displayed in the LogCat console. After the "Pick Date" and "Set Password" dialogs are functioning, you see the correct debug information here. Because the `onDestroyed()` method is called after `onPause()`, all changes to settings are reflected.

Summary

In this hour, you added a form to the settings screen of the Been There, Done That! trivia application. The form handles various fields, including text input of various kinds, using EditText controls, and a drop-down list, using a Spinner control. You also conserved screen space by implementing two Button controls, which can be wired up in the future to launch dialogs in the next chapter. Finally, you implemented a simple SharedPreferences mechanism to load and save game settings for use in the application.

Q&A

Q. *What is the* PreferenceActivity *class used for?*

A. The PreferenceActivity class can be used as a base activity class for handling simple preferences (much like the Android Settings hierarchy). This class is a reasonable option for simple application preferences. However, for the purposes of this tutorial, we wanted to illustrate how to use numerous Android user interface controls, so we do not use this mechanism. See the Android SDK documentation at http://goo.gl/adACH for details.

Q. *Why not use the typical Save and Cancel buttons that you'd see on a web form?*

A. Mobile input forms may certainly be designed using this traditional approach, but consider the overhead in terms of state management. (Activity life cycle events, such as suspend and resume, need to save and restore pending input.) A common approach for mobile input forms is to commit form fields automatically. This way, separate code is not needed for saving off intermediate values if the application is interrupted by a phone call, or some other action the user has no control over.

Q. *Does a* Spinner *control have to be populated from an array?*

A. No, the underlying data of a Spinner control can be populated from numerous data sources using a data adapter. For example, the contents of a Spinner control might instead come from a database.

Q. *How are application preferences stored on the device?*

A. Application preferences are stored on the Android file system as XML files. Preferences files can be accessed using the File Explorer of the Eclipse DDMS perspective. SharedPreferences files are found in the following directory: /data/data/<package name>/shared_prefs/<preferences filename>.xml

Workshop

Quiz

1. True or False: EditText controls are derived from TextView controls.

2. What types of button controls are available on the Android platform?

   A. Button

   B. TextButton

   C. ImageButton

3. True or False: You can store Calendar data in SharedPreferences.

Answers

1. True. The TextView class, with its familiar attributes and methods, such as getText() and setText(), is the base class of the EditText class.

2. A and C. There are two button controls in Android: Button is a simple button with a text label. ImageButton is a button with a Drawable graphic label.

3. False. The only types supported by SharedPreferences are Boolean, float, int, long, and String. To save dates or times, consider storing them as long values (milliseconds from epoch).

Exercises

1. Add a Toast to the gender Spinner control listener. Make it display the new value when the preferences are successfully saved, confirming that the value was saved. Think about if this is useful feedback to the user or not.

2. Implement a Clear button that, when clicked, resets or deletes all game preferences using the clear() method of SharedPreferences.Editor. Don't forget to call the commit() method to save your changes to the preferences after you clear them.

3. **[Challenging!]** Modify each EditText control to save its contents when the user presses the Enter key (KEYCODE_ENTER). Hint: Use an OnKeyListener with the EditText controls. Look up how it works in the Android reference documentation. It is similar in style to the Spinner listener.

4. **[Challenging!]** Experiment with the PreferenceActivity class discussed in the Q&A section of this chapter. Create an alternative settings activity class and try to design it using the PreferenceActivity class. How does this method differ from the method shown in this hour? Which method do you prefer? There is sample code provided in the class documentation to get you going if you have trouble.

5. **[Challenging!]** The settings layout file is quite complex and therefore not necessarily as efficient as it could be. Could you redesign the layout to make use of a single RelativeLayout control instead of the nested LinearLayout controls within the ScrollView? Give it a shot!

HOUR 11

Using Dialogs to Collect User Input

What You'll Learn in This Hour:

▶ Working with activity dialogs
▶ Using `DatePickerDialog`
▶ Handling and formatting date information
▶ Building custom dialogs

In this hour, you continue to add features to the Been There, Done That! settings screen. Specifically, you learn about Android activity dialogs and implement several within the `QuizSettingsActivity` class. Each dialog is specially designed to collect a specific type of input from the user. First, you implement a `DatePickerDialog` to collect the user's date of birth and then you build a custom dialog to enable the user to change his or her password.

Working with Activity Dialogs

There is only so much screen real estate available on a device, but it's cumbersome—both for the developer and the user alike—to have to transition between activities too frequently for simple tasks. Luckily, the Android SDK includes a concept called a *dialog*. An `Activity` class can use `Dialog` classes of various types to organize information and react to user-driven events without having to spawn full subactivities. For example, an activity might display a `Dialog` informing the user of an error or asking to confirm an action such as deleting a piece of information. Using the `Dialog` mechanism for simple tasks helps keep the number of `Activity` classes within an application manageable.

Exploring the Different Types of Dialogs

A number of different Dialog types are available in the Android SDK, including the following:

▶ Dialog—The basic class for all dialog types (see Figure 11.1a). The simplest type of dialog, this control can be used to inform the user.

▶ AlertDialog—A dialog with one, two, or three Button controls (see Figure 11.1b). This type of dialog is often used to get user confirmation (or denial) of an operation—for example, to confirm the deletion of a file.

▶ CharacterPickerDialog—A dialog for choosing an accented character associated with a base character (see Figure 11.1c). This type of dialog is often used to provide a subset of characters to the user for selection.

▶ DatePickerDialog—A dialog with a DatePicker control (see Figure 11.1d). This type of dialog is used to collect date input from the user.

▶ ProgressDialog—A dialog with a determinate or indeterminate ProgressBar control (see Figure 11.1e). This type of dialog is used to inform the user about the status, or progress, of an operation—for example, to inform the user that data is being transferred to or from the network.

▶ TimePickerDialog—A dialog with a TimePicker control (see Figure 11.1f). This type of dialog is used to collect time input from the user.

FIGURE 11.1
The different dialog types available in Android.

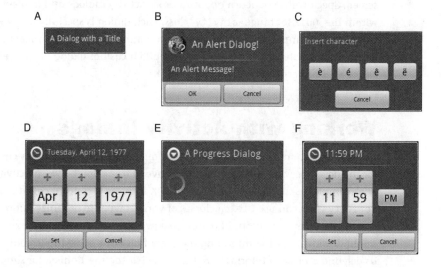

If none of the existing dialog types is adequate for your needs, you can use a dialog builder to create custom dialogs that meet your specific layout requirements. We discuss custom dialogs later in this hour when we implement the password dialog.

Tracing the Life Cycle of an Activity Dialog

Each dialog must be defined within the activity in which it is used; the dialog is exclusive to that Activity class. A dialog may be launched once or used repeatedly. Understanding how an activity manages the dialog life cycle is important to implementing a dialog correctly. Let's look at the key methods that an activity must use to manage a Dialog instance:

▶ The showDialog() method is used to display a Dialog instance.

▶ The dismissDialog() method is used to stop showing a Dialog instance. The Dialog is kept around in the activity's dialog pool. If the Dialog is shown again using the showDialog()method then the cached version is displayed again.

▶ The removeDialog() method is used to remove a Dialog instance from the Activity object's Dialog pool. The Dialog instance is no longer kept around for future use. If you call the showDialog() method again, the Dialog must be re-created.

Defining a Dialog

Dialogs must be defined in advance. Each dialog must have a unique dialog identifier (an integer that you define) associated with it. You must override the onCreateDialog() method of the Activity class and have it return the appropriate Dialog instance for the given identifier. If the activity has multiple dialogs, the onCreateDialog() method can use a switch statement to return the appropriate Dialog, based on the incoming parameter—the dialog identifier.

Initializing a Dialog

Because a Dialog instance may be kept around by an activity, it can sometimes be important to re-initialize or refresh the dialog each time it is shown instead of just when it is created the first time. We say "sometimes" because some dialogs do not require refreshes; for example, a static dialog that just shows a text label with some buttons does not need to be refreshed, whereas a complex dialog with input controls or progress bars likely does need to be reset. If you need a dialog to be re-initialized each time it is shown, you can override the onPrepareDialog() method of the Activity class and alter the dialog's contents.

Although the onCreateDialog() method may be called only once for initial dialog creation, the onPrepareDialog() method is called each time the showDialog() method is called, giving the activity a chance to initialize the dialog each time it is shown to the user.

Launching a Dialog

Any dialog already defined within an activity is shown by calling the showDialog() method and passing in a valid dialog identifier—in other words, one that is recognized by the onCreateDialog() method.

Dismissing a Dialog

Most dialogs have automatic dismissal circumstances in the form of Button controls. However, to force a dialog to be dismissed programmatically, simply call the dismissDialog() method and pass in the appropriate dialog identifier.

Removing a Dialog from Use

Dismissing a dialog does not destroy it or remove it from the activity's dialog pool. If the dialog is shown again using the showDialog() method, its cached contents are redisplayed. To force an activity to remove a dialog from its pool and not reuse it, call the removeDialog() method and pass in the valid dialog identifier.

Using the DatePickerDialog Class

Let's turn our attention to implementing a proper dialog in the on the settings screen of the Been There, Done That! application. You start with a simple dialog to collect the user's date of birth. To achieve this feature, you must add a DatePickerDialog to the QuizSettingsActivity class, which involves several steps:

1. Defining a unique identifier for the dialog within the QuizSettingsActivity class

2. Implementing the onCreateDialog() method of the activity to create and return DatePickerDialog when supplied the proper unique identifier

3. Implementing the onPrepareDialog() method of the activity to initialize DatePickerDialog with the date of birth preference or the current date

4. Updating the Pick Date Button control's click handler (called onPickDateButtonClick() in the sample code) to launch the DatePickerDialog using the showDialog() method, with the unique dialog identifier

Now that you know what steps to take to create your first dialog, let's walk through them individually.

Adding a DatePickerDialog to a Class

To create a DatePickerDialog instance within the QuizSettingsActivity class, first define a unique identifier to represent the dialog for the class, as follows:

```
static final int DATE_DIALOG_ID = 0;
```

Next, implement the onCreateDialog() method of the QuizSettingsActivity class and include a switch statement with a case statement for the new dialog identifier, like this:

```
@Override
protected Dialog onCreateDialog(int id) {
    switch (id) {
    case DATE_DIALOG_ID:
        // TODO: Return a DatePickerDialog here
    }
    return null;
}
```

Now let's look at how to construct a DatePickerDialog instance. Within the case statement for DATE_DIALOG_ID, you must return a valid DatePickerDialog instance. The constructor for the DatePickerDialog class includes a DatePickerDialog.OnDateSetListener parameter. This parameter can be used to provide an implementation of the onDateSet() method to handle when the user chooses a specific date within the picker. Use this method to save the date to the SharedPreferences, like this:

```
final TextView dob = (TextView) findViewById(R.id.TextView_DOB_Info);
Calendar now = Calendar.getInstance();
DatePickerDialog dateDialog =
    new DatePickerDialog(this,
        new DatePickerDialog.OnDateSetListener() {
            public void onDateSet(DatePicker view, int year,
                int monthOfYear, int dayOfMonth) {
                Time dateOfBirth = new Time();
                dateOfBirth.set(dayOfMonth, monthOfYear, year);
                long dtDob = dateOfBirth.toMillis(true);
                dob.setText(DateFormat
                    .format("MMMM dd, yyyy", dtDob));
                Editor editor = mGameSettings.edit();
```

```
                     editor.putLong(GAME_PREFERENCES_DOB, dtDob);
                     editor.commit();
            }
        }, now.get(Calendar.YEAR), now.get(Calendar.MONTH),
            now.get(Calendar.DAY_OF_MONTH));
```

A DatePicker control has three different input controls: a month picker, day picker, and a year picker. Therefore, to create a valid instance of a DatePickerDialog, you must set these values individually. Because the DatePickerDialog can be launched any number of times, do not initialize the picker date information within the onCreateDialog() method. Instead pass in default values (such as today's year, month, and day from the Calendar class). Then set the values to display in the onPrepareDialog() method. After you have a valid DatePickerDialog instance, return it:

```
return dateDialog;
```

Initializing a DatePickerDialog

To initialize the DatePickerDialog each and every time it is displayed, not just when it is first created, override the activity's onPrepareDialog() method to set DatePicker control's month, day, and year values to either today's date or the user's birth date as it is saved in the current game preferences.

The onPrepareDialog() method receives both the dialog identifier and the specific instance of the Dialog in order modify the related instance, as needed. To update the date values of DatePickerDialog, use the updateDate() method as shown in this implementation of the onPrepareDialog() method:

```
@Override
protected void onPrepareDialog(int id, Dialog dialog) {
    super.onPrepareDialog(id, dialog);
    switch (id) {
    case DATE_DIALOG_ID:
        // Handle any DatePickerDialog initialization here
        DatePickerDialog dateDialog = (DatePickerDialog) dialog;
        int iDay, iMonth, iYear;
        // Check for date of birth preference
        if (mGameSettings.contains(GAME_PREFERENCES_DOB)) {
            // Retrieve Birth date setting from preferences
            long msBirthDate = mGameSettings.getLong(GAME_PREFERENCES_DOB, 0);
            Time dateOfBirth = new Time();
            dateOfBirth.set(msBirthDate);
            iDay = dateOfBirth.monthDay;
            iMonth = dateOfBirth.month;
            iYear = dateOfBirth.year;
        } else {
            Calendar cal = Calendar.getInstance();
            // Today's date fields
            iDay = cal.get(Calendar.DAY_OF_MONTH);
```

```
            iMonth = cal.get(Calendar.MONTH);
            iYear = cal.get(Calendar.YEAR);
        }
        // Set the date in the DatePicker to the date of birth OR to the
        // current date
        dateDialog.updateDate(iYear, iMonth, iDay);
        return;
    }
}
```

Launching DatePickerDialog

You have configured DatePickerDialog, but it doesn't display unless the user clicks the appropriate Pick Date Button control on the main settings screen. The user triggers DatePickerDialog by pressing the Button control called Button_DOB. This triggers the onPickDateButtonClick() method previously implemented.

Replace the Toast message within the button handler. Call the showDialog() method, instead, which launches DatePickerDialog, as shown in Figure 11.2:

```
public void onPickDateButtonClick(View view) {
    showDialog(DATE_DIALOG_ID);
}
```

FIGURE 11.2
DatePicker Dialog used for date of birth input.

Voilà! You've completed your first dialog. Now turn your attention to the more complex password dialog.

Working with Custom Dialogs

When the basic dialog types do not suit your purpose, you can create a custom dialog. To create a custom dialog, begin with an `AlertDialog` instance and use an `AlertDialog.Builder` class to override its default layout and provide alternative functionality. To create a custom dialog this way, follow these steps:

1. Design a custom layout resource to display in `AlertDialog`.

2. Define the custom dialog identifier in the activity.

3. Update the `Activity` class's `onCreateDialog()` method to build and return the appropriate custom `AlertDialog`.

4. Launch the dialog using the `showDialog()` method.

Adding a Custom Dialog to the Settings Screen

The Been There, Done That! setting screen requires a password confirmation dialog. However, this type of dialog is not available within the Android SDK so you need to create a custom dialog to provide this functionality. Figure 11.3 shows how a password dialog might behave when passwords match or don't match.

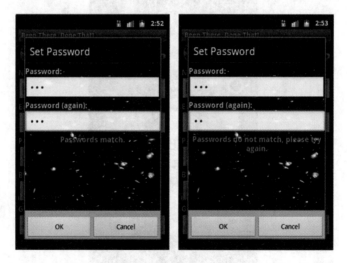

The custom dialog requires two text input fields for entering password data. When the two passwords match, the password is set. Figure 11.4 shows a rough design of the settings screen in this case.

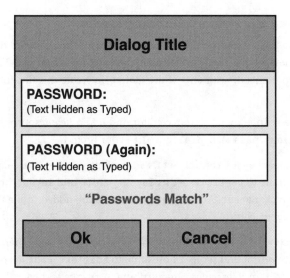

FIGURE 11.4
A custom dialog
used for han-
dling password
input.

The password dialog is simply a subform of the settings screen that contains two
EditText input fields as well as a TextView control below the input fields to inform
the user in real-time whether or not the passwords match.

Figure 11.5 shows the layout design of the password dialog.

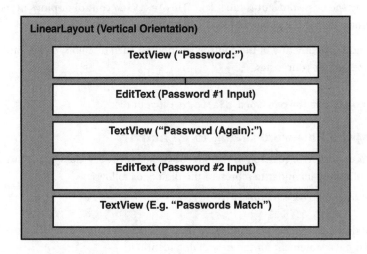

FIGURE 11.5
Layout design
for the custom
password dialog
of the Been
There, Done
That! settings
screen.

You can take advantage of the built-in Button controls that can be configured for
use with AlertDialog. The three (or fewer) buttons need not be included in your
custom dialog layout design.

Implementing the Password Dialog Layout

Now it's time to implement the new layout resource for the password dialog. Begin by creating a new layout resource file called `password_dialog.xml`. This layout resource file represents the contents of the dialog. To create this file, follow these steps:

1. Open the Eclipse layout resource editor and add a new resource file called `/res/layout/password_dialog.xml` to your project.

2. Add a `LinearLayout` control. Set its `id` attribute to `root` and set its `orientation` attribute to `vertical`. Set its `layout_width` and `layout_height` attributes to `match_parent`. All subsequent controls are added inside this `LinearLayout` control.

3. Add a `TextView` control to display the Password label text. Then add an `EditText` control and set its `id` attribute to `EditText_Pwd1`, its `maxLines` attribute to 1, and its `inputType` attribute to `textPassword`.

4. Add another `TextView` control to display the Password label text again. Then add another `EditText` control and set its `id` attribute to `EditText_Pwd2`, its `maxLines` attribute to 1, and its `inputType` attribute to `textPassword`.

5. Add a `TextView` control with the `id` attribute `TextView_PwdProblem` to display the password status label text. This `TextView` control displays in real time whether the two password fields match.

6. Finally, modify any of the controls' attributes, such as colors, styles, and text sizes to suit your tastes.

At this point, save the `password_dialog.xml` layout file.

Adding the Password Dialog to an Activity

To add a custom `AlertDialog` to the `QuizSettingsActivity` class, you must first declare a unique identifier to represent the dialog, as follows:

```
static final int PASSWORD_DIALOG_ID = 1;
```

Next, update the `onCreateDialog()` method of `QuizSettingsActivity` class to include a case statement for the new dialog identifier:

```
case PASSWORD_DIALOG_ID:
    // Build Dialog
    // Return Dialog
```

Now let's look at how to build the custom password dialog from the ground up. Begin by inflating (loading) the custom layout you created into a View control:

```
LayoutInflater inflater =
    (LayoutInflater) getSystemService(Context.LAYOUT_INFLATER_SERVICE);
final View layout =
    inflater.inflate(R.layout.password_dialog,
        (ViewGroup) findViewById(R.id.root));
```

To load the password_dialog.xml layout file into a View object, you must retrieve the LayoutInflater and then call its inflate() method, passing in the layout resource identifier as well as the root layout control's identifier (in this case, the LinearLayout encapsulating the EditText and TextView controls, called root).

After the custom layout has been inflated into a View, it can be acted upon programmatically much like a regular layout. At this point, you can populate controls can be populated with data and register event listeners. For example, to retrieve the EditText and TextView controls from the View instance called layout, use the findViewById() method for that View control (as opposed to the Activity as a whole), as follows:

```
final EditText p1 =
    (EditText) layout.findViewById(R.id.EditText_Pwd1);
final EditText p2 =
    (EditText) layout.findViewById(R.id.EditText_Pwd2);
final TextView error =
    (TextView) layout.findViewById(R.id.TextView_PwdProblem);
```

At this point, you can register any event listeners on the EditText fields, such as those discussed earlier to watch EditText input and match the strings as the user types.

Listening for EditText **Keystrokes**

When working with EditText controls, you can listen for keystroke events while the user is still typing. For example, you can check the text strings within two EditText password fields while the user is typing and report if they match or not. A third TextView control, called TextView_PwdProblem, provides "live" feedback about whether the passwords match.

First, register a TextWatcher with the second EditText control, using the addTextChangedListener() method, like this:

```
final TextView error =
    (TextView) layout.findViewById(R.id.TextView_PwdProblem);
p2.addTextChangedListener(new TextWatcher() {
    @Override
    public void afterTextChanged(Editable s) {
        String strPass1 = p1.getText().toString();
```

```
        String strPass2 = p2.getText().toString();
        if (strPass1.equals(strPass2)) {
            error.setText(R.string.settings_pwd_equal);
        } else {
            error.setText(R.string.settings_pwd_not_equal);
        }
    }

    // ... other required  overrides do nothing
});
```

The `TextWatcher` has a number of methods that require implementation. However, the one you're interested in is the `afterTextChanged()` method. Now the user can type the password into the `EditText_Pwd1` `EditText` control normally. However, each time the user types a character into the `EditText_Pwd2` control, the text is compared to the text in the first `EditText` control and the text of the `TextView` control called `TextView_PwdProblem` is updated to reflect whether the text matches.

Now that you have inflated the layout into a `View` object and configured it for use, you can to attach it to `AlertDialog`. To do this, use the `AlertDialog.Builder` class:

```
AlertDialog.Builder builder = new AlertDialog.Builder(this);
builder.setView(layout);
builder.setTitle(R.string.settings_button_pwd);
```

First, set the view of `AlertDialog.Builder` to the inflated layout using the `setView()` method and then set the title of the dialog with the `setTitle()` method (Set Password).

This dialog has two `Button` controls: a positive button (OK) and a negative button (Cancel). Because you do not want this dialog cached for reuse by the activity (which would cache typed-in password contents in the `EditText` controls), both `Button` handlers should call the `removeDialog()` method, which destroys the dialog:

```
QuizSettingsActivity.this
    .removeDialog(PASSWORD_DIALOG_ID);
```

The positive button (OK) requires some additional handling. When the user clicks this button, extract the password text from the `EditText` controls, compare the results, and, if two strings match, store the new password in the shared preferences of the application. Configure the positive button using the `setPositiveButton()` method of the builder, like this:

```
builder.setPositiveButton(android.R.string.ok,
    new DialogInterface.OnClickListener() {
        public void onClick(DialogInterface dialog, int which) {
```

```
    TextView passwordInfo =
        (TextView) findViewById(R.id.TextView_Password_Info);
    String strPassword1 = p1.getText().toString();
    String strPassword2 = p2.getText().toString();
    if (strPassword1.equals(strPassword2)) {
        Editor editor = mGameSettings.edit();
        editor.putString(GAME_PREFERENCES_PASSWORD,
            strPassword1);
        editor.commit();
        passwordInfo.setText(R.string.settings_pwd_set);
    } else {
        Log.d(DEBUG_TAG, "Passwords do not match. "
            + "Not saving. Keeping old password (if set).");
    }
    QuizSettingsActivity.this
        .removeDialog(PASSWORD_DIALOG_ID);
    }
});
```

The negative button (Cancel) simply returns the user to the main screen. Configure the negative button using the `setNegativeButton()` method of the builder, like this:

```
builder.setNegativeButton(android.R.string.cancel,
    new DialogInterface.OnClickListener() {
        public void onClick(DialogInterface dialog, int whichButton) {
            QuizSettingsActivity.this
                .removeDialog(PASSWORD_DIALOG_ID);
        }
});
```

When your dialog is fully configured using the `builder`, you call its `create()` method to generate the custom `AlertDialog` and return it:

```
AlertDialog passwordDialog = builder.create();
return passwordDialog;
```

Launching the Custom Password Dialog

A custom dialog, such as your password dialog, is launched the same way as a regular dialog: using the `showDialog()` method of the activity. On the settings screen of the Been There, Done That! application, the user triggers the custom password dialog to launch by pressing the `Button` control called `Button_Password`. Therefore, you can update this control's click handler (called `onSetPasswordButtonClick()` in the sample source code) to launch the password dialog accordingly:

```
public void onSetPasswordButtonClick(View view) {
    showDialog(PASSWORD_DIALOG_ID);
}
```

Figure 11.6 shows the resulting settings screen, with dialog controls.

FIGURE 11.6
The complete
Been There,
Done That! set-
tings screen.

Summary

In this hour, you learned how an activity can use dialog controls to simplify screen functionality and layout—specifically on the settings screen of the Been There, Done That! application. A dialog can be used to display appropriate information to the user in the form of a pop-up window. There are dialog types for inputting dates, times, and special characters as well as helper types for showing progress or display-ing alert messages. You can also create custom `Dialog` controls.

Q&A

Q. *How is dialog information saved within an activity?*

A. Each activity keeps a pool of dialog controls around for use and reuses the control when asked to be shown again. Basically, a dialog is shown using the `showDialog()` method and added to the pool. Each `Dialog` is dismissed but sticks around in the pool until either the activity is destroyed or the `removeDialog()` method is called explicitly.

Q. *How can I determine which activity launched a `Dialog` control?*

A. You can use the `getOwnerActivity()` method of the `Dialog` class to deter-mine the parent activity of a specific `Dialog` control.

Q. *What is the* `DialogFragment` *class used for?*

A. The Fragments API (http://goo.gl/0U25u), which was introduced in Android 3.0, or API Level 11, helps organize content on the screen in reusable modules appropriate for different device screens (notably, tablets). The `DialogFragment` class is just one small part of this API that helps integrate `Activity` class `Dialog` instances into a fragment-based design solution. We discuss fragments in more detail later in this book.

Workshop

Quiz

1. What class can be used to create pop-up windows within an activity?

   A. The `Popup` class

   B. The `ActivityWindow` class

   C. The `Dialog` class

   D. The `Toast` class

2. True or False: You can use the same dialog for multiple uses if the layout is the same.

3. True or False: Only certain layouts can be used with a dialog, such as `Alert` and `ContinueOrCancel`.

Answers

1. C and D. The `Dialog` class and its subclasses are used to create pop-up windows within an activity, using the `onCreateDialog()` and `showDialog()` methods. The `Toast` class can be used to display a temporary pop-up with some text, but the user does not interact with this type of message.

2. True. But if you want the data shown to be different, you need to override `onPrepareDialog()` in the activity.

3. False. You can use any layout you want for a dialog.

Exercises

1. Update the onDateSet() method of the DatePickerDialog to save the date of birth to a TextView control on the main settings screen.

2. Update the custom password dialog to display the status of the password (set or unset) in a TextView control on the main settings screen.

3. Update the custom password dialog to change the color of the status text in the TextView control based on whether the passwords match (green) or do not match (red). Hint: The TextView class has a setTextColor() method.

4. **[Challenging!]** Experiment with the onPrepareDialog() method. Try moving the password initialization code to the onCreateDialog() method and note how the dialog behaves differently and caches the contents of the controls when the dialog is launched multiple times.

HOUR 12

Adding Application Logic

What You'll Learn in This Hour:

▶ Designing the game screen
▶ Working with `ViewSwitcher` **Controls**
▶ Data structures and parsing XML
▶ Wiring up the game logic and keeping game state

In this hour, you wire up the screen at the heart of the Been There, Done That! application—the game play screen. This screen prompts the user to answer a series of questions and stores the resulting score information. Because the screen must display a dynamic series of images and text strings, you leverage several new `View` controls, including `ImageSwitcher` and `TextSwitcher` controls, to help transition between questions in the game. You also need to update the `QuizGameActivity` class with game logic and game state information, including the retrieval of batches of new questions, as a user progresses through the questions.

Numerous intermediate Java topics are referenced in this chapter, including the use of inner classes, class factories, and data structure classes such as the `Hashtable` class. Although these are not Android topics, per se, we try to provide some light explanation when we use these features. That said, readers are expected to either be familiar with such topics or be willing to go look them up in the Java reference of their choice.

Designing the Game Screen

The game screen leads the user through a series of questions and logs the number of positive responses as the score. Each question has text and a corresponding graphic to display. For example, the game screen might display a picture of a mountain, ask if the user has ever climbed a mountain and record one of two responses: Yes or No.

Unlike the screens you have developed in previous chapters, the game screen does not require the customary title bar. Instead, you should use the entire screen to display the game components. Figure 12.1 shows a rough design of the game screen.

FIGURE 12.1
Rough design for the Been There, Done That! game screen.

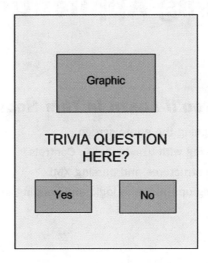

Despite the lack of header, you still want the game screen to share some common features with the rest of the application: It should use the same background graphic, font, and color scheme as the other screens. To translate this rough design into the appropriate layout design, update the /res/layout/game.xml layout file and the QuizGameActivity class.

The RelativeLayout control works especially well for displaying items, such as Button controls, in the bottom corners of the screen. You can also use a vertically oriented LinearLayout to display the text (in a TextView control) and graphic (in an ImageView control) related to each question to the user

Figure 12.2 shows the basic layout design of the game screen.

The buttons are used to handle the user responses and drive the application. Each time the user clicks a Button control, the game screen updates the ImageView and TextView controls to display the next question. To smoothly transition (and animate) from one question to the next, you can use the special view controls ImageSwitcher and TextSwitcher, which are subclasses of the ViewSwitcher class (android.widget.ViewSwitcher).

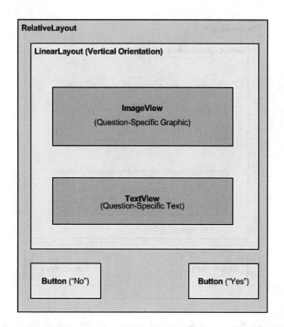

FIGURE 12.2
Layout design
for the Been
There, Done
That! game
screen.

A ViewSwitcher control can animate between two child View controls: the current
View control and the next View control to display. Only one View control is displayed at any time, but you can use animations, such as fades or rotates, during the
transition between View controls. These child View controls are generated using the
ViewFactory class. For example, you can use ImageSwitcher and its corresponding
ViewFactory to generate the current question ImageView and switch in the next
question's ImageView when the user clicks a Button control. Similarly, a
TextSwitcher control has two child TextView controls, with transitional animation
applying to the text.

Figure 12.3 shows the updated layout design of the game screen, which uses an
ImageSwitcher control and a TextSwitcher control. Each time the user clicks a
Button control, the two switcher controls generate a new TextView and ImageView
to display on the screen with the data for the next question.

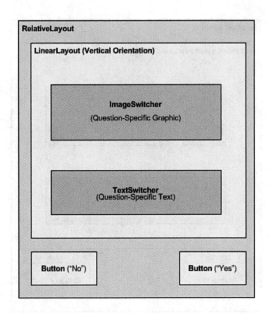

Implementing the Game Screen Layout

To implement the game screen, begin by adding numerous new resources to the project. Then update the game.xml layout resource to reflect the game screen design. Let's do this now.

Adding New Project Resources

For the game screen, add some new resources:

- String resources to display on Button controls and error messages
- Dimension resources needed to display the game screen controls
- Two XML resources with mock question batches

Adding New String Resources

The game screen relies on numerous new string resources. Add the following text resources to the strings.xml resource file:

- Text labels for each Button control (for example, Yes and No)
- Text to display when there are no questions available

Save the strings.xml resource file. For a complete list of the new strings required for the game screen, see the sample source code provided on the CD that accompanies this book, or download the source code from the book website.

Adding New Dimension Resources

The game screen relies on several new dimension resources. These dimensions are used to size the Button controls and display the question data. Therefore, add the following dimension resources to the `dimens.xml` resource file:

```
<dimen
        name="game_button_size">75dp</dimen>
<dimen
        name="game_padding">45dp</dimen>
<dimen
        name="game_image_size">225dp</dimen>
<dimen
        name="game_question_size">22dp</dimen>
```

Now save the `dimens.xml` resource file.

Adding New XML Resources

Eventually, the questions used by the Been There, Done That! application are retrieved from a server on the Internet as a chunk of XML data. XML is one of the most common mechanisms for transferring structured data, so you use it to store game question data, much as you did with the score data.

Just as you did for the score data, begin by creating two batches of mock questions that can be accessed locally as XML: `/res/xml/samplequestions.xml` and `/res/xml/samplequestions2.xml`.

In a future lesson when you add full network support to the application, you retrieve XML content in this same structure from a remote server. However, by including mock batches of questions for now, you have the opportunity to iron out the game logic without worrying about network connectivity, threading, or other more advanced topics that cannot be crammed into a one-hour lesson.

Regardless of whether the XML question batches are sourced locally or from a remote server, the XML content is the same. Here is what it looks like:

```
<?xml version="1.0" encoding="utf-8"?>
    <!-- This is a mock question XML chunk -->
<questions>
    <question
        number="1"
        text=
          "Have you ever been on an African safari?"
        imageUrl=
          "http://www.perlgurl.org/Android/BeenThereDoneThat/Questions/q1.png"
    />
    <question
        number="2"
        text=
          "Have you ever climbed a mountain?"
```

```
            imageUrl=
              "http://www.perlgurl.org/Android/BeenThereDoneThat/Questions/q2.png"
        />
        <question
            number="3"
            text=
              "Have you ever milked a cow?"
            imageUrl=
              "http://www.perlgurl.org/Android/BeenThereDoneThat/Questions/q3.png"
        />
</questions>
```

As you can see, the XML is very simple. It has one tag called <questions>, which can contain any number of <question> tags. Each <question> tag has three attributes: the question identifier (number), the question itself (text), and the URL to the image associated with the question (imageUrl). The images are remote graphics sourced from the Internet. Instead of adding each and every question graphic to the resources of the application, this saves time now because the images ultimately come from a server, anyway.

Updating the Game Screen Layout

The game.xml layout file dictates the user interface of the game screen. The Eclipse layout resource editor does not display TextSwitcher or ImageSwitcher controls in design mode, so you may want to work in XML mode. Follow these steps to generate the layout you want, based on your design:

1. Open the game.xml layout file in the Eclipse layout resource editor and remove all existing controls from the layout.

2. Add a new RelativeLayout control and set its background attribute to @drawable/bkgrnd. Set its layout_width and layout_height attributes to match_parent. All subsequent controls are added inside this control.

3. Add a LinearLayout control and set layout_width to match_parent and layout_height to wrap_content. Set its orientation to vertical and its gravity to center. Set its weightSum to 100 in order to specify the total weight sum for all child controls in this layout. Finally, set its layout_above attribute to @+id/Button_Yes.

4. Within the LinearLayout control, add an ImageSwitcher control with an id of @+id/ImageSwitcher_QuestionImage. Set its layout_width and layout_height attributes to the dimension resource @dimen/game_image_size. Also, set its clipChildren attribute to false. You can set the animations for switching between images directly via the XML using the inAnimation and outAnimation attributes. For example, you

could set the inAnimation attribute to @android:anim/fade_in and the outAnimation attribute to @android:anim/fade_out. Finally, set its lay-out_weight attribute to 75 to allocate 75% of the LinearLayout space to this control.

5. Below the ImageSwitcher control, add a TextSwitcher control with an id of @+id/TextSwitcher_QuestionText. Set its layout_width to match_parent and layout_height to wrap_content. Again, set its set inAnimation attrib-ute to @android:anim/fade_in and the outAnimation attribute to @android:anim/fade_out. Finally, set its layout_weight attribute to 25 to allocate 25% of the LinearLayout space to this control.

6. Outside the LinearLayout control, but inside the RelativeLayout, add a Button control with an id of @+id/Button_Yes. Set layout_width to wrap_content and layout_height to wrap_content. Also, set its layout_alignParentBottom and layout_alignParentRight attributes to true. Set its text attribute to a resource string (Yes) and tweak any other attributes to make the Button control look nice; specifically, you might want to set its textSize and minWidth to dimension resources created for this pur-pose. Finally, set its onClick to onYesButton; you then need to create this method within your activity class to handle clicks.

7. Add a second Button control with an id of @+id/Button_No. Set layout_width to wrap_content and layout_height to wrap_content. Also, set its layout_alignParentBottom and layout_alignParentLeft attributes to true. Set its text attribute to a resource string (No) and tweak any other attributes to make the Button control look nice; specifically, you might want to set its textSize and minWidth to dimension resources created for this pur-pose. Finally, set its onClick to onNoButton; you then need to create this method within your activity class to handle clicks.

At this point, save the game.xml layout file.

Working with ViewSwitcher Controls

For situations in which an activity is going to be updating the content of a View control repeatedly, the Android SDK provides a mechanism called a ViewSwitcher control. Using a ViewSwitcher is an efficient and visually interesting way to update content on a screen. A ViewSwitcher control has two children and handles transi-tion from the currently visible child view to the next view to be displayed. The child View controls of a ViewSwitcher control are generated programmatically using ViewFactory.

There are two subclasses of the ViewSwitcher class:

- ▶ TextSwitcher—A ViewSwitcher control that allows swapping between two TextView controls.

- ▶ ImageSwitcher—A ViewSwitcher control that allows swapping between two ImageView controls.

Although a ViewSwitcher control only ever has two children, it can display any number of View controls in succession. ViewFactory generates the content of the next view, such as the ImageSwitcher and TextSwitcher controls for iterating through the question images and text.

Initializing Switcher Controls

Now let's turn our attention to the QuizGameActivity class and wire up the switchers. Begin by defining two private member variables within the activity class:

```
private TextSwitcher mQuestionText;
private ImageSwitcher mQuestionImage;
```

You should initialize these switcher controls within the onCreate() method of the activity. To configure a switcher, use the setFactory() method and supply your custom ViewFactory class (android.widget.ViewSwitcher.ViewFactory). For example,

```
mQuestionText = (TextSwitcher) findViewById(R.id.TextSwitcher_QuestionText);
mQuestionText.setFactory(new MyTextSwitcherFactory());

mQuestionImage = (ImageSwitcher) findViewById(R.id.ImageSwitcher_QuestionImage);
mQuestionImage.setFactory(new MyImageSwitcherFactory());
```

Implementing Switcher Factory Classes

Now you need to create two classes: the MyTextSwitcherFactory and the MyImageSwitcherFactory. These can be inner classes within the activity itself and should implement the ViewSwitcher.ViewFactory class.

The ViewFactory class has one required method you must implement, the makeView() method. This method must return a View of the appropriate type. For example, ViewFactory for TextSwitcher should return a properly configured TextView, whereas ViewFactory for ImageSwitcher returns ImageView. You could implement the makeView() method to build up and return the appropriate TextView or ImageView control programmatically, or you could create a simple layout resource as a template for your control and load it using a layout inflater. The second method makes for cleaner code, so that's what you do here.

Begin with the ImageSwitcher. First, create a layout resource called
/res/layout/image_switcher_view.xml, as follows:

```
<?xml version="1.0" encoding="utf-8"?>
<ImageView
    xmlns:android="http://schemas.android.com/apk/res/android"
    android:layout_width="match_parent"
    android:layout_height="match_parent"
    android:scaleType="fitCenter">
</ImageView>
```

Now, within the QuizGameActivity class, here's an implementation of a
ViewFactory control for an ImageSwitcher control that you could use to generate
each question graphic on the game play screen:

```
private class MyImageSwitcherFactory implements ViewSwitcher.ViewFactory {
    public View makeView() {
        ImageView imageView = (ImageView) LayoutInflater.from(
            getApplicationContext()).inflate(
            R.layout.image_switcher_view,
            mQuestionImage, false);
        return imageView ;
    }
}
```

Note that the source data, or contents, of the view have not been configured in the
makeView() method. Instead, consider this a template that the ViewSwitcher control uses to display each child view.

Similarly, you must create a layout resource for your TextView, such as /res/lay-
out/text_switcher_view.xml, as follows:

```
<?xml version="1.0" encoding="utf-8"?>
<TextView
    xmlns:android="http://schemas.android.com/apk/res/android"
    android:layout_width="match_parent"
    android:textColor="@color/title_color"
    android:textSize="@dimen/game_question_size"
    android:gravity="center"
    android:layout_height="match_parent">
</TextView>
```

Next, implement the MyTextSwitcherFactory class (as an inner class within the
activity) such that it loads the TextView from the layout resource you just created:

```
private class MyTextSwitcherFactory implements ViewSwitcher.ViewFactory {
    public View makeView() {
        TextView textView = (TextView) LayoutInflater.from(
            getApplicationContext()).inflate(
            R.layout.text_switcher_view,
            mQuestionText, false);
        return textView;
    }
}
```

Much like the MyImageSwitcherFactory implementation, the MyTextSwitcherFactory also implements the makeView() method—this time generating the appropriate TextView control.

Updating the TextSwitcher Control

The TextSwitcher control enables an activity to animate between two TextView controls. So far you have

▶ Included a TextSwitcher control in your layout resource file

▶ Added a member variable for the TextSwitcher to your activity class

▶ Initialized the TextSwitcher and implemented its factory class

You're almost done wiring up your TextSwitcher control. All you need to do now is determine under what conditions the TextView control must be updated. It makes sense to update the question data in two circumstances: when the game screen is first loaded and after the user clicks one of the answer buttons, moving on to the next question. In both circumstances, your activity should determine which question to display and then update the TextSwitcher object, which then animates out the previous TextView control (if applicable) and animates in a newly generated TextView control in its place.

Whether you are initializing the TextSwitcher with the first question text, or the tenth question text, the method call is the same:

```
mQuestionText.setCurrentText("First Question Text");
```

Calling the setCurrentText() method causes MyTextSwitcherFactory to generate a new TextView control with the String parameter. Now, in the case of the QuizGameActivity class, you would not provide literal string data, but instead, determine the next question from the XML data and supply it to the TextSwitcher control.

Updating the ImageSwitcher Control

The ImageSwitcher control is wired up in a very similar fashion to the TextSwitcher control. You have already defined, configured, and initialized the control. All that's left is to update the image content under the right circumstances. These circumstances are the same as the TextSwitcher control: when the game screen is first loaded or after a user clicks a Button control. Whether you are initializing the ImageSwitcher with the first question image, or the tenth question image, the method call is the same:

```
mQuestionImage.setImageDrawable(drawable);
```

Calling the setImageDrawable() method causes MyImageSwitcherFactory to generate a new ImageView control with the Drawable parameter. The ImageSwitcher class also has methods for loading images via resource identifiers and other methods. In this case, you want to create a Drawable object by loading an image from a remote URL. To do this, you need to take some additional steps:

1. Retrieve the image address from the XML questions.

2. Generate a properly configured URL object.

3. Open and decode an input stream to the URL into a Bitmap object.

4. Create a BitmapDrawable from the Bitmap, for use as the Drawable parameter to the setImageDrawable() method.

These steps are easily consolidated into a helper function in the QuizGameActivity class:

```
private Drawable getQuestionImageDrawable(int questionNumber) {
    Drawable image;
    URL imageUrl;
    try {
        imageUrl = new URL(getQuestionImageUrl(questionNumber));
        InputStream stream = imageUrl.openStream();
        Bitmap bitmap = BitmapFactory.decodeStream(stream);
        image = new BitmapDrawable(getResources(), bitmap);
    } catch (Exception e) {
        Log.e(DEBUG_TAG, "Decoding Bitmap stream failed");
        image = getResources().getDrawable(R.drawable.noquestion);
    }
    return image;
}
```

The getQuestionImageDrawable() helper method takes a question number, retrieves the appropriate question image URL (using another helper method called getQuestionImageUrl() method, whose full implementation is provided in the sample source code), generates a URL object from the String representation of the web address, opens and decodes the data stream into a Bitmap object and finally generates a BitmapDrawable object for use by the ImageSwitcher. Finally, using the stream methods requires the android.permission.INTERNET permission, which needs to be added to your application Android manifest file in order for this method to function properly.

Wiring Up Game Logic

The Been There, Done That! application has an open-ended set of trivia questions. Therefore, you cannot save all the questions as resources but instead need to develop a simple way to get new questions on-the-fly. Also, by storing the complete (yet growing) set of trivia questions in a remote location, you streamline the application on the handset, saving disk space.

In the final version of the application, you will retrieve new batches of questions from the Internet. For now, though, you can retrieve two batches of questions from local XML files, simulating this effect without implementing the networking code required for the full solution. The application can keep a working set of questions in memory, and new batches of questions can be loaded as required.

To implement the game logic for the game screen, follow these steps:

1. Update SharedPreferences with game state settings.

2. Handle the retrieval and parsing batches of trivia questions (XML) into a relevant data structure, such as a Hashtable.

3. Implement Button click handling to drive the ImageSwitcher and TextSwitcher updates as well as the game logic.

4. Handle edge cases, such as when no more questions are available.

The following subsections describe these steps in more detail.

The full implementation of the game logic, including loading and parsing the XML question data, loading them into an appropriate data structure, such as a Hashtable of Question objects (a helper class you need to define), are too lengthy for complete coverage in this lesson, but we give you most of the basics in this section of the hour.

However, as the reader, you have everything you need to complete this task yourself. That said, if you get stuck or aren't looking for a challenge, just review and reproduce the implementation found in the QuizGameActivity class of the source code. For those looking for more of a challenge, feel free to make your own modifications or improvements to the game logic, but keep in mind we revisit this class in future lessons to add network support and other advanced features and you then have to support and modify this code.

Adding Game State Settings to the SharedPreferences

To keep track of game state, add two more Integer settings to the application SharedPreferences: the game score and the current question number. To add these

preferences, first declare the preference name `String` values to the
`QuizActivity.java` class:

```
public static final String GAME_PREFERENCES_SCORE = "Score";
public static final String GAME_PREFERENCES_CURRENT_QUESTION = "CurQuestion";
```

Next, define the `SharedPreferences` object as a member variable of the
`QuizGameActivity` class:

```
SharedPreferences mGameSettings;
```

Initialize the `mGameSettings` member variable in the `onCreate()` method of the
`QuizGameActivity` class:

```
mGameSettings = getSharedPreferences(GAME_PREFERENCES,
    Context.MODE_PRIVATE);
```

Now you can use `SharedPreferences` throughout the class, as needed, to read and
write game settings such as the current question and the game score. For example,
you could get the current question by using the `getInt()` method of
`SharedPreferences` as follows:

```
int startingQuestionNumber =
    mGameSettings.getInt(GAME_PREFERENCES_CURRENT_QUESTION, 0);
```

If you attempt to get the current question and it has not yet been set, then you are
at the beginning of the quiz and should start at the first question, and update the
current question number accordingly. Each time the user answers a question (and
clicks a `Button` control), the current question number should be updated. If the Yes
button is clicked then the score preference should also be incremented at the same
time.

Retrieving, Parsing, and Storing Question Data

We could load up every quiz question from the start, but this architecture is not terribly efficient. Instead, we aim for a more flexible approach: When the Been There,
Done That! application runs out of questions to display to the user, it attempts to
retrieve a new batch of questions. This architecture makes enabling networking for
the application more straightforward in future hours because the parsing of the
XML remains the same, but the application requires less memory as it manages
only a small, rolling "batch" of questions at a given time.

Each batch of questions arrives as a simple XML parcel, which needs to be parsed.

Declaring Helpful String Literals for XML Parsing

Take a moment to review the XML format used by the question batches, discussed earlier. To parse the question batches, you need to add several `String` literals to represent the XML tags and attributes to the `QuizActivity.java` class:

```
public static final String XML_TAG_QUESTION_BLOCK = "questions";
public static final String XML_TAG_QUESTION = "question";
public static final String XML_TAG_QUESTION_ATTRIBUTE_NUMBER = "number";
public static final String XML_TAG_QUESTION_ATTRIBUTE_TEXT = "text";
public static final String XML_TAG_QUESTION_ATTRIBUTE_IMAGEURL = "imageUrl";
```

While you are at it, define the default batch size, to simplify allocation of storage for questions while parsing the XML:

```
public static final int QUESTION_BATCH_SIZE = 15;
```

The size of the question batch is flexible, but works for our mock XML well.

Storing the Current Batch of Questions in a Hashtable

You can store the current batch of questions in memory by using a simple but powerful data structure—in this case, we recommend the `Hashtable` class (`java.util.Hashtable`). A hashtable is simply a data structure with key-value pairs, handy for quick lookups. For game logic purposes, it makes sense for the key to be the question number, and the value to be the question data (the question text and image URL). To store the question data, you need to create a simple data structure. Within the `QuizGameActivity` class, implement a simple helper class called `Question` to encapsulate a single piece of question data:

```
private class Question {
    int mNumber;
    String mText;
    String mImageUrl;

    public Question(int questionNum, String questionText, String
        questionImageUrl) {
        mNumber = questionNum;
        mText = questionText;
        mImageUrl = questionImageUrl;
    }
}
```

Next, declare a `Hashtable` member variable within the `QuizGameActivity` class to hold a batch `Question` objects in memory after you have parsed a batch of XML:

```
Hashtable<Integer, Question> mQuestions;
```

You can instantiate the Hashtable member variable in the onCreate() method of the QuizGameActivity class as follows:

```
mQuestions = new Hashtable<Integer, Question>(QUESTION_BATCH_SIZE);
```

Now, whenever questions are needed, retrieve the latest XML parcel, parse the XML, and stick the Question data into the Hashtable for use throughout the QuizGameActivity class. To save new key-value pairs to the Hashtable class, use the put() method. To retrieve a specific Question object by its question number, use the get() method. For example, to retrieve the current question information, check what the question number is (from the SharedPreferences setting you created earlier) and then make the following get() call:

```
Question curQuestion = (Question) mQuestions.get(questionNumber);
```

You can check for the existence of a specific question in the Hashtable member variable by question number, using the containsKey() method. This can be helpful for determining if it's time to retrieve a new batch of questions and to handle the case where no new questions are available.

For a full implementation of retrieving and parsing the XML question data and storing it within the Hashtable data structure, consult the source code that accompanies this lesson. This implementation, which is available primarily within the loadQuestionBatch() helper method of the QuizGameActivity class and relies solely on common Java classes and the XML parsing method, is covered in Hour 9, "Developing the Help and Scores Screens."

Handling Button Clicks and Driving the Quiz Forward

The two Button controls on the game screen are used to drive the ImageSwitcher and TextSwitcher controls which, in turn, represent the question displayed to the user. Each time the user clicks a Button control, any score changes are logged, the current question number is incremented and the ViewSwitcher controls are updated to display the next question. In this way, the Button controls drive the progress forward and the user progresses through the quiz.

Back when you were designing the game.xml layout, you set the onClick attributes of both Button controls; now it is time to implement these click handlers within the QuizGameActivity class. There is little difference between the handling of the Yes and No Button controls:

```
public void onNoButton(View v) {
    handleAnswerAndShowNextQuestion(false);
}
```

```
public void onYesButton(View v) {
    handleAnswerAndShowNextQuestion(true);
}
```

Both Button controls rely upon a helper method
handleAnswerAndShowNextQuestion(). This method is at the heart of the game
logic; here log the game state changes and handle all ImageSwitcher and
TextSwitcher update logic. Here is pseudo code for this method:

```
private void handleAnswerAndShowNextQuestion(boolean bAnswer) {
    // Load game settings like score and current question
    // Update score if answer is "yes"
    // Load the next question, handling if there are no more questions
}
```

Now let's work through the pseudo-code and implement this method. First, retrieve
the current game settings, including the game score and the next question number,
from SharedPreferences:

```
int curScore =
    mGameSettings.getInt(GAME_PREFERENCES_SCORE, 0);
int nextQuestionNumber =
    mGameSettings.getInt(GAME_PREFERENCES_CURRENT_QUESTION, 1) + 1;
```

Next, save off the current question number to the SharedPreferences. If the user
clicked the Yes button (and therefore the incoming parameter is true), update the
score and save it. Then commit these preference changes.

```
Editor editor = mGameSettings.edit();
editor.putInt(GAME_PREFERENCES_CURRENT_QUESTION, nextQuestionNumber);
if (bAnswer == true) {
    editor.putInt(GAME_PREFERENCES_SCORE, curScore + 1);
}
editor.commit();
```

Now it's time to move on to the next question. First, check whether the next question is available in the Hashtable using the containsKey() method. If there are
no remaining questions in the hashtable, retrieve a new batch of questions:

```
if (mQuestions.containsKey(nextQuestionNumber) == false) {
    // Load next batch
    try {
        loadQuestionBatch(nextQuestionNumber);
    } catch (Exception e) {
        Log.e(DEBUG_TAG, "Loading updated question batch failed", e);
    }
}
```

The loadQuestionBatch() helper method simplyretrieves the next XML parcel,
parses it, and shoves the new batch of Question data into the Hashtable for use by

the application. See the source code that accompanies this lesson for the full implementation of this method if you require another example of XML parsing.

Returning to the topic at hand, you should now have a fully loaded Hashtable of
question data, and a new question to pose to the user. Update the TextSwitcher
and the ImageSwitcher controls with the text and image for the next question. If
there is no question to display, handle this case as well:

```
if (mQuestions.containsKey(nextQuestionNumber) == true) {
    // Update question text
    TextSwitcher questionTextSwitcher =
        (TextSwitcher) findViewById(R.id.TextSwitcher_QuestionText);
    questionTextSwitcher.setText(getQuestionText(nextQuestionNumber));

    // Update question image
    ImageSwitcher questionImageSwitcher =
        (ImageSwitcher) findViewById(R.id.ImageSwitcher_QuestionImage);
    Drawable image = getQuestionImageDrawable(nextQuestionNumber);
    questionImageSwitcher.setImageDrawable(image);
} else {
    handleNoQuestions();
}
```

We discuss the handleNoQuestions() helper method in a moment. But for now, if
you have implemented all the bits described thus far, you should be able to run the
application and launch the game screen and answer some questions. The game
screen should look something like Figure 12.4.

FIGURE 12.4
The Been There,
Done That!
game screen.

Addressing Edge Cases

If there are no more questions available, you must inform the user. This case is handled by the `handleNoQuestions()` helper method. This method is quite simple. It does the following:

▶ Displays an informative text message to the user stating that there are no questions available using the `TextSwitcher` control.

▶ Displays a clear error graphic to the user, indicating that there are no questions available using the `ImageSwitcher` control.

▶ Disables both `Button` controls.

Here is the `handleNoQuestions()` implementation:

```
TextSwitcher questionTextSwitcher =
    (TextSwitcher) findViewById(R.id.TextSwitcher_QuestionText);
questionTextSwitcher.setText(getResources().getText(R.string.no_questions));
ImageSwitcher questionImageSwitcher =
    (ImageSwitcher) findViewById(R.id.ImageSwitcher_QuestionImage);
questionImageSwitcher.setImageResource(R.drawable.noquestion);
Button yesButton =
    (Button) findViewById(R.id.Button_Yes);
yesButton.setEnabled(false);

Button noButton =
    (Button) findViewById(R.id.Button_No);
noButton.setEnabled(false);
```

When the application runs out of questions, the game screen looks as shown in Figure 12.5. The user is informed that there are no more questions available and is not allowed to press any of the `Button` controls. Instead, the user must press the Back button and return to the main menu.

FIGURE 12.5
The Been There, Done That! game screen when no questions are available.

Summary

In this hour, you implemented the most important screen of the Been There, Done That! application—the game screen. You learned how to animate between View controls by using ImageSwitcher and TextSwitcher. You also got your first look at the various data structures available in the Android SDK and used a Hashtable member variable to store a batch of questions parsed from XML. Finally, you used the application's SharedPreferences to keep track of settings and game state information.

Q&A

Q. *If I'm storing images locally, can I use the* setImageURI() *method of the* ImageSwitcher *class instead of the* setImageDrawable() *method?*

A. Of course. In fact, we recommend it. If the graphic is locally available, use the setImageURI() method to greatly simplify the code for loading a graphic into an ImageSwitcher (or ImageView) control. There is no need for streams or Drawable objects in memory.

Q. *When using a* ViewSwitcher *control, can I set my own animations?*

A. Yes, you can set any animation resources for the "in" and "out" animations of a ViewSwitcher control, either programmatically or by using the animation attributes in the layout resource file.

Q. *How can I reset the quiz and start over with Question #1?*

A. There are two easy ways to "reset" the quiz for testing purposes. The first method is to delete the application's SharedPreferences file from the Android file system and restart the emulator. You use the Eclipse DDMS perspective to navigate to the data directory of the application and delete the associated SharedPreferences file. You can also uninstall and reinstall the application.

Workshop

Quiz

1. What subclasses are available for the ViewSwitcher class?

   A. TextSwitcher

   B. VideoSwitcher

   C. ImageSwitcher

   D. AudioSwitcher

2. True or False: The TextView controls used by a TextSwitcher control must be defined before the TextSwitcher control can be used.

3. True or False: A ViewSwitcher control has three states: the before View, the current View, and the next View.

Answers

1. A and C. The ViewSwitcher class has two subclasses: TextSwitcher (for animating between two TextView controls) and ImageSwitcher (for animating between two ImageView controls).

2. False. The TextView controls displayed by a TextSwitcher control can be created on-the-fly by using ViewFactory.

3. False. A ViewSwitcher control has two states: the current View and the next View.

Exercises

1. Review the sample code that accompanies this hour, especially the QuizGameActivity class. Make sure you understand each and every feature implemented in that class. If you are following along and building your own version of the application, ensure that all features are implemented in your own version of the activity as well.

2. Update the game screen to display the user's current score. This change requires the addition of a TextView control to the game.xml layout resource, which needs to be updated for each question displayed. Recall that the score is the number of Yes answers and is saved as a preference.

3. Modify the application to use a different data structure, such as a map or linked list, instead of a Hashtable.

4. **[Advanced]** Add a new option to the options menu of the game screen, created in Hour 8, "Implementing the Main Menu Screen," to reset the trivia quiz. Hint: We discuss resetting the quiz in the Q&A section. Make sure you clear only the appropriate game settings upon a reset, not all application preferences, in SharedPreferences.

HOUR 13

Working with Images and the Camera

What You'll Learn in This Hour:

▶ Designing the avatar feature
▶ Working with `ImageButton` controls and advanced `Button` features
▶ Launching activities and handling results
▶ Working with the camera and the Gallery
▶ Working with bitmap graphics

In this hour, you add a new feature to the Been There, Done That! settings screen—the ability for the user to add a small graphic or avatar. The user can set the avatar in two ways: by using the handset camera to take a photograph on-the-fly or by choosing an existing image from the handset using the Gallery.

Designing the Avatar Feature

Many mobile applications today are networked and have some social component. Some ways that users differentiate themselves from one another include giving themselves nicknames, or handles, and by setting custom icons to represent who they are, called avatars. To give users this ability, you implement an avatar feature on the settings screen of the Been There, Done that! application. Avatars come in many forms; an avatar might be a close-up photograph of the user's face, or it might be a funky graphic that speaks to the user's personality.

To incorporate the avatar feature into the Been There, Done That! Settings screen, you need to modify the screen design to accommodate the graphic as well as some mechanism by which the user can change the graphic. Figure 13.1 shows a rough design of how the avatar feature is incorporated into the settings screen.

FIGURE 13.1
Rough design
for the Been
There, Done
That! avatar
feature

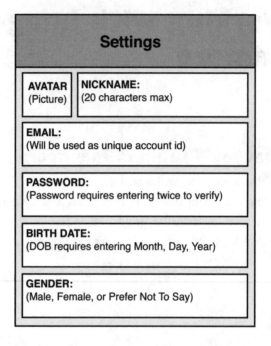

Space is at a premium in a mobile application. The settings screen for the Been There, Done That! application is no exception and must be kept as simple as possible. The avatar feature has two requirements. The user must be able to change the avatar and the chosen avatar must be displayed on the settings screen. Of the various controls available in Android, the `ImageButton` control is ideal for this purpose because

▶ An `ImageButton` control can display a graphic (for example, the current avatar).

▶ A regular click on an `ImageButton` control can trigger a type of avatar selection, such as launching the camera to take a photo to use as the avatar.

▶ A long click on an `ImageButton` control can trigger another type of avatar selection, such as launching the Gallery to enable the user to select an existing photo.

To incorporate your avatar design changes into the `/res/layout/settings.xml` layout file, you need to modify the region of the screen where the nickname controls reside. In order to add a control to the left of the nickname controls, you need to encapsulate all three controls (the avatar ImageButton, nickname label TextView, and nickname EditText controls) inside a layout control, such as a LinearLayout (horizontally oriented). Further nesting the nickname controls in their own vertically oriented LinearLayout control results in the intended look. Figure 13.2 shows the layout updates required by the avatar feature.

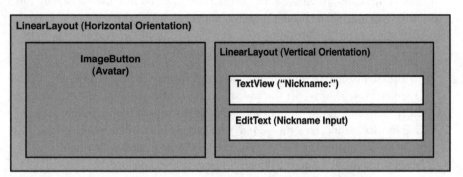

FIGURE 13.2
The settings screen layout updates required for the avatar feature.

Adding an Avatar to the Settings Layout

To add the avatar feature in the Been There, Done That! application settings screen, you need to add some new resources, including Dimension and Drawable resources, and then update the layout resource, settings.xml, to reflect the changes.

Begin by adding one new graphic resource (in various resolutions) to the /res/drawable directory hierarchy: avatar.png. The ImageButton control uses the avatar.png graphic as its default avatar, before one is chosen by the user.

Next, update the resources in /res/values/dimens.xml to include a dimension value for the size of the avatar. For example, the following dimension resource works well:

```
<dimen
        name="avatar_size">75dp</dimen>
```

Although this doesn't match the size of the avatar, it limits the size of the avatar that can be shown on the settings screen to something manageable. It also means that when the user replaces the avatar, the size of the replacement is irrelevant to the layout of the settings screen.

Save the resource files. After you have saved the files, you can use them in the layout resource files used by the settings screen layout.

Updating the Settings Screen Layout

The settings.xml layout file dictates the user interface of the settings screen. You need to reopen this layout file in the Eclipse layout resource editor and make the following changes:

1. First, find the TextView control called TextView_Nickname in the file. Above this control and inside the ScrollView control, add a new LinearLayout control and set its orientation attribute to horizontal. Set the layout_width and layout_height attributes to match_parent. Set its gravity attribute to fill as well, in order to grow its contents to fill the parent.

2. Within the LinearLayout control, add an ImageButton control called ImageButton_Avatar. Set the layout_width and layout_height attributes to wrap_content. You need to be able to scale the avatar graphic while preserving its aspect ratio, so set its adjustViewBounds attribute to true and its scaleType attribute to fitXY. You should also set its maxHeight and minHeight attributes to the dimension resource you created (@dimen/avatar_size). Finally, set its onClick attribute to onLaunchCamera; you also need to implement this method in your QuizSettingsActivity class. Unfortunately, you cannot register long-click handlers in the same way; they must be registered programmatically.

3. Below the ImageButton control, add another LinearLayout control. Set its orientation attribute to vertical and its layout_width attribute to match_parent and its and layout_height attribute to wrap_content. Now move the existing nickname controls (the TextView control called TextView_Nickname and the EditText control called EditText_Nickname) into this layout.

At this point, save the settings.xml layout file. If you rerun the application in the emulator, the settings screen should now look like Figure 13.3, complete with the new ImageButton control for the avatar feature.

FIGURE 13.3
The settings
screen with the
avatar feature.

Working with `ImageButton` **Controls**

The `ImageButton` control is a special type of `Button` control that displays a `Drawable` graphic instead of text in the area where the user normally clicks.

The `ImageButton` and `Button` controls are both derived from the `View` class, but they are unrelated to each other otherwise. The `Button` class is actually a direct sub-class of `TextView` (think of it as a line of text with a background graphic that looks like a button), whereas the `ImageButton` class is a direct subclass of `ImageView`.

Setting the Image of an `ImageButton` **Control**

As with `ImageView` controls, there are several different methods that you can use to set the graphic shown in an `ImageButton` control, including the following:

▶ `setImageBitmap()`—Use this method to set the graphic shown on the `ImageButton` control to a valid `Bitmap` object.

▶ `setImageDrawable()`—Use this method to set the graphic shown on the `ImageButton` control to a valid `Drawable` object.

▶ `setImageResource()`—Use this method to set the graphic shown on the `ImageButton` control to a valid `Resource` identifier.

▶ `setImageURI()`—Use this method to set the graphic shown on the `ImageButton` control to a valid `Uri` address.

Here's a handy trick for accessing application resources such as `Drawable` resources, using a specially constructed `Uri` address. This technique enables you to use the `setImageURI()` method of the `ImageButton` for both image resources and other graphics stored on the handset.

Resource URIs can be referenced by resource identifier or by resource type/name. The `Uri` address format for the resource identifier method is as follows:

```
android.resource://[package]/[res id]
```

For example, you could use the following `Uri` to access a `Drawable` resource called `avatar.png` by its resource identifier:

```
Uri path =
    Uri.parse("android.resource://com.androidbook.btdt.hour13/" +
    R.drawable.avatar);
```

The `Uri` address format for the resource type/name method is as follows:

```
android.resource://[package]/[res type]/[res name]
```

For example, you could use the following `Uri` to access a `Drawable` resource called `avatar.png` by its resource type/name:

```
Uri path = Uri.parse(
    "android.resource://com.androidbook.btdt.hour13/drawable/avatar");
```

When you have a valid `Uri` for the `Drawable` resource, you can use it with the `setImageURI()` method of an `ImageButton` control as follows:

```
ImageButton avatarButton = (ImageButton) findViewById(R.id.ImageButton_Avatar);
avatarButton.setImageURI(path);
```

Keep in mind that graphics displayed within an `ImageButton` control should generally be stored locally on the handset. Attempting to use remote `Uri` addresses is not recommended due to decreased application performance and responsiveness.

By the Way

> On some versions of the Android platform, the `ImageButton` control caches the graphic it is displaying and continues to do so even if you use one of the methods to change the graphic. One workaround for this is to call `setImageURI(null)` to flush the previous graphic and then call `setImageURI()` again with an appropriate `Uri` to the new graphic to display within the `ImageButton` control.

Handling ImageButton **Click Events**

ImageButton clicks are handled exactly the same way as with any View control—by using click listeners. For the avatar ImageButton control, you want to handle clicks and long-clicks.

Handling Regular Clicks

To listen and handle when a user clicks on the avatar ImageButton control, you must implement the onCameraLaunch() method within your activity class to match the onClick reference to it in the layout file:

```
public void onLaunchCamera(View v) {
        // TODO: Launch the Camera and Save the Photo as the Avatar
}
```

This should look familiar because you've already implemented a number of Button click handlers in prior lessons.

Handling Long-clicks

A long-click is a special type of click available on the Android platform. Basically, a long-click event is when a user clicks and holds his or her finger on a control for about one second. This type of click is handled separately from a regular, "quick" click. To handle long-clicks, you need to implement the click handler programmatically, as the current Android SDK does not include layout attributes for setting the click handlers in the resource files as it does for the android:onClick attribute.

To register a long-click handler programmatically, you must implement a View.OnLongClickListener class and pass it into the ImageButton control's setOnLongClickListener() method. The OnLongClickListener class has one required method you must implement: onLongClick(). Here is the implementation of OnLongClickListener for the avatar ImageButton control:

```
ImageButton avatarButton = (ImageButton) findViewById(R.id.ImageButton_Avatar);
avatarButton.setOnLongClickListener(new View.OnLongClickListener() {
    @Override
    public boolean onLongClick(View v) {
        // TODO: Launch Image Picker and Save Image as Avatar
        return true;
    }
});
```

The onLongClick() method has a return value, which should be true if long-click events are handled.

▼   **Try It Yourself**

Take a moment to try out clicks and long-clicks with an `ImageButton` control:

1. Navigate to the `QuizSettingsActivity.java` class file and add a click listener and a long-click listener to the `ImageButton_Avatar` control.

2. Within the button's `onClick` handler method, `onLaunchCamera`, add a `Toast` message that says "Short Click!".

3. Within the `onLongClick()` method of `OnLongClickListener`, add a `Toast` message that says "Long Click!".

4. Save your work and relaunch the application. Click the avatar `ImageButton` control on the settings screen and note how click and long-click events occur.

▲

Choosing and Saving the Avatar Graphic

Now that you have the avatar `ImageButton` control wired up, let's work on implementing the user click actions in their entirety. For now, when the user selects an avatar, the application saves the image locally on the handset. In future hours, you learn how the application can upload the avatar image to a remote server for safekeeping, and so that the user's avatar and login information persists across devices.

For now, let's work on the basics of avatar creation. To begin with, you need to add a new preference to the application `SharedPreferences`. Define this new preference in the `QuizActivity.java` class, as follows:

```
public static final String GAME_PREFERENCES_AVATAR = "Avatar";
```

Launching Activities and Handling Results

In order to support launching the Camera or Gallery applications and retrieving the avatar image from that application, you need to launch these systems activities via the use of an intent. When the user clicks the avatar button, the application configures the appropriate intent, launches the appropriate activity, and then handles the resulting image and sets it as an avatar.

If you think back to Hour 3, "Building Android Applications," when we talked about application life cycle, recall that there are several ways to launch an activity. The `Activity` class has two main methods for starting new activities. So far, you've been using the `startActivity()` method to transition between `Activity` classes (and screens) within your own application. Now you use the other method, called `startActivityForResult()`, which enables you to launch an activity and then handle the result by implementing the calling activity class's `onActivityResult()` callback method.

The `startActivityForResult()` method takes two parameters: a properly configured `Intent` object and a developer-defined request code. In order to implement the two click handlers, define two request codes, one for the Camera launch request and the other for the Gallery launch request, within the `QuizSettingsActivity` class:

```
static final int TAKE_AVATAR_CAMERA_REQUEST = 1;
static final int TAKE_AVATAR_GALLERY_REQUEST = 2;
```

We talk more about the `startActivityForResult()` method in a moment, but for now, let's focus on how the `QuizSettingsActivity` handles the results returned when the launched activity completes. Handle the result returned by the activity by implementing the `onActivityResult()` callback method of the `QuizSettingsActivity` class. Because you have more than one request code, use a `switch` statement to differentiate between the two cases, one for camera photo results and one for Gallery picker results:

```
protected void onActivityResult(int requestCode, int resultCode, Intent data) {
    switch(requestCode) {
    case TAKE_AVATAR_CAMERA_REQUEST:
        if (resultCode == Activity.RESULT_CANCELED) {
            // Avatar camera mode was canceled.
        } else if (resultCode == Activity.RESULT_OK) {
            // TODO: HANDLE PHOTO TAKEN WITH CAMERA
        }
        break;
    case TAKE_AVATAR_GALLERY_REQUEST:
        if (resultCode == Activity.RESULT_CANCELED) {
            // Avatar gallery request mode was canceled.
        } else if (resultCode == Activity.RESULT_OK) {
            // TODO: HANDLE IMAGE CHOSEN FROM GALLERY
        }
        break;
    }
}
```

The user might launch an activity and then cancel the operation. In this scenario, the `resultCode` parameter of the `onActivityResult()` method is `Activity.RESULT_CANCELED`. However, when the `resultCode` parameter is `Activity.RESULT_OK`, you should have a valid result to handle—the image the user wants as his or her avatar.

Working with the Camera

There are many ways to incorporate camera features into your application. You can build camera support directly into your application (and give your application the appropriate permissions), or you can integrate existing camera support functionality into your application by using the `Intent` mechanism to launch other applications that provide camera features. This second method is very straightforward, and for that reason you should use it in the Been There, Done That! application.

By far, the simplest way to include photo-taking abilities in an application is by using the `ACTION_IMAGE_CAPTURE` intent defined within the `android.provider.MediaStore` class. This intent can be used to launch the camera, capture an image, and return the image information to the calling application. This is exactly what you need for the camera support in your avatar feature.

Simply create an instance of the `ACTION_IMAGE_CAPTURE` Intent for use and then launch it with the `startActivityForResult()` method. Then retrieve the resulting image in the `onActivityResult()` callback method of your activity class. To do this, add the following code to the click handler of the avatar `ImageButton` control:

```
Intent pictureIntent = new Intent(
    android.provider.MediaStore.ACTION_IMAGE_CAPTURE);
startActivityForResult(pictureIntent, TAKE_AVATAR_CAMERA_REQUEST);
```

The `ACTION_IMAGE_CAPTURE` intent action causes the camera application to launch, enables the user to take a photograph, and returns the photo through the `onActivityResult()` callback method. By default, a small bitmap is returned, and it is suitable for your avatar. Within a specific `case` statement of the `onActivityResult()` method with the request code `TAKE_AVATAR_CAMERA_REQUEST`, you can retrieve the bitmap by inspecting the `Intent` parameter called `data`, as follows:

```
Bitmap cameraPic = (Bitmap) data.getExtras().get("data");
```

You can then process the bitmap graphic for use as an avatar. We discuss the details of how to achieve this in a moment or two. For now, save and run the application and observe the results. There is no camera available on the Android emulator. Instead, a mock camera screen is shown, and a fixed graphic is saved whenever the user chooses to take a picture. This is helpful for testing camera functionality using the Android emulator. When you run the application and click the avatar `ImageButton` control, the emulator screen should look something like Figure 13.4.

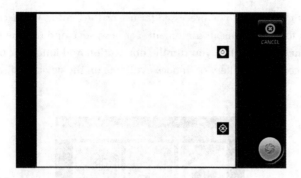

FIGURE 13.4
Taking a photo-
graph using the
camera applica-
tion in the
Android
emulator.

Working with the Gallery

Android has a standard intent action called ACTION_PICK
(android.intent.action.PICK) that enables the user to choose from a set of content. This type of intent is often used in conjunction with a URI, but it need not be.
You can also use the ACTION_PICK intent to create a set of all data of a given MIME
type on the handset and enable the user to choose an item from the set. Use the
setType() method of the Intent class to specify the type of media content to filter
the Gallery to. For example, you use the ACTION_PICK intent within the
ImageButton control's long-click handler to display all images in the Gallery for the
user to choose from, as follows:

```
Intent pickPhoto = new Intent(Intent.ACTION_PICK);
pickPhoto.setType("image/*");
startActivityForResult(pickPhoto, TAKE_AVATAR_GALLERY_REQUEST);
```

The ACTION_PICK Intent action causes a gallery of all images stored on the handset to launch, allows the user to choose one image, and returns a URI address to the
image's location on the device. Therefore, within the specific case statement of the
onActivityResult() method for the request code TAKE_AVATAR_GALLERY_REQUEST,
retrieve the Uri by inspecting the Intent parameter called data, as follows:

```
Uri photoUri = data.getData();
```

Then, to convert the Uri to a valid Bitmap object, use the Media class
(MediaStore.Images.Media) method called getBitmap():

```
Bitmap galleryPic = Media.getBitmap(getContentResolver(), photoUri);
```

The graphic is now ready to be processed for use as the avatar. We discuss the details of how to achieve this in a moment. For now, save and run the application and observe the results. When you run the application and long-click the avatar ImageButton control, a gallery of images available on the device is displayed (see Figure 13.5).

FIGURE 13.5
Choosing a photograph using the Gallery picker in the Android emulator.

Using Choosers to Provide Users with Options

When launching a "remote" activity—that is, an activity that is not necessarily part of your application—you are effectively sending out a message to the Android operating system that says, "I want to do this task. Figure out what app can do it for me and connect me to it, OK?" A number of other applications on the handset might have the ability to handle this operation. The Android operating system attempts to match the most appropriate activity to handle the request.

However, if you want the user to be shown a list of applicable activities (or applications) to handle the request, simply wrap your intent within another intent called ACTION_CHOOSER. You often see this mechanism used with common applications such as messaging applications (for example, "Which application do you want to use to send this message?"). You can wrap an intent within a chooser by using the createChooser() method, like this:

```
Intent.createChooser(innerIntent,
    "Choose which application to handle this");
```

Although most handsets have only one image-capturing application, as a developer, you are better off not making assumptions of this sort. For example, a user might have several email, image gallery, or social networking applications installed. It's generally a good idea to use the chooser technique when launching an activity outside your own application.

Working with Bitmaps

You now have two working mechanisms for retrieving bitmap graphics for the avatar image. However, you now need to save the graphic information to the Been There, Done That! application for use as the avatar. You can use the Bitmap class (android.graphics.Bitmap) to create, manipulate, and save graphics on the device.

> The Bitmap class encapsulates various bitmap-style graphics formats, including PNG and JPG. Do not confuse this with the bitmap file format (with a .bmp extension). You use the Bitmap class to create and manipulate PNG and JPG graphics on the Android handset.

By the Way

Because both the camera and gallery intents result in a Bitmap graphic object to save as the user's avatar, you can create a helper method called saveAvatar() in the QuizSettingsActivity class to handle these images. This helper method should take the Bitmap parameter, save it as a local application file, and treat it as the avatar within the Been There, Done That! application.

The pseudo-code for the saveAvatar() method might look like this:

```
private void saveAvatar(Bitmap avatar)
{
    // TODO: Save the Bitmap as a local file called avatar.jpg
    // TODO: Determine the Uri to the local avatar.jpg file
    // TODO: Save the Uri path as a String preference
    // TODO: Update the ImageButton with the new image
}
```

Saving Bitmap Graphics

The compress() method of the Bitmap class saves a bitmap in various image file formats and quality levels. For example, to save the avatar bitmap to a private application JPG file of high quality, use the following code (exception handling removed for clarity):

```
String strAvatarFilename = "avatar.jpg";
avatar.compress(CompressFormat.JPEG,
    100, openFileOutput(strAvatarFilename, MODE_PRIVATE));
```

Then determine the URI address of a local application file by using the fromFile() method of the Uri class. For example, to determine the URI for the avatar graphics file you just created using the compress() method, use the following code:

```
Uri imageUri = Uri.fromFile(new File(getFilesDir(), strAvatarFilename));
```

After the avatar is saved to a file and the appropriate URI generated, you can store the URI as an application preference and update the ImageButton control contents to display the new avatar image.

Now, if you run the application and choose an avatar (via the camera or the gallery), the ImageButton control contents are updated with the appropriate graphic, as shown in Figure 13.6.

FIGURE 13.6
The Been There, Done That! settings screen with a custom avatar.

Scaling Bitmap Graphics

The graphics returned by the two intents differ substantially in size. By default, the `ACTION_IMAGE_CAPTURE` intent returns a thumbnail of the original photo, which is appropriately sized for avatar use. However, the `ACTION_PICK` intent returns the full-size image, far too large for efficient avatar usage. In fact, on many devices, this image size is simply too large for use by the application.

For this reason, it's a good idea to scale large `Bitmap` graphics for use as the avatar. To do this, use the `createScaledBitmap()` method of the `Bitmap` class to generate thumbnail-sized graphics. Make sure to calculate the destination height and width appropriately to retain the original bitmap image's aspect ratio. Otherwise, the scaled graphic is stretched and shrunk in odd ways, which lessens its appeal.

To maintain the aspect ratio of a graphic, simply scale each axis (x and y) by the same percentage. Here's a helper method that creates a scaled bitmap image while maintaining its original aspect ratio:

```
private Bitmap createScaledBitmapKeepingAspectRatio(Bitmap bitmap, int maxSide)
{
    int orgHeight = bitmap.getHeight();
    int orgWidth = bitmap.getWidth();

    int scaledWidth = (orgWidth >= orgHeight) ? maxSide
        : (int) ((float) maxSide * ((float) orgWidth / (float) orgHeight));
    int scaledHeight = (orgHeight >= orgWidth) ? maxSide
        : (int) ((float) maxSide * ((float) orgHeight / (float) orgWidth));

    Bitmap scaledGalleryPic = Bitmap.createScaledBitmap(bitmap,
        scaledWidth, scaledHeight, true);

    return scaledGalleryPic;
}
```

Don't forget that if you apply scaling to all graphics, some may be downscaled and others may be upscaled, using the same code.

Summary

In this hour, you implemented a new avatar feature on the Been There, Done That! settings screen. The user can set an avatar by taking a picture with the built-in camera or by choosing an existing image from the Gallery. You learned how to launch an activity in another application via a properly configured `Intent` and retrieve its results by using the `startActivityForResult()` and `onActivityResult()` methods. Finally, you learned how to work with `Bitmap` graphics files in a variety of ways.

Q&A

Q. *By default, the* `ACTION_IMAGE_CAPTURE` *intent returns a small bitmap graphic of the photo taken by the camera. However, the full-size graphic captured by the camera is much larger. Can I access this photograph data?*

A. You can control the data returned by the camera application by supplying some extra data (specifically, the `EXTRA_OUTPUT` field) to the `Intent`.

Q. *Don't I need the* `android.permission.CAMERA` *permission to use the camera?*

A. Not always. For more fine-tuned control over the handset camera hardware and to access the `Camera` classes (such as `android.hardware.Camera`) and camera services of the Android, your application is required to have the `android.permission.CAMERA` permission. However, in this hour, you are using an `Intent` to launch a separate application that handles all camera-related features. That application requires the appropriate permissions, but your application does not. This is a fine, but important, distinction.

Workshop

Quiz

1. Activity results handled by the `onActivityResult()` method are differentiated from one another using which parameter?

    A. `requestCode`

    B. `resultCode`

    C. `data`

2. True or False: The `ImageButton` control is a subclass of the `Button` control.

3. True or False: The `Bitmap` class only creates traditional bitmap graphics with the `.bmp` extension.

Answers

1. A. The developer-defined `requestCode` is used to determine which activity (started with the `startActivityForResult()` method) is returning a result. `resultCode` provides information about that activity, such as whether it completed successfully or was canceled by the user.

2. False. The ImageButton control is actually a subclass of ImageView. However, a Button control behaves in a very similar fashion to an ImageButton control because they are both derived from the View class.

3. False. The Bitmap class encapsulates all bitmap-style graphics formats—specifically PNG (recommended) and JPG (supported).

Exercises

1. From the emulator, download several graphics from the web using the Browser application. To do this, browse to a website, find an image you like, and long-press on the image. Choose the Save image option. This image now appears in the Gallery for future use as an avatar. If the graphics don't show up immediately, launch the Dev Tools app (inside the emulator) and select Media Scanner to force the system to scan the media. Note: Your development machine needs an Internet connection to use the Browser application properly.

2. Install the application on the emulator and try setting the avatar setting using both methods: click and long-click. Note how the emulator "emulates" taking a photo. Choose one of the images you downloaded in Exercise 1 from the Gallery.

3. After setting the avatar in the emulator in Exercise 2, use the File Explorer in the DDMS perspective to see where the avatar.jpg file is stored in the application's data directory (for example, /data/data/com.androidbook.btdt.hour13/files/avatar.jpg). Copy the file to your hard drive and view it with a traditional graphics viewer.

4. Install the application on a test device (not an emulator) and try setting the avatar setting using both methods: click and long-click. Pay special attention to how the camera functions on a real device, and how that differs from the emulator. It is especially important to test on the device in this sort of situation, as the behavior is different.

5. **[Challenging!]** Redesign the settings.xml layout resource file to reduce the number of nested LinearLayout controls. Consider using a RelativeLayout control instead of the vertical and horizontal LinearLayout controls that make up the avatar feature section of the settings screen.

HOUR 14

Adding Support for Location-Based Services

What You'll Learn in This Hour:

▶ Designing the favorite place feature
▶ Using location-based services
▶ Using geocoding services
▶ Working with maps

In this hour, you add a new feature to the Been There, Done That! settings screen—the ability for the user to set his or her favorite place in the world. The user configures this information by using the current location provided by location-based services (LBS) on the handset or by supplying a place name (for example, The Grand Canyon) that can be resolved into the corresponding GPS coordinates using the geocoding services provided in the Android SDK.

Designing the Favorite Place Feature

Mobile users are always on the go, and location-aware mobile applications are incredibly popular. The Android SDK makes it fairly straightforward to add LBS support to applications. The degree to which location support is incorporated into an application is a design choice for the developer, and there are a number of options.

Because the Been There, Done That! application is primarily a game, its location-based features are secondary. However, there's no reason not to leverage some of the most common LBS features of the Android SDK to get a feel for the technology and to provide a richer experience for users. This can be achieved by adding a new feature to the settings screen: the ability for the user to specify his or her favorite place.

On the settings screen, you implement a new dialog that collects information about the user's favorite location. The user can choose to label and save the handset's last known location as his or her favorite place or type in a different place name, such as an address, a city, or a landmark (for example, New York City, Iceland, Yellowstone National Park, or 90210). The application then leverages the geocoding service providers available on the device to resolve these location strings into the appropriate GPS coordinates.

To incorporate this kind of feature into the Been There, Done That! Settings screen, you need to modify the screen design slightly to include the new favorite place feature. Figure 14.1 shows a rough design of how the favorite place feature is incorporated into the settings screen.

FIGURE 14.1
Rough design of the favorite place feature.

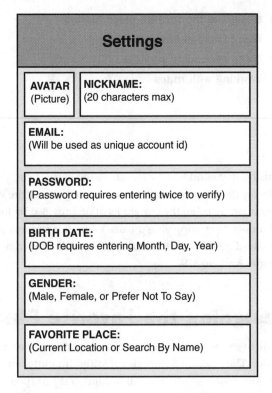

Determining Favorite Place Feature Layout Updates

Recall that the fields displayed on the settings screen are encapsulated within a `ScrollView` control. This makes it easy to add a new setting at the bottom of the screen for your new feature. The favorite place feature functions much like the date of birth and password settings: It relies upon TextView and Button controls, the latter of which launches a custom dialog to collect the user's favorite place data.

To incorporate the favorite place design changes into the /res/layout/settings. xml layout file, you need to add a new region to the settings screen below the gender Spinner control. Specifically, you add a TextView control to display the label of the new setting, followed by a LinearLayout control with a Button control to launch the dialog and a TextView control to display the resulting Favorite Place name. Figure 14.2 shows the layout updates required by the favorite place feature.

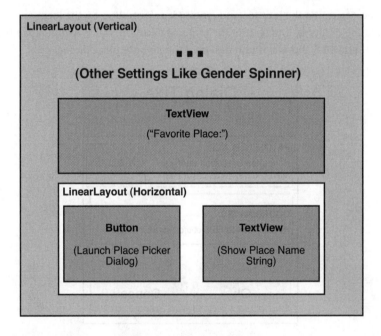

FIGURE 14.2
The settings screen layout updates required for the favorite place feature.

Designing the Favorite Place Dialog

You can build the favorite place picker dialog as a custom dialog based upon the AlertDialog class, much like you designed the password dialog in Hour 11, "Using Dialogs to Collect User Input."

The favorite place setting data is stored in the application preferences in three parts:

▶ The name of the location (a String value)

▶ The latitude of the location (a float value)

▶ The longitude of the location (a float value)

To keep the dialog simple, you can offer the user two location choices:

▶ Enter a string into an `EditText` control for the label of the current location. For the coordinates, use the last known location data, provided that GPS provider(s) available on the device exist and can determine this information.

▶ Enter a string into an `EditText` control and use the geocoding services available within the Android SDK to resolve the string into the appropriate GPS coordinates, provided geocoding services exist on the device.

After you determine the latitude and longitude information on the location, you can also add the ability to launch into the Maps application, if it is available on the device. Figure 14.3 shows a rough design of the favorite place dialog.

FIGURE 14.3
Rough design of the favorite place dialog.

Implementing the Favorite Place Feature

To implement the Favorite Place feature on the settings screen, you need to add new project resources, update the `settings.xml` layout resource to reflect the settings screen design, and create a new layout resource for the Favorite Place picker dialog.

Adding New Project Resources

You need to add a number of new resources to support the Favorite Place feature of the settings screen, including string and dimension resources as well as layout resource file updates and additions.

Adding New String Resources

The Favorite Place feature relies on numerous new string resources. Add the following text resources to the `strings.xml` resource file:

- ▶ Text label for the feature's `TextView` control (for example, Favorite Place:).

- ▶ Text label for the `Button` control (for example, Pick a Place).

- ▶ Text to display in a `TextView` control when the location is not set (for example, No Favorite Place Set).

- ▶ Text to display in a `TextView` control for the GPS coordinate data (for example, Coordinates:).

- ▶ Text to display in a `EditText` control when set to the current location (for example, (Current Location)). The user can overwrite this text with a more specific label.

- ▶ Text label for the `Button` control on the dialog to launch the Maps application (for example, Map It!).

Save the `strings.xml` resource file. For a complete list of the new strings required for the Favorite Place feature, see the sample source code provided on the CD that accompanies this book, or download the source code from the book website.

Adding New Dimension Resources

The Favorite Place feature relies upon at least one new dimension resource. This dimension resource dictates the width of the `EditText` control on the Favorite Place picker dialog:

```
<dimen
    name="fav_place_textbox_size">200dp</dimen>
```

Save the `dimension.xml` resource file. Now you are ready to update the layout resources for this feature.

Updating the Settings Screen Layout

The settings.xml layout file dictates the user interface of the settings screen. You need to reopen this layout file in the Eclipse layout resource editor and make the following changes to add the favorite place feature:

1. Below the Spinner control, add the Favorite Place settings region of the form. Start by adding another TextView control to display the Favorite Place label text. Set its id attribute to @+id/TextView_FavoritePlace and its layout_width and layout_height attributes to wrap_content. Set any text style attributes appropriately. Finally, set its text attribute to the string resource you just created called @string/settings_favoriteplace.

2. Add a horizontal LinearLayout control. Set its layout_height attribute to wrap_content and its layout_width attribute to match_parent. This LinearLayout has two child controls: a Button control and a TextView control.

3. Within the LinearLayout, add the Button control first. Set its id attribute @+id/Button_FavoritePlace and the text attribute set to the Favorite Place button text string resource you created called @string/settings_button_favoriteplace. Finally, set its layout_width and layout_height attributes to wrap_content. Finally, set its onClick attribute to the QuizSettingsActivity method named onPickPlaceButtonClick, which you need to implement to handle clicks from this control.

4. Configure the TextView control to display the Favorite Place setting state string ("No Favorite Place Set.", for now, until you wire up the dialog). Configure the control's properties to match those in the Password and Date of Birth regions. For example, set the textStyle attribute to bold, the gravity attribute to center, and so on.

At this point, save the settings.xml layout file.

Implementing the Favorite Place Dialog Layout

You need to create a new layout resource file for the Favorite Place dialog layout design. Begin by adding a new layout resource file to the project called /res/layout/fav_place_dialog.xml. Figure 14.4 shows the layout for the Favorite Place picker dialog.

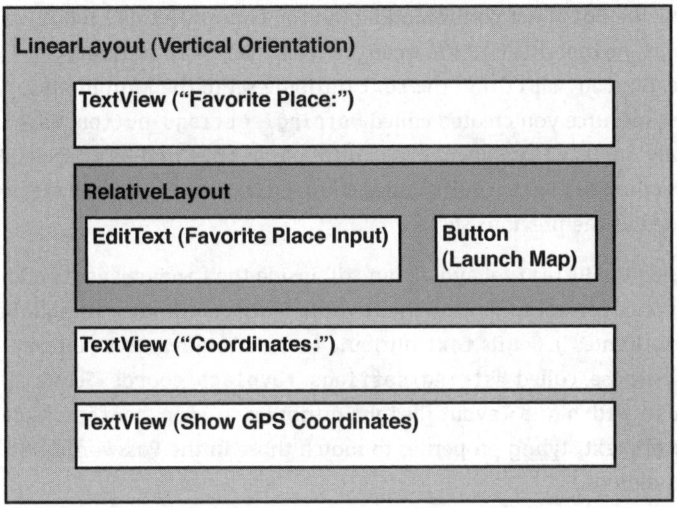

FIGURE 14.4
The favorite
place dialog
layout.

This layout file dictates the user interface of the Favorite Place dialog. Create this layout file in the Eclipse layout resource editor and take the following steps to build this resource:

1. Below the typical XML header that should exist within every layout resource file, add a vertically oriented LinearLayout control. Set its id attribute to @+id/root, its layout_width and layout_height attributes to match_parent, and its background attribute to the background drawable resource you created many lessons ago.

2. Within the LinearLayout control, add a TextView control with an id attribute of @+id/TextView_FavPlace. Set its layout_height and layout_width attributes to wrap_content. Set its text attribute to the string resource you created for this Favorite Place setting label: @string/settings_favoriteplace. Modify any text styling attributes (bold style, font size, etc.) to match the text with other settings.

3. Add a RelativeLayout control. Set its layout_width to match_parent and its layout_height attribute to wrap_content.

4. Within the RelativeLayout control, add an EditText control with an id attribute of @+id/EditText_FavPlaceName. Set its layout_height and layout_width attributes to wrap_content. Set its maxLines attribute to 1 and its inputType attribute to text. Set its width to the dimension resource you just created for this purpose, @dimen/fav_place_textbox_size. Set its default text attribute to the string resource you just created to label the current location, called @string/settings_favplace_currentlocation. Finally, set its layout_alignParentLeft attribute to true.

5. Below the `EditText` control, add a `Button` control. Set its `layout_width` and `layout_height` attributes to `wrap_content`. Set its `id` attribute `@+id/Button_MapIt` and the `text` attribute set to the Map It! button text string resource you created called `@string/settings_button_favplace_map`. Finally, set its `alignParentRight` attribute to `true` and its `alignRight` attribute to the `EditText` control called `@+id/EditText_FavPlaceName`, which you defined in the previous step.

6. Outside the `RelativeLayout`, but still inside the `LinearLayout`, add a `TextView` control to display the Favorite Place coordinates string label ("Coordinates"). Set its `text` attribute to the string resource you created for this purpose, called `@string/settings_favplace_coords`. Set its `layout_width` and `layout_height` attributes to `wrap_content`. Configure the control's text styling properties to match those in the Password and Date of Birth dialogs.

7. Finally, add a second `TextView` control to display the Favorite Place coordinates data. Set its `id` attribute to `@+id/TextView_FavPlaceCoords_Info`. Set its `layout_width` to `match_parent` and its `layout_height` attribute to `wrap_content`. Configure the control's text styling properties to match those in the Password and Date of Birth dialogs.

At this point, save the `fav_place_dialog.xml` layout file. This layout resource is inflated at runtime, much as the custom password dialog is.

Implementing the Favorite Place Dialog

Before you can turn your attention to the more interesting aspects of adding LBS support to the Been There, Done That! application, you need to leverage many of the skills discussed in previous hours to implement the new dialog used by the Favorite Place feature in the `QuizActivity` and `QuizSettingsActivity` classes. This is a great way to exercise some of your new skills.

Because each of these tasks has been covered in a previous hour, we do not go into too much detail here, but we discuss the basic steps to complete this task. If you require more detail, see the sample code that accompanies this lesson for the complete implementation, available on the book's CD or on the book website.

1. Define three new game preference `String` values in the `QuizActivity` class. These preferences are used by the application's `SharedPreferences` to store the user's favorite location name (`String`) as well as that location's latitude (`float`) and longitude (`float`).

2. Update the `QuizSettingsActivity` class to include a new dialog. First, define a dialog identifier (for example, `PLACE_DIALOG_ID`) in the class.

3. In the `QuizSettingsActivity` class, implement the `onPickPlaceButtonClick` method to handle button clicks for the Pick a Place button. This handler should simply use the `showDialog()` method to call your new Favorite Place Dialog (`PLACE_DIALOG_ID`).

4. Add a helper method called `initFavoritePlacePicker()` to the `QuizSettingsActivity` class to display the favorite place name (if it exists) from the application preferences. Call this method in the `onCreate()` method.

5. Implement the `PLACE_DIALOG_ID` case statement for the `onCreateDialog()` method. You build this dialog much as you did the password dialog. Inflate the layout resource called `fav_place_dialog.xml` using a `LayoutInflater`. Find the important view controls, such as the `EditText` (Place Name), `TextView` (Coordinates) and `Button` (Map It!) controls within that layout using the `findViewById()` method. Register an `onClick` handler for the Button control; for now, this button can simply grab the text from the `EditText` control and display it in a `Toast` message. Finish up by using the `AlertDialog.Builder` class to generate the custom dialog. Give the dialog a title. Set the negative button click handler to remove the dialog forcefully so it is not reused. Set the positive button click handler to save off the favorite place data into the application's shared preferences, using mock coordinate data for the moment. Create and return the dialog.

6. Implement the `PLACE_DIALOG_ID` case statement for the `onPrepareDialog()` method. You build this dialog much as you did the password dialog. Retrieve the favorite place data from the application preferences and update the `EditText` (Place Name) and `TextView` (Coordinates) textual data on the screen. If no preference data exists, set the `EditText` text to the current location string and add a `TODO` comment to calculate the current location, which we discuss in a moment.

7. Add a helper method called `formatCoordinates()` to the `QuizSettingsActivity` class to take two `float` coordinate values (latitude and longitude) and return a single `String` representation to display those coordinates on the screen (in that `TextView` control). Hint: Consider using the `StringBuilder` class.

8. Add a simple inner class called `GPSCoords` to the `QuizSettingsActivity` class. Give the class two member variables: `float` coordinate values (latitude and longitude, and a single constructor that sets the coordinate values.

If you run the Been There, Done That! application now, the settings screen should look like Figure 14.5.

FIGURE 14.5
The favorite place region of the settings screen.

Now that you have implemented the framework to support the favorite place feature, you can turn your attention to more interesting matters, such as calculating the user's last known location and mapping GPS coordinates on a map and use this knowledge to flesh out these functional areas of the Favorite Place picker dialog.

Using Location-Based Services

Developers who leverage LBS support in their applications need to be aware of a number of issues. First and foremost, a user's location is personal information and subject to privacy concerns. Second, using LBS on a handset takes a toll on the device in terms of network data usage and battery life. Finally, not every Android device has LBS hardware, so you should not assume that all devices are able to provide location information.

The Android system addresses these issues, in part, through permissions. That said, some of the burden of managing the impact of LBS features on the user and the user's device does fall on the developer. Therefore, here are some guidelines for using services such as LBS:

▶ Request appropriate LBS permissions for your application. The user needs to approve the use of such permissions as part of the application install process. Do not request permissions your application does not require.

▶ Enable LBS features and services only when they are needed and disable them as soon as they are no longer required.

▶ Offload LBS operations, which can consume resources and affect the responsiveness of your application, to a separate thread from the main UI thread. We discuss threading later in this book. You could also consider developing a background service to support these features, but working with Android services is beyond the scope of this book.

▶ Inform the user when collecting and using sensitive data, as appropriate. Many users consider their present or past locations to be sensitive. This may involve creating a privacy policy.

▶ Allow the user to configure and disable features that might adversely affect his or her experience when using your application. For example, develop a "roaming" mode for your application to enable the user to enjoy your application without incurring huge fees.

▶ Handle events such as low-battery warnings and adjust how your application runs accordingly.

▶ Consider including a custom privacy message as part of your application's usage terms, to explain how any data collected from the user, including the user's name and location information, will and will not be used.

A number of LBS features are available as part of the Android SDK, but there are also some exciting features within the Google APIs add-on as well. This add-on enables you to use raw LBS data and integrate powerful features such as Google Maps functionality directly into your applications. Developers using the Google APIs add-on must register for a special Google developer account and use a special API key.

Enabling Location Testing on the Emulator

Many basic LBS features are available to developers without the special Google developer accounts and API keys. For example, you need a special API key to use Google Maps directly within your applications, but you do not need any special permission to launch the Maps application on the device via an intent and have it load a specific location.

To develop and test LBS features fully, you need to use a combination of specially configured AVDs for use with the emulator and, as always, test thoroughly on the target devices.

Creating an AVD with Google APIs and Applications

You might have noticed that the basic Android installation (the target platform chosen when creating an AVD for use with the emulator) does not include the Maps application. To use Google's Maps application in the emulator, you need to create an Android AVD that includes the Google APIs as part of the target platform. Because you are adding some mapping features to the Been There, Done That! application, you need to create a new AVD for this target platform. For example, you might choose a target platform such as "Google APIs (Google, Inc.) - API Level 8" to create an AVD that emulates an Android 2.2 device with the proper Google APIs. Recall that we discussed creating AVDs for emulator testing in Hour 1, "Getting Started with Android."

Configuring the Location of the Emulator

Unfortunately, the Android emulator just pretends to be a real device—that is, it doesn't actually have any hardware internals, so it cannot determine its current location via satellite. Instead, you must seed the location information to the specific emulator instance. The easiest way to configure the location data of your emulator is to use the DDMS perspective in Eclipse. You need the latitude and longitude of the location for the emulator to use.

To seed the emulator with a specific latitude and longitude, follow these steps on AVDs featuring stable Maps support, such as Android 2.2:

1. Launch the emulator. If you're running an application, click the Home button.

2. In the Settings, ensure that you have Allow Mock Locations enabled. You can find this setting under the Settings, Applications, Development menu.

3. Click the Home button and then browse to the installed applications and launch the Maps application.

4. Click through any help dialogs until you see the map.

5. Click the Menu button and press the target icon labeled My Location to initiate polling for location data in the emulator. (see Figure 14.6). You should then see a Toast message saying "Waiting for location."

FIGURE 14.6
The Maps
application in
the Android
emulator.

6. Switch to Eclipse and click on the DDMS perspective.

7. Choose the emulator instance you want to send a location fix to.

8. In the Emulator Control pane, scroll down to the location control.

9. Enter the longitude and latitude of your desired location. Try the coordinates
   for Lassen Volcanic National Park: longitude 40.50931 and latitude -121.4331
   (see Figure 14.7).

10. Click the Send button.

Back in the emulator, notice that the Google map is now showing the location you
seeded. If you were not quick enough, set up the DDMS data first, then jump over to
the Maps app, click the My Location button, and hit Send again in DDMS. Your
screen should now display your location as Lassen Volcanic National Park, as shown
in Figure 14.8.

FIGURE 14.7
Setting the location of the emulator to Lassen Volcanic National Park with DDMS.

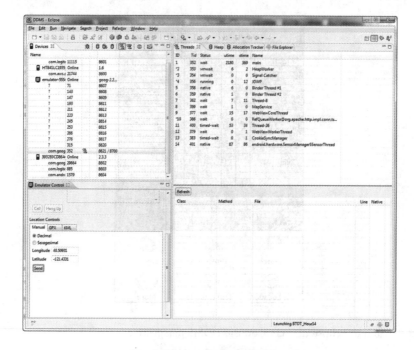

FIGURE 14.8
Setting the location of the emulator to Lassen Volcanic National Park.

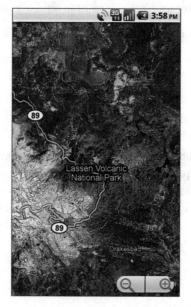

Accessing the Location-Based Services

To access LBS services (such as the user's location) on an Android device, you must have the appropriate permissions. Location-based services cannot be used by an Android application unless it is granted the appropriate <uses-permission> settings configured in the Android manifest file.

The most common permissions used by applications leveraging LBS are android.permission.ACCESS_FINE_LOCATION and android.permission.ACCESS_ COARSE_LOCATION. To use the GPS provider in the Been There, Done That! application, use the android.permission.ACCESS_FINE_LOCATION permission.

After you have registered the permission in your Android manifest file, you can access the LocationManager class (android.location.LocationManager) by using the getSystemService() method, as follows:

```
LocationManager locMgr =
        (LocationManager) getSystemService(LOCATION_SERVICE);
```

The LocationManager class enables you to access the LBS providers and their functionality, when it is available on the device.

Getting the Last Known Location

You can retrieve the last known location of the device (as calculated by a specific provider) by using the getLastKnownLocation() method of the LocationManager class. This location might not be current, but it often gives you a good enough starting point, and this data is returned quickly, whereas trying to get a current satellite fix can often take quite some time. It also bypasses the work of sorting through lots of location providers.

You need not start the provider to get the last known location; you simply need to request its last known result. The getLastKnownLocation() method returns a Location object:

```
Location recentLoc =
    locMgr.getLastKnownLocation(LocationManager.GPS_PROVIDER);
```

You can use the Location class (android.location.Location) to determine a number of interesting pieces of information regarding a location. For example, use the getLatitude() and getLongitude() methods to retrieve the coordinates from the Location object. The information available for a given location depends upon the LBS provider it came from. For example, most providers return latitude and longitude, but not all can calculate altitude. You could check for an altitude data using the Location class's hasAltitude() method and then call the getAltitude() method to retrieve the data.

This approximate location information is all that the Been There, Done That! application really needs for seeding the current location in the case where no Favorite place has been set by the user (the default). Finish implementing this functionality in the `QuizSettingsActivity` class at this time. Feel free to use the sample source code if you need extra help.

Working with Providers

A device might have any number of LBS providers available. You can get a list of all providers by calling the `getProviders()` method of the `LocationManager` class. You can limit the providers returned to only those that are enabled, or you can provide criteria for returning only providers with certain features (such as fine accuracy). You can also use the `getBestProvider()` method to return the most appropriate provider for a given set of criteria.

Both provider retrieval methods return a list of names of location providers. The best location provider for given set of criteria can be returned by name, using the `getProvider()` method. You can use the `LocationProvider` class (`android.location.LocationProvider`) to inspect a given provider and see what features it has, such as whether it supports altitude, bearing, and speed information and whether using it may incur a monetary cost to the user.

Receiving Location Updates

When you need more current information or want to know when the location changes, you can register for periodic location updates by using the `requestLocationUpdates()` method of the `LocationManager` class. This method allows an activity to listen to events from a specific provider (for example, the best provider given your criteria). The frequency of notifications can be adjusted by specifying the minimum time (in milliseconds) and the minimum distance interval (in meters) between updates.

To receive a notification when the location changes, your activity can implement the `LocationListener` class (`android.location.LocationListener`) interface. This interface has a number of helpful callback methods, which allow the activity to react when the provider is enabled and disabled, when its status changes, and when the location changes.

Using Geocoding Services

Now that you know how to determine the last known location of the user, let's turn our attention to another aspect of LBS support that we want to include in the Favorite Place dialog: geocoding.

Geocoding is the process of translating a description of a location into GPS coordinates (latitude, longitude, and sometimes altitude). Geocoding enables you to enter a place name, such as Eiffel Tower, into Google Maps (http://maps.google.com) and get the appropriate spot on the map. Many geocoding services also have reverse-geocoding abilities, which can translate raw coordinates into some form of address (usually a partial address).

Android devices might or might not have geocoding services available, and geocoding requires a back-end network service, so the device must have network connectivity to function. Different geocoding services support different types of descriptions, but the following are some of the most common ones:

- ▶ Names of towns, states, and countries

- ▶ Various forms of postal-style addresses (full and partial)

- ▶ Postal codes

- ▶ Airport codes (for example, LAX, LHR, JFK)

- ▶ Famous landmarks

Many geocoding services also allow input of raw coordinates (latitude and longitude). Finally, geocoding services are often localized.

Geocoded addresses are often ambiguous, so a geocoding service might return multiple records. For example, if you were to try to resolve the address "Springfield," you would likely get quite a few results because there is a town called Springfield in 35 of the states in the United States, and there are even more Springfields abroad. You might also get results for places called "East Springfield" or "Springfield by the Sea," for example. For the best results, choose a geocoding label, or address, that is the most specific. For example, use the zip code for your Springfield of choice instead of its name to resolve the coordinates.

Using Geocoding Services with Android

The Android SDK includes the `Geocoder` (`android.location.Geocoder`) class to facilitate interaction with the handset's geocoding and reverse-geocoding services, if they are present. Instantiating a `Geocoder` is simple:

```
Geocoder coder = new Geocoder(getApplicationContext());
```

When you have a valid `Geocoder` instance, you can begin to use any geocoding or reverse-geocoding services available on the device. Like other network operations, geocoding services are blocking operations. This means that you should put any calls to geocoding services in a thread separate from the main UI thread, otherwise you might run into problems if the results take too long to process.

> Geocoding services are not always reliable on the Android emulator at this time. If you try to geocode a location within the emulator, you are likely to see an exception such as `java.io.IOException: Service not Available`. Test geocoding features on actual devices.

Geocoding: Translating Addresses into Coordinates

You can use the `getFromLocationName()` method of the `Geocoder` class to resolve a location into coordinates. This method takes two parameters: the string containing the location information and the number of results you want returned. For example, the following code (exception handling removed for clarity) looks up a location called "Springfield" and limits the returned results to three addresses:

```
String strLocation = "Springfield";
List<Address> geocodeResults =
    coder.getFromLocationName(strLocation, 3);
```

Iterate through the results easily by using a Java iterator, like this:

```
Iterator<Address> locations = geocodeResults.iterator();
while (locations.hasNext()) {
    Address loc = locations.next();
    double lat = loc.getLatitude();
    double lon = loc.getLongitude();
    // TODO: Do something with these coordinates
}
```

Each resulting `Address` object (in this case, there are up to three) contains information about the location. You can use the `getLatitude()` and `getLongitude()` methods of the `Address` class to access the location's coordinates. Depending on your implementation, you might want to give the user the option to choose the right location, or simply take the first `Address` and use it.

The first `Address` object information is all that the Been There, Done That! application really needs for resolving the text from the `EditText` control of the dialog. Finish implementing this functionality in the dialog at this time. Gather the text from the user, resolve the location, and display the resulting coordinates in the `TextView` on the dialog for that purpose. Don't forget to save off the location data to the shared preferences when the dialog is dismissed (within the positive button click handler is a good place). Feel free to use the sample source code if you need extra help.

Reverse-Geocoding: Translating Coordinates into Addresses

You can use the Geocoder class's getFromLocation() method to translate raw latitude and longitude coordinates into address information. This method is much like the getFromLocationName() method. Again, you pass in the coordinates and the number of results to be returned.

Working with Maps

At this point, you have almost everything you need to finish up the Favorite Place picker dialog of the Been There, Done That! application. All that's left is adding a little bit of mapping support and wiring up the Map It! button on your dialog.

Most compelling map features on the Android platform are provided by the special Google API add-ons. For example, you can use the special MapView control in your layout files to tightly integrate Google Maps features into applications. You can also integrate with existing Maps applications available on the handset by way of the intent mechanism, much as you did with the camera in Hour 13, "Working with Images and the Camera."

Launching a Map Application by Using an Intent

Location applications such as the Maps application handle the ACTION_VIEW intent when supplied with a URI with geographic coordinates. This URI has a special format. You can launch the Maps application to a specific set of coordinates using the following URI format string:

```
geo:lat,lon
```

Here's an example of how to format this URI string:

```
String geoURI = String.format("geo:%f,%f", lat, lon);
```

This special URI could also include a zoom level, which is a number between 1 and 23, where zoom level 1 shows the whole planet, and zoom level 23 zooms in all the way (often way too far for map resolution). To include a zoom level, use the following URI format string:

```
geo:lat,lon?z=level
```

Here's an example of how to format a URI string with a specific zoom level:

```
String geoURI = String.format("geo:%f,%f?z=10", lat, lon);
```

When you have a properly formatted `Uri` object, use its `parse()` method to generate the `Uri` and use it with the `ACTION_VIEW` intent, as follows:

```
Uri geo = Uri.parse(geoURI);
Intent geoMap = new Intent(Intent.ACTION_VIEW, geo);
startActivity(geoMap);
```

If there are applications on the device that handle geo-format URIs, the appropriate application (most notably, the Google Maps application) launches as the new foreground activity and shows the location. After the user has looked at the map, he or she can return to the calling application simply by pressing the Back button.

Now you have everything you need to wire up the Map It! button on the Favorite Place picker dialog. Simply implement its click handler and use the appropriate GPS coordinates (as determined either by geocoding the `EditText` contents or using the last known location information) and launch an intent to display the location in the Maps application, as shown in Figure 14.9.

FIGURE 14.9
The favorite place picker dialog, launching the Google Maps application.

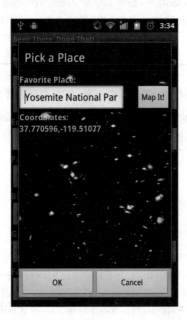
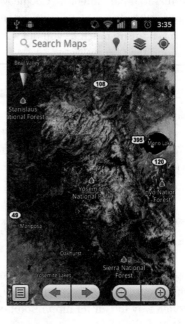

For example, let's say you typed "Great Pyramids" in the dialog. This is resolved to the appropriate coordinates. Click the Map It! button to launch the Maps application. If you press the Menu button in the Maps application, you can change the map mode to satellite view and zoom in to see the Great Pyramids clearly, as well as all the tour buses and the Sphinx, as shown in Figure 14.10.

FIGURE 14.10
Using the Google Maps application to zoom in satellite view.

Working with Third-Party Services and Applications

The built-in LBS features of the Android SDK are located in the android.location package. Basic LBS functionality, such as getting a location fix from satellite triangulation, is built into the Android SDK. However, many of the most interesting and powerful mapping and LBS-related features on Android phones are not actually built into the basic Android SDK but are part of the Google APIs that ship along with the Android SDK.

Working with Google APIs and Advanced Maps Features

Maps features can be built into applications using the Google API add-on. The following are some of the features available in the com.google.android.maps package:

▶ A MapView control for displaying an interactive map within a layout

▶ A MapActivity class to simplify MapView controls on a screen

▶ The GeoPoint class, which encapsulates position information

▶ Classes to support map overlays (drawing on top of the map)

▶ Classes for working with position projections and handling other common LBS-related tasks

For some Google APIs and features, you must sign up for a special account, agree to further terms of service, and receive an API key to use those services. These features are exciting and powerful, but they are unfortunately beyond the scope of this book. After you have mastered the basics of Android LBS support, consider consulting a more advanced Android manual, such as our book *Android Wireless Application Development* (Addison-Wesley Developer's Library), which contains extensive examples using the Google APIs. You can read more about these classes on the Google APIs Add-On Reference website at http://code.google.com/android/add-ons/google-apis/maps-overview.html.

Summary

In this hour, you implemented a new Favorite Place feature on the Been There, Done That! settings screen. You learned how to use built-in location-based services to determine the last known location, as well as how to translate addresses into geographical coordinates using geocoding services. You also learned how to launch the Maps application via an `Intent` and view a specific location. Finally, you learned about some of the advanced features of the location-based services functionality available within the Android SDK.

Q&A

Q. *Where can I get GPS coordinates for my favorite locations?*

A. You can use Google Maps to determine GPS coordinates. To find a specific set of coordinates, go to http://maps.google.com and navigate to the location you desire. Center the map on the location by right-clicking the map and then choose the option to link to the map (usually in the top-right corner of the screen, above the map). Copy the link URL—which has the GPS coordinates as part of the query string—to a text file. Find the last ll query variable, which should represent the latitude and longitude of the location. For example, the west edge of Yellowstone Lake in Yellowstone National Park has the ll value 44.427896,-110.585632. The ll value 44.427896,-110.585632 stands for latitude 44.427896 and longitude -110.585632. You can double-check these coordinates by pasting them into Google Maps and seeing if the map pinpoints the same place location again.

Q. *I want to use the* `MapView` *control. Where do I get a Google API key?*

A. Start at the Google API add-ons website, which lists all the steps you need to follow to register for the key: http://code.google.com/android/add-ons/google-apis/mapkey.html. As part of this process, you need to set up a Google account if you do not have one already.

Q. *How do I design an application that needs more robust location information, such as an update when the location changes?*

A. There are a number of ways to design LBS applications. For starters, the `LocationManager` object enables you to register an activity for periodic updates of location information, including the ability to launch an intent when a specific location event occurs. Make sure you move all LBS tasks off the main UI thread, as they are time-intensive; use a worker thread, the `AsyncTask` class, or a background process instead. Also, only listen for location events when you must, to avoid performance issues on the device.

Workshop

Quiz

1. Developers need to consider which of the following when working with location-based services?

   A. The user's privacy

   B. The user's phone bill

   C. The device's battery life

   D. The accuracy and validity of the information provided by LBS and geocoding services

   E. The time it takes for location information to be resolved

   F. All of the above

2. True or False: In addition to the `Button` controls provided with `AlertDialog`, other `Button` controls can be used as part of a custom layout.

3. Which services are provided as part of the Android SDK?

   A. Location-based services

   B. Geocoding and reverse-geocoding services

   C. Mapping services

4. True or False: Because the emulator is not the real device, there is no way to use LBS on the emulator.

Answers

1. F. Developers need to take all these concerns into account when developing LBS-enabled applications.

2. True. `Button` controls included as part of a custom layout for a dialog are acceptable. You should provide the appropriate `View.OnClickListener` click handlers as part of the dialog-building process. Note that this is slightly different from the `DialogInterface.OnClickListener` click handlers required to handle the basic three dialog buttons available with `AlertDialog`.

3. A and B. The Android SDK includes support for LBS, geocoding, and reverse-geocoding. The services provided by specific devices vary. Mapping services are provided as part of the Google API add-on, not as part of the stock Android SDK, and require a special API key as well as a shared library.

4. False. The emulator provides limited support for LBS services (for some services, such as installing the Maps application, the Google add-on is needed), and DDMS can be used to transmit mock location data to the emulator.

Exercises

1. Modify the favorite place picker dialog to enable the user to configure the zoom level of the map shown. Recall that the zoom level is configured using the URL sent to the Maps application, as discussed earlier in this lesson.

2. Modify the Been There, Done That! application to save altitude information along with the latitude and longitude settings. To do this, add another application preference for this information, and store it when you collect the latitude and longitude information.

3. Consider what alternative functionality the application could provide in the case where a device has no LBS or geocoding services available.

4. **[Advanced]** Modify the favorite place picker dialog to take GPS latitude and longitude input instead of a string label for geocoding. You may need to update the Favorite Place picker dialog controls to make this change.

HOUR 15

Adding Basic Network Support

What You'll Learn in This Hour:

▶ Designing network applications
▶ Running tasks asynchronously
▶ Working with progress bars
▶ Downloading data from an application server

In the next two hours, you enable the Been There, Done That! application to handle two-way network communication. In this hour, you concentrate your attention on downloading data from the Internet. Specifically, you learn the theory and design principles for networked applications. You learn about threading and progress bars. Finally, you modify the Been There, Done That! application to retrieve batches of quiz questions and live score data from a remote application server.

Designing Network Applications

Although mobile devices have come a long way in terms of computing speed and data storage, servers can still provide valuable processing power for backing up data or for providing ease of data portability between devices or access to portions of larger datasets that can't be retained on the local device. By design, today's mobile devices can easily connect to networks, the Internet, and many rely upon cloud-based services.

Most Android devices can connect to the Internet in multiple ways, including through 3G (and beyond) networks or Wi-Fi connections. Android applications can use many of the most popular Internet protocols, including HTTP, HTTPS, TCP/IP, and raw sockets. The

Android SDK gives developers access to these communication protocols, provided that the application has the appropriate permissions.

Working with an Application Server

Network-enabled applications often rely on an application server. The application server provides centralized data storage (a database) and high-performance processing power. Using a centralized server also enables the developer to implement a single server side with access from multiple client applications. For example, you could easily write iPhone, BlackBerry, and web versions of the Been There, Done That! application that use the same back-end application server. Score and friend data could then be shared across multiple client environments easily.

We have developed a simple application server for use with this book and the Been There, Done That! application, for your use. There are many ways to develop an application server, the details of which are far beyond the scope of this book. However, we wanted to provide you with a comprehensive networking example, beyond that of connecting to some third-party web service like a weather feed or something to that effect. Instead, we provide you with a fully functional open source server implementation, which you can choose to explore, or not. The choice is yours; after all, you are reading this book to learn Android, so you might want to keep focused on the business at hand. However, some readers cannot help but want to know every detail. We've tried to provide for both types of learners.

Here are the basics. Our network server implementation leverages a very simple, scalable server powered by Google App Engine (http://code.google.com/appengine/) with Java and servlets. The Google App Engine technology stores information using a schema-less object datastore, with a query engine and support for atomic transactions. While the implementation details of the application server are beyond the scope of this book, it can be helpful to understand how it was designed. We provide the source code in open source form at http://goo.gl/F9Fx5.

Think of this application server as a black box with the following attributes:

▶ The application server is always on and available for users. It's not in our broom closet.

▶ The application server is ours. We don't have to worry about some third party changing its services without warning and breaking the code. Because we control it, we can keep it stable.

▶ The application server is remotely accessed via HTTP, perhaps the most common communication protocol used by Internet-connected devices these days.

▶ The application server stores data, such as player settings, scores, and trivia questions.

▶ The application server can be queried for information, such as top scores or batches of questions.

▶ The application server uses JavaServer Pages (JSP) to handle HTTP requests and return the appropriate results in the XML format that the Been There, Done That! application expects; that is, the same XML schema that the mock data uses.

You could create an application server that has different characteristics than the one described here. For example, you could create a SQL database-driven application server using MySQL and PHP instead, or you could use a number of other technologies. You could run it out of your broom closet, if you were so inclined. However, creating a network server from scratch isn't something we'd expect our readers to do. (Although, depending on your background, you might be more than proficient at this.) Therefore, feel free to use the network server we have provided for the network portions of the sample application; in truth, we recommend doing so. Again, we are not expecting you to develop your own network server for use with this book.

Managing Lengthy Network Operations

Connecting, downloading, parsing, displaying content...network operations can take time. If an operation takes too long, the Android operating system may shut down the offending application for lack of response (the dreaded "force close"). Therefore, all network-related calls should be handled asynchronously, separately from the main UI thread. You can accomplish this by using the Java Thread class or by using the Android AsyncTask class, which we discuss later in this hour.

Informing the User of Network Activity

In this hour, we focus on the simple task of querying the application server and retrieving the XML returned from the query. Networking support does not necessitate any specific user interface or layout updates to the Been There, Done That! application. However, any time the user is required to wait for an operation that might take time—for example, for XML data to be downloaded from a remote server and parsed—it is important to inform the user that something is happening. Developers can use a visual mechanism such as an indeterminate ProgressBar control for this purpose. Otherwise, the user might sit there wondering what's going on and even abandon the application, thinking it's hung or crashed.

Developing Network Applications

Developers who enable network support in their applications need to be aware of a number of issues and follow a number of guidelines. These issues are very similar to those faced when enabling Location-Based Services (LBS) features in an application. User privacy concerns, device performance degradation, and unwanted network data charges are all common issues to consider when developing network applications. Also, network connectivity (availability, strength, and quality) is not guaranteed, so enabling network support gives your application a variety of opportunities to fail, so you want to design your application to fail gracefully.

Android devices address some of these issues, in part through permissions, but much of the burden of managing the effects of network features and performance falls upon the developer. Here are some guidelines for developers leveraging network features within applications:

▶ Use network services only when they are needed and cache data locally whenever possible.

▶ Inform the user when collecting and using sensitive data, as appropriate.

▶ Allow the user to configure and disable features that might adversely affect his or her experience when using your application. For example, develop an airplane mode for your application to enable the user to enjoy your application without accessing a remote server.

▶ Gracefully handle events such as no network coverage. Your application is more valuable to the user if it is useful even without an Internet connection.

▶ Review your application's network functionality after your application is stable and make performance improvements.

▶ Consider including a privacy message as part of your application's terms of use. Use this opportunity to inform the user about what data is collected from the user, how it will and will not be used, and where it is stored (for example, on a remote application server).

Enabling Network Testing on the Emulator

You do not need to make any changes to the emulator to write network-enabled applications. The emulator uses the Internet connection provided by your development computer and simulates true network coverage. Also, the emulator has a number of settings for simulating network latency and network transfer speeds, which can give you a better idea of the actual experience a user would have. For details on the network debugging features of the emulator, see the Android emulator documentation.

> **Did you Know?**
>
> Because the emulator uses your desktop Internet connection, including any proxy server settings, it is likely to be higher speed than a true Android device Internet connection will be. Make sure to test networking code on the target hardware before release, just to be safe.

Testing Network Applications on Hardware

As usual, the best way to test network-enabled applications is on the target Android device. There are a number of network-related settings on an Android device. You configure these settings through the Settings application on the device:

▶ **Airplane Mode**—This mode blocks all network activity according to most in-flight regulations.

▶ **Wi-Fi**—There are a number of Wi-Fi settings for when wireless networks are available for use.

▶ **Mobile Networks**—There are several settings for handling data services when roaming.

> **By the Way**
>
> Most Android devices on the market at this time are Internet-enabled phones and tablets, but the Android platform is not limited to just mobile devices. Not every Android device is guaranteed to have network support, although it's generally a pretty safe bet that some form of access to the Internet will be available. Keep this fact in mind when making assumptions about how much your application relies on a network.

You can also find a lot of information about the services available on the device by clicking the Settings application from the application tray and choosing About Phone (or About Device) and then Status from the menus. Here, you find important phone service information, such as the following:

▶ Phone number (for example, 888-555-1212)

▶ Wireless network (for example, Verizon, T-Mobile)

▶ Network type (for example, CDMA EVDO rev. A, or EDGE)

▶ Signal strength (for example, -81 dBm 0 asu)

▶ Service state (for example, In service)

▶ Roaming state (for example, Roaming or Not roaming)

▶ Mobile network state (for example, Connected)

> You can cause a mobile device to lose its signal by placing it inside a cookie tin, refrigerator, microwave, or in any other shielded area. Doing so can be helpful for testing signal and network service loss. Just don't leave a handset in the cold too long, or you will drain the battery. And don't use the microwave with the phone inside (common sense for all!).

Accessing Network Services

The Android platform has a wide variety of networking libraries. Those accustomed to Java networking will find the `java.net` package familiar. There are also some helpful Android utility classes for various types of network operations and protocols. Developers can secure network communication by using common technologies such as SSL and HTTPS.

Planning Been There, Done That! Network Support

So far, you have supplied only mock XML data in the Been There, Done That! application. Now it's time to modify the application to contact a remote application server to get live data. To do this, you need to learn about the networking features available on the Android platform, as well as how to offload tasks from the main UI thread and execute them asynchronously.

Two classes of the Been There, Done That! application need to download information from an application:

▶ `QuizScoresActivity`—This class needs to download score information.

▶ `QuizGameActivity`—This class needs to download each batch of trivia questions.

To enable the Been There, Done That! application to handle live data, you need to access an application server as well as add networking functionality to the client Android application. The fully functional sample code for this lesson is provided on the accompanying CD and on the book websites. Feel free to follow along.

Setting Network Permissions

To access network services on an Android device, you must have the appropriate permissions. An Android application can use most networking services only if it is granted the appropriate <uses-permission> settings configured in the Android manifest file. The following are three of the most common permission values used by applications leveraging the network:

- ▶ android.permission.INTERNET

- ▶ android.permission.ACCESS_NETWORK_STATE

- ▶ android.permission.CHANGE_NETWORK_STATE

There are a number of other permissions related to networking, including those that allow access and changes to Wi-Fi state and network state. Some applications might also use the android.permission.WAKE_LOCK permission to keep the device from sleeping.

The Been There, Done That! application does not require many network permissions in order to complete its networking tasks. The android.permission.INTERNET permission suffices.

Checking Network Status

The Android SDK provides utilities for gathering information about the current state of a network. This is useful for determining whether a network connection is available before trying to use a network resource. By validating network connectivity before attempting to make a connection, you can avoid many of the failure cases common in mobile device networking applications and provide your end users with a more pleasant user experience.

Retrieving Network Status Information Programmatically

Applications need to register the android.permission.ACCESS_NETWORK_STATE permission in the Android manifest file to read the network status of the device. To alter the network state of the device, the application must also have the android.permission.CHANGE_NETWORK_STATE permission.

Developers can leverage the ConnectivityManager class (android.net.ConnectivityManager) to access network status information about the device programmatically. You can get an instance of ConnectivityManager by using the familiar getSystemService() method of the application's Context object within your Activity class, like this:

```
ConnectivityManager conMgr = (ConnectivityManager)
    getSystemService(Context.CONNECTIVITY_SERVICE);
```

When you have a valid instance of ConnectivityManager, you can request the mobile (cellular) network information by using the getNetworkInfo() method:

```
NetworkInfo netInfo =
    conMgr.getNetworkInfo(ConnectivityManager.TYPE_MOBILE);
```

The NetworkInfo class (android.net.NetworkInfo) has a number of methods for retrieving important information about the network state, including whether the network is available, connected, and roaming:

```
boolean isMobileAvail = netInfo.isAvailable();
boolean isMobileConn = netInfo.isConnected();
boolean isRoamingConn = netInfo.isRoaming();
```

The NetworkInfo class also has many other methods for determining fine-grained network status information. Developers can use this information to modify application behavior in certain situations. For example, you might not want to initiate length downloads when the device user is roaming.

Checking Server Availability Programmatically

Even if a network is available and connected, there is no guarantee that the remote server you want to communicate with is accessible from the network. However, ConnectivityManager has a handy method called requestRouteToHost() that enables you to attempt to validate traffic, using a given network type (for example, mobile network, Wi-Fi) and IP address. This method acts as a sort of programmatic ping.

Using HTTP Networking

The most common network transfer protocol is Hypertext Transfer Protocol (HTTP). Most commonly used HTTP ports are open and available for use on Android device networks.

A fast way to get to a network resource is by retrieving a stream object to the content. Many Android data interfaces accept stream objects. One such example you should now be somewhat familiar with is XmlPullParser. The setInput() method of XmlPullParser class takes an InputStream object. Previously, you retrieved this stream from the XML resources. Now, however, you can get it from a network resource, using the simple URL class, as shown here:

```
URL xmlUrl = new URL("http://...xmlSourcepath...");
XmlPullParser questionBatch =
    XmlPullParserFactory.newInstance().newPullParser();
questionBatch.setInput(xmlUrl.openStream(), null);
```

That's it. The only magic here is determining what URL to use; in this case, the network server has a specially formatted URL for question batches (http://tqs. mamlambo.com/questions.jsp) and another for score data (http://tqs.mamlambo. com/scores.jsp).

After the appropriate URL is formatted and the XMLPullParser is created, the parsing of the XML remains unchanged, as the format is no different and the XmlResourceParser used previously was derived from the XmlPullParser class. After you have the question batches and score data downloading from the remote server, you can remove the mock XML resources from the project and the code that retrieves the XML resources.

Indicating Network Activity with Progress Bars

Network-enabled applications often perform lengthy tasks, such as connecting to remote servers and downloading and parsing data. These tasks take time, and the user should be aware that these activities are taking place. As discussed earlier in this lesson, a great way to indicate that an application is busy doing something is to show some sort of progress indicator. The Android SDK provides two basic styles of the ProgressBar control to handle determinate and indeterminate progress.

Displaying Indeterminate Progress

The simplest ProgressBar control style is a circular indicator that animates. This kind of progress bar does not show progress, per se, but informs the user that something is happening. Use this style of progress bar when the length of the background processing time is indeterminate.

Displaying Determinate Progress

When you need to inform the user of specific milestones in progress, use the determinate progress bar control. This control displays as a horizontal progress bar that can be updated to show incremental progress toward completion. To use this progress indicator, use the setProgress() method of the ProgressBar control.

As described later in this hour, you can put progress bars in the application's title bar. This can save valuable screen space. You often see this technique used on screens that display web content.

Displaying Progress Dialogs

To indicate progress in a dialog window, as opposed to adding a `ProgressBar` control to the layout of an existing screen, use the special `Dialog` class called `ProgressDialog`. For example, use `ProgressDialog` windows (see Figure 15.1) in the Been There, Done That! application to inform the user that data is being downloaded and parsed before displaying the appropriate screen of the application.

FIGURE 15.1
Informing the user that trivia questions are being downloaded.

Here is the code needed to programmatically create and display the `ProgressDialog` class:

```
ProgressDialog pleaseWaitDialog = ProgressDialog.show(
    QuizGameActivity.this,
    "Trivia Quiz",
    "Downloading trivia questions…",
    true);
```

Use the `dismiss()` method to dismiss `pleaseWaitDialog` control when the background processing has completed:

```
pleaseWaitDialog.dismiss();
```

By the Way

The pleaseWaitDialog control can be cancelled by the user if a fifth parameter is added to the show() method and set to true. In this case, we don't allow the user to cancel the dialog because we want it showing during the entire download. In the example code, which shows the final results for this hour, you see we do allow it to be cancelled, and you can read about it later in this hour.

Now you know how to create progress bars and display them in dialog windows using ProgressDialog control. Because the indicated progress is actually taking place asynchronously, it's time to turn our attention to background processing.

Running Tasks Asynchronously

Despite rapidly evolving technology, mobile wireless networks still provide relatively slow Internet connections compared to those found in personal computers. Your Android applications must be responsive, so you should always move all network operations off the main UI thread and onto a secondary, "worker," thread. The Android platform provides two easy methods for achieving this:

▶ AsyncTask—You can use this abstract class to offload background operations from the UI thread easily. Operations are managed by this helper class, making it the most straightforward for beginners and those not familiar with Java threading.

▶ Thread and Handler—You can use these classes together to handle concurrent processing and communicating with the UI thread's message queue. This advanced method allows more flexibility in terms of implementation, but you, as the developer, are responsible for managing thread operations appropriately.

For the Been There, Done That! application, the AsyncTask class is most appropriate because it's the most straightforward to implement.

Using AsyncTask

The Android SDK includes the AsyncTask class (android.os.AsyncTask) to help manage background operations that will eventually post back to the UI thread.

Instead of using handlers and creating threads, you can simply create a subclass of the AsyncTask class and implement the appropriate callback methods:

▶ onPreExecute()—This method runs on the UI thread before background processing begins.

▶ doInBackground()—This method runs in the background and is where all the real work is done.

▶ publishProgress()—This method, called from the doInBackground() method, periodically informs the UI thread about the background process progress. This method sends information to the UI process. Use this opportunity to send updated progress for a progress bar that the user can see.

▶ onProgressUpdate()—This method runs on the UI thread whenever the doInBackground() method calls publishProgress(). This method receives information from the background process. Use this opportunity to update a ProgressBar control that the user can see.

▶ onPostExecute()—This method runs on the UI thread once the background processing is completed.

When launched with the execute() method, the AsyncTask class handles processing in a background thread without blocking the UI thread.

Using Threads and Handlers

If you need to control a thread yourself, use the Thread class (java.lang.Thread) in conjunction with a Handler object (android.os.Handler). The Activity class that owns the thread is responsible for managing the lifecycle of the thread. Generally speaking, the Activity includes a member variable of type Handler. Then, when the Thread is instantiated and started, the post() method of the Handler is used to communicate with the main UI thread.

Downloading and Displaying Score Data

Let's begin by creating an asynchronous task for downloading the score data sets on the Been There, Done That! scores screen. Because the top scores and friends' scores data is very similar, there's no reason not to create just one kind of AsyncTask class to handle both types of downloads. You can then create two instances of the task: one for top scores, and another for friends' scores. This process involves extending the AsyncTask class, implementing the appropriate callbacks, creating two instances of the task (top scores and friends' scores) and then starting those tasks.

The network server has a JSP page for handling score requests. Define the appropriate URL strings in your `QuizActivity` class for use in the appropriate activities. For example

```
public static final String TRIVIA_SERVER_BASE = "http://tqs.mamlambo.com/";
public static final String TRIVIA_SERVER_SCORES = TRIVIA_SERVER_BASE +
➥ "scores.jsp";
```

This JSP page can take one parameter, when necessary: the user's player identifier. This identifier, which is stored on the network server in the next lesson, helps the network server filter to the player's friends' scores. For this lesson, you should supply a player identifier of 1. In the next hour, you flesh out this feature and are able to query for your own data. So, for example, to get the top scores, you would use the following URL for your query:

```
http://tqs.mamlambo.com/scores.jsp
```

Whereas, if you wanted the user's friends' scores, you would tack on the `?playerId=` query variable, with the player identifier, like this:

```
http://tqs.mamlambo.com/scores.jsp?playerId=2008
```

Extending AsyncTask **for Score Downloads**

Now let's work through the steps required to create an `AsyncTask` within the `QuizScoresActivity` class to handle the downloading and parsing of XML score information. Begin by creating a inner class within `QuizScoresActivity` called `ScoreDownloaderTask`, which extends the `AsyncTask` class within the `QuizScoresActivity` class:

```
private class ScoreDownloaderTask extends AsyncTask<Object, String, Boolean> {
    private static final String DEBUG_TAG = "ScoreDownloaderTask";
    TableLayout table;

    // TODO: Implement AsyncTask callback methods
}
```

Because you are populating a `TableLayout` control as part of this background task, it makes sense to add a handy member variable within `ScoreDownloaderTask` as well. While you're at it, override the `DEBUG_TAG` string so that events logged within the asynchronous task have a unique tag in LogCat.

At this time, you can also move the XML parsing helper methods from the `QuizScoresActivity` class, such as the `processScores()` and `insertScoreRow()`, to the `ScoreDownloaderTask` class. This allows all XML parsing and processing to occur within the asynchronous task instead of on the main thread. You should leave the `initializeHeaderRow()` and `addTextToRowWithValues()` methods in the `QuizScoresActivity` class, as they may be used even if the scores cannot be downloaded.

Finally, create two member variables within the `QuizScoresActivity` class to represent the two score sets to download:

```
ScoreDownloaderTask allScoresDownloader;
ScoreDownloaderTask friendScoresDownloader;
```

Starting the Progress Indicator with onPreExecute()

Next, you need to implement the `onPreExecute()` callback method of your `ScoreDownloaderTask` class, which runs on the UI thread before background processing begins. This is the perfect place to demonstrate adding an indeterminate progress indicator to the title bar:

```
@Override
protected void onPreExecute() {
    mProgressCounter++;
    QuizScoresActivity.this.setProgressBarIndeterminateVisibility(true);
}
```

There are two tabs of scores. Each tab's scores are downloaded separately, and you want the progress indicator to display until both are complete. Thus, you should create a counter member variable at the `QuizScoresActivity` class level (not the `ScoreDownloaderTask` level) called `mProgressCounter`, to track each download. In this way, you could add any number of tabs, and the indicator would still show and disappear at the correct time.

In order to use an indeterminate progress bar on the title bar of your screen, you need to add the following code to the `onCreate()` method of the `QuizScoresActivity`:

```
requestWindowFeature(Window.FEATURE_INDETERMINATE_PROGRESS);
```

You must call this method before you call the `setContentView()` method.

Clearing the Progress Indicator with onPostExecute()

Next, implement the `onPostExecute()` callback method, which runs on the UI thread after background processing completes. Specifically, when you have completed all parsing and displaying, you can hide the progress indicator shown in the title bar if all the tasks are complete, as determined by the mProgressCounter variable:

```
@Override
protected void onPostExecute(Boolean result) {
    Log.i(DEBUG_TAG, "onPostExecute");
    mProgressCounter--;
    if (mProgressCounter <= 0) {
        mProgressCounter = 0;
        QuizScoresActivity.this.
            setProgressBarIndeterminateVisibility(false);
    }
}
```

Again, all this callback does is decrement the counter and terminate the progress indicator, if necessary.

Handling Cancellation with onCancelled()

You can handle cancellation of the background processing by overriding the onCancelled() callback method. The onCancelled() method runs on the UI thread and, if it's called, it means that the onPostExecute() method is not called. Thus, any cleanup must be performed here. For this example, we perform the following operation:

```
@Override
protected void onCancelled() {
    Log.i(DEBUG_TAG, "onCancelled");
    mProgressCounter--;
    if (mProgressCounter <= 0) {
        mProgressCounter = 0;
        QuizScoresActivity.this.
            setProgressBarIndeterminateVisibility(false);
    }
}
```

The onCancelled() method is called when the cancel() method of AsyncTask is called. This does not happen automatically. Instead, good practice is for the Activity that owns the asynchronous task to cancel tasks when they are no longer needed. For the scores screen, you want to cancel the tasks if they're still running when the user leaves the screen for any reason. That is, you cancel them in the onPause() callback method of the QuizScoresActivity class, as shown here:

```
@Override
protected void onPause() {
    if (allScoresDownloader != null &&
        allScoresDownloader.getStatus() !=
        AsyncTask.Status.FINISHED) {
        allScoresDownloader.cancel(true);
    }
```

```
if (friendScoresDownloader != null &&
        friendScoresDownloader.getStatus() !=
        AsyncTask.Status.FINISHED) {
        friendScoresDownloader.cancel(true);
    }
    super.onPause();
}
```

Handling Processing with doInBackground()

Now it is time to identify what processing should run asynchronously. For this
example, it is the downloading and parsing of some XML from a network server.
Override the doInBackground() callback method, which is where all the background processing takes place. Any methods called within doInBackground() do
not block the main UI thread. Here's a sample implementation of the
doInBackground() method, with exception handling removed for clarity:

```
@Override
protected Boolean doInBackground(Object... params) {
    boolean result = false;
    String pathToScores = (String) params[0];
    table = (TableLayout) params[1];
    XmlPullParser scores = null;
    URL xmlUrl = new URL(pathToScores);
    scores = XmlPullParserFactory.newInstance().newPullParser();
    scores.setInput(xmlUrl.openStream(), null);
    if (scores != null) {
        processScores(scores);
    }
    return result;
}
```

Here we use the flexible incoming parameters to supply the appropriate URL to the
scores we want to download (top or friends). This string is used to generate the
appropriate URL to the application server and then an XMLPullParser is used to
download the score data and parse it, as discussed earlier in this lesson.

You now need to make one subtle change to the processScores() helper method,
which simply takes the XmlPullParser and parses the XML, to publish scores as
they are parsed within the task, using the publishProgress() method:

```
private void processScores(XmlPullParser scores)
    throws XmlPullParserException, IOException {
    int eventType = -1;
    boolean bFoundScores = false;

    // Find Score records from XML
    while (eventType != XmlResourceParser.END_DOCUMENT) {
        if (eventType == XmlResourceParser.START_TAG) {

            // Get the name of the tag (eg scores or score)
```

```
            String strName = scores.getName();

            if (strName.equals("score")) {
                bFoundScores = true;
                String scoreValue =
                    scores.getAttributeValue(null, "score");
                String scoreRank =
                    scores.getAttributeValue(null, "rank");
                String scoreUserName =
                    scores.getAttributeValue(null, "username");
                publishProgress(scoreValue, scoreRank, scoreUserName);
            }
        }
        eventType = scores.next();
    }

    // Handle no scores available
    if (bFoundScores == false) {
        publishProgress();
    }
}
```

The publishProgress() method can be called anytime within the doInBackground() method to cause the onProgressUpdate() callback method to be called. This allows the background process to communicate with the UI thread which can publish updates to the screen, whereas the background task cannot directly act upon the screen. Now let's implement the onProgressUpdate() callback method.

Handling Progress Updates with onProgressUpdate()

You can update the UI thread with background progress information by overriding the onProgressUpdate() callback method of the ScoreDownloaderTask class. This method enables you to display score data as it is parsed, instead of parsing all score data and then displaying it all in one go when the asynchronous task is completed. Users appreciate this, because, as you may have noticed, users are impatient.

Update the onProgressUpdate() method at this time. Pass in the new score just parsed using the flexible method parameters and insert a new row in the score TableLayout control, like this:

```
@Override
protected void onProgressUpdate(String... values) {
    if (values.length == 3) {
        String scoreValue = values[0];
        String scoreRank = values[1];
        String scoreUserName = values[2];
        insertScoreRow(table, scoreValue, scoreRank, scoreUserName);
    } else {
```

```
        final TableRow newRow =
            new TableRow(QuizScoresActivity.this);
        TextView noResults =
            new TextView(QuizScoresActivity.this);
        noResults.setText(
            getResources().getString(R.string.no_scores));
        newRow.addView(noResults);
        table.addView(newRow);
    }
}
```

The insertScoreRow() method simply creates a new TableRow control and adds it to the TableLayout control. The array of values must be passed in the same order each time. This is because of how the AsyncTask Java template works.

Starting the ScoreDownloaderTask

The ScoreDownloaderTask class is now complete. Now you just need to launch it. Do this by updating the onCreate() method of the QuizScoresActivity class to call the ScoreDownloaderTask class's execute() method when the screen first loads. The execute() method takes two parameters: the server web address and the table to populate with scores (a TableLayout control, as defined in the tabs):

```
public static final String TRIVIA_SERVER_BASE =
    "http://tqs.mamlambo.com/";
public static final String TRIVIA_SERVER_SCORES =
    TRIVIA_SERVER_BASE + "scores.jsp";
// ...
allScoresDownloader =
    new ScoreDownloaderTask();
allScoresDownloader.execute(TRIVIA_SERVER_SCORES, allScoresTable);

Integer playerId = 2008;

if (playerId != -1) {
    friendScoresDownloader = new ScoreDownloaderTask();
    friendScoresDownloader.execute(
        TRIVIA_SERVER_SCORES + "?playerId="
        + playerId, friendScoresTable);
}
```

Here we are doing a couple of things: We define the network server URL to use for downloading scores. We instantiate the two ScoreDownloaderTask instances, one for top scores and the other for friends' scores. We then call the execute() method for each task. Don't worry too much about the playerId value just yet. We discuss that next hour when you begin saving player data to the server. The player identifier is needed so that the appropriate friends' scores are downloaded. For now, feel free to use a player identifier with a value of 2008 to guarantee downloads from one of the test accounts on the server.

Downloading and Parsing Question Batches

Now that you understand how to download data asynchronously, you can use the AsyncTask again within the QuizGameActivity to handle downloading and displaying the question batches on the game screen. This process is very similar to the process involved in downloading score data. However, you do not publish progress as you go; instead, you simply display a progress bar until all questions in a given batch are downloaded.

The network server has a JSP page for handling question batch requests. Define the appropriate URL strings in your QuizActivity class for use in the appropriate activities. For example:

```
public static final String TRIVIA_SERVER_BASE = "http://tqs.mamlambo.com/";
public static final String TRIVIA_SERVER_QUESTIONS = TRIVIA_SERVER_BASE +
➥ "questions.jsp";
```

This JSP page can take two parameters: The max parameter specifies the question batch size and the start parameter specifies the starting question number to retrieve. Using these two values, you can request the "next" batch of questions, depending on where the user is in the quiz. The query parameters must be specified in this order. So, for example, to query for 15 questions starting at question number 16, you would use the following URL for your query:

```
http://tqs.mamlambo.com/questions.jsp?max=15&start=16
```

Extending AsyncTask for Question Downloads

Begin by creating an inner class called QuizTask within the QuizGameActivity class that extends the AsyncTask class, like this:

```
private class QuizTask extends AsyncTask<Object, String, Boolean> {
    private static final String DEBUG_TAG = "QuizGameActivity$QuizTask";
    int startingNumber;
    ProgressDialog pleaseWaitDialog;
    // TODO: Implement AsyncTask callback methods
}
```

The QuizTask class requires several member variables, including its own custom debug tag, the starting question number and a ProgressDialog to display background processing progress to the user when necessary.

Starting the Progress Dialog with onPreExecute()

Now you need to implement the onPreExecute() callback method. This is the perfect place to display a progress dialog that tells the user that the trivia questions are being downloaded. The user isn't able to do anything until the questions are downloaded. Although you put the indicator in the title bar when downloading the scores earlier, this time put a progress dialog over the game screen:

```
@Override
protected void onPreExecute() {
    pleaseWaitDialog = ProgressDialog.show(
        QuizGameActivity.this, "Trivia Quiz",
        "Downloading trivia questions", true, true);
    pleaseWaitDialog.setOnCancelListener(new OnCancelListener() {
        public void onCancel(DialogInterface dialog) {
            QuizTask.this.cancel(true);
        }
    });
}
```

Although we've used hardcoded strings here for clarity, a well-written application uses string resources for easy localization. A cancel listener is configured for the dialog. This enables the user to press the back button to cancel the dialog. When this happens, the cancel() method of the AsyncTask is called. This means that cancelling the dialog now cancels the task, which cancels the network activity.

Dismissing the Progress Dialog with onPostExecute()

Next, implement the onPostExecute() method. Now that the background processing has taken place, drop in the code you originally used to display the screen. This is also the perfect place to dismiss the progress dialog:

```
@Override
protected void onPostExecute(Boolean result) {
    Log.d(DEBUG_TAG, "Download task complete.");
    if (result) {
        displayCurrentQuestion(startingNumber);
    } else {
        handleNoQuestions();
    }

    pleaseWaitDialog.dismiss();
}
```

You also need to handle the cancel operation by implementing the onCancelled() callback method of the QuizTask class as well as the onPause() callback of the QuizGameActivity class, much as you did for the scores implementation.

Handling the Background Processing

Now you need to identify what processing should run asynchronously. Again, this is the downloading and parsing code. The following code (with exception handling removed for clarity) shows how to override the doInBackground() callback method:

```
@Override
protected Boolean doInBackground(String... params) {
    boolean result = false;
    startingNumber = (Integer)params[1];
    String pathToQuestions = params[0] +
        "?max=" + QUESTION_BATCH_SIZE + "&start=" + startingNumber;
    result = loadQuestionBatch(startingNumber, pathToQuestions);
    return result;
}
```

Here, the background processing simply involves determining the appropriate question batch to download and calling the helper method loadQuestionBatch(). We use the flexible parameters of the doInBackground() callback method to pass in the max and start criteria. You should move the loadQuestionBatch() method from QuizGameActivity into the QuizTask class and modify it to contact the application server at the appropriate URL. Again, this is simply a matter of generating the appropriate URL parameters, opening the stream to the remote application server, and using the XmlPullParser to process the XML data as before. The parsing details remain unchanged. Unlike the scores implementation, there is no need to post progress for this task.

Starting QuizTask

After you've implemented the QuizTask class, you can update the onCreate() method of the QuizGameActivity class to call the execute() method of the QuizTask class when the screen first loads. In this case, the execute() method takes two parameters: the server web address for question downloads and the starting question number (an Integer) for the batch to download:

```
QuizTask downloader = new QuizTask();
downloader.execute(TRIVIA_SERVER_QUESTIONS, startingQuestionNumber)
```

For the full implementation of the quiz question download task, including some code rearranging and cleanup, please see the sample code provided on the accompanying CD and the book websites.

Summary

In this hour, you modified the Been There, Done That! application to download data, including the quiz question batches and user scores, from a remote application server. You learned how to use the AsyncTask class to handle background processing and keep your application responsive. You also learned about many of the issues to be aware of when developing network-enabled mobile applications. Think of this hour as mastering the "building blocks" of networked applications. The next hour deepens your knowledge in this area and helps you to broaden the network support of the Been There, Done That! application.

Q&A

Q. *What is the optimum batch size for downloads?*

A. This is a tricky question. The short answer is: not so much data that the user is tapping his or her foot, waiting for the application to run, but enough so that the user doesn't have to wait for downloads too often. Ideally, all downloading would take place behind the scenes, while the user is doing something else, such as answering the questions that have downloaded.

Q. *Where can I find out more about the network protocol support available on the Android platform?*

A. Three good networking packages to browse within the Android SDK are android.net, java.net, and org.apache.

Q. *Can I easily display HTML content within my app?*

A. If your application needs to retrieve and display web content such as HTML, you can use the WebView control, which leverages the WebKit rendering engine to render HTML content onscreen. The WebView control can display local or remote sourced content.

Q. *What is a loader?*

A. The Loader class (android.content.Loader) was introduced in Android 3.0, (API Level 11, also known as Honeycomb). Loaders allow for easy asynchronous loading of data needed by an Activity. They also allow for the data to more easily persist across activity changes, such as when the screen rotates. Although introduced in API Level 11, they are available via the compatibility library for Android API Levels 4 and above. For more information, see the Android documentation on loaders at: http://goo.gl/VRCP0.

Workshop

Quiz

1. Where can you find out information about an Android handset's network status?

   A. On the status bar

   B. In the Android Settings application

   C. By calling the `getHandsetNetworkStatus()` method of the `NetStatus` class

2. True or False: The Android emulator cannot simulate network speed and latency similar to that found on real Android devices.

3. True or False: You must use Google App Engine for Android application servers.

4. Which of the following is a not a network protocol or technology that Android can use?

   A. HTTP

   B. HTTPS

   C. TCP

   D. IP

   E. Raw Sockets (RS)

Answers

1. A and B. Some basic information about the device's network status is indeed shown on the status bar, but you can get detailed network status information from the Android Settings application.

2. False. The Android emulator has a number of settings for simulating network speed and latency.

3. False. You can use any server technology standard you want to implement an application server to interact with the Android application. Google App Engine is only one of many such technologies.

4. Trick question! All of the listed protocols or network technologies can be used within Android applications. HTTP and HTTPS can be used for web technologies. TCP and IP are lower level network protocols used by Android and there are standard Java APIs for direct network socket use.

Exercises

1. Test the Been There, Done That! application in a variety of network situations using the emulator. Modify the emulator settings to simulate a slow network and then run the application and view the results.

2. Test the Been There, Done That! application in a variety of network situations using a device. Modify the device network settings (Airplane mode or try the cookie tin trick) and then run the application and view the results.

3. **[Advanced]** Modify the application to use the Thread and Handler methods for background processing instead of the AsyncTask method.

HOUR 16

Adding Additional Network Features

What You'll Learn in This Hour:

▶ Using Android services
▶ Using HTTP client services
▶ Performing HTTP GET and HTTP POST requests
▶ Adding third-party JAR files to your project
▶ Working with multipart MIME files

In this hour, you enhance the Been There, Done That! application to upload player data such as settings, scores, and avatars to the application server. You learn how to upload data to a network server, as well as a new way to offload important processing to a simple service that executes in the background. Finally, you learn how to add some external libraries to an Android project and work with multipart MIME entities.

Determining What Data to Send to the Server

So far, you have only downloaded data from the network server within the Been There, Done That! application. Now it's time to upload player information to the application server, creating a new account if necessary. To do this, you need to learn how to use the Apache HTTP client features available on the Android platform, as well as how to add extra Apache libraries to the project—libraries that aren't available with the Android SDK.

Three features of the Been There, Done That! application require uploading data to the application server or use related player data to retrieve the appropriate results:

▶ `QuizSettingsActivity`—This class needs to create a player record on the application server and upload player settings information, including the nickname, email address, and avatar information. This is a one-way upload, primarily because this is just a sample application. Some data is later used during score retrieval and the friend feature introduced in a later hour.

▶ `QuizGameActivity`—This class needs to upload the player's score. The player's score information is compiled with other players' data to compute the top scores and friends' scores data.

▶ `QuizScoresActivity`—This class needs to be updated to use a valid player identifier to retrieve friends' scores (even though we don't implement the friend feature until next hour).

The complete implementation of the sample code for this hour is provided on the CD that accompanies this book, or on the book's website. You might want to follow along.

Keeping Player Data in Sync

The Been There, Done That! application must be kept simple. Some of the player settings are uploaded to the application server, and others are only important to the application client. The application server needs to be able to track usage and installations. Therefore, the application must generate a unique identifier, store it, and send it with each request. The first time the server sees a new player it generates a player identifier and sends it down to the client. The player's identifier is the key upon which many features hinge: the ability to update the appropriate record on the server, the ability to retrieve the appropriate player's friends' scores, and the ability to tie a player name to a specific score.

There are many ways to create unique identifiers. One way is to use the `randomUUID()` method of the `UUID` class (`java.util.UUID`), like so:

```
String uniqueId = UUID.randomUUID().toString();
```

This method is preferable to some others, such as determining the device ID through the `TelephonyManager`, because it returns a valid identifier, regardless of whether the device is a smartphone, tablet, or Android-powered toaster. It also works on all versions of the Android SDK, unlike using the `Settings.Secure.ANDROID_ID` value that wasn't introduced until Android 2.2.

The next question is how to keep two copies of player data—the application shared preferences copy and the network server copy—in sync. For your simple application, you can keep the data "synchronized" by simply designating the application's version of the data as the "primary source," and the network server's version as a "read-only copy." In other words, you synchronize player data one-way only—from the application to the network server—but not in reverse. This helps avoid some of the design complexity of managing the player data. If you were to improve the application to allow the player to have multiple clients (different devices, web clients, and so on) then you would need to revisit and improve the data synchronization technique used by the application.

Uploading Settings Data to a Remote Server

In the previous hour, you learned how to use the AsyncTask class to handle downloading of data from the network server. In this hour, it's time to turn your attention to uploading data, including the player settings and current score, to the network server. These goals are best achieved in the following order:

1. Begin with the Settings screen and implement the functionality to generate a unique identifier for the player, and then upload and create a valid player record on the network server. This code is more complex than the simple network downloads of the previous hour.

2. After a valid player record with a unique identifier as been created, update the Game screen to send score data up to the server at regular intervals. As you have already generated an AsyncTask that routinely contacts the network server, adding this feature is trivial.

3. Update the Scores screen to retrieve the appropriate player's friend data by changing the hardcoded player identifier to the one stored in the application preferences. This is a trivial change.

As you can see, creating the valid player record is vital for all the other features to work properly. It is also the most complex feature and the basis of most of the work in this hour. In Hour 10, "Building Forms to Collect User Input," you began creating the settings screen and storing application data in SharedPreferences. Now you update the QuizSettingsActivity class to transmit the player settings to the server (in addition to storing it in SharedPreferences).

One fundamental difference between the networking features of the previous hour and the creation of the settings screen is the workflow. For the Game screen and the Scores screen, the user launched the appropriate activity, downloaded the data, and then used it. For the settings screen, the user launches the activity and sets any number of settings, which are immediately saved to the application preferences. You need to decide when it's the appropriate time to send all that information to the network server. You could send data piecemeal, each and every time there was a change, but that's not terribly efficient. Ideally, you want to send the data up to the server when the user is done entering any data he or she desires on the screen.

This is where things get a bit tricky. You might be tempted to add a little Button control to the screen to enable the user to initiate the network upload. This is not really the Android way. Instead, the user should be able to mosey on through the application at will. So perhaps you might consider launching an asynchronous task when the activity is winding down, such as in the onPause() or onDestroy() methods within the activity life cycle. You'd be on the right track. However, there's one problem: The AsyncTask class belongs to the activity and is therefore bound by the activity's lifecycle. In other words, when the activity goes away, you end up leaking the AsyncTask, as it cannot exist outside the activity.

What you really need is a way to spawn a background process that can live outside the activity. The Android SDK provides a mechanism for just this purpose, called an Android service.

Working with Android Services

A Service object is created by extending the Service class (android.app.Service) and defining the service within the AndroidManifest.xml file. The life cycle of a Service is different from that of an Activity class. Because you need a very simple service for the settings screen, this hour does not explore the complete life cycle of a service. However, generally speaking, the onCreate() method is called, followed by either the onStartCommand() or onBind() methods, depending on the type of service and how it was started. When the service is finished, either because it completed—and perhaps called the stopSelf() method—or because there is no process bound to it, the onDestroy() method is called.

So let's jump in and just create a service. What you want: a simple service to be used by the QuizSettingsActivity class to asynchronously upload player settings to the network server. For simplicity, you can give the service an AsyncTask class to encapsulate the networking code, much as we've done in previous occasions. The difference: The service runs the task, as opposed to the activity. This way, the service might do other things in the future, should you desire it to.

To create a service in the `QuizSettingsActivity` class, take the following steps:

1. Edit the `QuizSettingsActivity` class and add an inner class called `UploaderService`. This class should extend the `Service` class.

2. Create an inner class within the `UploaderService` called `UploadTask`. The `UploadTask` class should extend the `AsyncTask` class, much as you have seen in previous examples. This asynchronous task retrieves the application shared preferences, generates a unique identifier if the player record does not already exist, packages up the settings, and sends them off to the network server.

3. Give the `UploaderService` two member variables: a custom `DEBUG_TAG` for service-specific logging purposes and an `UploadTask` variable for the asynchronous task.

4. Override the `onStartCommand()` method of the `UploaderService` class. Have this method instantiate the `UploadTask` member variable and call the `execute()` method to start the task. Have this method return `START_REDELIVER_INTENT` so that the service only remains running for the duration of its current task.

5. Override the `onBind()` method of the `UploaderService` class to return `null`. No binding is required for this simple service.

After you have implemented the service, you must register it before it can be used. To register the service, update the Android manifest file for the project. The XML for this change would look like this:

```
<service android:name="QuizSettingsActivity$UploaderService"></service>
```

The resulting UploaderService class looks like this:

```
public static class UploaderService extends Service {
    private static final String DEBUG_TAG =
"QuizSettingsActivity$UploaderService";
    private UploadTask uploader;

    @Override
    public int onStartCommand(Intent intent, int flags, int startId) {
        uploader = new UploadTask();
        uploader.execute();
        Log.d(DEBUG_TAG, "Settings and image upload requested");
        return START_REDELIVER_INTENT;
    }

    @Override
    public IBinder onBind(Intent intent) {
        return null;
    }

    private class UploadTask extends AsyncTask<Object, String, Boolean> {
```

```
    // UPLOADTASK IMPLEMENTATION HERE
  }
}
```

You can then launch the `UploaderService` in the `onPause()` method of the `QuizSettingsActivity` class, like this:

```
Intent uploadService = new
Intent(getApplicationContext(),UploaderService.class);
startService(uploadService);
```

Implementing UploadTask

To communicate with the application server, you can leverage the `HttpClient` package (`org.apache.http`) included in the Android SDK. This package provides utilities for handling a variety of HTTP networking scenarios within your application. You can use `HttpGet` to post query variables in the same way a web form submission works, using the `HTTP GET` method, and you can use `HttpPost` to post form variables and upload the avatar graphic, in the same way a web form might use the `HTTP POST` method.

The application server was written with HTML web forms in mind. In fact, the server was tested using a standard HTML form before the Android client was written. By developing a web client before the Android client, you ensure that the client/server communication protocols used are standard and cross-platform compatible. When you use this procedure, you know that any platform—including Android—that can handle web form–style `HTTP GET` and `HTTP POST` methods is compatible with this application server. This way, the application can rely on the Apache HTTP libraries—primarily the `org.apache.http.client` package.

The `UploadTask` class is implemented much like the other asynchronous tasks you've already completed. It has a member variable of type `SharedPreferences` to access the application preferences. The `onPreExecute()` method retrieves the preferences. The bulk of the interesting part of the task involves the `doInBackground()` method, as usual. This method is broken down into two subtasks: uploading the primitive settings data using an `HTTP GET`, and uploading the avatar graphic using an `HTTP POST`. These subtasks are encapsulated in two helper methods we create, called `postSettingsToServer()` and `postAvatarToServer()`:

```
@Override
protected Boolean doInBackground(Object... params) {
    boolean result = postSettingsToServer();
    if (result && !isCancelled()) {
        result = postAvatarToServer();
    }
    Log.d(DEBUG_TAG, "Done uploading settings and image");
    return result;
}
```

Uploading Player Data with the HTTP GET Method

The primitive player data—that is the unique identifier, the nickname, the email, the password, the score, the gender, the birth date and the favorite place—is submitted to the application server by using the HTTP GET method via the HttpClient and HttpGet classes. To enable this feature, you need to take the following steps:

1. Begin by adding new shared preferences values to the QuizActivity class for the player's identifier and unique identifier. Also, add a definition for the network server URL for adding or editing player data on the server. This might look like the following.

   ```
   public static final String GAME_PREFERENCES_PLAYER_ID = "ServerId";
   public static final String GAME_PREFERENCES_UNIQUE_ID = "ClientId";
   public static final String TRIVIA_SERVER_ACCOUNT_EDIT = TRIVIA_SERVER_BASE
   ➥ + "receive";
   ```

2. Retrieve the appropriate player settings from the application shared preferences.

3. Generate a unique identifier if one has not been previously created and saved. Use the UUID class (java.util.UUID), as previously discussed. Save it to the preferences after creating it.

4. Package the settings in a Vector (java.util.Vector) of name-value pairs for easy transmission.

5. Generate the appropriate URL for adding or editing settings data. You can use the format() method of the URLEncodedUtils class (org.apache.http.client.utils.URLEncodedUtils) to include the vector data.

6. Create an HttpGet (org.apache.http.client.methods.HttpGet) request object using the URL.

7. Create an HttpClient (org.apache.http.client.HttpClient) and execute the HttpGet request.

Again, this is not Android-specific code, but standard Java using the common Apache libraries. The resulting postSettingsToServer() method of the UploadTask class looks like this:

```
private boolean postSettingsToServer() {
    boolean succeeded = false;

    String uniqueId = mGameSettings.getString(GAME_PREFERENCES_UNIQUE_ID, null);
    Integer playerId = mGameSettings.getInt(GAME_PREFERENCES_PLAYER_ID, -1);
    String nickname = mGameSettings.getString(GAME_PREFERENCES_NICKNAME, "");
    String email = mGameSettings.getString(GAME_PREFERENCES_EMAIL, "");
```

```java
String password = mGameSettings.getString(GAME_PREFERENCES_PASSWORD, "");
Integer score = mGameSettings.getInt(GAME_PREFERENCES_SCORE, -1);
Integer gender = mGameSettings.getInt(GAME_PREFERENCES_GENDER, -1);
Long birthdate = mGameSettings.getLong(GAME_PREFERENCES_DOB, 0);
String favePlaceName =
    ➥mGameSettings.getString(GAME_PREFERENCES_FAV_PLACE_NAME, "");

Vector<NameValuePair> vars = new Vector<NameValuePair>();

if (uniqueId == null) {

    String uniqueId = UUID.randomUUID().toString();
    Log.d(DEBUG_TAG, "Unique ID: " + uniqueId);
    // save it in the prefs
    Editor editor = mGameSettings.edit();
    editor.putString(GAME_PREFERENCES_UNIQUE_ID, uniqueId);
    editor.commit();
}
vars.add(new BasicNameValuePair("uniqueId", uniqueId));


if (playerId != -1) {
    // otherwise, we use the playerId to update data
    vars.add(new BasicNameValuePair("updateId", playerId.toString()));

    // and we go ahead and push up the latest score
    vars.add(new BasicNameValuePair("score", score.toString()));
}

vars.add(new BasicNameValuePair("nickname", nickname));
vars.add(new BasicNameValuePair("email", email));
vars.add(new BasicNameValuePair("password", password));
vars.add(new BasicNameValuePair("gender", gender.toString()));
vars.add(new BasicNameValuePair("faveplace", favePlaceName));
vars.add(new BasicNameValuePair("dob", birthdate.toString()));

String url = TRIVIA_SERVER_ACCOUNT_EDIT + "?"
    + URLEncodedUtils.format(vars, null);

HttpGet request = new HttpGet(url);

try {

    ResponseHandler<String> responseHandler = new BasicResponseHandler();
    HttpClient client = new DefaultHttpClient();
    String responseBody = client.execute(request,responseHandler);

    if (responseBody != null && responseBody.length() > 0) {
        Integer resultId = Integer.parseInt(responseBody);
        Editor editor = mGameSettings.edit();
        editor.putInt(GAME_PREFERENCES_PLAYER_ID, resultId);
        editor.commit();
    }
    succeeded = true;

} catch (ClientProtocolException e) {
    Log.e(DEBUG_TAG, "Failed to get playerId (protocol): ", e);
} catch (IOException e) {
```

```
        Log.e(DEBUG_TAG, "Failed to get playerId (io): ", e);
    }
    return succeeded;
}
```

This is a straightforward implementation of an HTTP GET request. It is typically not a good idea to send sensitive data across networks in plain text but it works for our simple example. There are equivalent classes for secure connections; consult the Java documentation for their usage.

> For this application, we store all data in the sample app database in plain text for readers to easily work with. Please do not use valid names and passwords when you are testing. We don't want to hear about anyone's information being exploited, so please, use dummy names, emails, passwords for testing purposes when working with the application server implementation provided with this book. While we limit the information readily available, it is just a test server and so few safeguards are in place. This is a purposeful design decision for readers' benefit such that they can inspect all aspects of the network process, if they so choose.

Uploading Avatar Data with the HTTP POST Method

The avatar data—that is a graphic file—is submitted to the application server by using the HTTP POST method. To enable this feature, you need to take the following steps:

1. Determine which classes (and third-party libraries) you need to package the avatar graphic data and send it to the server.

2. Add any third-party libraries to your Eclipse project and update project settings.

3. Implement the postAvatarToServer() method of the UploadTask class.

Again, this is not Android-specific code, but standard Java using common Apache libraries, including several MIME libraries you can download and include with your project.

Working with MIME Messages

The HttpClient class is ideal for uploading a multipart MIME message containing the avatar and some other important information for the application server. However, as of this writing, Apache HttpClient support within the Android SDK is incomplete. The Android SDK does not yet contain multipart MIME support, although this could change in a future version of the SDK. For now, to include multipart MIME support without writing the code yourself, you must add these Apache libraries to your project as JAR files. Specifically, you need to add the following JAR files to your project:

- Mime4j (http://goo.gl/7ASzA)
- HttpMime 4.0 (http://goo.gl/ISfHD)
- Apache Commons IO (http://goo.gl/VPb1J)

> Don't know what multipart MIME is? A great description is available on Wikipedia: http://goo.gl/EKOgb. Essentially, multipart MIME is a way of encoding multiple pieces of data—including binary data—in a single text message. Multipart MIME messages used with an HTML form correspond to the content encoding type multipart/form-data. Multipart MIME is not limited to HTTP. For example, email messages often use multipart MIME.

Adding JAR Files to Your Android Project

Now that you have identified the three JAR files the upload feature requires, add them to your project by following these steps:

1. Download the JAR file(s) you want to include in your project.

2. Create a directory called /libs in your project. This folder should be at the same level as the /src and /res folders.

3. Copy the JAR file(s) to the /libs directory. Refresh your project in Eclipse, if necessary, so that the /libs directory appears.

4. Under the Eclipse Project Properties, select the Java Build Path menu option and navigate to the Libraries tab.

5. Click the Add JARs button and choose the three JAR files you want to add to the project from the /libs directory. Click OK.

Packaging and Posting the Avatar to the Server

The avatar data—that is a graphic file—is submitted to the application server by using the HTTP POST method via the HttpClient and HttpPost classes. To enable this feature, perform the following steps:

1. Retrieve the avatar file location and player identifier settings from the application shared preferences.

2. Package the avatar graphic in a `MultipartEntity` (`org.apache.http.enti-ty.mime.MultipartEntity`) MIME message for easy transmission using some Apache libraries that are not part of the current Android SDK.

3. Create an `HttpPost` (`org.apache.http.client.methods.HttpPost`) request object using the same URL used for the settings (without the extra vector variables).

4. Create an `HttpClient` (`org.apache.http.client.HttpClient`) and execute the `HttpPost` request.

Here is the full implementation of the `postAvatarToServer()` method of the `UploadTask` class:

```java
private boolean postAvatarToServer() {
    boolean succeeded = false;
    String avatar = mGameSettings.getString(GAME_PREFERENCES_AVATAR, "");
    Integer playerId = mGameSettings.getInt(GAME_PREFERENCES_PLAYER_ID, -1);

    MultipartEntity entity =
        new MultipartEntity(HttpMultipartMode.BROWSER_COMPATIBLE);
    File file = new File(avatar);
    if (file.exists()) {
        FileBody encFile = new FileBody(file);
        entity.addPart("avatar", encFile);

        try {
            entity.addPart("updateId", new StringBody(playerId.toString()));
        } catch (UnsupportedEncodingException e) {
            Log.e(DEBUG_TAG, "Failed to add form field.", e);
        }

        HttpPost request = new HttpPost(TRIVIA_SERVER_ACCOUNT_EDIT);
        request.setEntity(entity);
        HttpClient client = new DefaultHttpClient();

        try {
            ResponseHandler<String> responseHandler = new
    BasicResponseHandler();
            String responseBody = client.execute(request,responseHandler);

            if (responseBody != null && responseBody.length() > 0) {
                Log.w(DEBUG_TAG, "Unexpected response from avatar upload: " +
    responseBody);
            }

            succeeded = true;

        } catch (ClientProtocolException e) {
            Log.e(DEBUG_TAG, "Unexpected ClientProtocolException",e);
        } catch (IOException e) {
            Log.e(DEBUG_TAG, "Unexpected IOException", e);
        }
    } else {
```

```
        Log.d(DEBUG_TAG, "No avatar to upload");
        succeeded = true;
    }
    return succeeded;
}
```

That concludes the implementation of the Settings screen data upload service. Now you can move on to the finishing touches in the other activities.

Uploading Score Data to a Remote Server

To upload the player score information to the application server, you could add yet another AsyncTask subclass to the QuizGameActivity class. But why not just update the existing QuizTask to communicate the player's score to the application server each time the game downloads new questions? This can help reduce latency and increase network efficiency. The only downside is that the score isn't updated at every answer and so may be slightly outdated.

The network server URL for retrieving new questions can simply include three extra query variables: a boolean value to turn on score updates (off by default), the player identifier, and the current score. The server then updates the user's score each time a new batch of questions is requested, doing double duty. To make this small change, update the doInBackground() method of the QuizTask class as follows:

```
SharedPreferences settings =
    getSharedPreferences(GAME_PREFERENCES, Context.MODE_PRIVATE);
Integer playerId = settings.getInt(GAME_PREFERENCES_PLAYER_ID, -1);
if (playerId != -1) {
    Log.d(DEBUG_TAG, "Updating score");
    Integer score = settings.getInt(GAME_PREFERENCES_SCORE, -1);
    if (score != -1) {
        pathToQuestions +=
            "&updateScore=yes&updateId="+playerId+"&score="+score;
    }
}
```

The code is added just after the URL string is created but before it's used so it can be updated. See the complete method implementation in the sample code that accompanies this book if you have further questions.

Downloading Friends' Score Data

Now that you have implemented the player identifier, you should take a moment to update the QuizScoresActivity class to use the real identifier instead of the hard-coded one. Replace the hardcoded (2008) identifier with the following code:

```
SharedPreferences prefs = getSharedPreferences(GAME_PREFERENCES,
    Context.MODE_PRIVATE);
Integer playerId = prefs.getInt(GAME_PREFERENCES_PLAYER_ID, -1);
```

Summary

In this hour, you modified the Been There, Done That! application to upload game data—including player settings, avatar, and score—to a remote application server. You also learned how to create a background service that can run outside your application's activity lifecycle, when necessary. In addition, you learned how to use the HTTP GET and HTTP POST methods with the HttpClient class when uploading data to a server. Finally, you learned how to add third-party packages to your application and use them much as you would Android SDK packages.

Q&A

Q. *Where can I learn more about Android services?*

A. For this particular service, which is simply started and left to complete, that's all you need to do. That said, services can be a pretty advanced topic for a beginner book. We discuss services in more detail in the next hour. We also cover services extensively in our more advanced book, *Android Wireless Application Development*, Second Edition (ISBN-13: 978-0321743015), but only briefly here, as services are often hard to avoid using. For a complete description of how services work on the Android platform, see the Android SDK documentation at http://goo.gl/TLOZu.

Q. *Is there a simpler way to provide a background work queue model for my application?*

A. Check out the IntentService class (android.app.IntentService). This class allows for a very simple Android service implementation which can be triggered by intent requests. The service handles all the details of asynchronous background processing for you.

Q. *How can I avoid uploading user data in plain text?*

A. There are many ways you can protect user data during transmission. For example, you can encrypt all data being sent over HTTP via SSL, using HTTPS. Check out the `java.net` and `java.net.ssl` packages for a start. Passwords that have already been shared through a secured channel can be sent in hashed form, using the `MessageDigest` class (`java.security.MessageDigest`).

Q. *Is JavaScript Object Notation (JSON) support available on the Android platform?*

A. Yes, you can find JSON libraries in the `org.json` package in the Android SDK.

Workshop

Quiz

1. True or False: The Android SDK comes complete with full multipart MIME handling support.

2. True or False: Network operations should always be performed on the UI thread so they are as fast as possible.

3. Which of the following are classes or objects that cannot be used to perform tasks in the background?

 A. BackgroundTask

 B. AsyncTask

 C. Thread

 D. AsyncActivity

4. True or False: An `AsyncTask` that is launched by an activity cannot run outside the lifecycle of the activity.

Answers

1. False. There is no built-in MIME support in the Android SDK at this time. Instead, you must add third-party MIME libraries to your Eclipse project.

2. False. Lengthy operations, such as networking operations, should never be performed on the UI thread to keep the handset as responsive as possible.

3. A and D. An `AsyncTask` is really a helper class that simplifies the use of a Thread. Both classes can be used. The other two are not SDK provided classes, if they exist at all.

4. True. The life of the asynchronous task is bounded by the lifecycle of its caller—in this case, the activity class. If you need something to run independent of the activity lifecycle, consider using a service.

Exercises

1. Modify the `QUESTION_BATCH_SIZE` variable defined within the `QuizActivity` class and make the value a lower number. The question batches are smaller, and thus retrieved more frequently, but the score data is uploaded more often as well.

2. Override the other callback methods of the `UploaderServer` such as `onDestory()` and add informational log messages to each.

3. **[Challenging!]** Add a new feature to the application that enables players to suggest new trivia questions—with images—by uploading them via multipart MIME POST to http://tqs.mamlambo.com/suggest, with a player identifier form field (`playerId`), question text form field (`question`), and question image form field (`questionImage`), with the image data done in the same way as for the avatar image used in this hour.

HOUR 17

Adding Social Features

What You'll Learn in This Hour:

▶ Enhancing applications with social features
▶ Adding friend request support
▶ Displaying friends' scores
▶ Integrating with third-party social networking services

In this hour, you enhance the Been There, Done That! application by adding some social integration. Specifically, you modify the application to allow the user to keep track of other players' scores by adding friends. This hour also discusses some of the many ways in which Android applications can use social features and third-party social networking sites to improve the game experience for users.

Enhancing Applications with Social Features

The Been There, Done That! application has really taken shape over the past few hours. However, it's not terribly fun to play a game all alone. Ideally, users want some friendly competition. At minimum, they want to be able to share the game experience with others. Applications that allow some sort of user interaction are more likely to become viral and more popular, thus ensuring success.

Social applications can be roughly divided into two categories: those that are designed to access social networks, such as Facebook or Twitter, directly and those that weave social information into the feature set in order to enhance the user's game experience. The Been There, Done That! game is ideal for this latter use. Indeed, we are only going to add very light social features to the application in order to enable a special listing filtering only the player's friends' scores. However, this only scratches the surface of the social features you could add to the application.

Tailoring Social Features to Your Application

Determining what social and interactive features to build into your application can be tricky business. As an application designer, you might ask yourself questions such as the following:

▶ What social features, if any, make sense in my application? Will the application use social features to encourage competition (high score comparisons, notifications to taunt a friend when a user surpasses a friend's high score, and so on)? Will the application use social networking features to broadcast game activity (post game wins to Facebook or a Twitter feed) and thus enable free promotional opportunities for the application?

▶ How will social relationships be defined for my application? How will the user invite contacts to play? Will users enter their friends' email addresses, phone numbers, or user names to connect with them? Will invitations be delivered via email? SMS? Will player relationships, such as Facebook friendships, need to be confirmed by both sides?

▶ What existing social networking sites are my target users a part of, and does it make sense for my application to integrate any of these sites' features? Does the social networking site I want to integrate with have a clearly defined API for development use? What licensing terms apply?

▶ How will my application protect its users' (and their friends') privacy? What guidelines will I use to determine what the application (and my company) can and cannot do with private user data?

Supporting Basic Player Relationships

Social applications rely on relationships between users. Different applications describe these relationships using different terminology. The terms contact and friend are the most widely used terms to describe user relationships, but some sites use unique terminology, such as user's circle or follower. Clever applications sometimes refer to friends or contacts within the theme of the game. For example, a clever war-themed game might use the phrase "recruit fellow warriors for the mission" instead of the more generic "invite your friends to play the game by giving us their email addresses."

Adding Friend Support to Your Application

For the Been There, Done That! application, you will add some light social integration to allow players to follow other players' game scores. This is a relatively simple way to encourage game play. By sharing only "public" score information, you can avoid having to implement robust support for friend validation and confirmation.

The simple social feature you add in this hour works as follows:

1. A player adds a friend's email address to identify another person as a friend.

2. If the email address matches that of another player record on the application server, a friendship link is established.

3. The players now see each other's scores on the Scores of Friends tab of the scores screen. Again, this is a one-way link akin to a "follow": that is, the user sees that friend's score listed on the scores tab. The other user does not automatically see anything in his score listing, unless he does the same by adding the first user's email address as one of his friends. See the exercises at the end of this hour for more details.

As always, the complete implementation of the code discussed in this hour is available on the accompanying CD and book websites for download. Feel free to follow along!

Enabling Friend Requests on the Settings Screen

To add this light social networking support to the Been There, Done That! application, you must update `QuizSettingsActivity` to allow the user to input friend email addresses. Specifically, you need to do the following:

▶ Add a new `Button` control to the settings screen to launch a new dialog.

▶ Implement another dialog within the `QuizSettingsActivity` class to allow the user to input a friend's email address.

▶ Add some networking code to communicate the friend request to the application server.

Adding New Project Resources

As with the other screens in the Been There, Done That! application, you need to add some string resources to your project to support the Add Friends feature on the

settings screen. Specifically for this implementation, add four string resources in
/res/values/strings.xml for the new setting and the related dialog:

```
<string
    name="settings_friend_email">Enter email address of friend:</string>
<string
    name="settings_friend_email_label">Friends</string>
<string
    name="settings_friend_email_tip">Add a new friend by email</string>
<string
    name="settings_button_friend_email">Add Friend</string>
```

Save the string resource file. The new strings can now be used in the layout resource
files used by the settings screen and friends dialog.

Updating the Settings Screen Layout

You must update the user interface of the Been There, Done That! application to
allow a player to enter friends' email addresses. There are a number of ways you
could go about doing this, of course. You could add a new activity and update the
menu screen, allowing for a whole new screen in the application, or you could just
update the settings screen with a new region. To keep things simple, add a new section for specifying friend email addresses at the bottom of the settings screen that
acts much like the other settings that rely on a dialog (see Figure 17.1).

FIGURE 17.1
The settings
screen updated
to allow for
friend requests.

By this time you have implemented several Button and dialog features on the settings screen, so you should find this task very straightforward. For example, you could add the following section of XML to the settings.xml layout resource file (just below the favorite place layout controls) to define a new region for the Add Friend feature:

```xml
<TextView
    android:id="@+id/TextView_Friend_Email"
    android:layout_width="wrap_content"
    android:layout_height="wrap_content"
    android:text="@string/settings_friend_email_label"
    android:textSize="@dimen/help_text_size"
    android:textStyle="bold"></TextView>
<LinearLayout
    android:id="@+id/LinearLayout_Friend_Email"
    android:orientation="horizontal"
    android:layout_height="wrap_content"
    android:layout_width="match_parent">
    <Button
        android:id="@+id/Button_Friend_Email"
        android:layout_width="wrap_content"
        android:layout_height="wrap_content"
        android:text="@string/settings_button_friend_email"
        android:onClick="onAddFriendButtonClick"></Button>
    <TextView
        android:layout_width="match_parent"
        android:layout_height="match_parent"
        android:textSize="@dimen/help_text_size"
        android:textStyle="bold"
        android:gravity="center"
        android:id="@+id/TextView_Friend_Email_Tip"
        android:text="@string/settings_friend_email_tip"></TextView>
</LinearLayout>
```

Like other settings on this screen, the layout updates involve adding several TextView labels and a Button control called Button_Friend_Email. Clicking this button launches a new dialog.

Implementing the Add Friend Dialog Layout

You can build the Add Friend dialog as a custom dialog based upon the AlertDialog class, much like the password dialog or favorite place dialog.

However, unlike previous user settings, we simplify the friend data by only using it on the server and not storing it locally as part of the application preferences. After all, this data is only used by the server to generate friends' scores listings.

To keep things simple, just create a dialog with a single EditText control to input a friend's email address. This address can be transmitted to the network server and stored there. The client need not store it at all for the social features at hand;

however, if you want to add more social features related to friend management, you might opt to store a local copy as well.

Again, you need to add a new layout resource to describe the Add Friend dialog user interface. This layout should be defined as follows in the XML layout file called `/res/layout/friend_dialog.xml`:

```xml
<?xml version="1.0" encoding="utf-8"?>
<LinearLayout
    xmlns:android="http://schemas.android.com/apk/res/android"
    android:id="@+id/root"
    android:orientation="vertical"
    android:layout_width="wrap_content"
    android:layout_height="wrap_content"
    android:background="@drawable/bkgrnd">
    <TextView
        android:id="@+id/TextView_Friend_Email"
        android:layout_width="wrap_content"
        android:layout_height="wrap_content"
        android:textSize="@dimen/help_text_size"
        android:textStyle="bold"
        android:text="@string/settings_friend_email"></TextView>
    <EditText
        android:id="@+id/EditText_Friend_Email"
        android:layout_height="wrap_content"
        android:maxLength="50"
        android:layout_width="match_parent"
        android:maxLines="1"
        android:inputType="textEmailAddress"></EditText>
</LinearLayout>
```

The contents of this layout are straightforward. The layout is a `LinearLayout` container with two controls: a `TextView` label that prompts the user to enter an email address and an `EditText` control to receive the email address string from the user.

Implementing the Friend Request Feature

Next, turn your attention to the `QuizSettingsActivity` class and implement the new dialog. This dialog is simpler than the password or favorite place dialog, but the steps to create it are basically the same. Begin by defining the new dialog identifier as a member variable for the class:

```java
static final int FRIEND_EMAIL_DIALOG_ID = 3;
```

Next, implement the click handler method referenced by the `Button` control called `Button_Friend_Email`, so that it launches the new dialog:

```java
public void onAddFriendButtonClick(View view) {
    showDialog(FRIEND_EMAIL_DIALOG_ID);
}
```

Now turn your attention to implementing the dialog. Begin by updating the onCreateDialog() method of the QuizSettingsActivity class to include a case statement for this new dialog:

```
case FRIEND_EMAIL_DIALOG_ID:
    LayoutInflater infl = (LayoutInflater) getSystemService(
        Context.LAYOUT_INFLATER_SERVICE);
    final View friendDialogLayout = infl.inflate(
        R.layout.friend_dialog, (ViewGroup) findViewById(R.id.root));

    AlertDialog.Builder friendDialogBuilder =
        new AlertDialog.Builder(this);
    friendDialogBuilder.setView(friendDialogLayout);
    final TextView emailText = (TextView)
        friendDialogLayout.findViewById(R.id.EditText_Friend_Email);

    friendDialogBuilder.setPositiveButton(
        android.R.string.ok, new DialogInterface.OnClickListener() {

        public void onClick(DialogInterface dialog, int which) {

            String friendEmail = emailText.getText().toString();
            if (friendEmail != null && friendEmail.length() > 0) {
                doFriendRequest(friendEmail);
            }
        }
    });
    return friendDialogBuilder.create();
```

This dialog implementation should look quite familiar. Again, you are building up an AlertDialog control by inflating a layout resource. The only implementation detail of note is the use of the doFriendRequest() method in the click handler of the positive dialog button. We discuss the implementation of this method a little later in this hour. For now, finish implementing the onPrepareDialog() method case statement for the Add Friend dialog. In this case, there is no real preparation to do.

The resulting Add Friend dialog should look like Figure 17.2.

Creating an Asynchronous Task to Handle Friend Requests

When the user clicks the OK button in the dialog, the email address needs to be sent to the application server. The application server is responsible for setting up the friend relationship if the friend's email address exists in the datastore.

There are numerous ways to implement this part of the add friend feature. If you were storing the user's friends' email addresses locally in the shared preferences, you could simply add this data to the simple background service you created in the previous hour. However, for simplicity, and because this feature is lightweight and not part of the core feature set of the application, you will simply spawn a new asynchronous task to communicate each email address to the server.

FIGURE 17.2
The friend
request dialog.

To achieve this, create a new inner class within the `QuizSettingsActivity` called `FriendRequestTask` that extends `AsyncTask`. This class is very simple and should look familiar. It simply grabs the appropriate player data from the shared preferences and the email supplied by the dialog and uses HTTP POST to transmit the information to the network server using a specially formulated URL:

```
private class FriendRequestTask extends AsyncTask<String, Object, Boolean> {
    @Override
    protected void onPostExecute(Boolean result) {
        QuizSettingsActivity.this.setProgressBarIndeterminateVisibility(false);
    }

    @Override
    protected void onPreExecute() {
        QuizSettingsActivity.this.setProgressBarIndeterminateVisibility(true);
    }

    @Override
    protected Boolean doInBackground(String... params) {
        Boolean succeeded = false;
        try {
            String friendEmail = params[0];

            SharedPreferences prefs = getSharedPreferences(GAME_PREFERENCES,
                Context.MODE_PRIVATE);
            Integer playerId = prefs.getInt(GAME_PREFERENCES_PLAYER_ID, -1);

            Vector<NameValuePair> vars = new Vector<NameValuePair>();
            vars.add(new BasicNameValuePair("command", "add"));
            vars.add(new BasicNameValuePair("playerId", playerId.toString()));
            vars.add(new BasicNameValuePair("friend", friendEmail));
```

```
            HttpClient client = new DefaultHttpClient();
            HttpPost request = new HttpPost(TRIVIA_SERVER_FRIEND_ADD);
            request.setEntity(new UrlEncodedFormEntity(vars));

            ResponseHandler<String> responseHandler = new
            ➥ BasicResponseHandler();
            String responseBody = client.execute(request, responseHandler);

            Log.d(DEBUG_TAG, "Add friend result: " + responseBody);
            if (responseBody != null) {
                succeeded = true;
            }

        } catch (MalformedURLException e) {
            Log.e(DEBUG_TAG, "Failed to add friend", e);
        } catch (IOException e) {
            Log.e(DEBUG_TAG, "Failed to add friend", e);
        }

        return succeeded;
    }
}
```

Don't forget to define the TRIVIA_SERVER_FRIEND_ADD URL in the QuizActivity
class:

```
public static final String TRIVIA_SERVER_FRIEND_ADD = TRIVIA_SERVER_BASE +
➥ "friend";
```

After you have implemented the FriendRequestTask class, you need to wire up the
QuizSettingsActivity to use it. To start, add a member variable to the class of
type FriendRequestTask:

```
FriendRequestTask friendRequest;
```

Next, update the onPause() method to cancel the friend request, if necessary:

```
if (friendRequest != null) {
    friendRequest.cancel(true);
}
```

Finally, implement the doFriendRequest() helper method, which is called when
the positive button is clicked on in the Add Friend dialog, such that it executes the
FriendRequestTask:

```
private void doFriendRequest(String friendEmail) {
    if (friendRequest == null ||
        friendRequest.getStatus() == AsyncTask.Status.FINISHED ||
        friendRequest.isCancelled()) {
        friendRequest = new FriendRequestTask();
        friendRequest.execute(friendEmail);
    } else {
        Log.w(DEBUG_TAG, "Warning: friendRequestTask already going");
    }
}
```

Note that we ensure that there is not another pending update before starting a new one.

Displaying Friends' Scores

Now that players can add friends, the `QuizScoresActivity` class automatically populates the Scores of Friends tab with live data from the application server as shown in Figure 17.3. You need to add some friends' email addresses that match users in the database first, of course.

FIGURE 17.3
The Scores of Friends tab.

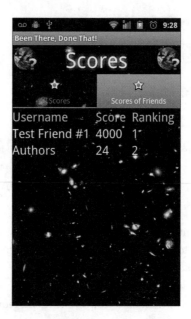

Enhancing Player Relationships

Enabling friend relationships can greatly enhance the experience for users in a variety of ways above and beyond what you have implemented thus far. Adding friend support may seem like a very lightweight social feature, but imagine how you can build up more social features from this simple starting point. Player relationships allow developers the flexibility to enhance applications in a variety of ways, such as the following:

▶ The application server could send an email invitation to any friend who did not already exist in the database.

▶ Players do not need to be restricted to the Android platform. You could easily add other platforms (web, iPhone, BlackBerry, and so on). This means friends could contact the same application server and play each other across platforms.

▶ Friend relationships could be one-way or two-way (showing up on one or both players' Friends lists). Different trust relationships could be established, allowing players access to different types of information about other players, including friends' answers to questions and their favorite place in the world.

▶ After a friend relationship has been established, more application features could be added, including challenges, messaging, notifications...the sky's the limit. Use your imagination.

The complete implementation of the friends feature as described in this hour might seem incomplete—and it is! Any application incorporating a similar friends feature should, at minimum, allow the player to manage (for example, view, delete) his or her existing friend relationships. However, these improvements are left as exercises for the overachieving reader.

Integrating with Social Networking Services

Social networking has really come into its own in the past few years, enabling people to connect, keep in touch, and share information (for better or worse) about their lives. Many social networking sites have developed APIs for third-party developers, many of which are web services based on representational state transfer (REST). There has been an explosion in the number of applications available for social networks, such as Facebook.

Android applications can integrate with a social networking site through development programs and the API provided by the specific site or service. The level of integration can range from lightweight to complete. Here are some examples of social networking integration you could consider in an Android application:

▶ Giving the user the option to automatically tweet on Twitter when he or she wins a game.

▶ Writing an application that enables the user to view and update his or her personal blog, Twitter feed, and Facebook status.

▶ Developing a fully featured Twitter client application that provides all the Twitter functionality to users of Android devices, in addition to any features you want to include above and beyond those found on other clients.

In each case, Twitter features are integrated into the Android application in different ways. Now let's look at adding support for some of the social networking services that are popular today.

Adding Facebook Support

Facebook is a popular social web service where people can connect, share pictures and video, and chat. Facebook provides a portal for developers who want to integrate Facebook functionality into their applications at http://goo.gl/GVe2P. You can find out more about the Facebook Platform for Mobile (Facebook Connect, Facebook SMS, and so on) at http://goo.gl/iB5Le.

Adding Twitter Support

Twitter is a popular social networking service where people share short text messages called tweets. Each tweet is at most 140 characters, making Twitter an ideal platform for mobile development. Twitter provides a portal for developers, with reference information about the Twitter API, at http://goo.gl/CnDr1.

Working with the OpenSocial Initiative

When you want to target more than one social networking site or reach as many end users as possible, you may want to look into the OpenSocial APIs: http://goo.gl/K3tnA. OpenSocial uses common APIs (instead of site-specific ones) to integrate with many popular social applications and services including (but not limited to) the following, which are in alphabetical order:

- friendster (still popular in Southeast Asia)

- hi5 (popular in Europe and Central and South America)

- Hyves (popular in the Netherlands)

- LinkedIn (business networking)

- Mail.ru (popular in Russia)

- mixi (popular in Japan)

- MySpace (popular in the United States and worldwide)

- Netlog (popular in Europe and the Middle East)

- orkut (popular in South America and India)

- RenRen (formerly Xiaonei, popular with students in China)

- XING (business networking, popular in Europe and China)

- Yahoo! (popular in the United States and worldwide)

Each of these social networks has daily and monthly active users in the millions.

Summary

In this hour, you learned how social features can be used to enhance the user experience of a mobile application. You worked through a short example of how to add social features to the Been There, Done That! application by adding the ability for a user to specify friends (by email address) and view friends' scores. Finally, you learned about many of the third-party social networking services you can consider integrating your application with.

Q&A

Q. How do I determine the best unique identifier to distinguish users?

A. Despite a number of initiatives to implement single-login services, there is still not a great answer to this question. Some candidates are unique username/password pairings, email addresses, or phone numbers. In the example application used in this book, we relied on the email address of the player as a unique identifier, and we allowed the user to set up a password. Many social networking sites use a similar mechanism, but this approach is not without problems—for example, email addresses change, users often have more than one account, and they have to keep track of yet another login and password combination. When you're integrating with a social networking website, you need to use whatever authentication and credentials are required by the site's API. And don't forget to use, store, and transmit that sensitive data securely.

Q. What are some of the privacy concerns I should consider when developing social applications?

A. When it comes to social applications, you should always include information about how you'll use any information supplied by the user. You're going to be safest when you follow these principles: Don't access, use, or store any information your application doesn't require and do assume that any and all information supplied by the user is private. Now, by this definition, even the lightweight friend support you added to the Been There, Done That! application is sharing private data: the user's nickname, score, and avatar. (See the exercises for accessing friends' avatar images from the server.) Technically, if you published this application, you would want to make it very, very clear to the player that this information is going to be uploaded to the application server and accessible to other players.

Q. *How do I find out if my application can integrate with a social network application that's not listed in this hour?*

A. Whether you want to integrate with a social networking service or some other web service (for example, Google, Amazon, eBay), the simplest way to find out if a service has an API is to browse the company's website. There you will often find a link for developers near the information about customer support, contact, and company information or within the customer support FAQ. Most companies require developers to agree to terms of use, and some companies require you to register for a special API key to use the services.

Workshop

Quiz

1. True or False: All Android applications can and should be enhanced using social features.

2. How does the Been There, Done That! application create friend relationships?

   A. By allowing the player to search the application server for friends he or she recognizes

   B. By allowing the player to input a friend's email address

   C. By launching the Contacts application and allowing the player to choose a contact

   D. By allowing the player to input a friend's phone number

3. True or False: The Android SDK has built-in support for social networking sites such as Facebook, Twitter, and MySpace.

Answers

1. False. Adding social features to an application can enhance the experience for users, but this is a design decision that requires thought and planning. Some types of applications benefit greatly from these features, and others do not. Add social features to an application only when doing so provides a clear benefit to both users and the developer.

2. B. Players can add friends in the Been There, Done That! application by inputting their email addresses. The application server tries to match each email address entered to an existing player. If the player exists, then a friend relationship is established.

3. False. You can use the networking features of the Android SDK to access the developer APIs provided by third-party social networking sites such as Facebook, Twitter, and MySpace.

Exercises

1. Review the development API documentation of the third-party social networking service of your choice. Sketch out how you could integrate this service with the Been There, Done That! application in an interesting way. For example, you might post a tweet to the player's Twitter feed each time that player answers a quiz question in the affirmative (for example, "Player X has climbed Mount Everest!").

2. Modify the scores screen to add a third tab that shows the scores of players who have added the player as a friend (in other words, players who are watching the player's score). The application server has the appropriate query implemented. Use the same URL but add the variable `followers` and set it to the string `true` (for example, "http://tqs.mamlambo.com/scores.jsp?playerId=##&followers= true").

3. Modify the Scores of Friends tab of the scores screen to display each friend's avatar as well as each score. (Hint: The URL for each friend's avatar is included in the XML score data downloaded from the application server.)

4. Add a feature to send an email message to the user's friend to invite him to install the Been There, Done That! application if they are not a registered user on the server when a user adds them as a friend. Hint: We talk about the appropriate intent for sending emails in this popular online article: http://goo.gl/USbnS.

HOUR 18

Creating a Home Screen App Widget

What You'll Learn in This Hour:

▶ Designing and implementing an App Widget
▶ Working with styles
▶ Handling App Widget user events
▶ Using services with App Widgets

In this hour, you create an App Widget for the Been There, Done That! application. Specifically, you create a simple App Widget control that can be added to the user's Home screen to display the user's avatar, nickname, and score information and remind her to continue playing the game.

Designing an App Widget

The Android SDK provides developers with an interesting way to provide functionality outside the traditional boundaries of a mobile application: App Widgets. Developers can use the App Widget API to create small controls that can be added to the Home screen of the user's device. These simple but powerful controls can provide a user with supplemental information about the application and remind the user to launch the application when necessary.

App Widgets can be useful for certain types of applications, such as those that might need to inform the user of some status or update. A weather application might include an App Widget that displays the current weather conditions at the given location. A task management application might include an App Widget that informs the user of the next task on his or her to-do list or how many tasks are left for the day. A picture gallery application might include an App Widget that acts as a slideshow of all the pictures stored in the gallery.

In this lesson, you create a simple App Widget for the Been There, Done That! application. This App Widget performs the following functions:

▶ Displays the user's avatar, nickname, and current score

▶ Displays the user's top friend's avatar, nickname, and current score

▶ Launches the Been There, Done That! application when clicked

Developing an App Widget

Developing an App Widget can be somewhat complex, compared to the tasks you've completed in previous lessons. You must draw upon many of the skills you've been learning in order to complete the implementation of a simple App Widget. The steps to create an App Widget are the following:

1. Create an App Widget configuration file.

2. Create an App Widget layout resource file.

3. Implement an App Widget Provider.

4. Implement an Android service to update the App Widget, where appropriate.

5. Register your App Widget and related service in the Android manifest file.

Now let's look at each of these tasks in more detail. The complete sample code for this hour is provided on the accompanying CD and is available for download on the book websites.

Configuring App Widget Properties

App Widget definition and configuration properties must be defined in a separate XML file and are then referenced from within the Android manifest file. The following are some of the common properties used to define an App Widget:

▶ **Size**—The width and height dimensions of the App Widget, defined in density-independent pixels (dp or dip), which correspond to the number of Home screen grid cells the App Widget requires to display correctly. The Android Home screen is organized in grid cells that usually correspond to a square of 74 by 74 dp. Only one item, such as an App Widget or application shortcut, can sit in any one cell within the grid. This way, items do not overlap.

▶ **Update Frequency**—The time (in milliseconds) between system calls to the App Widget provider to update the contents of the App Widget.

▶ **Initial Layout**—A layout file to use when the App Widget is initially added. This can be changed in code later.

▶ **Configuration Activity**—The definition for an activity to launch to configure various aspects of the App Widget before it is first displayed.

To add an App Widget definition to the Been There, Done That! application, add a new XML file called `widget_info.xml` under the `/res/xml` resource folder for the project. In this file, place the following App Widget definition. For example

```
<?xml version="1.0" encoding="utf-8"?>
<appwidget-provider
    xmlns:android="http://schemas.android.com/apk/res/android"
    android:minWidth="294dp"
    android:minHeight="146dp"
    android:updatePeriodMillis="10800000"
    android:initialLayout="@layout/widget">
</appwidget-provider>
```

This definition file defines an App Widget that updates every three hours and is 4 by 2 grid cells in size. If you've done the math, you might have noticed that the 294dp width and the 146dp height on the edges is not a multiple of the 74dp we previously defined a grid cell size to be. Although a grid cell is typically considered 74dp on edge, when calculating the size, you must subtract 2dp from the final result. In this example, we multiplied 74 by 2 to get 148. Then, we subtracted 2 from it to get to the 146 we put in the file. The same holds true of 294dp—here we multiplied 74 by 4 and then subtracted 2 for a result of 294. Without this, the App Widget might not draw in the expected number of cells.

This App Widget receives update calls every 10,800,000 milliseconds, which corresponds to three hours. In addition, this App Widget initially uses a predefined layout, referenced by `android:initialLayout="@layout/widget"`. Now turn your attention to creating this layout resource to represent the widget user interface.

Working with `RemoteViews`

App Widgets have specific layout requirements. To begin with, an App Widget is drawn through the `RemoteViews` interface, which limits the types of user interface controls that can be displayed. Next, the App Widget must conform to the size configured in its definition.

A `RemoteViews` object is used when the actual display of a view is performed from within another process. This is exactly what happens with an App Widget. App

Widgets are displayed in the App Widget host process, not your application's main process. `RemoteViews` objects are limited in the layout and view objects they may use. Some layout and view objects supported within App Widgets include the following:

- `LinearLayout`
- `FrameLayout`
- `RelativeLayout`
- `TextView`
- `ImageView`
- `Button`
- `ImageButton`
- `ProgressBar`
- `AnalogClock`
- `Chronometer`

Classes extending these controls cannot be used. This means that the design of the layout is limited. A number of additional controls and features were enabled for App Widget usage as part of Android 3.0 and 3.1. App Widgets are not meant to provide the same powerful features that a fully functional application can provide, though. The customary way of enhancing the features of an App Widget is to provide a simple way to trigger the launch of a full application activity in the event that more powerful features or complex screens are required because activities launched from an App Widget no longer carry the limitations that an App Widget has from the required use of a `RemoteViews` object.

Working with Styles

It can get tiresome, setting the same layout control attributes over and over again. Now that you are very familiar with controls such as `TextView`, let's look at one way you can simplify your layout designs: styles. We mentioned styles very briefly in Hour 4, "Managing Application Resources." Styles allow the easy encapsulation of specific control attributes, which can be set all at once. If you are familiar with web design, Android styles are a lot like CSS style sheets.

For the Been There, Done That! App Widget, we want some uniform text styling in different `TextView` controls. Therefore, create a new file called `/res/values/styles.xml` and define two styles within it:

```xml
<?xml version="1.0" encoding="utf-8"?>
<resources>
    <style
        name="WidgetTextShade">
        <item
            name="android:shadowDx">0</item>
        <item
            name="android:shadowDy">0</item>
        <item
            name="android:shadowRadius">6</item>
        <item
            name="android:shadowColor">@android:color/black</item>
    </style>
    <style
        name="WidgetText"
        parent="@style/WidgetTextShade">
        <item
            name="android:layout_width">wrap_content</item>
        <item
            name="android:layout_height">wrap_content</item>
        <item
            name="android:textSize">@dimen/widget_text_size</item>
        <item
            name="android:textColor">@color/title_color</item>
        <item
            name="android:gravity">center_horizontal</item>
    </style>
</resources>
```

Now, instead of setting each of the attributes listed individually within each
TextView control, you can simply set its style attribute to the style name of your
choice. Note that the WidgetTextShade style resource simply sets the shadow attributes. The WidgetText style resource inherits the WidgetTextShade style attributes
and adds several additional attributes, including textSize, textColor, and more.
Save the styles.xml style resource file. You can now use these styles in your layout
resource files, most importantly your new App Widget layout.

Designing the App Widget Layout

To design a layout for the App Widget, create a new layout file called /res/lay-
out/widget.xml, and place the following code in it:

```xml
<?xml version="1.0" encoding="utf-8"?>
<RelativeLayout
    xmlns:android="http://schemas.android.com/apk/res/android"
    android:layout_height="match_parent"
    android:layout_width="match_parent"
    android:id="@+id/widget_view">
    <LinearLayout
        android:layout_height="match_parent"
        android:layout_width="match_parent">
        <RelativeLayout
            android:layout_width="wrap_content"
            android:layout_height="match_parent"
```

```
        android:id="@+id/widget_left_view"
        android:layout_weight="50">
        <ImageView
            android:layout_centerInParent="true"
            android:layout_height="match_parent"
            android:layout_width="match_parent"
            android:id="@+id/widget_left_image">
                </ImageView>
                <TextView
            style="@style/WidgetText"
            android:layout_alignParentTop="true"
            android:layout_centerHorizontal="true"
            android:id="@+id/widget_left_nickname">
                </TextView>
                <TextView
            style="@style/WidgetText"
            android:layout_centerHorizontal="true"
            android:layout_alignParentBottom="true"
            android:id="@+id/widget_left_score">
        </TextView>
    </RelativeLayout>
    <RelativeLayout
    android:layout_width="wrap_content"
    android:layout_height="match_parent"
    android:id="@+id/widget_right_view"
    android:layout_weight="50">
    <ImageView
        android:layout_centerInParent="true"
        android:layout_height="match_parent"
        android:layout_width="match_parent"
        android:id="@+id/widget_right_image">
    </ImageView>
    <TextView
        style="@style/WidgetText"
        android:layout_alignParentTop="true"
        android:layout_centerHorizontal="true"
        android:id="@+id/widget_right_nickname">
        </TextView>
    <TextView
        style="@style/WidgetText"
        android:layout_centerHorizontal="true"
        android:layout_alignParentBottom="true"
        android:id="@+id/widget_right_score">
    </TextView>
    </RelativeLayout>
    </LinearLayout>
        <TextView
        style="@style/WidgetTextShade"
        android:layout_width="wrap_content"
        android:layout_height="wrap_content"
        android:id="@+id/textVersus"
        android:text="VS"
        android:layout_centerInParent="true"
        android:textStyle="bold"
        android:typeface="serif"
        android:textSize="60dp">
    </TextView>
</RelativeLayout>
```

Save this layout file. You have completed the configuration details required by the App Widget and can focus on the Java implementation.

Implementing an App Widget Provider

Now that the configuration is in place, you need to implement the App Widget Provider. To do this, you must create a new class within your project called `QuizWidgetProvider` that extends the `AppWidgetProvider` class. The `AppWidgetProvider` class has five callback methods that may be overridden:

▶ `onUpdate()`—This method is called at each update interval.

▶ `onDeleted()`—This method is called each time an App Widget is deleted.

▶ `onEnabled()`—This method is called the first time an App Widget is created, but not subsequent times.

▶ `onDisabled()`—This method is called when the last instance of an App Widget is deleted.

▶ `onReceive()`—This method is called for all received broadcast events; the default implementation calls each of the previous callback methods (for example, `onUpdate()`, `onDeleted()`, `onEnabled()`, and `onDisabled()`) when necessary. This method can be overridden when advanced behavior is required.

For the purposes of the Been There, Done That! App Widget, we need to perform some background processing in order to provide updates. Therefore, before we dive into the callback methods we must implement within the `AppWidgetProvider`, we need to start by creating a new service.

Handling App Widget Background Tasks

You might think that because the App Widget doesn't run within the application process, you don't have to worry about operations taking too long. You might also think that it would automatically perform its actions in the background. In both cases, you'd be wrong.

For lengthy operations, the normal solution is to handle the work asynchronously, as you do with activities. However, for App Widgets, this isn't feasible as there's no underlying activity to manage the task. The process the App Widget is in could go away at any time, even if an asynchronous task was running. Instead, you must again create an Android `Service` object and then, from the service, you can perform the background operations you require.

Creating an App Widget Update Service

Within the QuizWidgetProvider class, define an inner class called
WidgetUpdateService that extends the Service class.

The WidgetUpdateService class implementation is fairly straightforward:

```
public static class WidgetUpdateService extends Service {
    WidgetUpdateTask updater;
    private static final String DEBUG_TAG = "WidgetUpdateService";

    @Override
    public int onStartCommand(Intent intent, int flags, int startId) {
        updater = new WidgetUpdateTask();
        updater.execute(startId);
        return START_REDELIVER_INTENT;
    }

    @Override
    public void onDestroy() {
        updater.cancel(true);
        super.onDestroy();
    }

    @Override
    public IBinder onBind(Intent intent) {
        return null;
    }

    private class WidgetUpdateTask extends AsyncTask<Integer, Void, Boolean>
    {
        // Async Task Implementation here…
    }
}
```

The WidgetUpdateService has the expected member variables: the asynchronous
task to handle background operations and a custom log tag for service logging. The
callback methods of the service simply manage the asynchronous task called
WidgetUpdateTask. The onStartCommand() callback method starts the
WidgetUpdateTask and returns the START_REDELIVER_INTENT, which is used for
services that only remain running while processing commands. Because binding
does not occur with App Widget implementations, the onBind() callback method
simply returns null. Finally, the onDestroy() callback method cancels the
asynchronous task.

You can see all the services currently running on an Android handset or emulator
by selecting Settings, Applications, Running Services. From here, you can choose
to stop services, as well.

Implementing the `WidgetUpdateTask` Class

The processing of the `WidgetUpdateService` happens in its `WidgetUpdateTask` inner class. This class is responsible for retrieving and updating the App Widget `RemoteViews` data asynchronously. As you might expect, the only really interesting aspect of the `WidgetUpdateTask` is its `doInBackground()` callback method (exception handling removed for clarity and brevity). The method begins by retrieving the data to display in the App Widget:

```
Context context = WidgetUpdateService.this;
SharedPreferences prefs = getSharedPreferences(
QuizActivity.GAME_PREFERENCES, Context.MODE_PRIVATE);
Integer playerId = prefs.getInt(QuizActivity.GAME_PREFERENCES_PLAYER_ID, -1);

WidgetData playerData = getWidgetData(playerId);
WidgetData friendData = getTopFriendWidgetData(playerId);
```

The `getWidgetData()` and `getTopFriendWidgetData()` methods are simply helper methods that contact the network server and download the appropriate player and friend data as XML, and then parse that data for use within the App Widget. The `WidgetData` class is simply an inner class used to encapsulate a set of player data including the avatar, nickname, and score information. These tasks have been thoroughly covered in previous hours. Feel free to review the full source code implementation available on the CD or the book websites if you have further questions about how these methods function.

Next, retrieve the `RemoteViews` instance from the App Widget and set the appropriate control attributes using special methods. For example, to set the text within a `TextView` that belongs to a `RemoteViews` object, use the `setTextViewText()` method:

```
String packageName = context.getPackageName();
RemoteViews remoteView = new RemoteViews(
context.getPackageName(), R.layout.widget);

remoteView.setTextViewText(R.id.widget_left_nickname, playerData.nickname);
remoteView.setTextViewText(R.id.widget_left_score, "Score: " +
playerData.score);

remoteView.setTextViewText(R.id.widget_right_nickname, friendData.nickname);
remoteView.setTextViewText(R.id.widget_right_score, "Score: " +
friendData.score);
```

The `setWidgetAvatar()` method is a helper method that contacts the network server and decodes the appropriate avatar graphic into a `Bitmap` and then uses the `setImageViewBitmap()` method of the `RemoteViews` class to set the graphic. Again, see the sample source code for the complete implementation if you want a refresher on downloading a graphic file from a URL:

```
setWidgetAvatar(remoteView, playerData.avatarUrl, R.id.widget_left_image);
setWidgetAvatar(remoteView, friendData.avatarUrl, R.id.widget_right_image);
```

As it stands, the App Widget works but isn't terribly interactive. Recall that the list of views that an App Widget supports did not include any user input fields. Basically, the only event that an App Widget supports is a click event. Because the App Widget isn't displayed in the same process as the application, a new method is needed for getting the click event. The Android SDK provides an Intent type known as PendingIntent for this purpose. This is an Intent that is basically packaged to be sent at a future time and can be sent by another process. To create a PendingIntent, an Intent instance must first be created. Then the PendingIntent is created with some additional information, such as what to do on subsequent uses of the same Intent. That is, the exact same instance could be used, or a new instance could be created. After the PendingIntent object is created, it can be assigned to the RemoteViews object via a call to the setOnClickPendingIntent() method:

```
Intent launchAppIntent = new Intent(context,QuizMenuActivity.class);
PendingIntent launchAppPendingIntent = PendingIntent.getActivity(context, 0,
    launchAppIntent, PendingIntent.FLAG_UPDATE_CURRENT);
remoteView.setOnClickPendingIntent(R.id.widget_view,launchAppPendingIntent);
```

Finally, your RemoteViews object is properly configured and you are ready to update your live App Widget. Do this by using the updateAppWidget() method of the AppWidgetManager class (android.appwidget.AppWidgetManager).

```
ComponentName quizWidget = new ComponentName(context, QuizWidgetProvider.class);
AppWidgetManager appWidgetManager = AppWidgetManager.getInstance(context);
appWidgetManager.updateAppWidget(quizWidget, remoteView);
```

Round out the implementation of the doInBackground() method by returning the appropriate result.

Managing the App Widget Update Service

Now that you have implemented the background service to manage your App Widget updates, you need to have the App Widget Provider manage it. Begin by starting the service in the onUpdate() callback method of the QuizWidgetProvider class. In this case, use the startService() method by replacing the onUpdate() method with the following code:

```
@Override
public void onUpdate(Context context,
    AppWidgetManager appWidgetManager, int[] appWidgetIds) {
```

```
    Intent serviceIntent = new Intent(context, WidgetUpdateService.class);
    context.startService(serviceIntent);
}
```

> If you were paying close attention, you might have noticed that you didn't use two of the onUpdate() parameters: appWidgetManager and appWidgetIds. The appWidgetManager parameter isn't used because you are moving the code to a different method shortly, where an instance of it is retrieved separately. The appWidgetIds parameter is used when you want to support multiple unique App Widgets that show different data. In that case, the application must track the appWidgetIds values, which are assigned by the system, separately and pair them correctly to the data that needs to be shown in each App Widget. Typically, this is done using a distinct configuration activity for the App Widget so the user controls what they want displayed in each different instance of this App Widget.

If the App Widget is removed from its host, such as the Home screen, while an update is taking place, the service needs to be terminated in a different way. To accomplish this, include the following code for the onDeleted() method into the QuizWidgetProvider implementation:

```
@Override
public void onDeleted(Context context, int[] appWidgetIds) {
    Intent serviceIntent = new Intent(context, WidgetUpdateService.class);
    context.stopService(serviceIntent);
    super.onDeleted(context, appWidgetIds);
}
```

The call to the stopService() method triggers a call to the onDestroy() method of the Service class implementation, which then attempts to interrupt the thread to stop it.

Updating the Android Manifest File

Your project's Android manifest file needs to be updated to tell the system where to find the definition of the App Widget and the background service must be registered as well.

An App Widget is a specialized form of a BroadcastReceiver control. Therefore, you must place a <receiver> definition within the AndroidManifest.xml file that defines what Intent objects can be received and a couple other pieces of data specific to the App Widget. To accomplish this task, add the following <receiver> section to the application section of the AndroidManifest.xml file:

```
<receiver
    android:name="QuizWidgetProvider">
    <intent-filter>
```

```
    <action
        android:name="android.appwidget.action.APPWIDGET_UPDATE" />
  </intent-filter>
  <meta-data
      android:name="android.appwidget.provider"
      android:resource="@xml/widget_info" />
</receiver>
```

This `<receiver>` segment of the Android manifest file defines an intent filter for App Widget updates. In addition, it ties the App Widget, and its definition file, to the overall application.

Finally, the Android manifest file also needs to be updated so the system knows about the new background service. To do this, add a second `<service>` block to the `<application>` section of the manifest file, like this:

```
<service
    android:name="QuizWidgetProvider$WidgetUpdateService" />
```

This tells the system that there is a service and where to find it. You have now implemented everything you need to create a fully functional App Widget.

▼ Try It Yourself

To add an App Widget to the Home screen of an Android phone or the emulator, follow these easy steps:

1. Navigate to the Home screen.

2. Find a suitably empty area of the screen. (Remember that the App Widget needs 2x2 grid cells.)

3. Click and hold your finger (or the mouse button on the emulator) over the area where you want to add the App Widget.

4. When the pop-up menu appears, choose Add to Home Screen, Widgets. The App Widget should now appear in the Home screen's App Widget interface, as shown in Figure 18.1.

5. Select the App Widget you just created (or any other App Widget) from the list and add it to your Home screen, as shown in Figure 18.2.

▼

FIGURE 18.1
Adding the App
Widget to the
Home screen.

FIGURE 18.2
The Been There,
Done That! App
Widget.

Summary

In this hour, you built a simple App Widget for the Been There, Done That! application to display the user's avatar, nickname, and score. This hour covered all the implementation details of App Widget development, including designing the layout and defining the App Widget properties. You also added some simple event handling, allowing the user to click the App Widget to launch the Been There, Done That! application. Finally, you used a background service to handle processing of App Widget events and updates.

Q&A

Q. *Is the Home screen the only place I can include App Widget controls?*

A. No. Any App Widget host can hold App Widget controls. The Home screen is simply the place you most commonly see App Widgets used. See the documentation for `AppWidgetHost` and `AppWidgetHostView` for more details.

Q. *How do I add more interactive features, such as* `Button` *controls, to an App Widget?*

A. If you want to add configuration controls to an App Widget and allow the user to trigger updates to the App Widget content, you need to define each event separately and implement the appropriate click handlers to send specific event commands, via `PendingIntent` objects, to a registered receiver of the `Intent` objects. Then the App Widget application needs to receive the commands and process them accordingly, updating the App Widget content as necessary. You can find a complete example of an interactive App Widget provided in our article "Handling User Interaction with Android App Widgets," available at http://goo.gl/d4h0H.

Q. *Can I have multiple instances of an App Widget?*

A. Having multiple instances doesn't make sense with the App Widget you implemented for the Been There, Done That! application. However, in certain instances, it might make sense to allow the user to have multiple instances of an App Widget with different configurations. One way to accomplish this is to allow the user to configure each App Widget instance using the configuration activity defined for the App Widget. Then, the application must keep track of the differences between the instances by keeping track of the user configuration activity for each App Widget identifier. We also cover this advanced topic in our article "Handling User Interaction with Android App Widgets" (see the previous Q&A for details).

Q. *I've seen some resizable App Widgets as well as App Widgets with ListView controls and the like. How do I create those?*

A. Many new App Widget features were introduced in Android 3.0 and 3.1. See the release notes for these specific SDK versions for details on how to use these new APIs. That said, keep in mind that most devices are not yet running Android 3.0 (as of this writing), and so these new features are not compatible with most legacy devices.

Workshop

Quiz

1. True or False: App Widgets can reside only on the Home screen.

2. Which of the following is an example of a View widget that cannot be used with an App Widget?

   A. Button

   B. WebView

   C. ProgressBar

3. True or False: Although App Widgets are defined in density-independent pixels, their size must correspond directly to a certain number of cells.

4. For what reason is a service used in an App Widget?

   A. To handle lengthy background operations

   B. To handle drawing directly on the screen

   C. To access private data

Answers

1. False. App Widgets can reside within an application that implements an AppWidgetHost object.

2. B. Both Button and ProgressBar can be used, but not WebView.

3. True. Each cell is typically defined as 74 pixels, but when adding up the number for multiple cells, 2 pixels are subtracted. Thus, 2 cells wide would be (74x2) – 2, or 146 pixels.

4. A. An App Widget runs in another process so must be responsive to requests. A `thread` can't be used because it might be killed when the App Widget returns. Therefore, a service is started to perform background processing.

Exercises

1. Implement the rest of the App Widget Provider callbacks to log an informational message.

2. Modify the App Widget layout to make the App Widget more visually appealing using the limited controls available.

3. **[Advanced]** Add another feature to the App Widget. Perhaps a Button control that launches straight into the Game screen activity, bypassing the main menu screen.

4. **[Challenging!]** Modify the App Widget to display a different friend's data every 30 minutes. Hint: The current implementation stops at the first friend score data. You need to continue and read more.

HOUR 19

Internationalizing Your Application

What You'll Learn in This Hour:

▶ Languages supported by the Android platform
▶ Managing strings and other resources
▶ Localized formatting utilities
▶ Other internationalization concerns

The mobile marketplace is global—serving a variety of users in many countries and many locales. Developers need to keep this in mind when designing and developing applications for the Android platform; applications will likely be used by foreign-speaking users. In this hour, you learn about the localization features of the Android platform and how to prepare your application for publication in a variety of countries, regions, or locales.

> In Hour 24, "Publishing on the Android Market," you learn how to make your application available for distribution within the Android Market. This includes publishing to a variety of different countries and providing application descriptions in numerous languages and prices in different currencies.

By the Way

General Internationalization Principles

With a global marketplace, developers can maximize profits and grow their user base by supporting a variety of different languages and locales. Let's take a moment to clarify some terms. Although you likely know what we mean by *language*, you might not be aware that each language may have a number of different locales (dialects in laymen's terms). For example, the Spanish spoken in Spain is quite different from that spoken in the Americas; the French spoken in Canada differs from that spoken in Europe and Africa; and the English spoken in the United States differs from that spoken in Britain. English is a *language*, while English (United States), English (United Kingdom), and English (Australia) are *locales* (see Figure 19.1).

FIGURE 19.1
People who
speak the same
language often
have localized
dialects.

Applications are made up of data and functions (behavior). For most applications, the behavior is the same, regardless of the locale. However, the data must be localized. This is one of the key reasons resource files exist—to externalize application data. Locale and language differences go far beyond "accents"—to include different word spellings, meanings, slang, and format of regional data such as date and time and primary currency. The most common type of application data that requires localization is the strings of text used by the application. For example, a string of data might represent a user's name, but the text label for that value on an application screen needs to be shown in the proper language (for example, "Name," "Nom," "Nombre").

Development platforms that support internationalization typically allow for string tables, which can be swapped around so that the same application can target different languages. The Android platform is no exception.

Do not hard code localizable data such as string information into the application source files—Java and layout resource files especially—unless absolutely necessary. Doing so hinders internationalization efforts.

How Android Localization Works

Compared to other mobile platforms, the Android SDK provides extensive support for internationalization and the good news is that the Android SDK documentation has been updated and is now pretty comprehensive, so no more guesswork!

Android localization considerations fall into three main categories:

▶ The languages and locales supported by the Android platform (an extensive list—the superset of all available languages)

▶ The languages and locales supported by a specific Android handset (a list that varies—a subset of languages chosen by a handset manufacturer or operator)

▶ The countries, languages, and locales supported by the Android Market application (the countries and locales where Google can sell legally; this list grows continuously)

New locales are added with each new Android SDK, so for a complete list of the locales supported for a given Android SDK, see the specific platform documentation. For example, the Android 2.1 locale support is listed here: http://goo.gl/MIkAW. The complete list of locales supported by Android 3.0 is shown in Table 19.1.

TABLE 19.1   Languages and Regions Supported in Android 3.0

Language	Regions
Arabic (ar)	Egypt (ar_EG)
	Israel (ar_IL)
Bulgarian (bg)	Bulgaria (bg_BG)
Catalan (ca)	Spain (ca_ES)
Chinese (zh)	PRC (zh_CN)
	Taiwan (zh_TW)
Croatian (hr)	Croatia (hr_HR)
Czech (cs)	Czech (cs_CZ)
Danish (da)	Denmark (da_DK)
Dutch (nl)	Netherlands (nl_NL)
	Belgium (nl_BE)

TABLE 19.1   Continued

Language	Regions
English (en)	United States (en_US)
	Britain (en_GB)
	Canada (en_CA)
	Australia (en_AU)
	Ireland (en_IE)
	India (en_IN)
	New Zealand (en_NZ)
	Singapore (en_SG)
	Zimbabwe (en_ZA)
Finnish (fi)	Finland (fi_FI)
French (fr)	France (fr_FR)
	Belgium (fr_BE)
	Canada (fr_CA)
	Switzerland (fr_CH)
German (de)	Germany (de_DE)
	Austria (de_AT)
	Switzerland (de_CH)
	Liechtenstein (de_LI)
Greek (el)	Greece (el_GR)
Hebrew (he)	Israel (he_IL)
Hindi (hi)	India (hi_IN)
Hungarian (hu)	Hungary (hu_HU)
Indonesian (id)	Indonesia (id_ID)
Italian (it)	Italy (it_IT)
	Switzerland (it_CH)
Japanese (jp)	Japan (jp_JP)
Korean (ko)	South Korea (ko_KR)
Latvian (lv)	Latvia (lv_LV)
Lithuanian (lt)	Lithuania (lt_LT)
Norwegian bokmål (nb)	Norway (nb_NO)
Polish (pl)	Poland (pl_PL)

TABLE 19.1 Continued

Language	Regions
Portuguese (pt)	Brazil (pt_BR)
	Portugal (pt_PT)
Romanian (ro)	Romania (ro_RO)
Russian (ru)	Russia (ru_RU)
Serbian (sr)	Serbia (sr_RS)
Slovak (sk)	Slovakia (sk_SK)
Slovenian (sl)	Slovenia (sl_SI)
Spanish (es)	Spain (es_ES)
	United States (es_US)
Swedish (sv)	Sweden (sv_SE)
Tagalog (tl)	Philippines (tl_PH)
Thai (th)	Thailand (th_TH)
Turkish (tr)	Turkey (tr_TR)
Vietnamese (vi)	Vietnam (vi_VN)

How the Android Operating System Handles Locale

Much like other operating systems, the Android platform has a system setting for locale. This setting has a default setting that can be modified by the mobile operator. For example, a German mobile operator might make the default locale Deutsch (Deutschland) for its shipping handsets. An American mobile operator would likely set the default locale to English (American) and also include an option for the locale Español (Estados Unidos)—thus supporting American English and Spanish of the Americas. Individual devices may filter the locales to only those relevant to the device. For example, a device targeted at Americans might only support the relevant English (en_US) and Spanish (es_US) locales.

A user can change the system-wide setting for locale in the Settings application. The locale setting affects the behavior of applications installed on the handset.

▼   **Try It Yourself**

To change the locale on a handset, perform the following steps. Take care to remember the steps (or related icons), as you have to navigate back to the locale settings in the foreign language you chose.

1. From the Home screen, click the Menu button and choose Settings.

2. From the Settings menu, select the Language & Keyboard option.

3. Choose Select Locale and select a locale. The Android platform immediately changes the locale on the system. For example, if you choose Español, you see that many of the menus on the Android platform are now in Spanish.

▲

How Applications Handle Locales

Now let's look at how the system-wide locale setting affects each Android application. When an Android application uses a project resource, the Android operating system attempts to match the best possible resource for the job at runtime. In many cases, this means checking for a resource in the specific language or regional locale. If no resource matches the required locale, the system falls back on the default resource.

Developers can include language and locale resources by providing resources in specially named resource directories of the project. You can localize any application resource, whether it is a string resource file, a drawable, an animation sequence, or some other type.

Specifying Default Resources

So far, just about every resource in the Been There, Done That! application is a default resource (the exception being the icon.png file, which does not have a default resource in the /drawable directory, only pixel-density specific versions). A default resource is simply a resource that does not have specific tags for loading under different circumstances.

Default resources are the most important resources because they are the fallback for any situation when a specific, tailored resource does not exist (which happens more often than not). In the case of the Been There, Done That! application, the default resources are all in English.

Specifying Language-Specific Resources

To specify strings for a specific language, you must supply the resource under a specially named directory that includes the two-letter language code provided in ISO

639-1 (see http://goo.gl/ToTSo). For example, English is en, French is fr, and German is de. Let's look at an example of how this works.

Say that you want the Been There, Done That! application to support English, German, and French strings. You would take the following steps:

1. Create a strings.xml resource file for each language. Each string that is to be localized must appear in each resource file with the same name, so it can be programmatically loaded correctly. Any strings you don't want to localize can be left in the default (English) /res/values/strings.xml file.

2. Save the French strings.xml resource file to the /res/values-fr/ directory.

3. Save the German strings.xml resource file to the /res/values-de/ directory.

Android can now grab the appropriate string, based on the system locale. However, if no match exists, the system falls back on whatever is defined in the /res/values/ directory. This means that if English (or Arabic, or Chinese, or Japanese, or an unexpected locale) is chosen, the default (fallback) English strings are used.

Similarly, you could provide German-specific drawable resources to override the default graphics in the /res/drawable/ directory by supplying versions (each with the same name) in the /res/drawable-de/ directory.

Specifying Region-Specific Resources

You might have noticed that the previous example specifies high-level language settings only (English, but not American English versus British English versus Australian English). Don't worry! You can specify the region or locale as part of the resource directory name as well.

To specify strings for a specific language and locale, you must store the localized resource under a specially named directory that includes the two-letter language code provided in ISO 639-1 (see http://goo.gl/ToTSo), followed by a dash, then a lowercase r, and finally the ISO 3166-1-alpha-2 region code (see http://goo.gl/Qqfgx). For example, American English is en-rUS, British English is en-rGB, and Australian English is en-rAU. Let's look at an example of how this works.

If you want the Been There, Done That! application to support these three versions of English, you do the following:

1. Create a strings.xml resource file for each language. You can leave any strings you don't want to localize in the default (American English) /res/values/strings.xml file.

2. Save the British English `strings.xml` resource file to the `/res/values-en-rGB/` directory.

3. Save the Australian English `strings.xml` resource file to the `/res/values-en-rAU/` directory.

To summarize, start with a default set of resources—which should be in the most common language your application will rely on. Then add exceptions—such as separate language and region string values—where needed. This way, you can optimize your application so it runs on a variety of platforms. For a more complete explanation of how the Android operating system resolves resources, check out the Android developer website: http://goo.gl/qUP0h.

How the Android Market Handles Locales

The Android Market supports a subset of the locales available on the Android platform. Because the Android Market uses the Google Checkout system for payments, only countries where this online marketplace is legal can be supported for paid applications.

New countries are being added to the Android Market all the time. Locale affects a number of different features of the Android Market:

▶ Paid Android applications can be sold by developers who reside in specific countries. For a list of supported developer countries for paid apps, see http://goo.gl/U07uq. If you are developing in a country such as Argentina, Brazil, Israel, Mexico, Russia, South Korea, or Taiwan, you may need to manage your own tax rates with your developer account for legal reasons.

▶ Free Android applications can be distributed by developers who reside in a much larger number of countries. For a list of supported developer countries for free applications, see http://goo.gl/CNz77.

▶ Android applications can be sold in different currencies. For more information on selling apps in different currencies, see http://goo.gl/cj4uj.

▶ Each currency has a range that is allowable on the Android Market. You can find these ranges at http://goo.gl/6aPpp.

Developers must register to sell applications on the Android Market. As the developer, you are responsible for being aware of any export compliance law that applies to your situation.

Android Internationalization Strategies

Don't be overwhelmed by the permutations available to developers when it comes to internationalizing an application. Instead, give some thought to how important internationalization is to your application during the design phase of your project. Develop a strategy that suits your specific needs and stick to it.

Here are some basic strategies to handle Android application internationalization:

- Forgo internationalization entirely
- Limit internationalization
- Implement full internationalization for target audiences

Now let's talk about each of these strategies in more detail.

Forgoing Application Internationalization

Whenever possible, save your development and testing teams a lot of work—don't bother to internationalize your application. This is the "one size fits most" approach to mobile development, and it is often possible with simple, graphic-intensive applications such as games that do not have a lot of text to display. If your application is simple enough to work smoothly with internationally recognized graphical icons (such as play, pause, stop, and so on) instead of text labels, or "Sims" language (garbled mumbles that get the point across to speakers of any language) then you may be able to forgo internationalization entirely. Games such as tic-tac-toe and chess are games that require little, if any, text resources.

Some of the pros of this strategy are the following:

- Simplified development and testing
- Smallest application size (only one set of resources)

Some of the cons of this strategy are the following:

- For text- or culture-dependent applications, this approach greatly reduces the value of the application. It is simply too generic.
- This strategy automatically alienates certain audiences and limits your application's potential marketplaces.

This technique works only for a subset of applications. If your application requires a help screen, for example, you're likely going to need at least some localization for your application to work well all over the world.

Limiting Application Internationalization

Most applications require only some light internationalization. This often means internationalizing string resources only, but other resources, such as layouts and graphics, remain the same for all languages and locales.

Some of the pros of this strategy are the following:

▶ Modest development and testing requirements

▶ Streamlined application size (specialized resources kept to a minimum)

Some of the cons of this strategy are the following:

▶ This strategy might still be too generic for certain types of applications. Overall design (especially screen design) might suffer from needing to support multiple target languages. For example, text fields might need to be large enough to support verbose languages such as German but look odd and waste valuable screen real estate in less verbose languages.

▶ Because you've headed down the road of providing language-specific resources, your users are more likely to expect other languages you haven't supported. In other words, you're more likely to start getting requests for your app to support more languages if you've supported some. That said, you've already built and tested your application on a variety of languages, so adding new ones should be straightforward.

Implementing Full Application Internationalization

Some types of applications require complete internationalization. Providing custom resources for each supported language and locale is a time-intensive endeavor, and you should not do it unless you have a really good reason to do so because the size of the application grows as you include more resources. This approach often necessitates breaking the individual languages into separate APK files for publication, resulting in more complex configuration management. However, this allows a developer to tailor an application for each specific marketplace to a fine degree.

Some of the pros of this strategy are the following:

▶ The application is fully tailored and customized to individual audiences; this strategy allows for tweaks to individual locales.

▶ It builds user loyalty by providing users with the best, most customized experience. (This is also a technique used by Google.)

Some of the cons of this strategy are the following:

▶ It is the most lengthy and complicated strategy to develop.

▶ Each internationalized version of the application must be fully tested as if it were a completely different application (which it might well be, if you are forced to split it into different APK files due to application size).

Beware of over-internationalizing an application. The application package size grows as you add language- and locale-specific resources. There is no reason to head down this road unless you have a compelling reason to do so—and unless you have the development, testing, and product team to manage it. Having a poorly localized version of an application can be worse to your image than having no localization at all.

Using Localization Utilities

The Android SDK includes support for handling locale information. For example, the Locale class (java.util.Locale) encapsulates locale information.

Determining System Locale

If you need to modify application behavior based on locale information, you need to be able to access information about the Android operating system. You can do this by using the getConfiguration() method of the Context object, as follows:

```
Configuration sysConfig = getResources().getConfiguration();
```

One of the settings available in the Configuration object is the locale:

```
Locale curLocale = sysConfig.locale;
```

You can use this locale information to vary application behavior programmatically, as needed.

Formatting Date and Time Strings

Another aspect of internationalization is displaying data in the appropriate way. For example, U.S. dates are formatted MM/DD/YY and October 26, 2011, whereas much of the rest of the world uses the formats DD/MM/YY and 26 October 2011. The Android SDK includes a number of locale-specific utilities. For example, you can use the DateFormat class (android.text.format.DateFormat) to generate date and time strings in the current locale, or you can customize date and time information

as needed for your application. You can use the `TimeUtils` class
(`android.util.TimeUtils`) to determine the time zone of a specified country
by name.

Handling Currencies

Much like dates and times, currencies and how they are formatted differ by locale.
You can use the standard Java `Currency` class (`java.util.Currency`) to encapsulate currency information. Use the `NumberFormat` class (`java.text.NumberFormat`)
to format and parse numbers based on locale information.

Summary

In this hour, you reviewed basic internationalization principles such as externalizing
project resources and knowing your target markets. You learned how the Android
platform handles different countries, languages, and locales. Finally, you learned
how to organize Android application resources for a variety of different countries
and regions, for maximum profit, using a number of different internationalization
strategies.

Q&A

Q. *Which languages and locales should I target in my Android applications?*

A. The answer to this question depends on a variety of factors and is something
of a numbers game. The short answer is this: the fewest you can get away
with. The number of mobile users who use a specific language should not be
the only factor in deciding which languages to support. For example, there are
many more Spanish- and Chinese-speaking mobile users than English-speak-
ing ones, but generally, English market users are willing to pay much higher
prices for applications. The answer really boils down to knowing your user
audience(s)—which should be part of your business plan to begin with.

Q. *Why does my Android handset show only a subset of the languages and
locales listed in this hour?*

A. Although the Android platform supports a variety of languages and locales,
mobile handset manufacturers and operators can customize the locale support
available on specific devices. This may be done for resource efficiency. For
example, a phone available through a U.S. operator might support only
English (American) and Spanish (Americas).

Q. *What language should I use for default resources such as strings?*

A. Your default resources should be in the language/locale used by your largest target audience—the most generic/likely values that appeal to the most users. If you're targeting the world at large, the choice is often English, but it need not be. For example, if your application allows turn-based directions anywhere in China, then you'd probably want your default language/locale to be one of the Chinese options (and even within China, different locale settings are more widely used than others)—unless you were targeting business types who are visiting China, in which case, you're back to using English, which is still "the international language of business" (at least, for now).

Q. *I changed the locale to Spanish. Why are some applications still displaying in English?*

A. If an application has its default strings in English and has no Spanish resources available, then the defaults are used, regardless of the language chosen.

Workshop

Quiz

1. True or False: An Android application can support multiple languages within a single APK file.

2. True or False: The number of languages supported by the Android platform and the Android Market is fixed.

3. What language should your default resources be?

A. English

B. Chinese

C. The language that appeals most to your target audience

D. Another language

Answers

1. True. An application can be compiled with resources in several different languages. The Android platform can switch between these resources on-the-fly,
   based upon the locale settings of the handset.

2. False. Android language support is being updated continuously. New languages and locales are being added all the time.

3. C. Your default resources should be the ones that are most likely to load and
   be used. Therefore, it makes sense to design these resources to be in the language and locale that appeals to the most number of users.

Exercises

1. Add a new set of string resource values to the Been There, Done That! application in the language or locale of your choice. Test the results in the Android
   emulator and on a real handset (if it supports the language/locale you chose).

2. Change the Been There, Done That! application so that it loads a custom
   drawable or color resource for a specific language or locale. For example,
   change the planet graphic on the main menu to something more specific to
   that language/locale. Test the results in the Android emulator and on a real
   handset (if it supports the language/locale you chose).

3. Review the qualifier types listed in the table in the alternative resources
   Android SDK documentation: http://goo.gl/E8v1d.

4. Create two alternative icon resources for the larger sized screens and higher
   density screen resolutions: xlarge and xhdpi.

HOUR 20

Developing for Different Devices

What You'll Learn in This Hour:

▶ Designing for different handset configurations
▶ Handling screen orientation changes
▶ Working with different Android SDK versions

The Android platform is maturing at an accelerating rate. We're seeing revisions of the Android SDK rolling out every few months, with new handsets showing up all the time. In this hour, you learn how to develop Android applications for different targets. Android devices vary in terms of hardware and software features, as well as the version of the Android SDK they run.

Configuration Management for Android

Developers must try to support the widest possible range of devices without biting off more than they can chew in terms of maintenance and configuration management. The following are some factors to consider when determining target platforms:

▶ What hardware features does the application require? Does the application require a touch screen? A hardware keyboard? A directional pad? Specific screen dimensions?

▶ What software features does the application require? Does the application support different screen orientations?

▶ What Android SDK does the application require?

Although some of these decisions necessitate changes in the project libraries and the Android manifest file, many can be handled using the same resource directory qualifier strategy used for application internationalization.

Resource directories can be qualified to provide resources for a number of different application configurations (see Table 20.1). You can apply these directory name qualifiers to the resource subdirectories, such as /res/values/. Qualifiers are concatenated onto the existing subdirectory name, in a strict order, shown in precedence order in Table 20.1. You can combine multiple qualifiers by separating them with dashes. Qualifiers are always lowercase, and a directory can contain only one qualifier of each type. Custom qualifiers are not allowed.

TABLE 20.1   Important Resource Directory Qualifiers

Directory Qualifier Type	Values	Comments
Language	`en, fr, es, zh, ja, ko, de,` and so on	ISO 639-1 two-letter language codes
Region/locale	`rUS, rGB, rFR, rJP, rDE,` and so on	ISO 3166-1-alpha-2 region code in ALL UPPERCASE, preceded by a lowercase r
Screen dimensions	`small, normal, large, xlarge`	Screen size and density ratio
Screen aspect ratio	`long, notlong`	Screen aspect ratio to handle "wide screen" devices
Screen orientation	`port, land`	Portrait mode, landscape mode
Dock mode	`car, desk`	Device is in a specific dock state
Night mode	`night, notnight`	Device is in night or day mode
Screen pixel density	`ldpi, mdpi, hdpi, xhdpi, nodpi`	Screen density that the resource is for
Touch screen type	`notouch, stylus, finger`	No Touch screen, Stylus-only, Finger Touch screen
Is keyboard available	`keysexposed, keyshidden, keyssoft`	Keyboard available, Keyboard not available to user, resources used only with software keyboard
Primary non-touch screen navigation method	`nonav, dpad, trackball, wheel`	Four-key directional pad, trackball, scroll wheel
SDK version	`v1, v2, v3, v4, v5, v6, v7, v8, v9, v10, v11, v12,` and so on	The SDK version's API level (for example, v4 is Android SDK 1.6, while v11 represents Android SDK 3.0)

There are a number of other, less commonly used qualifiers as well. You can concatenate different resource directory qualifiers together using dashes. Here are some good examples of properly qualified directories:

```
/res/values-en-rUS-port-finger
/res/drawables-en-rUS-land
/res/values-en-v11
```

The following are some incorrectly qualified directories:

```
/res/values-en-rUS-rGB
/res/values-en-rUS-port-FINGER
/res/values-en-rUS-port-finger-custom
```

For an exhaustive list of the qualifiers available for resource customization (mobile country code, carrier, screen size, and so on), see the Android developer website: http://goo.gl/pOIPn.

Handling Different Screen Orientations

Android applications can run in landscape or portrait mode, depending on how the user tilts the device screen. Besides internationalization, one of the most common situations in which applications might want to customize resources is to provide different layout details for portrait and landscape screen orientations.

Strategies for Handling Screen Orientation

The best way to support different orientations is to design simple enough layouts that work in either portrait or landscape mode, without modifications. For example, the settings screen of the Been There, Done That! application works fine in both landscape and portrait modes because each setting is stacked in a `LinearLayout` control, within a scrolling area that can scale well to any size. However, some layouts, such as the splash or game screen, might need some special tweaking for each orientation.

There are many strategies for supporting different screen sizes and orientations. Here are some tips for developing layouts that work for multiple types of screens:

- ▶ Don't crowd screens. Keep them simple.
- ▶ Use scalable container views such as `ScrollView` and `ListView`.
- ▶ Scale and grow screens in only one direction (vertically or horizontally), not both.
- ▶ Don't hard code the positions of screen elements. Instead, use relative positions and layouts, such as `RelativeLayout`.
- ▶ Avoid `AbsoluteLayout` and other pixel-specific layout settings.
- ▶ Use stretchable graphics, such as Nine-Patch.

▶ Keep resources as small as possible, so they load fast when the screen orientations change.

Adding Custom Layouts for Screen Orientations

Thus far, you have been developing and testing the Been There, Done That! application primarily in portrait mode (the default). Run the application now and change to landscape mode. Review each screen. Note that some screens, such as the settings, scores, and help screens, display well because they have flexible layouts that work well in either landscape or portrait mode. Other screens, such as the splash, menu, and game screens could certainly use some improvement.

Did you Know?

> You can toggle the orientation of the emulator by pressing Ctrl+F11 and Ctrl+F12.

Figure 20.1 illustrates some of the flaws that the Been There, Done That! application displays in landscape mode.

Did you Know?

> The Android developer website contains a helpful set of guidelines for supporting multiple screens: http://goo.gl/BOl37.

FIGURE 20.1
Some screens of the Been There, Done That! application do not display well in landscape mode.

Modifying how a screen displays based on the orientation of the device is as simple as adding a new set of layout resource files. To do this, you need to do the following:

▶ Create a new landscape-specific layout file to the `/res/layout-land/` directory.

▶ Make sure to include all the controls defined in default layout resources that are referenced in the Java code or other files.

▶ Design a new version of the layout that also looks nice in landscape mode.

Let's give this a shot by providing different versions of the layout files for the three screens that do not currently display well in landscape mode: the splash screen, the main menu screen, and the game screen. As always, recall that the full layout implementation for the landscape mode changes and handset differences discussed in this hour are available on the CD that accompanies this book as well as on the book's websites.

Designing a Landscape-Mode Splash Screen Layout

Let's begin with the splash screen. The layout for this screen is defined in the /res/layout/splash.xml resource file. By running the application in landscape mode, we see that the graphics push the version and copyright information off the bottom of the screen, obscuring it. Ideally, we want to create a landscape-specific layout resource that rearranges the existing controls without losing any of the features we've built into the splash screen. To do this, follow these steps:

1. Create a new layout resource file called `/res/layout-land/splash.xml`.

2. Copy the original contents of the `/res/layout/splash.xml` to the new file.

3. Modify the contents of the landscape-specific layout file to accommodate landscape mode devices. For example, you might modify the layout to have all four images display in one `TableRow` control, instead of two.

4. You might also modify the referenced dimensions of the `TextView` controls slightly by creating alterative dimension resources in the `/res/values-land/dimens.xml` resource file. Make sure the alterative dimension resources are named the same as the default versions stored in the `/res/values/dimens.xml` file.

If you now run your application in landscape mode, you see a greatly improved splash screen that no longer has display problems, as shown in Figure 20.2. These improvements were achieved entirely by the judicious rearrangement of resources. No Java code changes were necessary. That said, all controls that were referenced in the QuizSplashActivity class are required to be present in both the default and landscape-mode version of the splash.xml layout resource file.

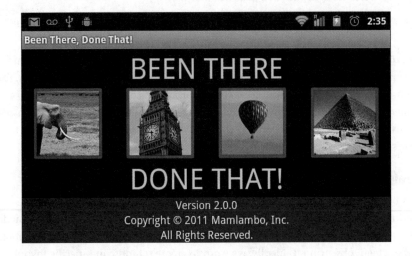

Designing a Landscape-Mode Main Menu Screen Layout

Next, let's turn our attention to the main menu screen. The layout for this screen is defined in the /res/layout/menu.xml resource file. By running the application in landscape mode, we see that the giant Earth graphic is obscuring the menu items. In this case, we have several options: rearrange the screen controls in a new way, make the Listview fonts substantially smaller, or simply remove the ImageView with the Earth graphic entirely. Because the ImageView is little more than "eye candy" and not a functional part of the screen—that is, not a control that is referenced in other parts of the application—we can safely create an alternative layout called /res/layout-land/menu.xml, copy the contents of the default layout, and remove that ImageView control.

You might have noticed the background was stretched. This might be acceptable to some, but for completeness you should fix this. Create three new drawable folders named /drawable-land-hdpi, /drawable-land-mdpi, and /drawable-land-ldpi. Inside each of these, place a new version of the bkgrnd.png file in an appropriate resolution for the screen density and orientation. We used 854×480, 480×320, and 360×240, respectively. Adding the updated background resource now affects all screens in landscape mode, even those layouts without specific landscape-only resource files.

If you now run your application in landscape mode, you see a simplified main menu screen that no longer has display problems, as shown in Figure 20.3.

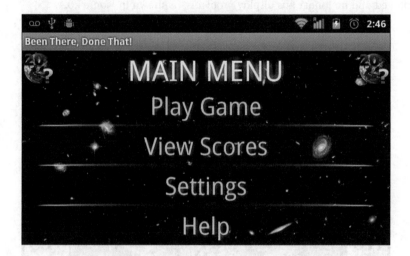

FIGURE 20.3
The newly improved main menu screen in landscape mode.

Designing a Landscape-Mode Game Screen Layout

Finally, we must update the game screen for proper landscape mode display. The layout for this screen is defined in the /res/layout/game.xml resource file. By running the application in landscape mode, we see that the question graphic and text are clipped at the bottom of the screen. Ideally, we want to create a landscape-specific layout resource that rearranges the existing controls without losing any of the features we've built into the splash screen. To achieve this, take the following steps:

1. Create a new layout resource file called /res/layout-land/game.xml.

2. Copy the original contents of the /res/layout/game.xml to the new file.

3. Modify the contents of the landscape-specific layout file to accommodate landscape mode devices. For example, modify the LinearLayout control that contains the question graphic and text; make this control's orientation horizontal, such that the question graphic displays to the left of the question text, instead of above it. Adjust any other properties until you are happy with the layout design. Provided you do not change the unique identifiers of the important controls, the application functionality remains unchanged.

4. You might also modify the referenced dimensions of the `ImageView` controls slightly by creating alterative dimension resources in the `/res/values-land/dimens.xml` resource file.

Now run your application in landscape mode. The look of the game screen is greatly improved and no longer has display problems, as shown in Figure 20.4.

FIGURE 20.4
The newly improved game screen in landscape mode.

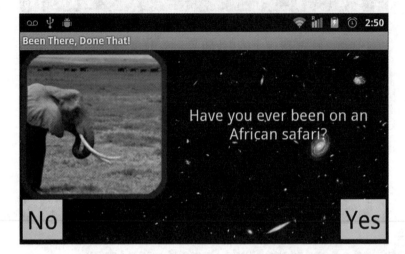

You might notice that the image coming from the server could use some improvement. We could place some logic on the server to improve the served up size of the images. This task is beyond the scope of this Android-oriented book. However, for your own solutions, we recommend always trying to deliver optimal graphics from servers.

Handling Orientation Changes Programmatically

Orientation changes cause the current activity to be restarted, so any processing tasks such as image decoding or network operations begin again unless you implement the `onRetainNonConfigurationInstance()` method of the `Activity` class. For more information on this type of situation, see the write-up at the Android developer website: http://goo.gl/M4uwd.

In addition to providing different resources such as layouts for different orientations, activities can register to listen for screen orientation events and react with different program functionality. To do this, use the `SensorManager` class (`android.hardware.SensorManager`) to query for the current orientation with the `getOrientation()` method. Alternatively, you can implement the `OrientationEventListener` class (`android.view.OrientationEventListener`) and override its onOrientationChanged() callback method to register for orientation changes.

However, listening for these changes is necessary only when applications require special internal handling of orientation events. An application that defines a landscape layout resource in the /res/layout-land/ directory and a default portrait layout resource in the /res/layout/ directory works seamlessly, without the need for a listener.

Supporting Different Screen Characteristics

Android devices come with a variety of display settings, including different screen sizes, densities, aspect ratios, resolutions and default orientations. Also, different devices have different default settings for display purposes, including themes and styles. Make sure you run your application on all target platforms prior to release. Your application will likely behave and display slightly differently on each device. Screen characteristics are major design factors to consider when developing user interfaces.

Figure 20.5 shows how the same layout might appear differently on different screens. On the top, we have a generic high-density WVGA screen and on the bottom, we have the Galaxy tab, which has a high-density WSVGA screen. Note the rather obvious differences.

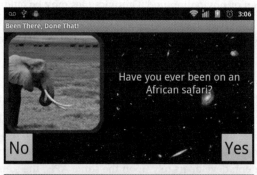

FIGURE 20.5
A layout may display differently on different devices.

Don't despair, though. Fixing these sorts of problems is straightforward. Some ways to prevent display problems associated with screen density and the like in the first place include the following:

► Only set attributes you require (no unnecessary settings to maintain).

► Keep all dimension values in a dimension value resource file, not in individual layout files.

► Specify font sizes in dp or sp, as opposed to pt.

► Specify pixel dimensions in dp, as opposed to px.

► Add custom alternative resources when needed (but sparingly).

By making these changes to the Been There, Done That! project—or better yet, designing the layouts using these guidelines from the start—we help ensure that the application displays properly on a wider variety of devices, from the smallest smartphones to the largest tablets.

Supporting Different Device Features

As you saw in Table 20.1, developers can provide custom resource files for a number of different handset configuration situations. A game might customize certain resources if the handset has no hardware keyboard or if the handset has a specific type of touch screen or navigation pad. Graphics files may be enlarged for very capable handsets with high-resolution screens, whereas on basic handsets they may be reduced to save space. In extreme cases, a game may be 2D on one handset and 3D on another.

One particular kind of Android device that might merit special attention is the Android tablet. There are numerous tablets on the market today, with more shipping every quarter. These large-screened, high-resolution devices offer developers a lot of "screen real estate" and can pose special challenges from a UI design perspective. That said, Android tablet development is really no different from normal Android development; developers rely upon the same APIs, the sample underlying operating system, and the same programming paradigms. For more on targeting Android tablets, check out our article on Tablet tips and tricks on InformIT (http://www.informit.com/articles/article.aspx?p=1708160).

Developing for Different Android SDKs

At the time of this writing, there are eight primary versions of the Android SDK in users' hands: Android 1.5, Android 1.6, Android 2.1, Android 2.2, Android 2.3-2.3.2, Android 2.3.3-2.3.4, Android 3.0, and Android 3.1. The upcoming release (code-named Ice Cream Sandwich) will add to this list, as will any minor SDK revisions. From time to time, Google publishes a breakdown of the usage of various Android versions on handsets, which stand at the following:

▶ 1.9% of users are using Android SDK 1.5.

▶ 2.5% of users are using Android SDK 1.6.

▶ 21.2% of users are using Android SDK 2.1.

▶ 64.6% of users are using Android SDK 2.2.

▶ 1.1% of users are using Android SDK 2.3.

▶ 8.1% of users are using Android SDK 2.3.3-2.3.4.

▶ 0.3% of users are using Android SDK 3.1.

This data was collected and provided online by the Android developer website during the two weeks prior to June 1, 2011. You can check for updated statistics at the following Android developer website: http://goo.gl/jKRKw. One particularly interesting factor is that some versions of the SDK are effectively skipped by most devices, such as 2.0, because they are quickly replaced, and updates (like 2.3.3) are pushed out to users over time. This data can be invaluable for reducing testing load to just platforms where it matters.

It may not be feasible for certain phones, especially older models, to receive the latest firmware updates. As you can see, if you want to hit the broadest range of users, you might need to develop for several different versions of the SDK. This data can be invaluable for reducing the testing load to only those platforms where it matters.

Looking for new data, watching the market news, and surveying your target users ultimately helps you determine which devices to target.

As mobile developers who have been working with and writing about Android since long before the first devices hit the market, we'd like to take a moment to discuss the Android SDKs in terms of backward compatibility.

In general, the Android team strives to keep new Android versions compatible with previous versions so that applications written to previous SDKs run smoothly on the latest firmware. They have done an admirable job. That said, despite claims to the contrary, the reality is that backward compatibility in the Android platform is not guaranteed and developers need to take some responsibility for keeping their apps up-to-date.

Developers regularly find it necessary to update their applications when a new SDK is released. Classes are sometimes changed or deprecated, and methods might appear unchanged in terms of API level or parameters, but their underlying functionality may be modified. In the past, the Android team has claimed that any backward-compatibility issues should be considered "bugs" and should be filed so they can be fixed, but reality has shown that it takes many months before fixes arrive in end-user handsets (if they ever do; some Android handsets have already had their manufacturer support terminated), this sort of guarantee doesn't help the developer who has an application in the user's hands that is failing because "something has changed."

This can be very frustrating to developers and users alike, but it's the reality of the platform. Stay on top of things by retesting your applications when a new SDK is released, so that you can provide updates to users as they upgrade their devices.

Choosing an Application's Target Platform

To appeal to the most users, you need to give some thought to your target platform before you develop any Android application. Will your application support some of the older, more established handsets or just the newest ones? Do some market research and determine what versions of the SDK your target users are using in the field.

Specifying a Project's Target SDK

You can specify an application's SDK support by compiling against the appropriate SDK version, which is set in the project settings, as well as the Android manifest file. You can also specify certain application resources to work with certain SDK versions by using the appropriate resource directory qualifiers listed in Table 20.1.

Designing Applications for Backward Compatibility

To target the largest number of handsets, you need to target multiple versions of the SDK. However, setting required SDK versions in the Android manifest file limits the versions of the SDK on which your application can be installed.

There is a workaround here, though. Because Java uses reflection, you can query classes and methods without including them in the import statements. You could therefore set the minimum SDK version to the lowest possible version that your application can reasonably use. Then application logic can be used—by determining what's actually available at runtime—to enhance any functionality or features that are available. This method can also be used on devices that include specialized features or functions not found on other devices but that your application might want to leverage when they are available. A great example of how to use reflection to support multiple Android SDK versions is available at http://goo.gl/YUBlU.

Detecting the Android SDK Programmatically

You can programmatically determine the version of Android by using the `Build` class (`android.os.Build`). Specifically, you can check the `Build.VERSION` class's `SDK_INT` value, as defined in `android.os.Build.VERSION_CODES`.

Defining Android SDK–Specific Application Resources

Much as developers can provide resources for specific language, region, and handset configuration options in applications, they can also provide resources for specific versions of the Android SDK. Recall from Table 20.1 that resource paths can also specify a particular Android API level number.

Summary

In this hour, you learned how to customize application resources for a variety of handset configurations, including hardware and software requirements. You also learned how to design applications to smoothly handle orientation changes. Finally, you learned how to develop applications for a variety of Android SDK versions.

Q&A

Q. *A firmware upgrade broke my application. What can I do?*

A. First, dry your tears and delete that angry ranting email you were about to send off to the Android development team. This kind of thing is annoying and sometimes downright embarrassing, but it happens. In some cases, you can avoid surprises like this by testing your application against the open source project for the upcoming Android SDK release, but there's no guarantee that a specific handset (or operator) won't modify the firmware release, adding and removing features at will. Sometimes, you won't know there's a problem until you get a complaint from someone in Sao Paulo or Beijing or, perhaps most cringe-worthy, from your boss. Here, a solid response plan is a must. Designate someone in advance to stay on top of Android SDK releases—to fix bugs and to publish application updates to users.

Q. *How can I listen for orientation changes and load the appropriate portrait or landscape layout so my application screens always look nice?*

A. Your application does not have to listen for orientation changes to do this. Instead, just make sure you have the appropriately qualified layout resources (using the `port` or `land` qualifier). The Android operating system automatically loads the appropriate layout whenever the orientation of the device changes. As with any other resource, make sure the portrait and landscape resources contain the same child views (so you don't run into cases where a referenced view is undefined in one orientation).

Workshop

Quiz

1. True or False: The following is a correctly qualified resource directory name: `/res/drawables-rUS-en`.

2. For which of the following handset configurations can resources be defined?

   A. Language and region/locale

   B. Input methods, such as keyboards, touch screens, and navigation keys

   C. Screen size, resolution, and orientation

   D. Whether the keyboard and navigation keys are hidden

   E. All of the above

3. True or False: You can provide alternative resources for a specific version of the Android SDK, such as Honeycomb (Android 3.0).

Answers

1. False. The region must follow the language. Therefore, the directory would appropriately be named `/res/drawables-en-rUS`.

2. E. All these qualifiers are available for application resources. There are also others. For a complete list, see the list at the Android developer website (http://goo.gl/87cUS).

3. True. The SDK version resource directory qualifier is the final (last) qualifier at the end of a string of applicable qualifiers.

Exercises

1. Provide alternative string resources so that the name of the Been There, Done That! application has the Android SDK version built into its application name—for example, "Been There, Done That! (Honeycomb Edition) versus "Been There, Done That! (Gingerbread Edition).

2. Update the Been There, Done That! application and provide an alternative look-and-feel for day versus night mode. For example, the defaults could be used for night mode. Day mode changes might include different text colors and a different background graphic that is brightly colored instead of the dark space background.

3. Implement an orientation listener in one of your Activity classes. Log an information message each time an orientation event occurs.

4. **[Challenging]** Interested in tablet development? See our series of online articles on the new Fragments API and how it can be used to leverage that "screen real estate" more effectively on tablets. Start with this tutorial: http://goo.gl/cDEwK.

HOUR 21

Diving Deeper into Android

What You'll Learn in This Hour:

▶ Exploring more advanced Android features
▶ Designing advanced user interfaces
▶ Working with multimedia
▶ Managing and sharing data
▶ Accessing underlying device hardware

When you are becoming familiar with a new mobile platform, it can be helpful to know what is feasible and what is not. This hour provides a crash-course in some of the more advanced features of the Android SDK. Specifically, you will more about using core application features, designing advanced user interfaces, using multimedia, managing storage and data, and accessing the underlying device hardware.

Exploring More Core Android Features

This might come as something of a surprise, but 24 hours is not enough time to cover all the interesting and useful features of the Android platform and Android SDK. You've already packed tons of features into the Been There, Done That! application over the course of this book.

Now that you have mastered the basics of Android development, you might find your attention returning to your own application ideas. Perhaps you find yourself wondering if certain features we have not covered in this basic book are feasible and where to start looking for more information. In this hour, you learn about many of the advanced features of the Android platform. These topics are covered in further detail in the Android SDK documentation as well as more advanced Android programming books, including those written by these authors.

Declaring and Enforcing Application Permissions

As you know, applications must register the appropriate permissions they require within the Android manifest file. Applications can also declare and enforce their own custom permissions with the <permission> tag. Each permission must be defined in the Android manifest file and can be applied to specific components— notably an activity or a service—within the application. You can also apply permissions at the method level.

Alerting the User with Notifications

An application can alert the user even when the application isn't actively running in the foreground using a notification. For example, a messaging application might notify users when a new message is delivered, as shown in Figure 21.1.

FIGURE 21.1
Several notifications in the status window.

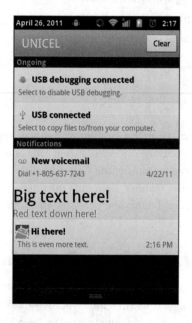

Notifications come in a variety of forms. An application can use several different kinds of notifications, provided that it has the appropriate permissions registered in the Android manifest file:

▶ Display a text notification on the status bar

▶ Play a sound

▶ Vibrate the device

▶ Change the indicator light color and blinking frequency

Not all devices support every notification type. For example, some devices might not have the ability to vibrate, play sounds, or have an indicator light.

Notifications are created and triggered using the `NotificationManager` system service (`android.app.NotificationManager`). After it is requested, you can create a `Notification` object (by setting the appropriate notification text, vibration, light, and sound settings) and use the `notify()` class method to trigger the notification.

Take special care to use notifications appropriately, so as not to be a nuisance to the user. Some notification methods, such as vibration, must be tested on the device because the Android emulator does not simulate this type of action.

Watch Out!

Designing Advanced User Interfaces

The best and most popular applications on the Android platform have one thing in common: Each has an excellent, well-designed user interface. You've worked with many of the common user interface features of Android, such as layouts and user interface controls. However, the Android SDK has many other exciting user interface features, including the following:

▶ A Fragments API that helps componentize user interface functionality separate from a specific Activity class

▶ The ability to apply consistent settings across many controls or entire screens using styles and themes

▶ The ability to design and reuse custom user interface components

▶ A powerful input method framework

▶ The ability to detect various screen gestures

▶ A text-to-speech (TTS) engine

▶ Speech recognition support

Using Styles and Themes

The Android SDK provides two powerful mechanisms for designing consistent user interfaces that are easy to maintain: styles and themes.

A style is a grouping of common View attribute settings that you can apply to any number of View controls. For example, you might want all View controls in your application, such as TextView and EditText controls, to use the same text color, font, and size. You could create a style that defines these three attributes and apply it to each TextView and EditText control within your application layouts.

A theme is a collection of one or more styles. Whereas you apply a style to a specific control, such as a TextView control, you apply a theme to all View objects within a specified activity. Applying a theme to a set of View objects all at once simplifies making the user interface look consistent; it can be a great way to define color schemes and other common View attribute settings across an application. You can specify a theme programmatically by calling the Activity class's setTheme() method. You can also apply themes to a specific activity in the Android manifest file.

> The Android SDK includes a number of built-in themes, which you can find in the android.R.style class. For example, android.R.style.Theme is the default system theme. There are themes with black backgrounds, themes with and without a title bar, themes for dialog controls, and more.

Designing Custom View and ViewGroup Controls

You are already familiar with many of the user interface controls, such as layout and View controls, that are available in the Android SDK. You can also create custom controls. To do so, you simply start with the appropriate View (or ViewGroup) control from the android.view package and implement the specific functionality needed for your control or layout.

You can use custom View controls in XML layout files, or you can inflate them programmatically at runtime. You can create new types of controls, or you can simply extend the functionality of existing controls, such as TextView or Button controls.

For more information on implementing custom View controls, see http://goo.gl/InF05.

Working with Input Methods

The Android platform provides a user-friendly software keyboard (see Figure 21.2) for devices that do not have hardware keyboards. The Android SDK also includes powerful text input method support for predictive text and downloadable input method editors (IMEs).

FIGURE 21.2
The Android
software
keyboard.

Handling User Gestures

You already know how to listen for click events. You can also handle gestures, such as flings, scrolls, and taps, by using the GestureDetector class (android.view.GestureDetector). You can use the GestureDetector class by implementing the onTouchEvent() method within an activity.

The following are some of the gestures an application can watch for and handle:

▶ onDown—Occurs when the user first presses the touch screen

▶ onShowPress—Occurs after the user first presses the touch screen but before the user lifts up or moves around on the screen

▶ onSingleTapUp—Occurs when the user lifts up from the touch screen as part of a single-tap event

▶ onSingleTapConfirmed—Called when a single-tap event occurs

▶ onDoubleTap—Called when a double-tap event occurs

▶ onDoubleTapEvent—Called when an event within a double-tap gesture occurs, including any down, move, or up action

▶ onLongPress—Similar to onSingleTapUp but called if the user has held his or her finger down just long enough to not be a standard click but also didn't move the finger

▶ onScroll—Called after the user has pressed and then moved his or her finger in a steady motion and lifted up

▶ onFling—Called after the user has pressed and then moved his or her finger in an accelerating motion just before lifting it

In addition, the android.gesture package enables an application to recognize arbitrary gestures, as well as store, load, and draw them. This means almost any symbol a user can draw could be turned into a gesture with a specific meaning. Some versions of the SDK have a Gesture Builder application that can simplify the process of creating gestures for applications that don't have a gesture-recording feature.

For more information about the android.gesture package, see http://goo.gl/MqgN4.

Converting Text to Speech

The Android platform includes a TTS engine (android.speech.tts) that enables devices to perform speech synthesis. You can use the TTS engine to have your applications "read" text to the user. You might have seen this feature used frequently with Location-Based Services (LBS) applications that allow for hands-free directions. Other applications use this feature for users who have reading or sight problems.

The Android TTS engine supports a variety of languages, including English (in American or British accents), French, German, Italian, and Spanish. The synthesized speech can be played immediately or saved to an audio file, which can be treated like any other audio file.

Watch Out!

To provide TTS services to users, an Android device must have both the TTS engine (available in Android SDK 1.6 and higher) and the appropriate language resource files. In some cases, the user must install the appropriate language resource files (assuming that the user has space for them) from a remote location. The users can do this themselves by going to Settings, Text-to-speech, Install Voice Data. You might also need to do this on your devices. Additionally, the application can verify that the data is installed correctly or trigger the installation if it's not. See the documentation for the android.speech.tts package at http://goo.gl/4zUsl.

Converting Speech to Text

You can enhance an application with speech recognition support by using the speech recognition framework (android.speech.RecognizerIntent). You use this intent to record speech and send it to a recognition server for processing, so this feature is not really practical for devices that don't have a reasonable network connection.

> On Android SDK 2.1 and later, speech recognition is built in to most on-screen keyboards. Therefore, an application may already support speech recognition, to some extent, without any changes. However, directly accessing the recognizer can allow for more interesting spoken word control over applications.

Did you Know?

Working with Multimedia

Mobile devices are increasingly being used as multimedia devices. Many Android devices have built-in cameras, microphones, and speakers, allowing playback and recording of multimedia in a variety of formats. The Android SDK provides comprehensive multimedia support, allowing developers to incorporate audio and visual media (still and video) into applications. These APIs are part of the android.media package.

> The Android emulator cannot record audio or video. Testing of audio and video recording must be done using a real Android device. Also, the recording capabilities of a given device will vary based upon the hardware and software components used. For instance, Android devices that aren't phones often lack microphones and cameras.

Watch Out!

Playing and Recording Audio

The Android SDK provides mechanisms for audio playback and recording in various formats. Audio files may be resources, local files, or URI objects to shared or network resources. You can use the MediaPlayer class (android.media.MediaPlayer) to play audio, and the MediaRecorder class (android.media.MediaRecorder) can be used to record audio. Recording audio requires the android.permission.RECORD_AUDIO permission.

Playing and Recording Video

You can use the `VideoView` control to play video content on a screen. You can use the `MediaController` control to provide the `VideoView` control with basic video controls, such as play, pause, and stop (see Figure 21.3).

As with audio recording, you can use the `MediaRecorder` class to record video content using the built-in camera. Applications that access the camera hardware must have the `android.permission.CAMERA` permission registered, and those that record audio using `MediaRecorder` must register the `android.permission.RECORD_AUDIO` permission in the Android manifest file. Thus, to record video, which uses the microphone and camera, you must add both permissions to the Android manifest file.

Working with 2D and 3D Graphics

If you're familiar with computer graphics programming, you will be pleased to note that Android has fairly sophisticated graphics capabilities for a mobile device.

Using the Android Graphics Libraries

The Android SDK comes with the android.graphics package, which includes a number of handy classes for drawing on the screen (see Figure 21.4). Some features of the Android graphics package include bitmap graphics utilities and support for typefaces, fonts, paints, gradients, shapes, and animation. There are also helper classes, such as the Matrix class, that can help perform graphics operations.

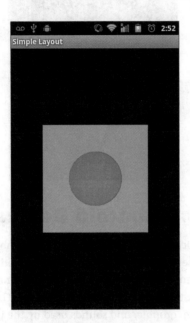

FIGURE 21.4
A simple two-dimensional graphic created with Android.

Using the OpenGL ES Graphics API

For more advanced graphics, Android uses the popular OpenGL ES graphics API (1.0), and it provides limited support for OpenGL ES 1.1. Applications can use Android's OpenGL ES support to draw, animate, light, shade, and texture graphical objects in three dimensions (see Figure 21.5).

FIGURE 21.5
An OpenGL ES
graphic created
with Android.

Personalizing Android Devices

Personalization of a device involves enabling the user to change the look and behavior of his or her user experience. From the software side, personalization involves configuring features such as the wallpaper, ringtone, and such. Android allows a deep level of customization and personalization. The user can customize their home screen, theme, graphic, and sounds used by the platform. Android applications can provide many of these personalization features to users. For instance, a branded application might allow the users to set ringtones and wallpapers that support the brand.

Setting the Ringtone

An application can change the handset ringtone by using the `RingtoneManager`. To modify the ringtone, an application must have the appropriate permission (`android.permission.WRITE_SETTINGS`) registered in the Android manifest file. You can also launch the ringtone picker by using the `ACTION_RINGTONE_PICKER` intent.

Setting the Wallpaper

An application can set a wallpaper for the background of the Home screen by using the `WallpaperManager` class. Various methods are provided to retrieve the current wallpaper and set a new one using a bitmap, a resource, or another form of wallpaper.

In addition to using static images as wallpapers, Android supports live wallpapers, which are essentially animated wallpapers but can contain almost anything an application can draw on a surface. For example, you could create a wallpaper that visually shows the current weather, time of day, information about music playing, a slideshow, or some sort of video or animated demonstration. Live wallpapers are similar to widgets in that they are surfaces; however, the implementation details are different.

For more information on wallpapers, see the Android SDK documentation related to the `android.service.wallpaper` package at http://goo.gl/IFcbg.

Creating a Live Wallpaper

A live wallpaper can display anything that can be drawn on a surface using the full graphical capabilities of the device and the Android SDK (as described in the section on 2D and 3D graphics from earlier in this hour).

A live wallpaper is similar to an Android Service, but its result is a surface that the host can display. You can create a live wallpaper as complex as you like, but you should take into account handset responsiveness and battery life. Some examples of live wallpapers include

- ▶ A 3D display showing an animated scene portraying abstract shapes

- ▶ A service that displays a slideshow of images found on an online image sharing service

- ▶ An interactive pond with water that ripples with touch

- ▶ Wallpapers that change based on the actual season, weather, and time of day

To learn more about how to implement live wallpapers, see the article on live wallpapers at the Android developer website (http://goo.gl/mvn3K) and the Cube Live Wallpaper sample application included with the Android SDK.

By the Way

Managing and Sharing Data

You are already familiar with some of the ways applications can store data persistently:

- ▶ They can store simple, primitive data types within `SharedPreferences` at the application and activity levels.

- ▶ They can store data on a remote application server.

Applications can also store and share data by doing the following:

▶ They can leverage the file and directory structure on the device to store private application files in any format.

▶ They can store structured data in private SQLite databases.

▶ They can access data within other applications that act as content providers.

▶ They can share internal application data by becoming content providers.

You already know how to work with SharedPreferences and how to store data on a network application server, so let's talk about other ways of managing and sharing data.

Working with Files and Directories

Each Android application has its own private application directory and files. You can use the standard java file I/O package called java.io to manipulate files and directories.

Android application files are stored in a standard directory hierarchy on the Android file system. Android application data is stored on the Android file system in the following top-level directory:

/data/data/<package name>/

Several special-purpose subdirectories are created beneath the top-level application directory to store databases, preferences, and files. You can also create private directories and files here, as needed, using the appropriate methods of the application's Context object. The following are some of the important file and directory management methods of the Context class:

▶ openFileInput()—Opens an application file for reading in the /files subdirectory

▶ openFileOutput()—Creates or opens an application file for writing in the /files subdirectory

▶ deleteFile()—Deletes an application file by name from the /files subdirectory

▶ fileList()—Lists all files in the /files subdirectory

▶ getFilesDir()—Retrieves a File object for the /files subdirectory

▶ getCacheDir()—Retrieves a File object for the /cache subdirectory

▶ getDir()—Creates or retrieves a File object for a subdirectory by name

> You can browse the Android file system (of the emulator or a connected device) by using the DDMS File Explorer.

Storing Structured Data in a SQLite Database

Android applications can have a locally accessible, private application database powered by SQLite. SQLite relational databases are lightweight and file based—ideal for mobile devices. The Android SDK includes a number of useful SQLite database management classes. The SQLite support available on the Android platform is found in the android.database.sqlite package. Here, you can find utility classes for the following:

▶ Creating, versioning, and managing databases

▶ Building proper SQL queries

▶ Iterating through query results with Cursor objects

▶ Processing database transactions

▶ Handling specialized database exceptions

> Android has built-in SQLite support. However, you can also find generic database classes within the android.database package.

In addition to programmatically creating and using SQLite databases, developers can use the sqlite3 command-line tool, which is accessible through the ADB shell interface for debugging purposes.

Sharing Data with Other Applications

An application can leverage the data available within other Android applications if the other applications expose specific data by becoming content providers. You can also enable your application to share data within other applications by making it a content provider.

Using Content Providers

The Android platform ships with some useful applications—such as a contacts application and a browser application—that expose some or all of their data by acting as content providers. An application can access the content of these applications by using the content provider data interface. Some content providers provide only "read" access to data, and others allow applications to create, update, and delete records, such as contacts.

Most access to content providers comes in the form of queries to specific predefined URI object-contained addresses. Once formulated, a query might return a list of contacts or missed calls, or it might return a specific record, such as all contact information for John Smith. Applications can access content provider interfaces much as they would access any database.

You can think of a URI as an address to the location where content exists. You can use the managedQuery() method to retrieve data from a content provider and then iterate through the query results by using a cursor, just as you would any database query result.

Exploring Some Commonly Used Content Providers

You can find the content providers included with Android in the android.provider package. Here are some of the most useful content providers:

- ▶ MediaStore—Used to access media (audio, video, and still images) on the phone and on external storage devices

- ▶ CallLog—Used to access information about dialed, received, and missed phone calls

- ▶ Browser—Used to access the user's browsing history and bookmarked websites

- ▶ Contacts—Used to access the user's contacts database

- ▶ UserDictionary—A dictionary of user-defined words for use with predictive text input

You can bind data from a database or content provider cursor directly to user interface View controls such as ListView. To do so, use a data Adapter control, such as ArrayAdapter or CursorAdapter, and a View control derived from AdapterView, such as a ListView or Spinner control.

Acting as a Content Provider

An application can expose internal data to other applications by becoming a content provider. To share information with other applications, an application must implement a content provider interface and register as a content provider within the Android manifest file.

Organizing Content with Live Folders

A live folder is a special type of object that, when clicked, shows data from an application acting as a content provider. For example, a music application might enable the user to create live folders for specific music playlists, which could be placed on the Home screen (via a long-click on the home screen, then choosing Folders). To create a live folder, an application must create an `Activity` class that responds to the intent action `ACTION_CREATE_LIVE_FOLDER` and have a corresponding `ContentProvider` object for the data contents of the live folder. See the documentation for the `android.provider.LiveFolders` package at http://goo.gl/n7d5H for more details.

Integrating with Global Search

Android allows applications to be searchable at a system-wide level. This is done by configuring the application and providing custom `Activity` classes that handle the various commands required to handle the search actions and search results. Additionally, applications can provide search suggestions that display when a user is typing their search criteria in the search field (the Quick Search Box).

If your application is content rich, either with content created by users or with content provided by the developer, then integrating with the global search mechanism of Android can provide many benefits and add value to the user. The application data becomes part of the overall handset experience, is more accessible, and your application may be presented to the user in more cases than just when he or she launches it.

> To learn how to incorporate global search functionality into Android applications, see the documentation for the `SearchManager` class (`android.app.SearchManager`) at http://goo.gl/MEYEB and the Searchable Dictionary sample application found with the Android SDK and online at http://goo.gl/eeFzO.

By the Way

Accessing Underlying Device Hardware

Android developers have unprecedented access to the underlying hardware on a device. In addition to hardware such as the camera and LBS services, the Android SDK has a variety of APIs for accessing low-level hardware features on the handset, including the following:

- Reading raw sensor data (such as the magnetic and orientation sensors)
- Accessing Wi-Fi and Bluetooth sensors
- Monitoring battery usage and power management

> Not all sensors and hardware are available on each Android device. Many of these features are optional hardware. Be sure to programmatically test for device features before attempting to use them.

The sensors available on a given device vary in terms of availability and sensitivity. Some sensors provide raw sensor data, but others are backed by services or software to provide useful data to the application.

Reading Raw Sensor Data

The following are some of the device sensors that the Android SDK supports:

- `Accelerometer`—Measures acceleration in three dimensions
- `Light sensor`—Measures brightness (which is useful for camera flashes)
- `Magnetic field sensor`—Measures magnetism in three dimensions
- `Orientation sensor`—Measures a device's orientation
- `Temperature sensor`—Measures temperature
- `Proximity sensor`—Measures the distance from the device to a point in space

> The Android emulator does not simulate any device sensors natively, but OpenIntents provides a handy sensor simulator (http://goo.gl/Ousse). This tool simulates accelerometer, compass, and orientation sensors, as well as a temperature sensor, and it transmits data to the emulator. You can also test sensor functionality on the target device.

The SensorManager object is used to gather data from the device sensors. You can retrieve an instance of SensorManager by using the getSystemService() method.

Working with Wi-Fi

Applications with the appropriate permissions (ACCESS_WIFI_STATE and CHANGE_WIFI_STATE) can access the built-in Wi-Fi sensor on a device by using the WifiManager object. You can retrieve an instance of WifiManager by using the getSystemService() method.

The Android SDK provides a set of APIs for retrieving information about the Wi-Fi networks available to a device as well as Wi-Fi network connection details. This information can be used for tracking signal strength, finding access points, or performing actions when connected to specific access points.

> The emulator does not emulate Wi-Fi support, so you need to perform all testing of Wi-Fi APIs on a device.

Working with Bluetooth

The Android SDK includes Bluetooth support classes in the android.bluetooth package. Here, you find classes for scanning for Bluetooth-enabled devices, pairing, and handling data transfer.

Managing Power Settings and Battery Life

Most mobile devices operate primarily using battery power. To monitor the battery, an application must have the BATTERY_STATS permission, register to receive Intent.ACTION_BATTERY_CHANGED BroadcastIntent, and implement BroadcastReceiver to extract the battery information and take any actions required. The following are some of the battery and power settings that can be monitored:

▶ Whether a battery exists

▶ The battery health, status (charging state), voltage, and temperature

▶ The battery charge percentage and associated icon

▶ Whether the device is plugged in via AC or USB power

An application can use the information about the device power state to manage its own power consumption. For example, an application that routinely uses a lot of processing power might disable features that use a lot of power when little battery life remains.

Summary

In this hour, you learned about more advanced features of the Android platform. You learned about some of the more advanced architectural components of Android applications, such as how you can use services and notifications and how applications can define and enforce their own permissions. You learned how to design consistent user interfaces by using styles and themes. You now know that Android devices have many powerful multimedia features, including the ability to play and record audio and video, and that it is feasible to develop 3D graphics-intensive applications by using OpenGL ES. Android applications can take advantage of the handy SQLite database features and can share data with other applications by accessing a content provider or by becoming a content provider. Finally, applications can access and interact with myriad underlying hardware sensors on a device.

Q&A

Q. *What multimedia formats are supported on the Android platform?*

A. Different Android devices support different formats. The platform supports a number of core formats, but specific devices might also extend this list as they see fit. For a complete list of supported formats, see the Android documentation at http://goo.gl/xe1wG.

Q. *Where can I see code examples of the advanced features covered in this chapter?*

A. The implementation details of the features discussed in this chapter are beyond the scope of this book. However, we have written an advanced Android book titled *Android Wireless Application Development*. We have also written countless articles and online tutorials on a variety of Android subjects—find out more at our website, http://androidbook.blogspot.com. You can also find many Android SDK examples on the Android developer website, http://developer.android.com.

Q. *Can my application use Near Field Communication (NFC)?*

A. Android 2.3 introduced NFC APIs for use by app developers. As of this writing, there are few Android devices that support NFC, most notably the Nexus S. You can find out more about the NFC support in Android in the `android.nfc` package.

Q. *Can I develop USB accessories for Android?*

A. A new Android Open Accessory Development Kit was introduced in Android 3.1 (compatible also with Android 2.3.4). Find out more about it at: http://goo.gl/7IXOt.

Workshop

Quiz

1. True or False: Content providers always require an Android application to declare permissions in the Android manifest file.

2. Which multimedia features are feasible on Android?

   A. Ability to play audio

   B. Ability to play video

   C. Ability to record audio

   D. Ability to record video

   E. All of the above

3. True or False: The indicator light on an Android device is accessible using the Android SDK.

4. True or False: This chapter covers all additional features of the Android SDK not covered elsewhere in this book.

Answers

1. False. Content providers may require specific permissions. However, the enforcement of permissions depends on the content provider. Check the specific content provider documentation for what specific permissions are required to access its provider interface.

2. E. The android.media package includes support for playing and recording audio and video in a variety of formats. Different Android devices have different hardware available, so check specific target devices to make sure they support the multimedia features an application requires.

3. True. You can use the NotificationManager class to access the LED indicator light on an Android device.

4. False. The Android SDK has many more features and nuances. In addition, the framework is being updated and enhanced very rapidly. You can find various resources, blogs, articles, and developer guides at http://developer.android.com. Also see our blog for tips, tricks, guides, and pointers to other resources: http://androidbook.blogspot.com.

Exercises

1. Think of three different ways you could use a local SQLite database to enhance the Been There, Done That! application.

2. Review the various system services that can be requested by using the getSystemService() method. The various services are defined in the android.content.Context class.

3. Review the Been There, Done That! application and identify three functional areas where you could design and use custom View controls. What would those custom controls do?

4. Many Android applications have the same look because they rely on the default theme provided by the platform. Add theme definitions to the layout screens in the Been There, Done That! application. This way, the application has a custom look that is consistent across Android devices, regardless of what the default theme is.

HOUR 22

Testing Android Applications

What You'll Learn in This Hour:

▶ Best practices for testing mobile applications
▶ Developing a mobile test framework
▶ Handling other testing concerns

Every mobile developer dreams of developing a "killer app." Many people think that if they could just come up with a great idea, success is guaranteed. This is, unfortunately, not the case. The truth is, people come up with great ideas all the time. The trick is to act on the idea with a clear vision, a concise "pitch" to users, and an intuitive user interface. There's also a time component—you have to get that app into users' hands quickly—before someone else does! A killer app must have the right mix of these ingredients, but a poor implementation of an excellent idea isn't going to become a killer app, so it's important to test each application thoroughly before publication. In this hour, you learn how to test mobile applications in a variety of ways.

Testing Best Practices

Mobile users expect a lot from today's mobile applications. They expect the applications they install to be stable, responsive, and secure. Stable means that the application works and doesn't crash or mess up the user's device. Responsive means the device always responds to button presses and tap events, and long operations use progress bars or other forms of activity indicators. Secure means that the application doesn't abuse the trust of the user, either intentionally or unintentionally. Users expect an application to have a reasonably straightforward user interface, and they expect the application to work 24/7 (especially when it comes to networked applications with a server side).

It might seem like users expect a lot for an application that might be priced at $0.99, but really, do any of these expectations seem that unreasonable? We don't think so. However, they do impose significant responsibilities on a developer in terms of testing and quality control.

Whether you're a project team of one or one hundred, every mobile development project benefits from a good development process with a solid test plan. The following are some quality measures that can greatly improve the development process:

▶ Coding standards and guidelines

▶ Regular versioned builds

▶ A defect tracking system with a process for resolving defects

▶ Systematic application testing using a test plan

You can outsource application testing to a third party. Keep in mind that the success of any outsourced project depends heavily on the quality of the documentation you provide (for example, functional specifications, use cases) to the outsourcing facility.

Developing Coding Standards

When developers have and follow a set of predetermined guidelines, their code is more cohesive, easier to read, and easier to maintain. Developing a set of well-communicated coding standards for developers can help drive home some of the important requirements of mobile applications we've been discussing. For example, developers should

▶ Discuss and come up with a common way for all developers to implement error and exception handling

▶ Move lengthy or process-intensive operations off the main UI thread

▶ Release objects and resources that aren't actively being used

▶ Practice prudent memory management and track down memory leaks

▶ Use project resources appropriately. For example, don't hard-code data and strings in code or layout files

Performing Regular Versioned Builds

Implementing a reproducible build process is essential for a successful Android project. This is especially true for applications that include support for multiple Android SDK versions, devices, or languages. To perform regular, versioned builds, do the following:

▶ Use a source control system to keep track of project files

▶ Version project files at regular intervals and perform routine, reproducible builds

▶ Verify (through testing) that each build performs as expected

There are many wonderful source control systems out there for developers, and most that work well for traditional development work fine for a mobile project. Many popular source control systems—such as Perforce, Subversion, Git, and CVS—work well with Eclipse, including through plug-ins that provide integration right with Eclipse.

Because of the speed at which mobile projects tend to progress, iterative development processes are generally the most successful strategies for mobile development. Rapid prototyping gives developers and quality assurance personnel ample opportunities to evaluate an application before it reaches users.

Did you Know?

Using a Defect Tracking System

A defect tracking system provides a way to organize and keep track of application bugs, or defects, and is generally used along with a process for resolving these issues. Resolving a defect generally means fixing the problem and verifying that the fix is correct in a future build.

With mobile applications, defects come in many forms. Some defects occur on all devices, but others occur only on specific devices. Functional defects—that is, features of an application that are not working properly—are only one type of defect. You must look beyond these and test whether an application works well with the rest of the Android operating system in terms of performance, responsiveness, usability, and state management.

Developing Good Test Plans

Testers rely heavily on an application's functional specification, as well as any user interface documentation, to determine whether features and functionality have been properly implemented. The application features and workflow must be thoroughly documented at the screen level and then validated through testing. It is not uncommon for interpretive differences to exist between the functional specification, the developer's implementation, and the tester's resulting experience. These differences must be resolved as part of the defect-resolution process.

Android application testers, or quality assurance personnel, have a variety of tools at their fingertips. Although some manual testing is essential, there are now numerous opportunities for automated testing to be incorporated into testing plans.

Test plans need to cover a variety of areas, including the following:

▶ **Functional testing**—This type of testing ensures that the features and functions of the application work correctly, as detailed in the application's functional specification.

▶ **Integration testing**—This type of testing ensures that the software integrates well with other core device features. For example, an application must suspend and resume properly, and it must gracefully handle interruptions from the operating system (for example, incoming messages, phone calls, powering off).

▶ **Client/server testing**—Networked mobile applications often have greater testing requirements than stand-alone applications. This is because you must verify the server-side functionality in addition to the mobile client.

▶ **Upgrade testing**—Upgrades come in many forms. Android devices receive frequent firmware updates, which may necessitate application upgrades. When possible, perform application upgrade testing of both the client and the server to ensure that any upgrades go smoothly for users.

▶ **Internationalization testing**—This type of testing ensures internationalization support—especially language support—early in the development process. If an application supports multiple languages, problems tend to arise related to screen real estate, string manipulation, and issues with currency, date, and time formatting.

▶ **Usability testing**—This type of testing identifies any areas of the application that lack visual appeal or are difficult to navigate or use, usually from a user interface perspective. It verifies that the application's resource consumption model matches the target audience. For example, gamers might accept shorter battery life for graphic-intensive games, but productivity applications should not drain the battery unnecessarily.

▶ **Performance testing**—This type of testing uses the debugging utilities of the Android SDK to monitor memory and resource usage; it also identifies performance bottlenecks as well as dangerous memory leaks and fixes them.

▶ **Conformance testing**—This type of testing reviews any policies, license agreements, terms and laws (including export laws) that an application must conform to and verifies that the application complies.

▶ **Edge-case testing**—An application must be robust enough to handle random and unexpected events. We've all forgotten to lock our devices on occasion, only to find that the device has received random key presses, launched random apps, or made unnecessary phone calls from the comfort of our pocket. An application must handle these types of events gracefully. That is to say, it shouldn't crash. You can use the monkey tools, Monkey and monkeyrunner, that come with the Android SDK to stress-test an application in both random and reproducible ways.

Maximizing Test Coverage

While 100% test coverage is unrealistic, the goal is to test as much of an application as possible, in as many different conditions as possible. To do this, you are likely to need to perform tests on the emulator with numerous AVDs as well as on many target devices, and you might want to consider using both manual and automated testing procedures.

Managing the Testing Environment

Don't assume that mobile applications are simpler to test just because they are "smaller" than desktop applications and have fewer features. Testing mobile applications poses many unique challenges to testers, especially in terms of configuration management. Let's discuss some of these challenges.

Identifying and Acquiring Target Devices

The earlier you can decide on and get your hands on the devices you are targeting for your application, the better. Sometimes, this is as easy as going to the store and grabbing a new device (sometimes with a new service plan); other times, it's more complicated.

*Did you
Know?*

Some companies, including device manufacturers, run developer programs with device labs. Here, developers can rent time on specific devices—by mail, remotely (via the Internet), or by traveling to the lab. This gives developers access to a wide variety of devices on many different networks, without requiring them to own each and every one. Some labs are even staffed with experts to help iron out device-specific problems.

For preproduction devices, it can take months to get the hardware in-hand from the manufacturer or operator through developer program loaner services. Cooperating with carrier device loaner programs and buying devices from retail locations is frustrating but sometimes necessary. Don't wait until the last minute to gather the test hardware you need.

*Watch
Out!*

There is no guarantee that a preproduction device will behave exactly the same as the production model that eventually ships to consumers. Features are often cut at the last minute to make the production deadline.

Dealing with Device Fragmentation

One of the biggest challenges a mobile application tester faces is the explosion of new Android devices on the market. This problem—sometimes called device fragmentation—makes the task of keeping track of the devices available—running the different versions of the Android SDK and having different screen sizes, features, and hardware—increasingly complex (see Figure 22.1).

Managing a Device Database

It is a good idea to use a database to keep track of device information for development, testing, and marketing purposes. Such a database might contain information such as the following:

▶ Device information (models, features, SDK version, hardware specifics such as whether a device has a camera or built-in keyboard)

▶ Which devices you have on hand (and where they are, if they are owned or loaned, and so on)

▶ Which devices you want to target for a given application

▶ The devices on which your applications are selling best

FIGURE 22.1
Device
fragmentation.

Testing on the Emulator

A test team cannot be expected to set up testing environments on every carrier or in every country where users will use an application. There are times when using the Android emulator can reduce costs and improve testing coverage. The following are some of the benefits of using the emulator:

▶ Rapidly testing when a target device is not available (or is in short supply) using AVD configuration settings

▶ Simulating devices when they are not yet available (for example, preproduction devices)

▶ Testing difficult or dangerous scenarios that are not feasible or recommended on live devices (such as tests that might somehow break a device or invalidate a service agreement)

The emulator provides a useful but limited simulation of a generic Android device. By using AVD configuration options, you can customize an emulator to closely represent a target device. However, an emulator does not rely on the same hardware—or software—implementation that is on an actual device. An emulator simply pretends. The more hardware features an application relies on (for example, making calls, networking, LBS, the camera, Bluetooth, sensor data), the more important it is to test on an actual device.

Watch Out!

Testing on Target Devices

Here is a mobile mantra that is worth repeating: Test early, test often, test on the actual device.

It's important to get target devices in-hand as soon as you can. This cannot be said enough: Testing on the emulator is helpful; testing on the device is essential. In reality, it doesn't really matter if your application works on the emulator; users run the applications on devices.

Watch Out!

> It's important to test application assumptions early and often, on the target device(s). This is called *feasibility testing*. It is disheartening to design and develop an application and then find that it doesn't work on the actual device. Just because your application works on the emulator does not guarantee that it works on the device.

Testing on a target device is the safest way to ensure that an application works correctly because you are running the application on the same hardware that your users are going to use. By mimicking the environment your users use, you can ensure that your application works as expected in the real world.

Watch Out!

> Although it can be convenient to test with the device plugged in, this is not the way most users will use your application. Normal users typically use battery power only. Be sure to unplug the device and test an application the way users will most likely encounter it. Pay special attention to how your application affects battery life.

Performing Automated Testing

Collecting application information and building automated tests can help you build a better, more bulletproof application. The Android SDK provides a number of packages related to code diagnostics. Application diagnostics fall into three categories:

- ▶ Logging application information for performance or usage statistics
- ▶ Automated test suites based on the JUnit framework
- ▶ Automated testing based on scripts using the monkeyrunner tool

Logging Application Information

The beginning of this book covered how to leverage the built-in logging class Log (`android.util.Log`) to implement different levels of diagnostic logging. You can monitor the output of log information from within Eclipse or by using the LogCat utility provided with the Android SDK.

Don't forget to strip any diagnostic information, such as logging information, from the application before publication. Logging information and diagnostics can negatively affect application performance.

Automated Testing with JUnit and Eclipse

The Android SDK includes extensions to the JUnit framework for testing Android applications. Automated testing is accomplished by creating test cases, in Java, that verify that the application works the way you designed it. You can use automated testing techniques for both unit testing and functional testing, including user interface testing.

This discussion is not meant to provide full documentation for writing JUnit test cases. For that, look to online resources, such as http://www.junit.org, or books on the subject. However, we provide a simple example of how to use JUnit with Android projects in Eclipse.

Some people follow a paradigm of creating the test cases first and then writing code that causes the test cases to pass. This method can work well in an environment where all application results and behavior are known before coding begins and will change little or not at all.

Automated testing for Android involves just a few straightforward steps:

1. Create a test project.

2. Add test cases to the new project.

3. Run the test project.

The following sections walk you through how to perform each of these steps to test a specific feature of the Been There, Done That! settings screen.

Creating the Test Project

Recall from Hour 1, "Getting Started with Android," when you first created a project using Eclipse, that the wizard has an option for creating a test project. You're now going to leverage that option to get up and running quickly with creating test cases. Conveniently, the option for creating a test project is also available after a project already exists. To create a test project for an existing Android project in Eclipse, follow these steps:

1. Select the appropriate project, right-click on it, choose Android Tools, New Test Project.

2. In the section labeled Test Target, choose An Existing Android Project and select the application project to test (for example, BTDT_Hour22).

3. The wizard fills in the rest of the fields with reasonable default values based upon the test project details, as shown in Figure 22.2. Change any final details you'd like (we used the defaults).

FIGURE 22.2
Test Application
Project Wizard
defaults in
Eclipse.

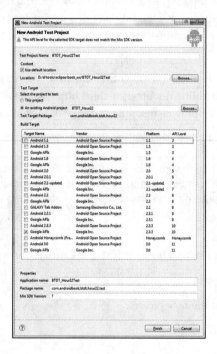

4. Click Finish. Your new test project is created and shows up in the Eclipse Package Explorer.

Creating a Test Case

After you have your test project in place, you can write test cases. Let's create a test case that tests the behavior of the Nickname field of the settings screen controlled by the QuizSettingsActivity class. To do this, first follow these steps to create the empty test case file:

1. Within your test project, right-click the package name within the `src` folder of your test project.

2. Choose New, JUnit Test Case.

3. Set the Name field to `QuizSettingsActivityTests`.

4. Modify the Superclass field to be `android.test.ActivityInstrumentation` `TestCase2<QuizSettingsActivity>`. (Ignore any warning that says "Superclass does not exist.")

5. Modify the Class Under Test field to be `com.androidbook.btdt.hour22.QuizSettingsActivity`.

6. Click Finish.

7. In the newly created file, manually add an import statement for `QuizSettingsActivity` (or organize your imports).

8. Finally, add the following constructor to the newly created class:

```
public QuizSettingsActivityTests() {
    super("com.androidbook.triviaquiz22", QuizSettingsActivity.class);
}
```

Now that your test case file is ready, you can test the Nickname field and make sure it matches the value of the nickname in `SharedPreferences` and that it updates after a new string is entered. You first need to modify the `setUp()` method to perform some common behavior. You get the nickname `EditText` object for use in the other two tests. The following code does just that:

```
import com.androidbook.btdt.hour22.R;
...
private EditText nickname;
...
@Override
protected void setUp() throws Exception {
    super.setUp();
    final QuizSettingsActivity settingsActivity = getActivity();
    nickname =
        (EditText) settingsActivity.findViewById(R.id.EditText_Nickname);
}
```

The import statement is at the file level, and needs to be added manually. The class field is within the test class. The method call for `getActivity()` retrieves the activity being tested. Within an instance of an `ActivityInstrumentationTestCase2` class (our `QuizSettingsActivityTests`, for instance), the activity is created as it would normally be when the activity is launched.

Normally, you also override the tearDown() method. However, for these tests, you have no lingering items that need to be cleaned up.

JUnit tests must begin with the word test. So, to write specific tests, you need to create methods that begin with the word test, followed by what you are testing. First, make sure the displayed Nickname field is consistent with the stored value in SharedPreferences. Add the following code to QuizSettingsActivityTests to implement this test:

```
public void testNicknameFieldConsistency() {
    SharedPreferences settings =
        getActivity().getSharedPreferences(QuizActivity.GAME_PREFERENCES,
            Context.MODE_PRIVATE);
    String fromPrefs =
        settings.getString(QuizActivity.GAME_PREFERENCES_NICKNAME, "");
    String fromField = nickname.getText().toString();
    assertTrue("Field should equal prefs value",
        fromPrefs.equals(fromField));
}
```

The first few lines are all standard Android code that you should be familiar with. By using the Android testing framework, you are enabling using the various Android objects within the testing code. The last line, however, is where the real test is performed. The assertTrue() method verifies that the second parameter actually is true. If it's not, the string is output in the results. In this case, the two strings are compared. They should be equal.

The next test is to verify that editing the field actually updates the Shared Preferences value. Add the following code to QuizSettingsActivityTests to test that this is true:

```
private static final String DEBUG_TAG = "QuizSettingsActivityTests";
private static final String TESTNICK_KEY_PRESSES = "T E S T N I C K ENTER";
// ...
public void testUpdateNickname() {
    Log.w(DEBUG_TAG, "Warning: " +
        "If nickname was previously 'testnick' this test is invalid.");
    getActivity().runOnUiThread(new Runnable() {
        public void run() {
            nickname.setText("");
            nickname.requestFocus();
        }
    });
    sendKeys(TESTNICK_KEY_PRESSES);
    SharedPreferences settings =
        getActivity().getSharedPreferences(QuizActivity.GAME_PREFERENCES,
            Context.MODE_PRIVATE);
    String fromPrefs =
        settings.getString(QuizActivity.GAME_PREFERENCES_NICKNAME, "");
    assertTrue("Prefs should be testnick", fromPrefs
        .equalsIgnoreCase("testnick"));
}
```

As before, most of this is standard Android code that you should be familiar with. Not obvious in print, however, is that each letter in the String constant TESTNICK_KEY_PRESSES is separated by a space, except for the command "ENTER"— that is, this is a string of key presses, letters representing the keys corresponding to each letter of the word (testnick) and "ENTER" representing the Enter key. However, notice that this code is performing a couple calls on the UI thread. This is required for these particular calls; if you remove those calls from the UI thread, the test case fails.

To run an entire test method on the UI thread, add the @UiThreadTest annotation before your method implementation. But note that this won't work in the example shown here because the sendKeys() method can't be run on the main thread. (You get the "This method cannot be called from the main application thread" exception error.) Instead, just portions of the test can be run on the UI thread, as shown.

Running Automated Tests

Now that your tests are written, you need to run them to test your code. There are two ways of doing this. The first method is the most straightforward and provides easy-to-read results right in Eclipse: Simply select Debug, Debug As, Android JUnit Test. The Console view of Eclipse shows the typical installation progress for both the test application and the application being tested (see Figure 22.3).

```
Console                                                                    🖫 ⬚ ⬚ ⬚ ⬚
Android
[2011-04-27 11:34:28 - BTDT_Hour22Test] ------------------------------
[2011-04-27 11:34:28 - BTDT_Hour22Test] Android Launch!
[2011-04-27 11:34:28 - BTDT_Hour22Test] adb is running normally.
[2011-04-27 11:34:28 - BTDT_Hour22Test] Performing android.test.InstrumentationTestRunner JUnit launch
[2011-04-27 11:34:28 - BTDT_Hour22Test] Automatic Target Mode: Several compatible targets. Please select a target device.
[2011-04-27 11:34:31 - BTDT_Hour22Test] Uploading BTDT_Hour22Test.apk onto device '393
[2011-04-27 11:34:31 - BTDT_Hour22Test] Installing BTDT_Hour22Test.apk...
[2011-04-27 11:34:32 - BTDT_Hour22Test] Success!
[2011-04-27 11:34:32 - BTDT_Hour22] Project dependency found, installing: BTDT_Hour22
[2011-04-27 11:34:32 - BTDT_Hour22] Uploading BTDT_Hour22.apk onto device '39
[2011-04-27 11:34:32 - BTDT_Hour22] Installing BTDT_Hour22.apk...
[2011-04-27 11:34:38 - BTDT_Hour22] Success!
[2011-04-27 11:34:38 - BTDT_Hour22Test] Launching instrumentation android.test.InstrumentationTestRunner on device 393
[2011-04-27 11:34:38 - BTDT_Hour22Test] Collecting test information
[2011-04-27 11:34:39 - BTDT_Hour22Test] Sending test information to Eclipse
[2011-04-27 11:34:39 - BTDT_Hour22Test] Running tests...
[2011-04-27 11:34:40 - BTDT_Hour22Test] Attempting to connect debugger to 'com.androidbook.btdt.hour22' on port 8611
[2011-04-27 11:34:44 - BTDT_Hour22Test] Test run finished
```

FIGURE 22.3
Eclipse console output while running JUnit tests on Android.

If the test project is not selected, Eclipse may try to run a regular application as a JUnit test application, resulting in a bunch of warnings and errors. To avoid this problem, right-click on the project name in the Package Explorer pane of Eclipse, choose Debug As, and then choose Android JUnit Test. Alternatively, you can go to the Debug Configurations menu, double-click on Android JUnit Test to create a new test configuration, and then fill in the details.

With the LogCat view, you see the normal Android debug output as well as new output for the tests that are performed. In this way, you can better debug problems or errors that result from failures, or even find new failures that should be tested for.

The JUnit view, though, might be the most useful. It summarizes all the tests run and how long each one takes, and it includes a stack trace for any failures found. Figure 22.4 shows what this looks like in Eclipse.

FIGURE 22.4
Eclipse JUnit view running Android tests.

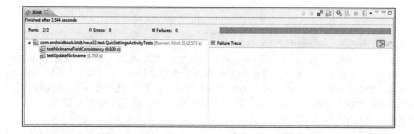

The second way of running the tests is available only in the emulator. To use this method, launch the Dev Tools app, found installed on the emulator, and then choose Instrumentation. If you've followed along and don't have any other tests installed, you likely see `android.test.InstrumentationTestRunner` as the only item shown. Clicking this launches the tests. When you use this method, the only way to see results (other than a visual indication during user interface tests) is to watch the LogCat output.

The description of the item in the list can be changed. In the `AndroidManifest.xml` file of the test app, in the instrumentation section, modify it to read as follows:

```
<instrumentation
    android:targetPackage="com.androidbook.btdt.hour22"
    android:name="android.test.InstrumentationTestRunner"
    android:label="BTDT Hour 22 Tests" />
```

Now when you launch Dev Tools and go to the Instrumentation section, the easier-to-understand label displays rather than the name.

Adding More Tests

Now you have all the tools you need to add more unit tests to your application. The Android SDK includes a variety of classes that you can implement for performing a wide range of tests specific to Android. Among these are the following:

▶ `ActivityUnitTestCase`—Similar to the example testing in the preceding section in that it tests on `Activity`, but at a lower level. This class can be used to unit test specific aspects of an activity, such as how it handles `onPause()`, when it has called onFinished(), and so on. This is a great way to test the life cycle of an activity.

▶ ApplicationTestCase—Like ActivityUnitTestCase, this class allows testing of Application classes in a fully controlled environment.

▶ ProviderTestCase2—Performs isolated testing on a content provider.

▶ ServiceTestCase—Performs isolated testing on a service.

In addition to these test case objects, there are helper classes for providing mock objects (that is, objects that aren't the real ones but can be used to better trace calls to the real objects), helper classes for simulating touch screen events, and other such utilities. You can find full documentation on these classes in the android.test package.

Summary

In this hour, you learned about the many different ways in which you can test and improve an Android application, which results in a higher-quality, polished product users appreciate. You learned many best practices for testing mobile applications, including the importance of creating a solid, complete testing plan. You learned about some of the ways you can acquire devices for testing purposes. You also learned how to create automated tests using the Android JUnit framework. Finally, you learned about some other specialized testing concerns that should be part of any good product test plan.

Q&A

Q. *Are there any certification programs for Android applications?*

A. There are currently no certification programs for Android applications. However, providers, operators, and mobile marketplaces often impose their own application quality standards, as they see fit.

Q. *Where can I find out more about creating automated test suites with JUnit?*

A. Visit the JUnit organization website, at www.junit.org, or find one of the many books on JUnit.

Q. *Is there a way I can easily write scripts to control emulators and test suites and develop a robust automated test environment?*

A. There is a tool called monkeyrunner that uses python scripts. You can use this test API to automate the installation and uninstallation of applications on emulators and devices. You can also use it to send keystrokes and capture screen shots and run JUnit test suites. You can find out more about the monkeyrunner tool on the Android developer website: http://goo.gl/uioB7.

Workshop

Quiz

1. True or False: Developers can create automated tests to exercise Android applications programmatically.

2. Which of the following should be considered an application defect or bug?

   A. An application takes a long time to start up.

   B. An application crashes when there is an incoming call.

   C. German text is too long to display onscreen and overflows.

   D. Buttons are too small or close together to push with a finger.

   E. An application enters an infinite loop when certain criteria are reached.

   F. All of the above.

3. True or False: Automated testing for Android applications can be performed only on the emulator.

4. The JUnit framework included with Android can be used for testing many things. Which of the following can it not do?

   A. Run repeated tests all day long, without tiring

   B. Test on old devices

   C. Move the device around the country to test GPS signals

   D. Test behavior on multiple carriers/operators

Answers

1. True. The Android SDK includes a variety of packages for developing test suites for automated application testing.

2. F. These are all defects of different kinds—performance, integration, internationalization, usability, and functional defects. (A) An application that takes too long to start up is a serious performance issue that may cause the Android operating system to kill the app—which is not good. (B) Many Android devices are phones first; an application must interact well with the rest of the system, which means gracefully handling incoming calls and text messages. (C) A well-written application does not short-change users in foreign languages by providing a substandard user interface. (D) A well-done user interface is essential to the success of an application. (E) A functional defect—that is, a problem with the core application logic—is always a defect, no matter how unlikely the event.

3. False. Automated tests can be performed on any Android device that can be connected for debugging.

4. C and D. Unfortunately, the JUnit framework alone can't physically move devices around the world. In addition, it can't simulate nuances to specific carriers around the world. However, emulator options can be used to mimic certain network performance characteristics but not the specifics of a different networking environment.

Exercises

1. Develop a high-level test plan for the Been There, Done That! application.

2. Write a test case for validating that a user's avatar uploads correctly.

3. Review the various agreements you have encountered in beginning to develop Android applications (such as the Android SDK License Agreement and Google Maps API Terms and Conditions). Identify any test cases that might be required for compliance with these agreements.

4. Read up on the Monkey Test tools available as part of the Android SDK at http://goo.gl/5xJlv.

5. **[Advanced]** Know python? Interested in developing a robust automated testing system for your app? Check out the monkeyrunner tool: http://goo.gl/uioB7.

HOUR 23

Getting Ready to Publish

What You'll Learn in This Hour:

▶ Preparing for application publication

▶ Testing and verifying a release build

▶ Packaging and signing your application for release

An application might be functionally complete, but you need to take one final step before you can publish: You must package the application so that it can be deployed to users safely and securely. In this hour, you learn how to prepare and package an application for release on the most popular Android publishing venue: the Android Market.

Understanding the Release Process

Preparing and packaging an application for publication is called the release process (see Figure 23.1). The release process is an exciting time: The application is stable and working as expected, all those troublesome bugs have been resolved (within reason, at least), and you feel that you're ready to put your app in front of users.

The final build you perform—the build you expect to deliver to users—is called the *release candidate build*. The release candidate build should be rigorously tested and verified before it reaches users' hands. If the release candidate build passes every test, it becomes the *release build*—the official build for publication.

FIGURE 23.1
An overview of
the release
process.

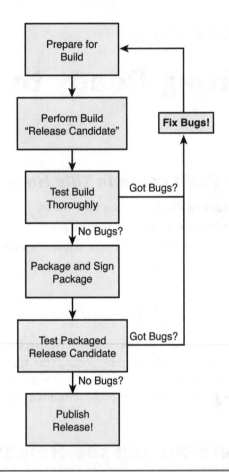

Different people use different terminology for the release process. Different software methodologies impose different terms. Some companies have code names
for such events, such as "going gold." Over the years, we've settled on release
and release candidate because, regardless of the methodology of choice, the
terms are pretty self-explanatory to most developers.

To publish an Android application, follow these steps:

1. Prepare and perform a release candidate build of the application.

2. Test the application release candidate thoroughly.

3. Package and digitally sign the application.

4. Test the packaged application release thoroughly.

5. Publish the application.

Let's explore each of these steps in more detail.

Preparing the Release Candidate Build

It's important to polish your application and make it ready for public consumption. This means you have to resolve any open or outstanding problems or issues with the application that might block the release. All features must be implemented and tested. All bugs must be resolved or deferred. Finally, you need to remove any unnecessary diagnostic code from the application and verify that the application configuration settings in the Android manifest file are appropriate for release.

Here's a short prerelease checklist for a typical Android application:

❏ Sufficiently test the application as described in the test plan, including testing on target handsets.

❏ Fix and verify all defects and bugs in the application.

❏ Turn off all debugging diagnostics for release, including any extraneous logging that could affect application performance.

Preparing the Android Manifest File for Release

Before release, you need to make a number of changes to the application configuration settings of the Android manifest file. Some of these changes are simply common sense, and others are imposed by marketplaces such as the Android Market.

You should review the Android manifest file as follows:

❏ Verify that the application icon (various sizes of PNG) is set appropriately. This icon is seen by users and is often used by marketplaces to display the application.

❏ Verify that the application label is set appropriately. This represents the application name as users see it.

❏ Verify that the application version name is set appropriately. The version name is a friendly version label that developers (and marketplaces) use.

> The Android SDK allows the android:versionName attribute to reference a string resource. The Android Market does not. You will encounter an error during the upload process when your package is validated. The package will not be accepted.

Watch Out!

❏ Verify that the application version code is set appropriately. The version code is a number that the Android platform uses to manage application upgrades.

Consider incrementing the version code for the release candidate in order to differentiate it from the prerelease version of the application.

❏ Confirm that the application uses-sdk setting is set correctly. You can set the minimum, target, and maximum Android SDK versions supported with this build. These numbers are saved as the API level of each Android SDK. For example, Android 2.1 is API level 7.

> The Android Market filters applications available to specific users based on the information provided in each application's manifest file, including the information provided in the uses-sdk settings. Read more about market filters at http://goo.gl/L8DOA and at the website of any alternative market you use to publish.

❏ Disable the debuggable option.

❏ Confirm that all application permissions are appropriate. Request only the permissions the application needs with uses-permission, and make sure to request permissions the application uses, regardless of handset behavior without them.

Protecting Your Application from Software Pirates

You spent a lot of time, effort, and resources developing your application. The last thing you want is for software pirates to steal your hard work and intellectual property. The Android Eclipse tool-chain includes built-in support for the ProGuard tool to help you secure your application against theft and misuse.

Some of ProGuard's benefits include

▶ Shrinking and optimizing your application source code. Unused code is removed, making for a leaner package for users to download.

▶ Obfuscating, or scrambling, your source code, including renaming classes, fields, and methods. This makes "reverse-engineering" your application code more difficult.

Some of ProGuard's drawbacks include

▶ Your release build code is obfuscated, making legitimate debugging more of a challenge, but still feasible.

▶ More advanced ProGuard configurations are needed for applications that use external libraries, paths with spaces, and other coding specifics.

Enabling ProGuard is simple; there is a proguard.cfg configuration file associated with your application project in Eclipse where you can modify its settings. Then you must update the proguard.config setting within the application's default.properties configuration file to point at the proguard configuration file, like this:

```
proguard.config=proguard.cfg
```

For more information on using ProGuard, see its documentation at the Android developer website: http://goo.gl/0Lo0G. We have also written this helpful online article on tips and tricks for using ProGuard to protect your Android applications, available here: http://goo.gl/cF9UM.

Readying Related Services for Release

If the Android application relies on any external technologies or services, such as an application server, then these must be readied for release as well.

Many large projects have a "mock" application server (often called a sandbox) as well as a real "live" server. The release build needs to be tested against the live server, just the way users would use it.

Testing the Application Release Candidate

After you address all the prerelease issues, you're ready to perform the release candidate build. There is nothing particularly special about the general build process here, except that you launch a Run Configuration, rather than a Debug Configuration, in Eclipse.

You should test the release candidate rigorously. In addition to any regular testing, you should verify that the application meets the criteria of the application marketplaces (such as the Android Market) where you want to publish the app. For example, the Android Market currently limits application package sizes to 50MB.

If you find any defects or issues with the release candidate build, you must decide whether they are serious enough to stop the release process. If you decide that an issue is serious enough to require another build, you simply start the release process over again after you have addressed the issue (see Figure 23.2).

FIGURE 23.2
The release
candidate
testing cycle.

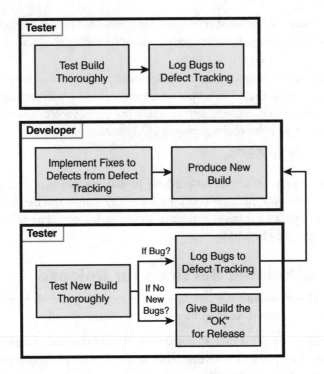

Packaging and Signing an Application

Now that you have a solid release candidate build that's tested and ready to go, you need to package the application for publication. This process involves generating the Android package file (the .apk file) and digitally signing it.

The process of packaging and signing an application has never been easier. Everything you need to package and sign your application is available within the Android plug-in for Eclipse as a simple wizard.

Digitally Signing Applications

Android application packages must be digitally signed for the Android package manager to install them. Throughout the development process, Eclipse has used a debug key to manage this process. However, for release, you need to use a real digital signature—one that is unique to you and your company. To do this, you must generate a private key.

A private key identifies the developer and is critical to building trust relationships between developers and users. It is very important to secure private key information.

You can use the private key to digitally sign the release package files of your Android application, as well as any upgrades. This ensures that the application (as a complete entity) is coming from you, the developer, and not someone pretending to be you.

You don't need to use a certificate authority, such as VeriSign, Equifax, or any of the other companies that certify that you are who you say you are before providing a certificate. Self-signing is standard for Android applications, which simply means that you aren't proving who you are, but the next time you publish something, if the keys match, then users (and Android) know it's been signed by the same person or entity. So don't share your private key!

Application updates must be signed with the same private key. For security reasons, the Android package manager does not install the update over the existing application if the key is different. This means you need to keep the key corresponding with the application in a secure, easy-to-find location for future use.

Exporting and Signing the Package File

You are now ready to export and sign your Android package file. To do this using the wizard provided as part of the Eclipse ADT plug-in, perform the following steps:

1. In Eclipse, right-click the appropriate application project and choose the Export option.

2. Under the Export menu, expand the Android section and choose Export Android Application.

3. Click the Next button.

4. Select the project to export. The one you right-clicked is the default, but you can use the Browse button to change to other open Eclipse projects as well.

5. Click the Next button.

6. On the keystore selection screen, choose the Create New Keystore option and enter a file location (where you want to store the key) as well as a password for managing the keystore. (If you already have a keystore, choose browse to pick your keystore file and then enter the correct password.)

7. Click the Next button.

8. On the Key Creation screen, enter the details of the key, including information about your organization. See the note on key validity below. If you need help with other particular fields, see the Android developer website documentation on application signing at http://goo.gl/LWtFj. Your details might look something like what is shown in Figure 23.3.

FIGURE 23.3
Exporting an Android application using the Eclipse plug-in.

9. Click the Next button.

10. On the Enter Destination and Key/certificate Checks screen, enter a file destination for the application package file.

11. Click the Finish button.

You have now created a fully signed and certified application package file.

Testing the Signed Application Package

Now that you signed and packaged the application, and now that it's ready for production, you should perform one last test cycle, paying special attention to subtle changes to the installation process for signed applications.

> Before installing the release version of your application on the emulator or handset, you must uninstall the debug version completely, as it uses a different signature and the new one can't be directly installed over it. Uninstall apps from the Home screen by clicking Menu, Settings, Application, Manage Applications, choosing the application from the list, clicking the Uninstall button, and verifying that you want to uninstall the application.

Installing the Signed Application Package

Up until now, you've allowed Eclipse to handle the packaging and delivery of the application to handsets and emulators for debugging purposes. Now you have the application release version sitting on your hard drive, and you need to load it and test it.

The simplest way to manually install (or uninstall) an application package (.apk) file on a handset or the emulator is to use the adb command-line tool. The following is the command for installing a package using adb:

```
adb install <path_to_apk>
```

If there is only one device or emulator, this command works. However, if you have multiple devices and emulators floating around, you need to direct the installation command to a specific one. You can use the devices command of the adb utility to query for devices connected to your computer:

```
adb devices
```

The list this command returns includes any emulators or handsets attached to the computer. The results might look like this:

```
$ adb devices
List of devices attached
emulator-5554   device
HT9CSP801234    device
```

You can then target a specific device on which to install the application package file by using the -s option. For example, to install the BeenThereDoneThat.apk application package file on the emulator, you use the following:

```
adb -s emulator-5554 install BeenThereDoneThat.apk
```

For more information about the adb command-line tool, see the website http://goo.gl/jqXK3.

Verifying the Signed Application

You're almost done. Now it is time to perform a few last-minute checks to make sure the application works properly:

▶ Verify smooth installation of the signed application package.

▶ Verify that all debugging features have been disabled.

▶ Verify that the application is using the "live" services as opposed to any "mock" services.

▶ Verify that application configuration data such as the application name and icons, as well as the version information, displays correctly.

If you find any issues with the signed application functionality, you must decide whether they are serious enough to stop the release process and begin again. After you've tested the application package thoroughly and are confident that users will have a positive experience using your application, you are ready to publish!

Summary

In this hour, you learned how to prepare an application for publication. Specifically, you learned about the steps to take to verify that your application is ready for publication, such as stripping debugging information, verifying application configuration settings, and performing a release build. You then learned to export an unsigned application package file, generate a private key, and digitally sign the application for publication.

Q&A

Q. *Will the release process described in this hour work for any Android application marketplace?*

A. Generally speaking, yes. We have focused on the Android Market requirements. For details on the requirements imposed by other marketplaces, see those specific developer programs. Typically, any differences are in the requirements imposed on the application's Android manifest file and the specifics of the digital signature that accompanies the application.

Q. *Why must the key be valid until October 22, 2033?*

A. The digital signature of an application will persist through various application upgrades. By enforcing a date far in the future, trust relationships between the application provider and third parties (including users) can be established and maintained for the long term.

Q. *Can I programmatically obtain information about an application package?*

A. Yes, you can use the `getPackageInfo()` method of the `PackageManager` class (`android.content.pm.PackageManager`) to obtain information about an application package. This method returns a `PackageInfo` object (`android.content.pm.PackageInfo`), which contains all the information of that application's manifest file, from configuration details to the list of specific activities and permissions of the application.

Q. *I want to know what my users are doing. Is there an easy way to collect statistics from within my application?*

A. There is! There is a Google Labs project called the Google Analytics SDK for Android, which you can use to collect and analyze information about your applications. For more information, check out the Google code page: http://goo.gl/yvu2z.

Workshop

Quiz

1. True or False: The release process is important only for big projects.

2. Which version fields in the application's Android manifest file should you verify for release purposes?

   A. `android:versionCode`

   B. `android:versionLabel`

   C. `android:versionName`

   D. `android:version`

   E. All of the above

3. True or False: You cannot publish an application that includes a debug signature.

Answers

1. False. Whether you're a hobbyist working on your own or a member of a large development team, taking the time to verify whether an application is ready for release is important to the success of the application.

2. A and C. The Android platform uses the version code to perform upgrades, and the version name is a string field that developers and markets use for product support purposes.

3. True. The Android package manager installs only applications that have been properly signed.

Exercises

1. Choose one of the Been There, Done That! builds from this book (from any hour, or your own version). Export the APK package file and digitally sign it.

2. Review the package file created in Exercise 1. How large is it? List several ways you might make the package file smaller and leaner. Hint: Application resources are a big part of the package size.

3. Install the Been There, Done That! application package on a device (or emulator, if you do not have a device) by using the adb command-line utility.

4. Uninstall the Been There, Done That! application package on a device (or emulator, if you do not have a device) by using the Manage Applications features in the device settings.

HOUR 24

Publishing on the Android Market

What You'll Learn in This Hour:

▶ Selling Android applications on the Android Market
▶ Exploring Android application publishing options
▶ Protecting your intellectual property

Congratulations! You've made it to the final hour, and you've learned how to design, build, and test an Android application from start to finish. The next logical step is to publish your application. In this hour, you learn how to publish an Android application on the popular Android Market and explore other publishing options. The Android platform supports paid distribution, free distribution, and even self-distribution options. This gives a developer great flexibility for getting applications into the hands of users, with fewer hurdles than most platforms.

Selling on the Android Market

At this time, Google's Android Market is the most popular mechanism for distributing Android applications with approximately 5 billion downloads as of June 2011 (Source: Wikipedia: http://goo.gl/apEkM). The Android Market is available as an Android application (installed on the device) as well as a website (http://market.android.com) that can push apps to devices linked to a user's Google account. The Android Market is where most users purchase and download applications. As of this writing, the Android Market is available on most Android handsets, although the website component is only compatible for devices running Android 1.6 and newer platform versions. Due to Android Market's popularity, in this hour, we focus our attention on how to check a package for preparedness, sign up for a developer account, and submit your application for sale on the Android Market.

Signing Up for a Developer Account

To publish applications through the Android Market, you must register as a developer. Registering as a developer verifies who you are to Google and signs you up for a Google Checkout account, which the Android Market uses to disperse revenue from applications sales back to developers.

To sign up for Android Market, follow these steps:

1. Browse to http://market.android.com/publish/signup (http://goo.gl/CSKNw), as shown in Figure 24.1.

2. Sign in with the Google Account you want to use.

3. Enter you developer information, including your name, email address, and website, as shown in Figure 24.2.

4. Confirm your registration payment (as of this writing, $25 USD). Note that Google Checkout is used for registration payment processing.

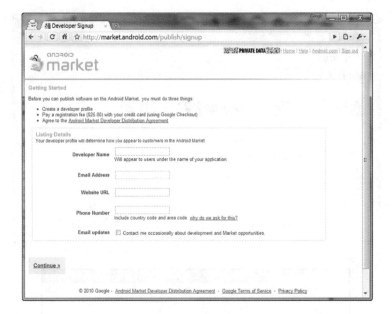

FIGURE 24.2
The Android
Market publish-
er profile page.

5. Provide information for a Google Checkout Merchant account. This is manda-
tory when signing up and paying to be an Android Developer.

6. Agree to link your credit card and account registration to the Android Market
Developer Distribution Agreement.

When you successfully complete these steps, you are presented with the home screen
of the Android Market, which also confirms that the Google Checkout Merchant
account was created.

Uploading an Application to the Android Market

Now that you have a Google account with an associated Google Checkout Merchant
account registered, you can begin publishing applications through the Android
Market. First, you must upload a signed application package. From the main page
of the Android Market website, sign in and click the Upload Application button, as
shown in Figure 24.3.

You now see a form, as shown in Figure 24.4, for uploading the application package
and marketing materials. Upload your signed application package. You should
also upload a number of application screenshots, icons, and other promotional
materials.

FIGURE 24.3
Android Market
listings.

FIGURE 24.4
Android Market
Application
Upload Form.

If you scroll down this form you find the Listing details. Figure 24.5 shows the listing
details, where you specify the title and description of your application in a variety of
languages, as well as set the application type and category information.

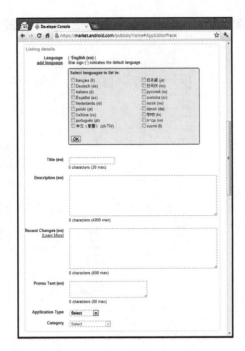

FIGURE 24.5
Android Market
Application
Upload Form:
Listing Details.

Some of the important information you must enter on this part of the form includes the following:

▶ **Application title and description in several languages**—English is the default language.

▶ **Application type**—At this time, the Android Market supports two types of applications: Applications (everything but games) and Games.

▶ **Application category**—Spend the time to set the category field appropriately, as defined by the Android Market, so that your application reaches its intended audience. Incorrectly categorized applications do not sell well.

Keep scrolling down on the form and fill out the Publishing options. Figure 24.6 shows the publishing options details, where you specify the content rating, pricing mechanism (free or paid), and set any pricing information of your application in a variety of currencies.

FIGURE 24.6
Android Market
Application
Upload Form:
Publishing
Options.

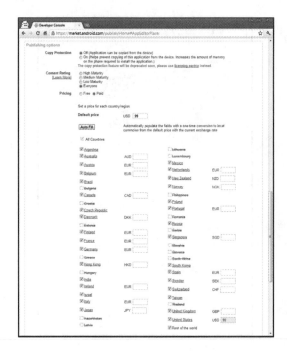

Some of the important information you must enter on this part of the form includes the following:

▶ **Countries (locations) where the application will be published**—These locations are subject to export compliance laws, so choose your locations carefully. As of this writing, nearly 50 locations are available, and new locations are being added regularly. In addition, you can choose specific carriers for each location to further limit application distribution. Alternatively, you can choose All Locations to include any future locations supported by the market. For a complete list of locations where Android applications can be sold or published for free, see http://goo.gl/43AGh.

▶ **Application price**—Note that the Android Market currently imposes a 30% transaction fee for hosting applications within the Android Market. Prices can range from $0.99 to $200 USD, with similar ranges in other currencies.

▶ **Copy protection information**—Choosing this option, if it is available, might help prevent the application from being copied from the device and distributed without your knowledge or permission. You might also want to look into the Android Licensing Server solution for use with the Android Market. Find out more here: http://goo.gl/gCDNX.

At the bottom of the form, you must fill out some developer contact information. You must also verify that your application meets all Android Market guidelines and complies with law in all countries in which you plan to publish.

Some of the important information you must enter on this part of the form includes the following:

▶ **Developer support contact information**—Set the website, email, and phone number for the developer here. This option defaults to the information you provided for the developer account. You can change it on an app-by-app basis, though, which allows for great support flexibility when you're publishing multiple applications.

▶ **Consent to the Android Content Guidelines**—You must click the checkbox to agree to the terms of the current (at the time you click) Android Content Guidelines as specified by the Android Market policy.

▶ **Consent to the Export Compliance**—You must click the checkbox to verify that your application complies with any United States export laws as well as the laws of the countries you wish to publish in, regardless of your location or nationality.

You can then save the application details as a draft (to update later) or publish it immediately.

Did you Know?

After you have successfully uploaded an application package, you can save the information you entered as a draft, which is great for verification before final publishing. Also, the application icon, name, version, localization information, and required permissions are shown so you can verify that you have configured the Android manifest file properly.

Publishing on the Android Market

After you click the Publish button, the application appears in the Android Market almost immediately. After your app is published, you can see statistics including ratings, reviews, downloads, active installs, and so on in the Your Android Market Listings section of the main page on your developer account. These statistics aren't updated as frequently as the publish action, and you can't see review details directly from the listing.

By clicking the application listing, you can edit the various fields. Although some details can be edited, pricing information can't be changed. For example, if your app starts as a free application, you cannot make it a paid app later. You can always upload a different version for a paid version of the application with new features. On the Android Market, paid application pricing can be changed at any time but must fall within certain limits. For example, in USD, the range is from $0.99 to $200, and in Japanese Yen, the range is from ¥99 to ¥20000. As you can see, the ranges vary depending on the currency in use. A list of ranges is maintained at http://goo.gl/IuVbM.

Understanding Billing

Android Market uses Google checkout for processing payments. After an application is purchased, the user owns it. If your application requires a service fee or sells other goods within the application (for example, ringtones, music, ebooks), you need to develop an in-app billing mechanism.

The Android Market has a specific in-app billing mechanism that requires fairly extensive modifications to your application source code. For more information, check out the Android developer website documentation on this subject: http://goo.gl/kMV3a.

Watch Out!

> Because most Android devices can leverage the Internet, using online billing services and APIs—PayPal, Google, and Amazon, to name a few—is also technically feasible. Check with your preferred billing service to make sure it specifically allows mobile use. Also, make sure to check the guidelines for the app stores (such as the Android Market) you are considering publishing to, as they may have limitations on the billing mechanisms your application can employ internally.

Another method for making money from users is to have an ad-supported mobile business model. This shouldn't come as too much of a surprise, considering the popularity of Google's AdSense. The Android platform has no specific rules against using advertisements within applications, but again, check the guidelines of your specific target markets to make sure they allow ad-driven applications.

Understanding the Android Market Application Return Policy

Although it is a matter of no small controversy, the Android Market has a 24-hour refund policy on applications. That is to say, a user can use an application for 24 hours and then return it for a full refund. As a developer, this means that sales aren't final until after the first 24 hours. However, this only applies to the first download and first return. If a particular user has already returned your application and wants to "try it again," he or she must make a final purchase—and can't return it a second time. Although this limits abuse, you should still be aware that if your application has limited reuse appeal or if all its value can come from just a few hours (or less) of use, you might find that you have a return rate that's too high, and you'll need to pursue other methods of monetization.

Removing Your Application from the Android Market

You can use the unpublish action in your developer account to remove an application from the Android Market. The unpublish action has an immediate effect but might take a few moments to become unavailable across the entire system.

Using Other Developer Account Benefits

Having a registered Android developer account enables you to manage your applications on the Android Market. In addition, if you have a developer account, you can purchase development versions of Android handsets. These handsets are useful for general development and testing but might not be suitable for final testing on actual target handsets because some functionality might be limited, and the firmware version is different than that found on consumer handsets.

Exploring Other Android Publishing Options

The Android platform is an open platform, and publishing options are also very open. You've learned how to publish on the Android Market, but there are other options available as well. You might want to take advantage of these alternatives to target handsets and devices that do not come with the Android Market, distribute handsets to a narrower target audience, distribute applications that don't comply with the Android Market rules, or simply control distribution on your own.

Selling Your Application on Your Own Site

You can distribute Android applications directly from your own website or server. This method is most appropriate for vertical market or enterprise applications, content companies developing mobile marketplaces, and big-brand websites that want to drive users to their branded Android applications. It can also be a good way to get beta feedback from end users before going "live."

Although self-distribution is perhaps the easiest method of application distribution, it is also the most challenging in terms of marketing, protecting your application, and making money. The only requirement for self-distribution is to have a place to host the application package file online.

One serious downside of self-distribution is that the end user must configure his or her device to allow installation of applications from unknown sources. This setting is found under the Application Settings section of the device Settings application, as shown in Figure 24.7.

FIGURE 24.7
The Application
Settings screen,
showing the set-
ting for down-
loading from
unknown
sources.

After that, the user must enter the URL of the application package into the web browser on the handset and download the file (or click a link to it). After the file is downloaded, the standard Android installation process occurs, during which the user needs to confirm the permissions and, optionally, confirm an update or replacement of an existing application if a version is already installed.

> Not all devices include the option for enabling installation from unknown sources. Some manufacturers or operators disable this feature, making it difficult or impossible for users to download applications from markets other than the Android Market.

Selling Your Application on Other Markets

The Android Market is not the only market available for selling your Android applications. Because Android is an open platform, there is nothing preventing a handset manufacturer or an operator (or even you) from running an Android marketplace website or building an Android application that serves as a market. Anyone can develop a new Android application store and market applications on his or her own terms.

Here are a few marketplaces where you might consider distributing your Android applications:

- ▶ **Amazon Appstore**—This recently launched app store has a big brand name behind it and a solid platform for digital content distribution. They distribute free and paid Android applications across a wide range of devices (http://www.amazon.com/appstore).

- ▶ **GetJar**—This app store has impressive download statistics. They distribute free and paid mobile applications for a wide range of devices and platforms (http://getjar.com).

- ▶ **Handango**—This site distributes free and paid mobile applications for a wide range of devices and platforms (http://www.handango.com).

- ▶ **V CAST Apps**—Run by Verizon, this is an example of a carrier-specific app store (http://developer.verizon.com/jsps/devCenters/Smart_Phone/index.jsp (http://goo.gl/N8n5h)).

- ▶ **MiKandi.com**—Marketed as the "World's First App Market for Adults," this app store is an example of a specialty app store that does not limit adult materials in its content guidelines that many other app stores do.

This list is not complete, and we don't specifically endorse any one market over another, but it is important to note that there are a number of alternative distribution mechanisms available to developers. Application requirements, content guidelines, and royalty rates vary by store. In addition to these markets, many manufacturers and wireless operators have their own stores, especially for devices that don't include the "Google experience" (that is, devices that don't ship with built-in Google apps, such as the Android Market).

Third-party application stores are free to enforce whatever rules they want on the applications they accept, so read the fine print carefully at each site. Only you and your project team can determine which sites are suitable for your specific needs.

There are numerous app stores out there. Some are app "superstores," and others are specialty markets. Check out our article on where to sell your killer Android apps at http://goo.gl/tWNG7 for a more thorough discussion of the options out there today.

By the Way

Summary

In this final hour, you learned how to publish an Android application for the world to see and use. You now know there are numerous distribution opportunities for Android developers, including self-publishing from your website and a variety of third-party application stores that can help you sell your work (for a cut of the profit). You've set yourself up for success by learning how to work with the most popular Android application store: Google's Android Market. You learned how to set up a developer account with the Android Market and can now begin to sell your own applications there.

Perhaps you already have some great app ideas in mind. It's time to fire up Eclipse and start coding! When you start building applications, drop us a note and tell us about them. (Our contact information is available in Appendix C, "Supplementary Materials.") We'd love to hear from you!

Q&A

Q. *How can I limit my application to only specific types of devices?*

A. The Android Market attempts to filter applications available to those compatible with the specific user's device. The Android Market inspects each application package and derives important information from the Android manifest file. Certain manifest file settings can be used to specify what types of devices your application supports or does not support. These configuration details are called market filters. For more information on Android Market filters that can be specified within the Android manifest file, visit http://goo.gl/Leicq. These filters are not used by other Android app stores at this time.

Q. *What languages are supported by the Android Market in terms of marketing?*

A. The Android Market currently supports application descriptions in over a dozen languages, and more are added all the time. The following are some of the languages currently supported by the Android Market:

- ▶ English (en)
- ▶ French/français (fr)
- ▶ German/Deutsch (de)
- ▶ Italian/italiano (it)
- ▶ Spanish/Español (es)

- ▶ Dutch/Nederlands (nl)

- ▶ Polish/polski (pl)

- ▶ Czech/ čeština (cs)

- ▶ Portugese/português (pt)

- ▶ Taiwanese/中文（繁體）(zh_TW)

- ▶ Japanese/日本語 (ja)

- ▶ Korean/한국어 (ko)

- ▶ Russian/ русский (ru)

- ▶ Swedish/ svenska (sv)

- ▶ Norwegian/norsk (no)

- ▶ Danish/dansk (da)

- ▶ Hindi/हिंदी (hi)

- ▶ Hebrew/עברית (iw)

- ▶ Finnish/ suomi (fi)

Q. *How can I protect my hard work from software piracy?*

A. After you spend time, money, and effort building a valuable Android application, it makes sense to protect yourself against reverse engineering of trade secrets and software piracy. Because Android applications are compiled for the Dalvik virtual machine, most traditional Java obfuscation tools won't work. Some tools, such as ProGuard (http://proguard.sourceforge.net), do support Android. The Android Market application publication screen also includes a mysterious (undocumented) checkbox for copy protection when publishing your application.

Q. *Where can I find a list of other app markets for comparison purposes?*

A. Finding reasonable market statistics is challenging. We find Wikipedia's entry called the "List of digital distribution platforms for mobile devices" a good starting point: http://goo.gl/0kU8G.

Workshop

Quiz

1. True or False: You don't need an account to sell on the Android Market.

2. Which of the following statements are true?

A. The Android Market allows for paid and free applications.

B. The Android Market allows developers to sell applications only in the United States.

C. The Android Market is the only Android application store available.

D. The Android Market imposes a 30% transaction fee on applications sold.

E. All of the above.

3. True or False: You can sell Android applications from your own website.

4. Before submitting an application to the Android Market, which of the following must you do?

A. Certify your application through an approved certification program.

B. Provide a notarized Statement of Testing Completeness, proving you've tested every single aspect of the application in all scenarios.

C. Sign your application package with a well-known certificate authority approved for use with the Android Market.

D. Record a video of your application in action.

E. Provide a Word document with thorough documentation of application flows and a complete user manual.

F. Get certified carrier and operator approval from each carrier your application will be launching on before uploading your application package.

Answers

1. False. You must create an authenticated developer account with Google before you can publish Android applications on the Android Market.

2. A and D. The Android Market, the most popular Android application store, allows developers to publish free and paid applications in a number of different countries, and it takes a 30% transaction fee for hosting applications.

3. True. You can sell your Android applications from a number of application shops, including your own site. Keep in mind that users need to enable installation of applications from unknown sources to install applications from unknown websites.

4. None! Although none of these are required, some of them, such as thoroughly testing your application, are advisable. Others, such as a video demo, might be useful for marketing purposes, but are optional. However, none of the items listed are actually required by the Android Market. It's very open!

Exercises

1. Create a developer account for yourself on the Android Market.

2. Browse through the Android Market (on a handset or on the Android Market website). Think of an idea for an application and determine what category and price range is appropriate for that application.

3. Browse through the Android Market (on a handset or on the Android Market website). Focus on two applications—perhaps those similar to your idea or in the same category (for example, Games). Try to find one popular application (high ratings, downloads) and one not-so-popular application. Perform a comprehensive review of these applications' market features. Pay special attention to the marketing support materials provided, such as the screenshots, description, and user reviews and ratings. What do they do right? What would you do differently?

4. [Thrilling!] Go write a fabulous and exciting application and then share it with the world. Email us about your experiences and your app at androidwirelessdev+apps@gmail.com.

APPENDIX A

Configuring Your Android Development Environment

This appendix walks you through the steps needed to install and configure all the appropriate tools you need to get started developing Android applications:

- ▶ The appropriate Java Development Kit (JDK)
- ▶ The Eclipse Integrated Development Environment (IDE)
- ▶ The Android Software Development Kit (SDK) and tools
- ▶ Any drivers required by specific Android devices

These software packages are available free of charge from their vendors' websites.

Development Machine Prerequisites

Android developers may use a number of different operating systems and software configurations. This appendix walks you through the installation of the tools used in this book. If you're installing from scratch, you should choose the latest versions of the software packages required for development.

For a complete list of software and system requirements, see the Android developer website: http://goo.gl/F7i3K.

Supported Operating Systems

You can write Android applications on the following operating systems:

- ▶ Windows XP (32-bit), Vista (32- or 64-bit), or Windows 7 (32- or 64-bit)
- ▶ Mac OS X 10.5.8 or later (x86 only)
- ▶ Linux (see http://developer.android.com/sdk/requirements.html for details)

Available Space

You need approximately 2GB of space to safely install all the tools you need to develop Android applications. This includes installing the JDK, the Eclipse IDE, the Android SDK, and the tools and plug-ins.

Installing the Java Development Kit

Most Android applications are written in Java, and this book focuses on Android Java development for this reason. You can develop Android applications using Oracle's JDK 5 or JDK 6, which you must install on the development machine. You can read the license agreement and download the latest version of the Java Standard Edition JDK at Oracle's website: http://goo.gl/yhhaL. Make sure you choose the full Java Development Kit (JDK) for development purposes, not simply the Java Runtime Environment (JRE). Simply follow the directions of the appropriate installer to install the Java development environment on your machine. For specific installation for your operating system, see the documentation available with the installation package you choose.

Installing the Eclipse IDE

This book uses the popular Eclipse integrated development environment (IDE) for development purposes. Many, if not most, developers use Eclipse for Android development because the Android SDK includes plug-ins that allow tight integration with the IDE.

> If you don't want to use Eclipse, you can find more information about configuring your computer for Android development with other IDEs at the Android website: http://goo.gl/KXcZj. Keep in mind that the exercises in this book rely upon the assumption that the reader is using the Eclipse IDE.

Eclipse is available for Windows, Mac, and Linux operating systems. Make sure you choose a compatible Eclipse installation, such as

- ▶ Eclipse IDE for Java Developers
- ▶ Eclipse IDE for Java EE Developers

You can read the license agreement and download the Eclipse IDE at http://goo.gl/49qml. The Eclipse package comes as a compressed zip file. There is no installer. You unzip the package into the desired folder and then follow the specific instructions in the following sections for your target operating system.

Notes on Windows Installations

After you install the files in the appropriate location, navigate to the Eclipse.exe executable and create a shortcut on your desktop. Edit the shortcut and modify the target field with any command-line arguments you desire.

Notes on Mac OS X Installations

If you are installing Eclipse on a Mac OS X system, make sure to review the README.html file included with the Eclipse package. This readme file covers how to pass command-line arguments to Eclipse using the eclipse.ini file and how to run more than one instance of Eclipse so that you can work with multiple project workspaces simultaneously.

Installing the Android SDK Starter Package

Now we're getting to the good stuff. You need to install the Android SDK to develop Android applications.

The Android SDK Starter Package is available from the Android Developer website, http://goo.gl/PFaxh. Some versions of the Android SDK have a helpful installer—feel free to use it if it's available for your platform, or download the compressed file and unzip it into the desired folder. The compressed SDK files require about 33MB of hard drive space and uncompress to a size of approximately 46MB.

The Android SDK, as a whole, includes the Android JAR file (Android application framework classes) as well as Android documentation, tools, and sample code for different versions of the Android platform. However, the SDK Starter Package only includes the core tools needed to retrieve the components you desire—we'll discuss this further in a moment.

Notes on Windows Installations

To update your PATH variable to include the Android tools directory, right-click Computer and choose Properties. In Vista, you also need to click Advanced System Settings. You continue by clicking the Advanced tab of the System Properties dialog and clicking the Environment Variables button. In the System Variables section, edit the PATH variable and add the path to the tools directory.

> At the time of this writing, the installer did not always properly detect the existence of the JDK installation on 64-bit versions of the Windows operating system. If you run into this problem or any others with the installer, simply use the downloadable compressed zip file instead.

Notes on Mac OS X Installations

To update your PATH variable to include the Android tools directory, you need to edit your .bash_profile file in your Home directory.

Notes on Linux OS Installations

To update your PATH variable to include the Android tools directory, you need to edit your ~/.bash_profile, ~/.bashrc, or ~/.profile file.

Installing and Configuring the Android Plug-in for Eclipse (ADT)

The Android plug-in for Eclipse allows seamless integration with many of the Android development tools. If you're using Eclipse, it's highly recommended that you install this tool, as it makes life much easier—this book assumes you use this tool. The plug-in includes various wizards for creating and debugging Android projects and project resources.

To install the Android Development Tools plug-in for Eclipse (ADT), you must launch Eclipse and install a custom software update. The steps required depend on the version of Eclipse you use. For complete instructions, see the Android developer website: http://goo.gl/SDoC5.

To install Android Plug-in on Eclipse 3.6 (Helios), follow these steps:

1. Launch Eclipse.

2. Select Help, Install New Software.

3. Click the Add button.

4. Add a repository with the Name "ADT" and the Location https://dl-ssl.google.com/android/eclipse/.

5. Click OK. If this fails to resolve to the appropriate repository, try using "http" in the Location URL instead of "https."

6. You should see items listed in the Available Software listing. Check the check-box next to Developer Tools to download all available tools.

7. Click the Next button and follow the wizard for installing the tools. Accept the terms of the license agreement and click the Finish button.

8. You might see a warning that you are installing unsigned content. You need to click OK to proceed and install the plug-in.

9. After the software update completes, restart Eclipse as prompted.

The Android tools and SDK versions are componentized. This means that instead of installing one large package for development for all supported versions of Android, you can pick and choose the Android SDK versions you want to install and work with using the Android SDK and AVD Manager. This tool enables developers to easily upgrade their development environments when a new version of Android comes out (which, historically, has happened quite frequently). In addition to various Android target versions to choose from, you can download other tools and support, such as USB drivers for Windows.

After you install the ADT plug-in, you need to choose and install the specific Android platforms you will develop for, as well as any other components you'd like. To do this, use the Android SDK and AVD Manager as follows:

1. Launch Eclipse.

2. Select Window, Android SDK and AVD Manager.

3. Click the Available Packages option on the left-hand menu.

4. You should see at least two options: Android Repository and Third Party Add-ons. Most readers should download all items, including all sample code, offline documentation, and the tools. However, if you have limited disk space, feel free to limit the components you download to those you require and add others as needed. Select the checkboxes next to the items you want to download.

For this book, you need the following components: Under the Android Repository, you need the platform tools and several Android platforms (for example, Android 1.6, 2.1, 2.3, 3.0, and so on.). The documentation and samples are highly recommended, but not required. Similarly, under Third Party Add-ons, you need the Google add-ons only. For an explanation of each component, see http://goo.gl/50xlq.

5. Click the Install Selected button.

6. Choose the Accept All radio button and click the Install button.

7. You may need to restart components, when prompted.

8. When the installation has completed, click Close. If you navigate to the Installed Packages menu item, you should see numerous components and platform versions are now installed.

Finally, after you use the Android SDK and AVD Manager to download all the Android components for development purposes, update your Eclipse preferences to point at the Android SDK components you just downloaded and installed using the following steps:

1. Launch Eclipse.

2. Select Window, Preferences (or Eclipse, Preferences in Mac OS X).

3. Click the top-level Android preferences and set the SDK Location to where you installed the Android SDK on your computer initially.

If you have configured this setting correctly, you should see a number of different Android SDK Target platforms listed, along with their API Level information.

You should check back in the Android SDK and AVD Manager frequently to check for updates and new versions of the Android SDK, tools and components as they become available. Before doing this, make sure to first update the components of Eclipse, which might include plug-in updates. (For instance, the Android SDK and AVD Manager is updated through the Eclipse update mechanism.)

Configuring Development Hardware for Device Debugging

Much of Android development involves designing applications on your computer and then downloading, running, and debugging them onto Android devices via a USB connection. Most devices have these development options disabled by default for security purposes.

Configuring Android Devices for Development Purposes

Each Android device may have different debugging settings, but here are the generic steps for enabling Android development settings on an Android device:

1. On the device Home screen, select Menu, Settings, Applications.

2. Click the checkbox to enable Unknown sources. This enables you to install your applications, as opposed to only applications available on the Android Market.

3. Select the Development menu (Menu, Settings, Applications, Development).

4. Click the checkbox to enable USB debugging. This enables you to debug your applications while they are running on this device from within Eclipse.

5. Click the checkbox to enable Stay Awake. This keeps the device from going to sleep during long debugging sessions.

6. Finally, click the checkbox to enable Allow Mock Locations. This setting facilitates development of applications that leverage location-based services—a topic covered in Hour 14, "Adding Support for Location-Based Services."

Configuring Your Operating System for Device Debugging

To install and debug Android applications, you might need to configure your operating system drivers such that you can connect to devices via USB. This is especially true of Windows machines. The Android SDK ships with drivers compatible with most Android devices.

> If the basic drivers do not work for your specific Android device, check the device's manufacturer website for the latest drivers.

By the Way

Notes on Windows Installations

If you develop on a Windows operating system, you will need to install Android USB drivers compatible with your Android devices before you can access them via a USB connection. Most drivers can be downloaded from the Available Packages section of the Android SDK and AVD Manager; other specialty drivers may need to be acquired from the device manufacturer's website. After you have downloaded the appropriate drivers, you can use the Device Manager and point at the google-usb_driver folder under the Android SDK directory. Alternatively, you can download the latest Google USB drivers from the Android website at http://goo.gl/TkqjL and get a list of sources to find specific manufacturer USB drivers at http://goo.gl/ecNHn. After you unzip the drivers, connect your phone to your computer via the USB cable and select the drivers you want to install.

Notes on Mac OS X Installations

On a supported Mac, all you have to do is plug in the USB cable to the Mac and the device. There is no additional configuration needed.

APPENDIX B

Eclipse IDE Tips and Tricks

In this appendix, a variety of tips and tricks for Eclipse are offered for your enjoyment and benefit. These tips and tricks are geared toward tasks performed frequently while developing Android applications but some also apply to other Java development in Eclipse.

> Do you have your own tips or tricks for Android development in Eclipse? If so, email them to us (with permission to publish them) at androidwirelessdev@gmail.com, and they might be included on our blog at http://androidbook.blogspot.com. Get your moment of geekly fame!

By the Way

Creating New Classes and Methods

You can quickly create a new class and corresponding source file by right-clicking the package to create it and choosing New, Class. Then you enter the class name, pick a superclass and interfaces, and choose whether to create default comments and method stubs for the superclass for constructors or abstract methods.

Along these lines, you can quickly create method stubs by right-clicking a class or within a class in the editor and choosing Source, Override/Implement Methods. Then you choose the methods to create stubs for, where to create them, and whether to generate default comment blocks.

Organizing Imports

When referencing a class in your code for the first time, you can hover over the newly used class name and choose "Import 'Classname' (package name)" to have Eclipse quickly add the proper import statement.

In addition, the Organize imports command (Ctrl+Shift+O in Windows or Cmd+Shift+O on a Mac) causes Eclipse to automatically organize your imports. Eclipse removes unused imports and adds new ones for packages used but not already imported.

If there is any ambiguity in the name of a class during automatic import, such as with the Android Log class, Eclipse prompts you with the package to import.

Finally, you can configure Eclipse to automatically organize the imports each time you save a file. This can be set for the entire workspace or for an individual project. Configuring this for an individual project allows better flexibility when you're working on multiple projects and don't want to make changes to some code, even if they are an improvement. To configure this, perform the following steps:

1. Right-click the project and choose Properties.

2. Expand Java Editor and choose Save Actions.

3. Check Enable Project Specific Settings, Perform the Selected Actions on Save, and Organize Imports.

Documenting Code

Regular code comments are useful (when done right). Comments in Javadoc style appear in code completion dialogs and other places, thus making them even more useful. To quickly add a Javadoc comment to a method or class, simply press Ctrl+Shift+J in Windows (or Cmd+Alt+J on a Mac). Alternatively, you can choose Source, Generate Element Comment to prefill certain fields in the Javadoc, such as parameter names and author, thus speeding up the creation of this style of comment.

Using Auto-Complete

Auto-complete is a great feature that speeds up text entry. If this feature hasn't appeared for you yet or has gone away, you can bring it up by pressing Ctrl+spacebar.

Auto-complete not only saves time in typing but can be used to jog your memory about methods—or find a new method. You can scroll through all the methods of a class and even see the associated Javadocs with them. You can easily find static methods by using the class name or the instance variable name. You follow this name with a dot (and maybe Ctrl+spacebar) and then scroll through all the names. Then you can start typing the first part of a name to filter the results.

Editing Code Efficiently

Sometimes, you might find that the editor window is just too small, especially with all the extra little metadata windows and tabs surrounding it. Try this: Double-click the tab of the source file that you want to edit. Boom! It's now nearly the full Eclipse window size! Just double-click to return it to normal.

Ever wish you could see two source files at once? Well, you can! Simply grab the tab for a source file and either drag it over to the edge of the editor area or to the bottom. You then see a dark outline, showing where the file will be docked—either side-by-side with another file or above or below another file. This creates a parallel editor area where you can drag other file tabs, as well.

Ever wish you could see two places at once in the same source file? You can! Right-click the tab for the file in question and choose New Editor. A second editor tab for the same file comes up. With the previous tip, you can now have two different views of the same file.

Ever feel like you get far too many tabs open for files you're no longer editing? We do! There are a number of solutions to this problem. First, you can right-click a file tab and choose Close Others to close all other open files besides the chosen one. You can quickly close specific tabs by middle-clicking with a mouse on each tab. (This even works on a Mac with a mouse that can middle click, such as one with a scroll wheel.) Finally, you can use the Eclipse setting that limits the number of open file editors:

1. Open Eclipse's Preferences dialog.

2. Expand General, choose Editors, and check Close Editors Automatically.

3. Edit the value in Number of Opened Editors Before Closing.

We find eight to be a good number to use for the Number of Opened Editors Before Closing option to keep the clutter down, but have enough editors open to still get work done and have reference code open. Note also that if you check Open New Editor under When All Editors Are Dirty or Pinned, more files will be open if you're actively editing more than the number chosen. Thus, this setting doesn't affect productivity when you're editing a large number of files all at once but can keep things clean during most normal tasks.

Renaming Almost Anything

Eclipse's Rename tool is quite powerful. You can use it to rename variables, methods, class names, and more. Most often, you can simply right-click the item you want to rename and then choose Refactor, Rename. Alternatively, after selecting the item, you can press Ctrl+Alt+R in Windows (or Cmd+Alt+R on a Mac) to begin the renaming process. If you rename a top-level class in a file, you must change its filename as well. Eclipse usually handles the source control changes required to do this, if the file is being tracked by source control.

If Eclipse can determine that the item is a reference to the identically named item being renamed, all instances of the name are renamed as well. Occasionally, this even means comments are updated with the new name. Quite handy!

Formatting Code

Eclipse has a built-in mechanism for formatting Java code. Formatting code with a tool is useful for keeping the style consistent, applying a new style to old code, or matching styles with a different client or target (such as a book or an article).

To quickly format a small block of code, select the code and press Ctrl+Shift+F in Windows (or Cmd+Shift+F on a Mac). The code is formatted to the current settings. If no code is selected, the entire file is formatted. Occasionally, you need to select more code—such as an entire method—to get the indentation levels and brace matching correct.

The Eclipse formatting settings are found in the Properties pane under Java Code Style, Formatter. You can configure these settings on a per-project or workspace-wide basis. Dozens of rules can be applied and modified to suit your own style.

Organizing Code

Sometimes, formatting code isn't enough to make it clean and readable. Over the course of developing a complex activity, you might end up with a number of embedded classes and methods strewn about the file. A quick Eclipse trick comes to the rescue: With the file in question open, make sure the outline view is also visible. Simply click and drag methods and classes around in the outline view to place them in a suitable logical order. Do you have a method that is only called from a certain class but available to all? Just drag it in to that class. This works with almost anything listed in the outline, including classes, methods, and variables.

Fun with Refactoring

Do you find yourself writing a whole bunch of repeating sections of code that look, for instance, like this:

```
TextView nameCol = new TextView(this);
nameCol.setTextColor(getResources().getColor(R.color.title_color));
nameCol.setTextSize(getResources().
    getDimension(R.dimen.help_text_size));
nameCol.setText(scoreUserName);
table.addView(nameCol);
```

This code sets text color, text size, and text. If you've written two or more blocks that look like this, your code could benefit from refactoring. Eclipse provides two very useful tools—Extract Local Variable and Extract Method—to speed up this task and make it almost trivial.

Follow these steps to use the Extract Local Variable tool:

1. Select the expression getResources().getColor(R.color.title_color).

2. Right-click and choose Refactor, Extract Local Variable (or press Ctrl+Alt+L).

3. In the dialog that appears, enter a name for the variable and leave the Replace All Occurrences check box selected. Then click OK and watch the magic happen.

4. Repeat steps 1–3 for the text size.

The result should now look like this:

```
int textColor = getResources().getColor(R.color.title_color);
float textSize = getResources().getDimension(R.dimen.help_text_size);
TextView nameCol = new TextView(this);
nameCol.setTextSize(textSize);
nameCol.setText(scoreUserName);
nameCol.setTextColor(textColor);
table.addView(nameCol);
```

All repeated sections of the last five lines also have this change made. How convenient is this?

Now you're ready for the second tool. Follow these steps to use the Extract Method tool:

1. Select all five lines of the first block of code.

2. Right-click and choose Refactor, Extract Method (or choose Ctrl+Alt+M).

3. Name the method and edit the variable names anything you want. (Move them up or down, too, if desired.) Then click OK and watch the magic happen. By default, the new method is below your current one.

If the other blocks of code are actually identical, meaning the statements of the other blocks must be in the exact same order, the types are all the same, and so on, they are also replaced with calls to this new method! You can see this in the count of additional occurrences shown in the dialog for the Extract Method tool. If that count doesn't match what you expect, check that the code follows exactly the same pattern.

Now you have code that looks like the following:

```
addTextToRowWithValues(newRow, scoreUserName, textColor, textSize);
```

It is easier to work with this code than with the original code, and it was created with almost no typing! If you had ten instances before refactoring, you've saved a lot of time by using a useful Eclipse tool.

Resolving Mysterious Build Errors

Occasionally, you might find that Eclipse is finding build errors where there were none just moments before. In such a situation, you can try a couple quick Eclipse tricks.

First, try refreshing the project: Simply right-click the project and choose Refresh or press F5. If this doesn't work, try deleting the R.java file, which you can find under the /gen directory under the name of the particular package being compiled. (Don't worry: This file is created during every compile.) If the Compile Automatically option is enabled, the file is re-created. Otherwise, you need to compile the project again.

A second method for resolving certain build errors involves source control (which is covered at the end of this appendix). If the project is managed by Eclipse by using Team, Share Project, this enables Eclipse to manage files that are to be read-only or automatically generated. Alternatively, if you can't or don't want to use source control, make sure all of the files in the project are writeable (that is, not read-only).

Finally, you can try cleaning the project. To do this, choose Project, Clean and choose the projects you want to clean. Eclipse removes all temporary files and then rebuilds the project(s).

Creating Custom Log Filters

Every Android log statement includes a tag. You can use these tags with filters defined in LogCat. To add a new filter, click the green plus sign button in the LogCat pane. Name the filter—perhaps using the tag name—and fill in the tag you want to use. Now there is another tab in LogCat that shows messages that contain this tag. In addition, you can create filters that display items by severity level.

Android convention has largely settled on creating tags based on the name of the class. You see this frequently in the code provided with this book. Note that we create a constant in each class with the same variable name to simplify each logging call. Here's an example:

```
public static final String DEBUG_TAG = "MyClassName";
```

This convention isn't a requirement, though. You could organize tags around specific tasks that span many activities or you could use any other logical organization that works for your needs.

Moving Panes Around in a Workspace

Eclipse provides some pretty decent layouts with the default perspectives. However, not everyone works the same way and, with Android, a few perspectives have poor default layouts for us.

For instance, the Properties pane is usually found on the bottom of the Eclipse workspace. For code, this works fine because this pane is only a few lines high. But for layouts in Android, this doesn't work so well.

Luckily, in Eclipse this is easy to fix: Simply drag the pane by left-clicking and holding on the pane (the title) itself and dragging it to a new location, such as the vertical section on the right side of the Eclipse window. This provides the much-needed vertical space to see the dozens of properties often found there.

You can experiment to find a pane layout that works well for you. Each perspective has its own layout, too, and the perspectives can be task oriented. If you completely mess up a perspective, or just want a clean start, you can simply choose Window, Reset Perspective.

Customizing Panes in a Workspace

Eclipse provides some pretty decent layouts with the default perspectives. However, most of the workspaces are designed for general Java development—the DDMS perspective being the noted exception. In addition to rearranging the panes within your workspace, as discussed in the previous tip, you can also customize your workspace by adding or removing panes altogether.

Eclipse calls these panes views (confusing for Android developers). Eclipse has numerous panes available for use. You can add panes to your workspace in Eclipse by choosing Window, Show View, and choosing a specific functional view pane. You can simply close view panes that are already open using the little X next to the pane title. And again, if you completely mess up a perspective, or just want a clean start, you can simply choose Window, Reset Perspective.

Integrating Source Control

Eclipse has the ability to integrate with many source control packages through add-ons. This allows Eclipse to manage checking out a file—making it writable—when you first start to edit a file, checking a file in, updating a file, showing a file's status, and a number of other tasks, depending on the support of the add-on. Common source control add-ons are available for CVS, Subversion, Perforce, git, and many other packages.

Generally speaking, not all files are suitable for source control. For Android projects, any file with the bin and gen directories shouldn't be in source control.

To exclude these generically within Eclipse, go to Preferences, Team, Ignored Resources. Add *.apk, *.ap_, and *.dex by clicking the Add Pattern button and adding one at a time.

APPENDIX C

Supplementary Materials

This book introduces Android, but this 24-hour "crash" course barely scratches the surface of the platform. This book is meant to be used along with the supplementary book materials, including the accompanying source code, the publisher's website, the authors' book website, and the up-to-date documentation provided with the Android SDK.

A number of supplementary materials have been developed especially for this book. These materials, such as source code for many of the examples provided, are available online or as part of the accompanying CD. There are also a number of other online resources available for Android developers.

Using the Source Code for This Book

The source code for this book is designed with the assumption that you'll follow along with the accompanying chapter text. The source code downloads are not the "answers" to the lessons and exercises. Due to the length restrictions, we are not able to provide pages and pages of code listings in the book text. Instead, we provide code snippets on the topics at hand and expect the reader to see the source code if they require further clarification. The source code for this book is available in several locations: on the accompanying CD, on the publisher's website, and on the authors' book website.

We make every effort to make the code in this book both forward and backward compatible, but we have no control over the changes made by the Android team.

The source code for this book functioned as designed when this book was published and was tested with the exact versions of the tools and Android SDK referenced in this book's introduction. However, subsequent Android SDK and tool releases sometimes introduce changes; therefore, you may want to check for the latest version of the source code or the authors' website if you run into problems.

The source code is especially helpful for

▶ Understanding the full scope of a feature's implementation, beyond what is discussed in the code excerpt in the book text

▶ Clarifying Java implementation details for those with limited (or rusty) Java experience

▶ Providing a fully functional implementation of the concepts for a given lesson

▶ Providing hints or even implementations of material from the Exercises

Accessing the Android Developer Website

Just as you wouldn't get very far learning a foreign language without a textbook and a dictionary for translation, it is impossible to master Android without using the SDK class documentation. The Android Developer website and SDK documentation is available at http://developer.android.com, as discussed in Hour 2, "Mastering the Android Development Tools." The Android Developer website is especially helpful for

▶ Researching Android SDK APIs, classes, and methods used in this book

▶ Finding additional tutorials or articles on topics discussed in this book

▶ Keeping up with the latest trends and revisions of the Android SDK

▶ Diving deeper into a topic not covered in detail in this introductory book

Accessing the Publisher's Website

The source code that accompanies this book is available for download from the publisher's website (see Figure C.1), http://www.informit.com/store/product.aspx?isbn=0672335697.

Here's what you can find on the publisher's website:

▶ A thorough description of this book

▶ Downloadable source code

▶ Errata and book updates

▶ InformIT users' reviews of the book

▶ Sample content

▶ Other related books

FIGURE C.1
The InformIT
website.

Accessing the Authors' Website

The authors' book website, at http://androidbook.blogspot.com, is a complementary guide for designing, developing, debugging, and distributing Android applications (see Figure C.2); the source code is available for download here as well.

Here's what you can find on the authors' website:

▶ Downloadable source code

▶ Clarification regarding book exercises and reader questions

▶ Information about Android SDK updates and revisions, especially if a change affects readers

▶ Market news and information related to Android and mobile

▶ Tips, tricks, and pitfalls of Android development

▶ Links to reviews of the authors' books

▶ Supplemental code examples

▶ Informal discussions of more advanced Android development topics

▶ Links to other Android materials written by the authors, including their more advanced Android book and technical articles, many of which are available online

FIGURE C.2
The Android
Mobile
Application
Development
website.

Contacting the Authors

We do our best to answer each and every query and often post commonly asked questions and their answers on the book website at http://androidbook.blogspot.com.

As always, we welcome your feedback! If you have comments, questions, or concerns about the content of this book, you can email us (Lauren and Shane) at androidwirelessdev+s2e@gmail.com (see Figure C.3).

FIGURE C.3
Send us
feedback!

Leveraging Online Android Resources

The Android developer community is friendly and helpful. Here are a number of useful websites for Android developers and followers of the wireless industry in general:

▶ **Android Developer Website**—The Android SDK, developer reference site, and forums: http://developer.android.com

▶ **Open Handset Alliance**—Android manufacturers, operators, and developers: http://www.openhandsetalliance.com

▶ **Android Market**—Buy and sell Android applications: http://market.android.com/publish

▶ **OpenIntents**—An Android developer resource with a public intent registry as well as a source for third-party Android libraries and extensions: http://openintents.org

▶ **anddev.org**—An Android developer forum: http://www.anddev.org

▶ **FierceDeveloper**—A weekly newsletter for wireless developers: http://www.fiercedeveloper.com

▶ **Stack Overflow: Android**—A collaborative site for programmers, with an official section for Android: http://stackoverflow.com/questions/tagged/android

▶ **Wireless Developer Network**—A daily news digest for the wireless industry: http://www.wirelessdevnet.com

▶ **Developer.com**—A developer-oriented site that publishes technical articles: http://www.developer.com

Index

ListView, 135

main menu screens, 140-143

templates, 139

ProgressBar, 277

RelativeLayout, 135, 206

ScrollView, 173

Spinner, 182, 250

configuring, 182

events, 183

selections, 183

TabHost

adding, 158

configuring, 163

TextSwitcher, updating, 214

TextView, 20, 173, 230

VideoView, 378

View, 119

ViewGroup, 374

ViewSwitcher, 211-215

converting text to speech, 376

coordinates, translating addresses, 262-263

Copy button, 38

copying files, 35-36

costs, development, 11-12

coverage, test, 395-405

createScaledBitmap() method, 241

currencies, handling, 352

customizing

avatars, 227

adding, 229-230

bitmaps, 239-241

ImageButton controls, 231-234

selecting, 234-238

dialogs, 196-201

dividers, adding, 143

help screens, 151-152

applying files, 155-157

implementing, 153-155

interfaces, 373

input methods, 374

styles and themes, 373

user gestures, 375

views, 374

log filters, 451

main menu screens, 133-136

adding resources, 136-137

ListView control, 140-143

types of menu mechanisms, 144-147

updating, 138-139

network applications, 269-271

accessing, 274-276

developing, 272-273

downloading score data, 280-286

parsing question batches, 287-289

progress bars, 277-279

running tasks asynchronously, 279-280

panes, 452

password dialogs, launching, 201-202

preferences, 110

scores screens, 157

applying XML, 165-167

building with tabs, 163-164

implementing, 160-162

requirements, 158

screen orientations, 357-362

selectors, adding, 143

splash screens, 117-118

adding resources, 120-122

animation, 126-130

layouts, 118-119

updating layouts, 122, 125

D

Dalvik Debug Monitor Service. *See* DDMS

data management, 381

content providers, 384-385

files and directories, 382-383

integrating global searches, 385

databases, managing devices, 396

DatePickerDialog class, 192-195

How can we make this index more useful? Email us at indexes@samspublishing.com

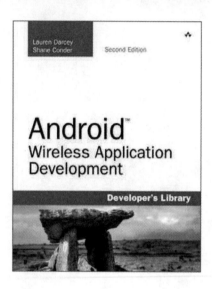

Sams Teach Yourself

When you only have time
for the answers™

FREE Online Edition

Your purchase of **Sams Teach Yourself Android Application Development in 24 Hours** includes access to a free online edition for 45 days through the Safari Books Online subscription service. Nearly every Sams book is available online through Safari Books Online, along with more than 5,000 other technical books and videos from publishers such as Addison-Wesley Professional, Cisco Press, Exam Cram, IBM Press, O'Reilly, Prentice Hall, and Que.

SAFARI BOOKS ONLINE allows you to search for a specific answer, cut and paste code, download chapters, and stay current with emerging technologies.

Activate your FREE Online Edition at www.informit.com/safarifree

> **STEP 1:** Enter the coupon code: LNWCWFA

> **STEP 2:** New Safari users, complete the brief registration form.
> Safari subscribers, just log in.

If you have difficulty registering on Safari or accessing the online edition, please e-mail customer-service@safaribooksonline.com